First X, Then Y, Now Z

LANDMARK THEMATIC MAPS

First
X
Then
Y
Now
Z

AN INTRODUCTION TO

Landmark Thematic Maps

by

John Delaney

PRINCETON, NEW JERSEY
PRINCETON UNIVERSITY LIBRARY
2012

COPYRIGHT © 2012
BY PRINCETON UNIVERSITY LIBRARY

This Volume is dedicated to
ARTHUR H. ROBINSON
(1915–2004)

true pioneer of early thematic mapping in the history of cartography. It was written to accompany an exhibition of historic maps and rare books, held in the main gallery of Firestone Library from 24 August 2012 through 10 February 2013, and its publication is due to the generosity of the Friends of the Princeton University Library.

The author greatly appreciates the professional attentions and contributions of digital photographer John Blazejewski, copyeditor Beth Gianfagna, and designer Mark Argetsinger.

FRONTISPIECE FOLDOUT:

First three pages of William C. Woodbridge's *Modern School Geography, on the Plan of Comparison and Classification* ... (Hartford: Wm. Jas. Hamersely, 1854) [courtesy of John Delaney]. An introductory geography lesson that leads from the concept of pictures, views, and plans to a simple thematic map. (For more on Woodbridge, see the Meteorology section.)

COVER IMAGE:

"Alexander von Humboldt in seiner Bibliothek." Chromolithograph copy of watercolor drawing by Eduard Hildebrant, 1856 (Berlin: Storch & Kramer) [Graphic Arts Collection]. Rooms in Humboldt's apartment at 67 Oranienburger Strasse in Berlin, where he lived from 1827 to the end of his life.

HIGH RESOLUTION IMAGES OF MANY OF THE MAPS
SHOWN HERE CAN BE FOUND VIA THE ONLINE CATALOG OF THE
PRINCETON UNIVERSITY LIBRARY

CONTENTS

PERSPECTIVE: *Maps & Geographic Information Systems Technology* by Wangyal Shawa	vii
INTRODUCTION: *Map Keys*	3
FRANCIS BACON, 1561–1626	15
ALEXANDER VON HUMBOLDT, 1769–1859	19
LANDMARK THEMATIC ATLASES	31

Quantitative Thematic Maps — 55

METEOROLOGY — 57
- Edmond Halley, 1656–1742 — 57
- Alexander von Humboldt, 1769–1859 — 59
- William Channing Woodbridge, 1794–1845 — 61
- James Pollard Espy, 1785–1860 — 64
- Elias Loomis, 1811–1889 — 66
- Léon Lalanne, 1811–1892 — 69
- John Chappelsmith, 1807?–1885? — 72
- Francis Galton, 1822–1911 — 74

GEOLOGY — 79
- Martin Lister, 1638?–1712 — 79
- Jean Etienne Guettard, 1715–1786 — 79
- William Smith, 1769–1839 — 83
- Georges Cuvier, 1769–1832 / Alexandre Brongniart, 1770–1847 — 88
- William Maclure, 1763–1840 — 90
- Edward Hitchcock, 1793–1864 — 93

HYDROGRAPHY — 101
- Athanasius Kircher, 1602–1680 — 101
- Eberhard Werner Happel, 1647–1690 — 101
- Benjamin Franklin, 1706–1790 — 103
- August Petermann, 1822–1878 — 106
- Georg Bauerkeller, *fl.* 1830–1870 — 106

NATURAL HISTORY — 111
- Eberhard August Wilhelm von Zimmermann, 1743–1815 — 111
- Joakim Frederik Schouw, 1789–1852 — 114

Medicine

- Giovanni Maria Lancisi, 1654–1720 — 119
- Valentine Seaman, 1770–1817 — 119
- Amariah Brigham, 1798–1849 — 123
- Edwin Chadwick, 1800–1890 — 125
- Thomas Shapter, 1809–1902 — 128
- John Snow, 1813–1858 — 131
- Henry Wentworth Acland, 1815–1900 — 132
- Florence Nightingale, 1820–1910 — 134

Sociology & Economics ("Moral Statistics")

- William Playfair, 1759–1823 — 141
- Charles Dupin, 1784–1873 — 146
- André-Michel Guerry, 1802–1866 — 150
- George Poulett Scrope, 1797–1876 — 151
- Adolphe Quetelet, 1796–1874 — 156
- Adolphe d'Angeville, 1796–1856 — 159
- Joseph Fletcher, 1813–1852 — 161
- Charles Joseph Minard, 1781–1870 — 165
- Henry Mayhew, 1812–1887 — 165

Qualitative Thematic Maps — 171

Communication & Transportation — 173
Ethnography — 189
Linguistics — 193
Military History — 195
Urban Planning — 197

Theme Maps (Fanta "Z") — 199

Literature — 201
Love & Marriage — 207
Utopia — 217

Conclusion — 223
Sources Consulted — 229

PERSPECTIVE

Maps and Geographic Information Systems Technology

by TSERING WANGYAL SHAWA

Geographic Information Systems and Map Librarian and Head,
Digital Map and Geospatial Information Center,
Princeton University

WHEN I WAS a student studying for a degree in cartography in the early 1980s, all the maps that I created for my classes were done manually. It was a laborious job. To draw a map, I used such things as tracing paper, rapidograph pens, rulers, and letter and symbol stencils. When I made a mistake, I had to remove the ink with a razor blade and then redraw the line or symbol again on tracing paper. Thanks to the development of geographic information systems, it became much easier to analyze geographic data and create a map.

What is a geographic information system (GIS), and what does it do? Geographic information systems can be defined in many ways because they mean different things to different people. GIS is most commonly described as a computer system that allows a person to create, analyze, and display geographically referenced data. Geographically referenced data mainly consist of two components: (1) the location, geometry, shape, or pixel, which is determined in relation to the Earth's surface, and (2) the attribute data associated with that location. Because of this, different geographically referenced data, such as property boundaries, land-use patterns, roads, rivers, and population density, can be overlaid on top of each other using GIS. Such a system allows researchers to conduct a variety of what-if scenarios and communicate their analyzed results through maps, tables, graphs, and animation.

GIS technology has become a critical research tool for essentially every discipline that studies or analyzes location-based information. For example, in Geo/Env 499: Investigating Natural Disasters, an undergraduate Princeton course taught by Professor Gregory van der Vink, students used GIS to discover the main reasons behind the apparent increase in the frequency and severity of federally-declared natural disasters. Integrating insurance rates, building codes, census data, and congressional districts, they developed vulnerability maps that included the distributions of hurricanes, tornadoes, earthquakes, and floods. Their GIS analysis (see map overleaf) demonstrated that the increase in disaster declarations was due not to any increase in the frequency of severity of events but, rather, to the changes in the population characteristics that had inadvertently been encouraged through earlier disaster management policies.

The history of geographic information systems and use of the acronym GIS can be traced back to the early 1960s, when the manual process of analyzing and creating maps was still very time-consuming. Researchers were working on options to use computers to capture, analyze, and create maps. The term "GIS" is widely believed to have first been used by Dr. Roger Tomlinson, a leader of the Canada Land Inventory program. This program was created by the Canadian government to identify national land resources and their potential uses. In order to record and analyze the Canadian geographic data, it developed a system called the Canada Geographic Information System after considering a few other names such as "spatial data system" and "land information system." Later the word "Canada" was dropped, and it was simply called a "geographic information system."

In the United States, a computer-mapping revolution was taking place in government departments and universities. In the early 1960s, Dr. Edgar Horwood of the University of Washington was developing mapping software packages called CARD MAPPING

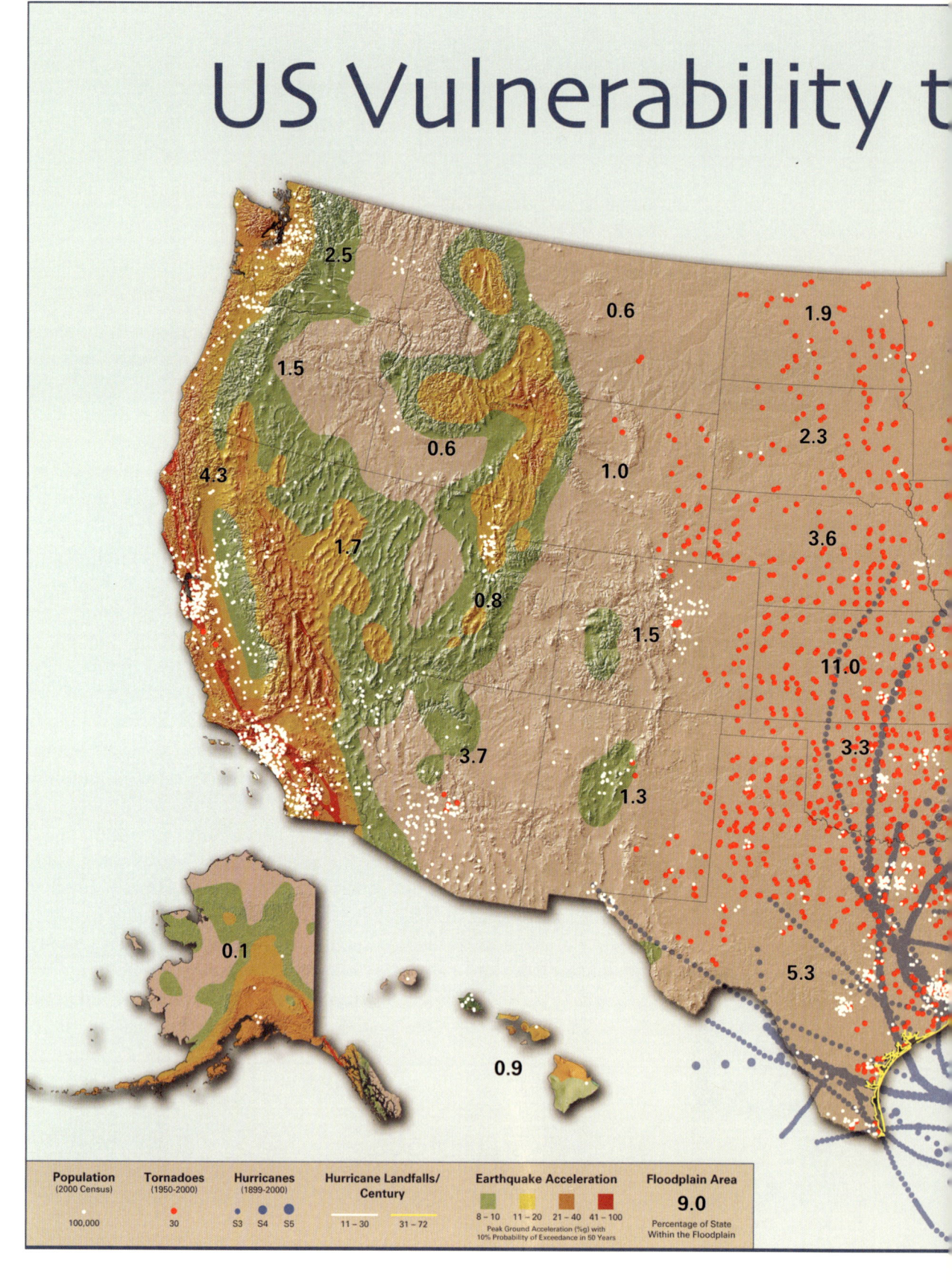

Natural Hazards

Population (2000 Census)	Tornadoes (1950-2000)	Hurricanes (1899-2000)	Hurricane Cen...
• 100,000	• 30	• S3 • S4 • S5	11 – 30

and TAPE MAPPING. These were used for producing choropleth maps and map symbols. Howard Fisher, who took Dr. Horwood's computer-mapping workshop, saw the potential of computer mapping and thought he could create a better mapping program. In 1965, Fisher received a grant from the Ford Foundation to develop a computer-mapping program. With this grant, he established a new computer graphics laboratory at Harvard University's Graduate School of Design, and within a year his group produced mapping software called SYMAP ("synagraphic" mapping package), which was distributed widely to academic institutions. This software allowed the user to produce rudimentary maps with a line printer. The laboratory was later named the Harvard Laboratory for Computer Graphics and Spatial Analysis, and it produced more mapping software such as CALFORM, GRID, and ODYSSEY. Many students who worked or studied in this lab became leaders in the geographic information system software world.

The development of SYMAP and other mapping software packages has fostered the use of computers to capture, process, analyze, and map geographic data. In the late 1960s, the United States Census Bureau was planning the 1970 census and started a project to develop software that would input the address information for every citizen in the 1970 census data collection. Before the 1970 census, all the population census data were collected either by interviewers who went from door to door asking questions or via mailed questionnaires that were later individually picked up by census workers. The new software that the Census Bureau was developing could reduce the number of people needed to collect the questionnaires. It could be used for address-matching of every person who returned the census questionnaire, and those matched addresses could be mapped and tied to census block and tract boundaries. The mapping software could also be used to report addresses from which census information had not been returned, thus allowing the bureau to send workers only to targeted addresses to collect missing questionnaires. This new computer software was called DIME (Dual Independent Map Encoding).

Later, in the 1980s, the Census Bureau started digitizing the United States Geological Survey's 1:100,000-scale topographic map series to create nationwide digital census tract boundaries and road networks. With the collection of nationwide digital data on road networks, census geography boundaries, and other physical and cultural geographic data, it later created a more advanced software program called TIGER (Topologically Integrated Geographic Encoding and Referencing), which was used for the 1990 census.

The United States Census Bureau is one of the leading government agencies that has helped the advancement of geographic information systems in the United States. After the 1990 census, large amounts of population and census geography data in digital format were not only made freely accessible online but were also distributed at no cost to all the federal depository libraries, which disseminate the data to the public. At the same time, other federal agencies, such as the United

*Eighty percent of digital information is location-based.**

* D.R. Fraser Taylor, "Global Geographic Information Management: Some Institution and Data Sharing Issues in Integrating Geospatial and Statistical Data," a paper presented at the Second Preparatory Meeting of the Proposed United Nations Committee on Global Geographic Information Management, New York, May 10–11, 2010.

States Geological Survey and the National Geospatial-Intelligence Agency (previously known as the Defense Mapping Agency), were converting their paper maps into digital geographic data and putting those datasets in the public domain. A variety of geographic data from the United States and the world now became accessible to the public and could be visualized and analyzed using geographic information systems. In the same decade, personal computers became more powerful and more affordable, and geographic information system software packages became more user-friendly. Once these large datasets that covered the whole world entered the public domain, private companies started making products based on this free information and began to market different geographic data products, digital maps, and software packages. This development led to more usage of geographic information systems in federal, state, and local governments, as well as in academic and nonprofit organizations.

In the late 1990s, commercial satellite companies got government approval to sell high-resolution images of the world to the public. In the early 2000s, Keyhole Corporation took advantage of this new development and designed an Internet application that integrated high-resolution satellite images with other geographic datasets released by the U.S. government and already in the public domain to create a seamless view of Earth, which it called Earth Viewer. This viewer was purchased by Google in 2004 and released in 2005 with the new name Google Earth, thus giving the public unprecedented access to high-resolution images of the earth that they had never seen before. Google Earth made it possible for a person to search for a location and see it at different scales, from a global view down to that of a local place—and in many cases even to an individual house. The technology that allows Google Earth to seamlessly overlay images at different resolutions onto geographic datasets and to zoom in at different scales is possible because of GIS technology.

GIS has not only changed mapmaking techniques but has also stimulated new ideas of mapmaking. With the development of GIS and related technologies such as Web 2.0, people can now generate whatever kinds of thematic maps they desire by meshing different map services over the Internet. These specialized maps can then be embedded in web pages and shared with anyone by providing the URL links, thus creating new possibilities for fashioning personalized maps. Such possibilities have democratized the mapmaking process. Before the development of GIS and related technologies, creating maps and collecting geographic data were mostly the purview of governments, but that is changing. Private citizens are now creating the Internet portals that are embedded with GIS technology to update and create maps and geographic data for their localities, thereby not only empowering the local residents but also enriching geographic information of their area. Now when I create a map, it takes much less time because I use geographic information systems, and the map can be shared with anyone in the world through different web mapping sites.

First X, Then Y, Now Z

LANDMARK THEMATIC MAPS

INTRODUCTION

Map Keys

THEMATIC MAPS are ubiquitous today. Think *National Geographic*. They are so common, in fact, that simple geographic maps have become rarities. (Think historic maps.) Their coming-of-age was the mid-1800s, after centuries of exploration and discovery, the rise of the Industrial Revolution and scientific inquiry, and technological improvements in printing. As will be seen, the instigators in the development of thematic maps were scientists, statisticians, and educators—not exclusively, as in the past, geographers, cartographers, or explorers.

First, however, we need a definition. What am I talking about? What is a thematic map? A geographic map is a reference map of somewhere—Africa, for example. For my purposes, a thematic map is simply *a map of something somewhere*, such as the AIDS epidemic *in* Africa—something *in* some place. Hence, thematic maps add a Z dimension to an existing, or even fictional, X-Y (latitude-longitude) landscape. Topographic, or relief, maps might also fit under this wide umbrella, but they constitute such a large, self-contained set that they are not considered here. Most of these kinds of maps are issued in series—they are part of larger families—and, I would argue, are more about "dressing" space than interpreting it.

Maps are always more than geography. Early ones sometimes bore effusive dedications to their sponsors, elaborate and imaginative cartouches, scales and superimposed grids or compass lines, as well as notations and comments—their thematic nature was subtle, almost invisible, more a tone than a feature. Here, the thematic qualities will seem blatant. The maps often take geography for granted, simplifying it to clear room for the graphic display of data. A thematic map, then, marries data and geography visually. To accomplish that, it needs something that is measurable, a method by which to measure it, and some way of visually exhibiting the results over a selected geographic region. And so, historically, the creation of thematic maps has required the development of new symbol systems and graphic methods of representation, more accurate base maps, and more systematic data collection.

In the world of maps, the notion of "where," over time, has given way to "what," or, more accurately, to the hybrid idea of "what/where." Just as geographic maps usually need a title, the development of data-driven maps also has necessitated the creation of data legends or keys to the symbols and graphic techniques employed in the maps. One way to approach the development of thematic maps, therefore, is to follow the historical trend in cartographic complexity in which map keys assume an increasingly significant role in conveying a map's purpose. Consider these aspects of maps:

1. PLACE NAMES
(X marks the spot)
Showing the relative location of places.

✼ [*Opposite*] Untitled manuscript chart on vellum, ca. 1575–1600, roughly 40 × 30 cm. From an atlas of four small portolan charts attributed to Jaume Olives because its style is similar to known portolanos by him [Kane Ms. 57, Manuscripts Division].

Portolan charts (or portolanos, from the Italian adjective *portolano*, "related to ports/harbors") were early navigational aids for merchants and explorers, particularly in the Mediterranean region. They indicated the sequence of places along the coasts and provided lines of compass bearings, called rhumb lines, for directional guidance, showing the thirty-two points of the mariner's compass.

This chart, for example, shows the order of cities/towns/villages along the western coast of Africa that one would expect to encounter when sailing south from the Strait of Gibraltar to the mouths of the Senegal and Gambia Rivers. Note the radiating rhumb lines and the latitude markers. Three Atlantic Ocean island groups (Azores, Madeiras, Canaries) on the top half,

4   *Introduction: Map Keys*

and one (Cape Verde) on the bottom, complement the continental focus of the chart.

✶ [*See opposite*] "The West-Road from London to Bristol; and Its Branches to Several of the Principal Towns, with Their Computed Distances." Letterpress table, 37.5 × 32.7 cm [Historic Maps Collection]. From John Speed's *The Theatre of the Empire of Great-Britain ...* (London: printed for Thomas Basset ... and Richard Chiswel ..., 1676). (For more on Speed, see the Military History part of the Qualitative Maps section.)

A stripped-down "map" that combines place names and relative distance with some sense of direction. Here, roads consist of stacks of place names; the title one ("West-Road") runs up the spine of the page from London at the bottom. The names of larger towns are printed in bold, 𝔒𝔩𝔡 𝔈𝔫𝔤𝔩𝔦𝔰𝔥 typeface letters. In the seventeenth century, one's options for leaving London by foot or horse were few. Heading west on this road towards Bristol—which everyone would know ("you need to take the West Road...")—one would expect to arrive in Hammersmith after four miles and reach Brentford via Turnham-Green after four more. (These localities are part of Greater London today.) From Maidenhead and Marlborough, other roads are shown going north. This hybrid approach, similar to a subway map today, has been an effective travel tool for over three hundred years.

2. DISTANCE SCALES
(distance × direction = itinerary)
Showing the distance between places.

✶ [*Right*] "Aphricae...." Table with a woodcut border, 13.5 × 10.1 cm. Verso of "Aphricae Tabula I" map from Sebastian Münster's edition of Ptolemy's *Geographia* (Basel: apud Henricum Petrum, mense martio anno 1540) [Rare Books Division]. (For more on Ptolemy, see section 3 below).

For each listed North African location, the data in the table show the length of its longest day (in hours and minutes) and its distance (in hours and minutes, hence time) west from Alexandria, Egypt.

✶ [*See overleaf*] "Neu vermehrter curioser Meilen-Zeiger der vornehmsten Staedte in Europa besonders in Teutschland wie-viel gemeine Teutsche Meilen solche voneinander entlegen ... = Tabula poliometrica ac praecipuorum quorundam locorum Europae." Copperplate table, with added color, 45.8 × 54 cm. (Nuremberg: Homannische Officin, 1731) [courtesy of John Delaney].

One of the most decorative tables of distances (in Roman miles) between major European cities printed in the eighteenth century. Not only were the data extremely useful for traveling but also for sending a letter, because distance, not weight, determined the price.

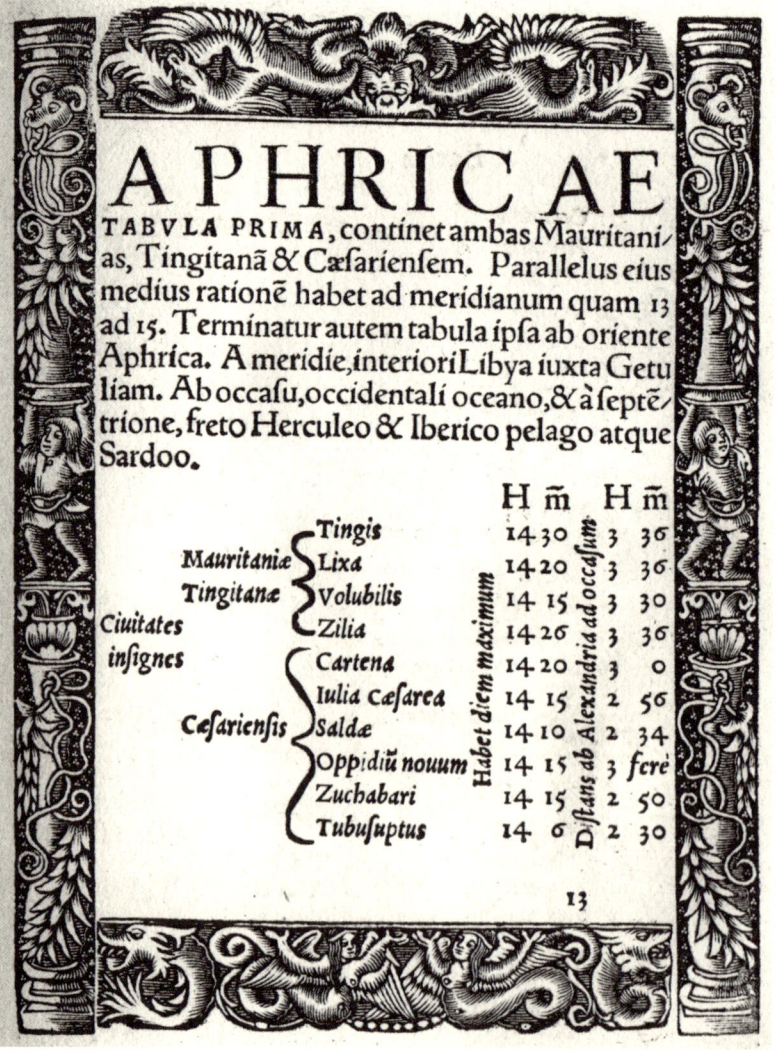

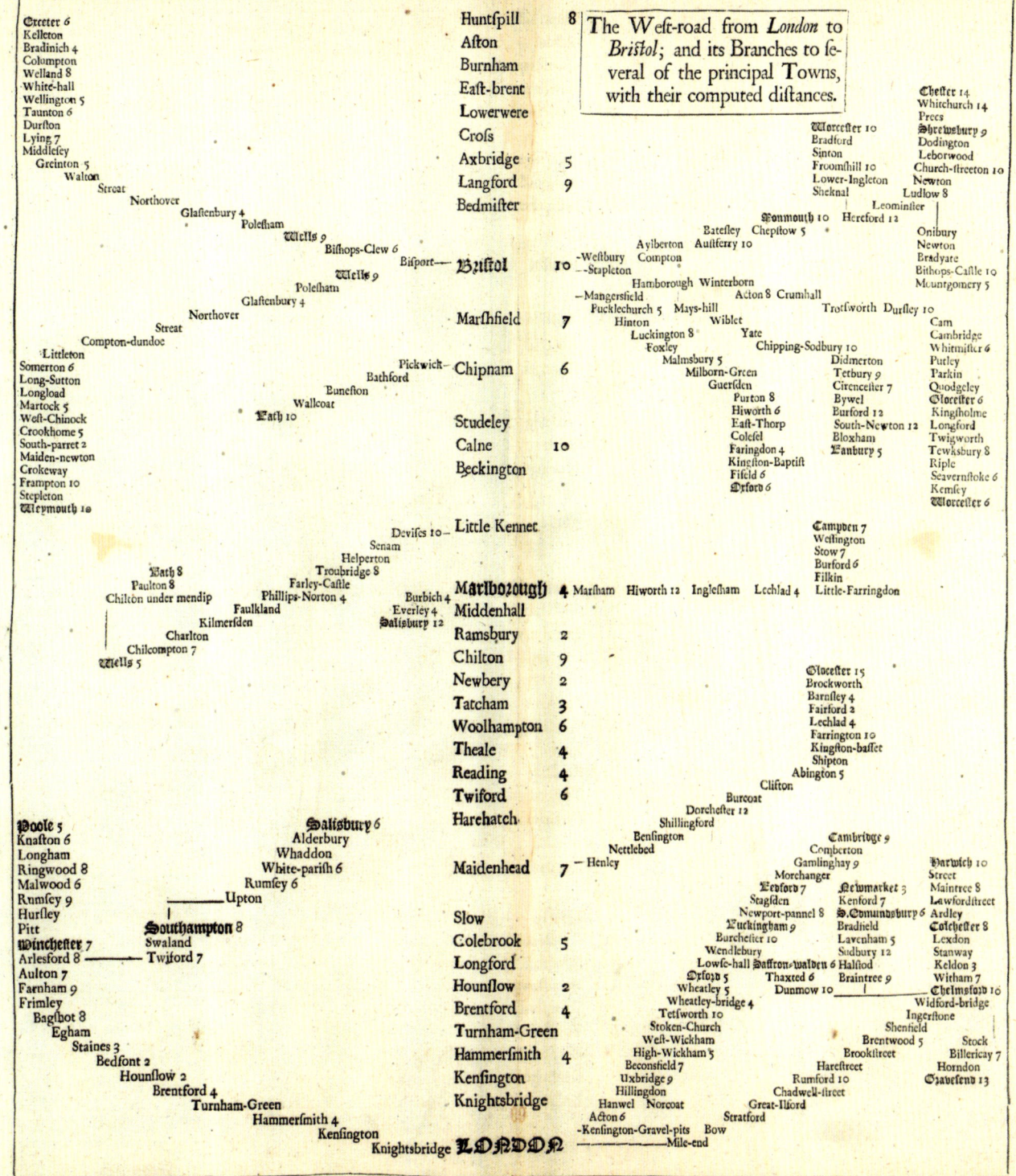

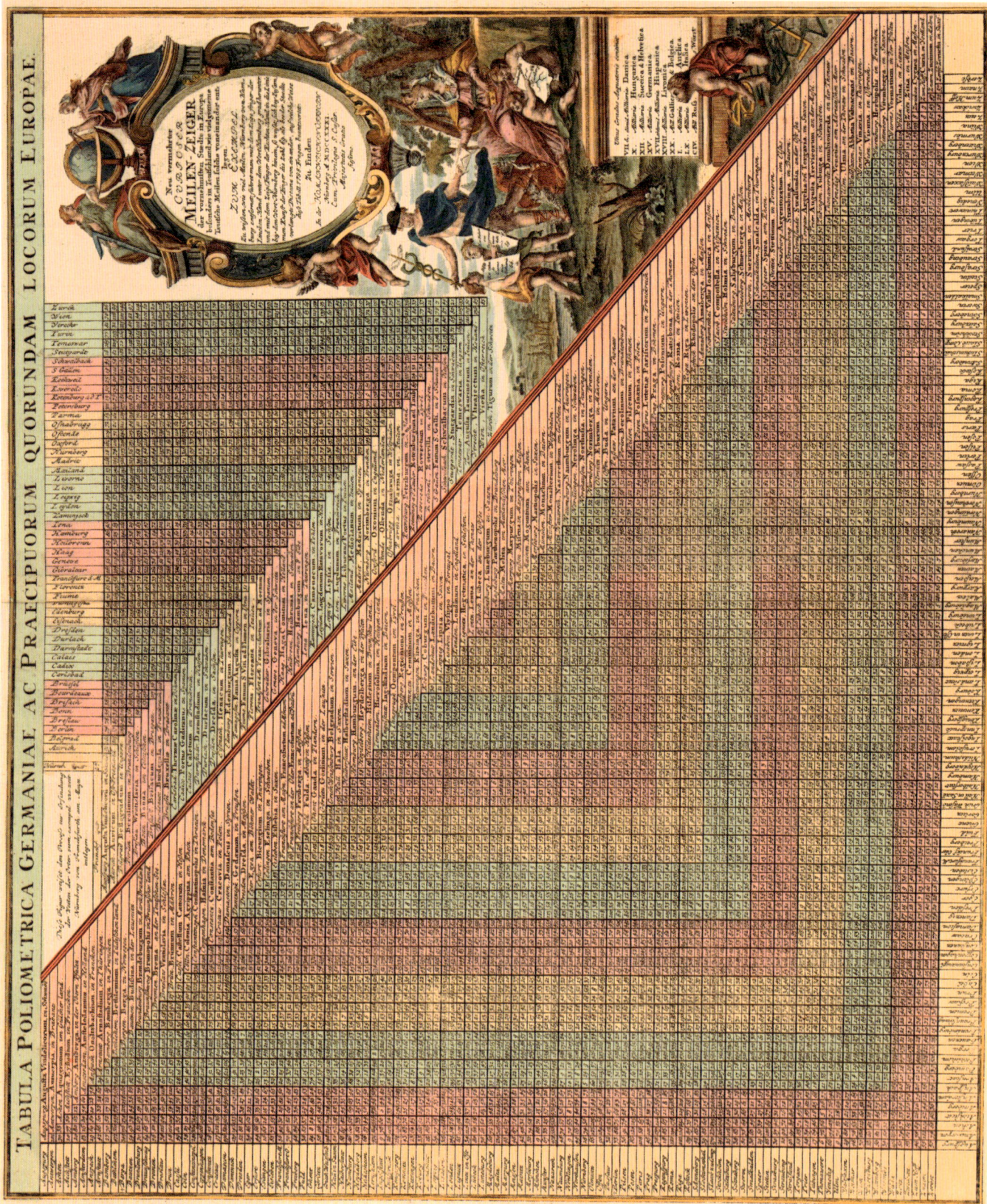

Introduction: Map Keys

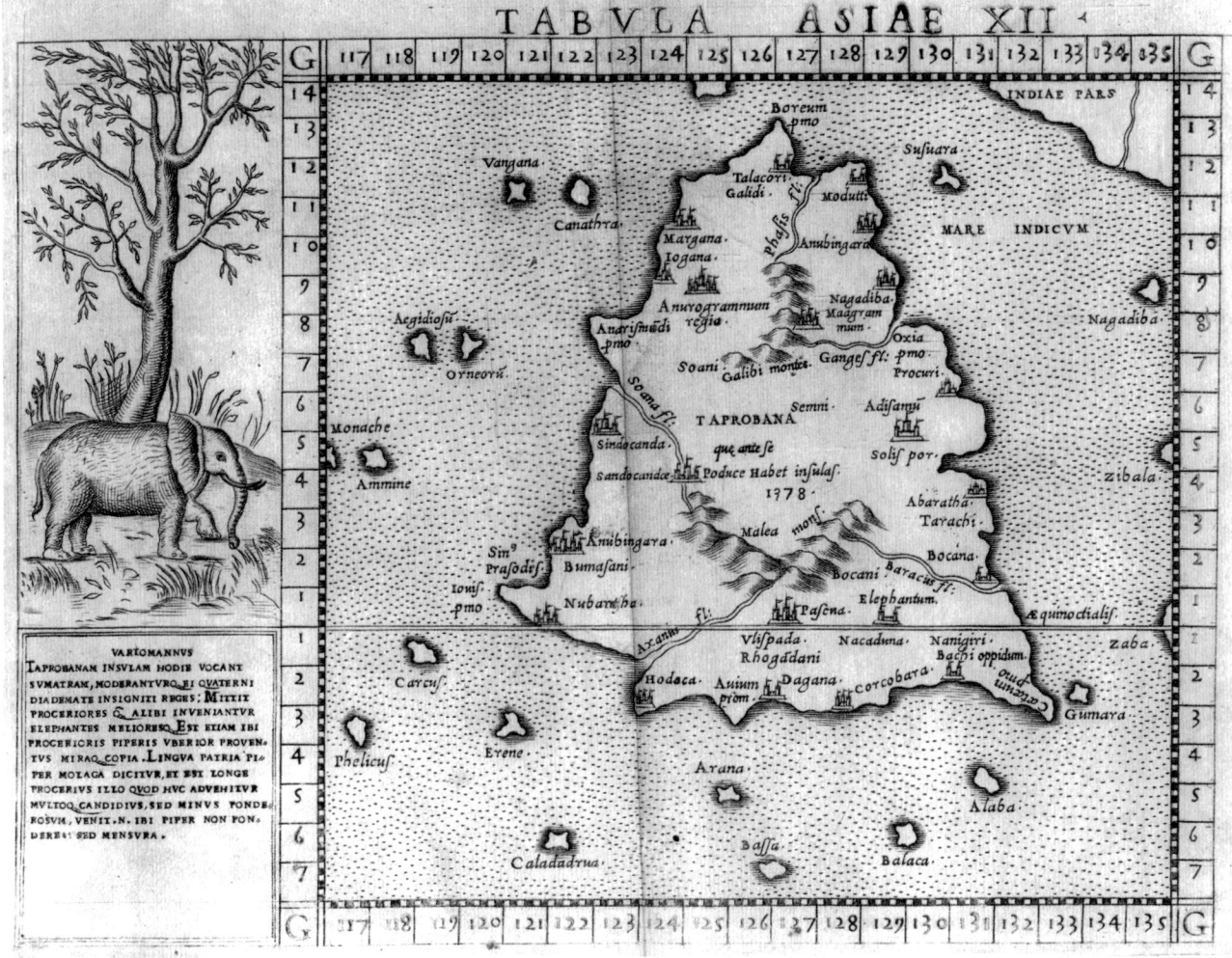

(Notice the letter being exchanged in the cartouche.) Provided in the box at the lower right are distance equivalents of an equatorial compass degree (*Unus gradus Aequatoris continet* = One degree at the equator contains ...), given in *millaria* (miles), for different countries; each used a different scale.

3. LATITUDE-LONGITUDE GRIDS
(X and Y coordinates)
Showing the standard skeleton on which the "organs" of place hang.

✳ [*Above*] "Tabula Asiae XII." Copperplate map, 16 × 17 cm, on sheet 19 × 26 cm [Historic Maps Collection]. From Girolamo Ruscelli's *Geographia Cl. Ptolemaei Alexandrini* (Venice: apud Vincentium Valgrisium, 1562).

Latitude and longitude lines began with the *Geographia*, a manual on the construction and drawing of maps, written in Alexandria, Egypt, about A.D. 160 by the mathematician, astronomer, and geographer Claudius Ptolemy (ca. A.D. 90–168). The European rediscovery of this work during the Renaissance, along with its numerous subsequent editions with maps created from its instructions, was a major milestone in cartographic history—the rest, as they say, is geography. On maps, the round earth soon acquired a girdle of 360° longitude (180° east and 180° west of a starting point, called the meridian) and a cap and bowl of 180° of latitude (90° north and 90° south of the equator).

This map of Sri Lanka (here called Taprobana, later, Ceylon), taken from Ruscelli's edition of Ptolemy's *Geographia*, places it roughly on the equator and near India, between 120 and 132 degrees east of the edge of Ptolemy's known world (Canary Islands). The cartographer has added some *interior* place names and the most rudimentary topographic features of generalized mountains and rivers. Descriptive text and the decorative charm of an elephant shown in its natural environment, and presumably native to this island country, enrich the cartographic experience.

4. TOPOGRAPHIC FEATURES
("dressing" space)
Showing "fully clothed" places.

✳ [*Right*] "Introduction aux Cartes qui se trouvent dans le Conducteur François [sic]." Key to Louis Denis's *Le conducteur français: Contenant les routes desservies par les nouvelles messageries, diligences & autres voitures publiques avec un détail historique & topographique des endroits par où elles passent & de ceux qu'on peut appercevoir, des notes curieuses sur les Chaînes de Montagnes que l'on traverse, relativement au système physique de Philippe Buache, premier Géographe du Roi: Enrichi de cartes topographiques, dont les routes seront distinguées par une coleur: Dressées & dessinées sur les lieux* (Paris: Chez Ribou, 1776–1780) [Rare Books Division].

Road maps might constitute another set of thematic maps in the widest sense, but this work has been chosen for its rich, and early, topographic treatment. Here in the general map key, a combination of color, shading, and symbols provides guidance to the usefulness of Denis's route maps. These are early precursors of today's familiar AAA TripTik maps, where striplike itineraries are annotated with descriptions of the interesting places encountered along the way. In 1675, British cartographer John Ogilby pioneered strip maps of English roads in his atlas *Britannia*, but his simple maps bore only rudimentary symbols. And Ogilby's work followed a long tradition of printed itineraries, dating back to Flemish cartographer Abraham Ortelius's version (1598) of the *Tabula Peutingeriana* (Peutinger Table), a thirteenth-century manuscript of the *cursus publicus* of the Roman emperors. (For more on this map, see the Ortelius entry in the Communication and Transportation section.)

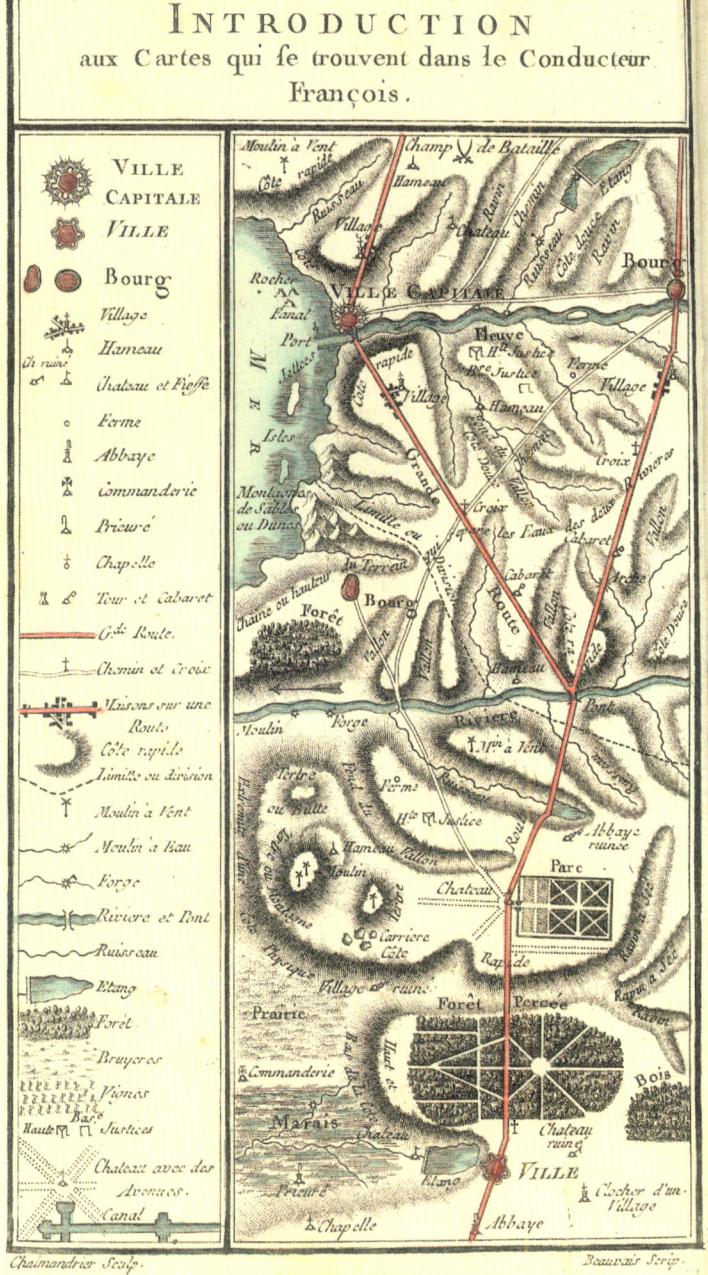

5. COLORING/SHADING/SYMBOLS
(adding a thematic Z layer)
Showing related, often more conceptual, aspects of places.

✳ [*Opposite*] "Designatio orbis Christiani." Copperplate map, with added color, 15 × 19 cm [Historic Maps Collection]. From Jodocus Hondius's *Atlas Minor* ... (Amsterdam: excusum in aedibus Iodoci Hondii,

10   Introduction: Map Keys

veneunt etiam apud Corneliu[m] Nicolai, item apud Ioannem Ianssonium Arnhemi, [1609]). Reference: Shirley, *Mapping of the World*, 260.

    Devoted to religion, this is one of the very earliest thematic maps. Three symbols (cross, crescent, arrow/spear) are used to designate Christian, Muslim, and idolatrous regions of the world. The map key, similar to a decision table, begins with the premise that everyone everywhere believes in a god, then breaks such spiritual faith into its various true/false permutations: true faith seems to be associated with organized religions—Christianity, Islam, Judaism (Christianity, of course, is the really true faith)—false with the worship of material bodies (stars/animals/vegetation) or good/bad spirits. Clearly, Christianity is in the minority. The moral of the map, addressed to its European audience, is that much proselytizing work needs to be done.

✸ [*Above*] Section of, and key to, "Quangsi, Sinarum Imperii Provincia Decimatertia." Copperplate map, with added color, 37.7 × 40 cm. From Martino Martini's *Novus atlas Sinensis* (Amsterdam: Blaeu, 1655) [Historic Maps Collection].

    This map is from the first Western atlas of China. The keys to the province maps may be the earliest to contain symbols for geological purposes—here, for example, locating silver and iron mines.

✸ [*Opposite*] "A Map of the King of Great Britain's Dominions in Europe, Africa, and America." Copperplate map, with added color, 26 × 31 cm [Historic Maps Collection]. From George Bickham's *A Short Description of the American Colonies Belonging to the Crown of Great Britain, in the British Monarchy ...* (London: G. Bickham, [1743–1749]).

    In this early thematic map, Bickham cleverly uses a different script (*Round hand*) to identify British possessions, which he explains in a note on the sides at the top of the map: "All those Countries, Islands, Forts, and Settlements, which are in the Round-hand Character, belong to the King."

A MAP of the King of GREAT BRITAIN's Dominions in Europe, Africa, and America.

N.B. All those Countries, Islands, Forts, and Settlements which are in the Round-hand Character, belong to the King.

To follow Plate 7.

G. Bickham Fecit.

To his most sacred Majesty GEORGE II. This Map Is most humbly Inscribed By his Majesty's most obedient Subject Geo. Bickham.

GUINEA
Gold Coast
NEGROLAND
BARBARY
Kingdom of Fez
Streights of Gibraltar
SPAIN
PORTUGAL
FRANCE
GERMANY
ENGLAND
Ireland
Denmark
Tropick of Cancer
Madeira I.
Canary I.
Azores I.
Cape Verd Isles
The First Meridian
The Equator or the Line
Polar Circle
Hudson's Bay
The Great Bank
The Little Bank
Cape Cod
Bermudas I.
Bahama Islands
CUBA
HISPANIOLA
Jamaica
Port Royal
CARIBE ISLANDS
Barbados
CARACOS
GUIANA
Tropick of Cancer

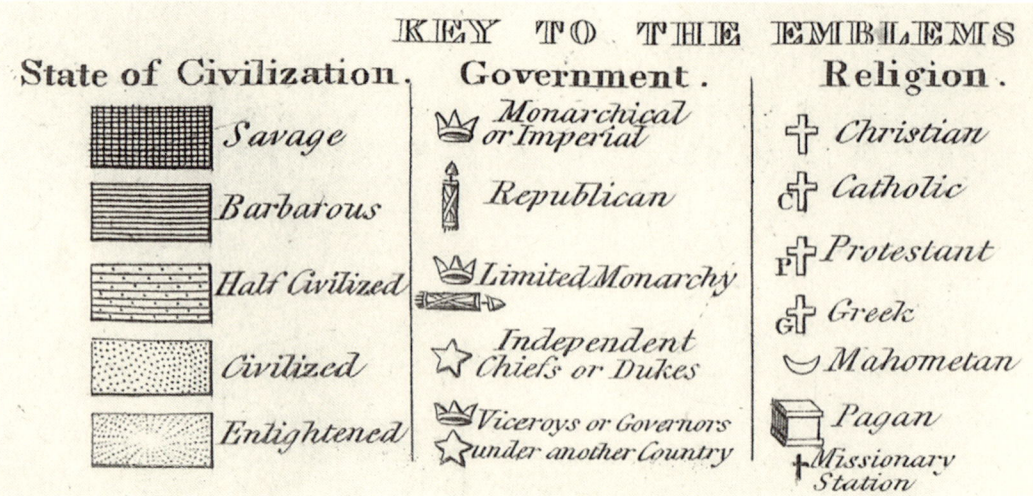

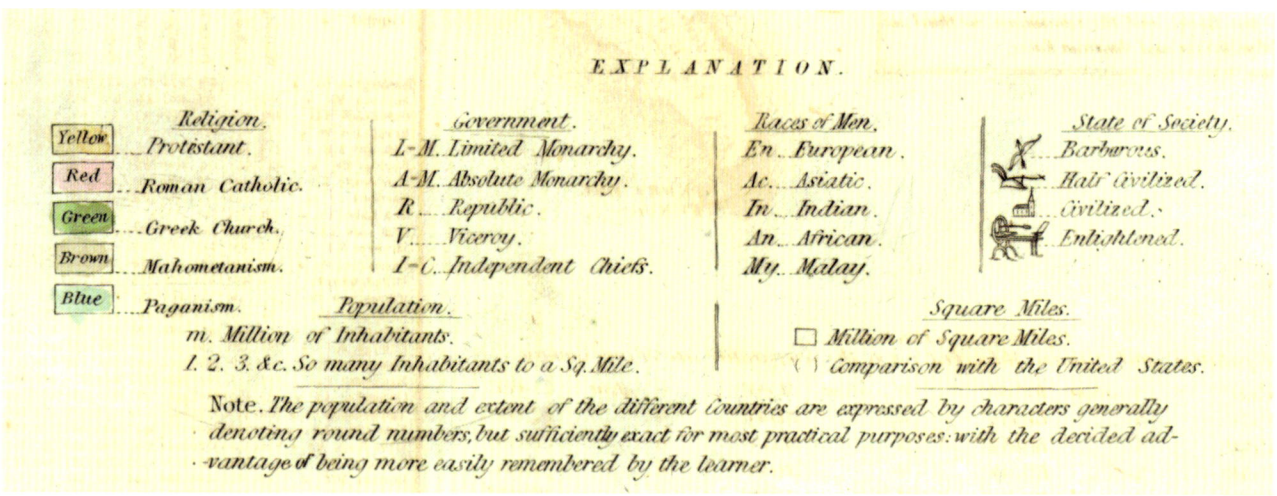

✳ [*Above, top*] "Key to the Emblems" in William C. Woodbridge's "Moral and Political Chart of the Inhabited World Exhibiting the Prevailing Religion, Form of Government, Degree of Civilization and Population of Each Country," dated 1821. From his *Woodbridge's School Atlas, an Improved Edition* … (Hartford [Conn.]: Oliver D. Cooke and Co., 1831) [Historic Maps Collection].

✳ [*Above, bottom*] "Explanation" key to Roswell Chamberlain Smith's "A Chart Exhibiting the Actual and Comparative Size of Each Country, Nation, and Kingdom…" ([Philadelphia: W. Marshall, 1837, c1835]) [Historic Maps Collection].

Subjective data. Woodbridge used shading to characterize countries as either savage, barbarous, half-civilized, civilized, or enlightened—the lighter the shade, the more enlightened the country. Smith's world map rates the "State of Society" of each country, reducing the categories to four and substituting symbols—bow and arrow, plough, church, and printing press—for each state. Neither map, nor Woodbridge's text, defines its terms. Intuitively, the reader must know what constitutes a savage or barbarous state and what separates a civilized country from an enlightened one. Curiously, Woodbridge used what appears to be a crate or box to indicate pagan religions, as if he were anticipating by half a century the idea of "cargo cults."

✳ [*Opposite*] "Explanation" to the frontispiece map "Liverpool, Ecclesiastical and Social." From Abraham Hume's *Condition of Liverpool, Religious and Social, Including Notices of the State of Education, Morals, Pauperism, and Crime* (Liverpool: T. Brakell, 1858) [Historic Maps Collection].

Map Keys

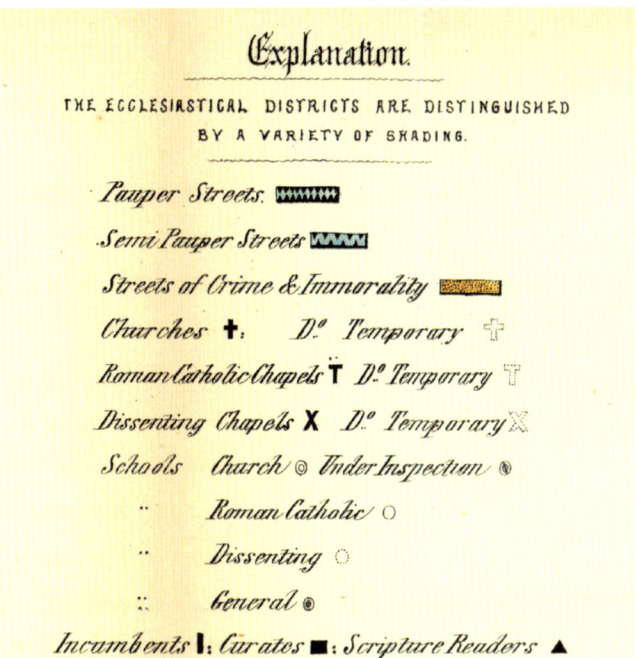

As seen from its key, this map from the "golden age" of thematic mapping, the mid-nineteenth century, offers a combination of coloring, shading, and symbols to convey its thematic purposes. Of course, the data behind Hume's decisions are invisible.

* * *

This brief summary of cartographic evolution suggests how maps and charts developed, first to help us navigate our way around the geographical world by (1) naming places, (2) plotting their relative order and distance from each other, (3) locking their locations on a universal, scientific grid, and (4) describing their natural (and some man-made) features—and then took another step by (5) adding interpretative layers of information about them, which usually *required* map keys. Voilà: thematic maps.

* * *

In this volume, you will find early, if not the earliest, thematic maps in various disciplines; in some cases the maps literally changed the world in the sense that new scientific avenues of investigation resulted. An obvious example of this would be German naturalist Alexander von Humboldt's isotherms map (1817), which showed contour lines of equal temperature—seemingly innocuous when it first appeared in a small journal but revolutionary in nature and infinitely useful since. Think of its application to the current global warming debate, almost two hundred years later.

My thinking in organizing the sections of this book is that English philosopher and scientist Francis Bacon provided the theory, Alexander von Humboldt the interdisciplinary methodology and vision. Brief biographical sketches of these two luminaries immediately follow this introduction. The rest of the men (and one woman) featured are their intellectual disciples and descendants, reaping the initial "crops" of their respective fields.

There are two basic classes of thematic maps: quantitative, those that rely on numerical data (for example, population density), and qualitative, those that emphasize non-numeric features of a geographic area (locations of hospitals, for instance). In the volume's main section, fundamental areas of quantitative maps—meteorology, geology, hydrography, natural history, medicine, and sociology and economics—are treated first, followed by a selective number of categories of qualitative maps. There are almost unlimited sources for the latter; the topics I have chosen—communication and transportation, ethnography, linguistics, military history, and urban planning—offer interesting opportunities for the use of thematic maps, suggesting the tremendous possibilities of the genre.

Preceding these two classes of thematic maps is a section devoted to landmark nineteenth-century atlases that revolutionized cartography. The emphasis is not only on the unique sorts of maps that these collections showcased, but also on the men who saw the need for them.

Wait. There's more. The last section, Theme Maps (Fanta "Z"), suggests that when imagination meets geography, the need for data disappears, and the result is symbolic cartography, where places are named and shaped according to a subjective theme. Literature, love and marriage, utopia—these have been historically rich fields for this kind of Ur-thematic map, often referred to as a cartographic curiosity.

FRANCIS BACON, 1561–1626

CALLED the father of empiricism, Sir Francis Bacon is credited with establishing and popularizing the "scientific method" of inquiry into natural phenomena. In stark contrast to deductive reasoning, which had dominated science since the days of Aristotle, Bacon introduced inductive methodology—testing and refining hypotheses by observing, measuring, and experimenting. An Aristotelian might logically deduce that water is necessary for life by arguing that its lack causes death. Aren't deserts arid and lifeless? But that is really an educated guess, limited to the subjective experience of the observer and not based on any objective facts gathered about the observed. A Baconian would want to test the hypothesis by experimenting with water deprivation under different conditions, using various forms of life. The results of those experiments would lead to more exacting, and illuminating, conclusions about life's dependency on water.

Throughout his life, Bacon lived mostly on the incline to success but beyond his means. He entered Trinity College at Cambridge at the age of twelve, traveled on the Continent, wrote significant and influential philosophical treatises and essays on reforming learning and reclassifying knowledge, served in Parliament, secured political appointments from Queen Elizabeth and King James I, was knighted in 1603, and became attorney general in 1613 and lord chancellor in 1618. However, always in debt, Bacon finally lost favor in 1621: he was convicted of corruption, heavily fined, and sentenced to the Tower of London (but was imprisoned only a few days). On a personal level, he was spurned for a wealthier man by the woman he loved, and he eventually married a fourteen-year-old when he was forty-five. Their marriage was fractious and soured, and he disinherited her in his will.

✻ Portrait of Francis Bacon. Frontispiece from his *Francisci Baconi ... Opera omnia quae extant, philosophica, moralia, politica, historica ...* (Frankfurt on Main: Impensis J. B. Schonwetteri, 1665) [Rare Books Division].

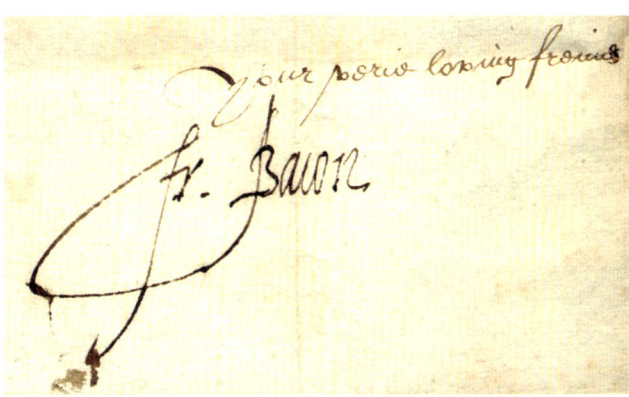

✻ Bacon's signature. From a letter from Bacon to "Mr. Auditor Sutton," dated 14 July 1614 [Robert H. Taylor Collection, Manuscripts Division].

After the disgraceful end to his public life, Bacon devoted himself more fully to study and writing. Among his later works was a short piece of science fiction, *New Atlantis: A Work Unfinished* (published in Latin, 1624; posthumously in English, 1627), in which he envisioned a utopian society that embodied his aspirations for mankind. The setting is an island called Bensalem, discovered by a European ship that is lost in the Pacific west of Peru. The centerpiece of the model society is a state-sponsored college, "Salomon's House," instituted "for the Interpreting of Nature, and the Producing of Great and Marvelous Workes for the Benefit of Men." Among its achievements are new foodstuffs and threads for apparel, artificial minerals and cements, accelerated germination of seeds, improved instruments of destruction (ideal societies are never safe), chambers where diseases are cured, and the creation of new and beneficial species. As one would expect in a Baconian world, there is a lot of experimentation conducted on the island and, more important, practical application of the knowledge gained. (For utopian maps, see the Utopia section of Theme Maps.)

Ironically, but perhaps not surprisingly, Bacon died from pneumonia while experimenting with snow as a way to preserve meat. His estate's debts were substantial.

{15}

Francis Bacon

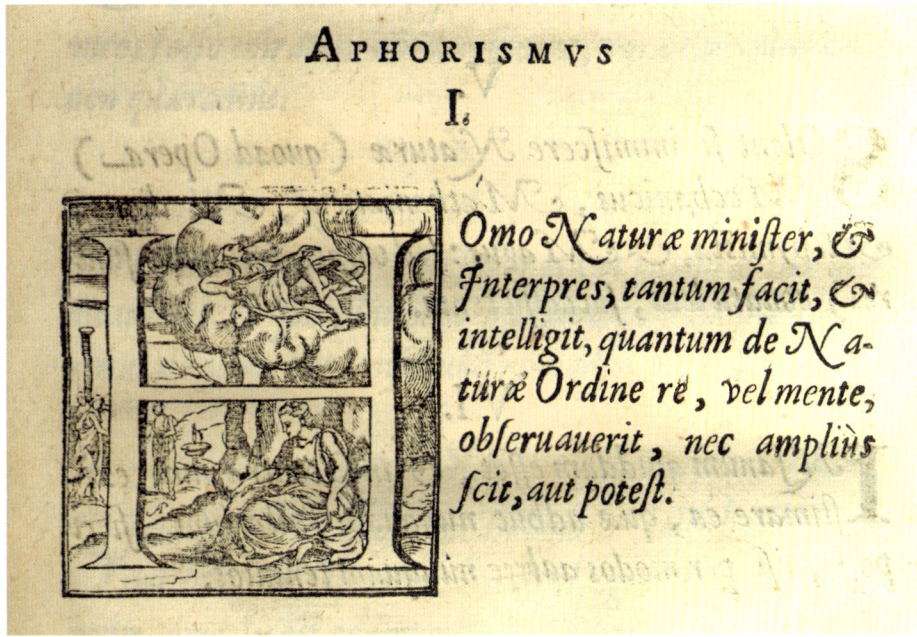

✱ [*Opposite*] Title page of Bacon's *Francisci de Verulamio, summi Angliae cancellarii, Instauratio magna* (London: apud Joannem Billium, Typographum Regium, anno 1620) [Scheide Library].

This copy contains only the second of the six parts of Bacon's planned great intellectual "restoration," the *Novum organum*, followed by a sketch of the third part. (Works that represent the first and third parts were published later; of the fourth and fifth parts only prefaces were written; the sixth was never begun.) The *Novum organum*, or "new instrument," a reference to Organon, Aristotle's work on logic, is Bacon's most significant work, laying out his guidelines for interpreting nature. Unlike the ancients, who often contended that nothing can be known, he argues here that there are progressive stages of certainty, and he will show how through inductive reasoning they can be achieved.

The title page exhibits a galleon exiting into the Atlantic Ocean from between the mythical Pillars of Hercules that stand on either side of the Strait of Gibraltar—hence, beyond the boundaries of the Mediterranean, or known world. The implications to the reader are clear: boldly embark on a voyage of discovery in which empirical investigation will lead to a greater understanding of the world. As the hopeful Latin caption states, "Many will pass through and scientific knowledge will increase."

Departing for the New World from Spain in 1799 in a vessel not unlike the one pictured here, the German naturalist Alexander von Humboldt robustly would begin the realization of that dream.

✱ [*Above*] "Aphorism I." From Bacon's *Novum organum* (1620).

Probably the most famous Baconian quote, usually translated from the Latin thus:

> Man, being the servant and interpreter of Nature, can do and understand so much and so much only as he has observed in fact or in thought about the order of Nature: beyond this he neither knows anything nor can do anything [p. 47].

The statement is the foundation of his scientific approach to acquiring knowledge. Later in the book, Bacon writes that printing, gunpowder, and the compass have revolutionized the world. But, of course, his scientific "method" (he never actually used that word) would have even more far-reaching effects. From our perspective today, what hasn't it touched?

Bacon's thinking, applied to cartography, leads logically to thematic maps—particularly the quantitative variety—for they are visual hypotheses, either posed or proven, created from measurable, hence verifiable, data about the natural (physical and social) world.

ALEXANDER VON HUMBOLDT, 1769–1859

ALEXANDER was the younger brother of the successful Prussian diplomat and linguist Wilhelm von Humboldt (1767–1835), the founder of Humboldt University. But he was not destined to live in his brother's shadow. Born in Berlin to privileged aristocracy during Frederick the Great's reign, Humboldt was nine when his father died, and the brothers were reared, according to biographers, in an emotional wasteland by a puritanical mother: work and achievement ruled over love and play. As a result, the boys became as close as twins.

While Wilhelm's studiousness put him on the fast track in training for a high public office, Alexander's restlessness and outdoor wanderings—collecting and labeling beetles, flowers, shells, and stones were favorite pastimes—led his mother to choose for "the little apothecary" a more bureaucratic career. In 1789, he matriculated at Göttingen University, where he met and formed a strong friendship with naturalist-ethnologist-revolutionary Georg Forster, who had accompanied his father on Captain James Cook's second voyage of exploration around the world. After spending time with Forster, traveling to London and back through revolutionary Paris, Humboldt seemed to have found his calling: thereafter he pursued a relentless, self-imposed program of study, both curricular and extracurricular, to become a scientific explorer himself. He studied commerce, geology, botany, foreign languages, anatomy, astronomy, and scientific instruments as if possessed by a demon. Among his prominent instructors were geologist Abraham Gottlob Werner, anatomist Justus Christian Loder, and astronomers Franz Xaver von

✺ Portrait of Alexander von Humboldt. From vol. 1 of Evert A. Duyckinck's *Portrait Gallery of Eminent Men and Women of Europe and America* ... (New York: Johnson & Miles, ca. 1873) [General Library Collection].

German naturalist Alexander von Humboldt lived to see the new direction taken by geographic studies, which his own work had initiated. By the time of his death, thematic mapping had already passed its golden age.

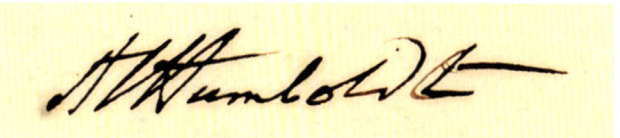

✺ Humboldt's signature. From a letter to an unidentified correspondent, dated 8 December 1840 [General Manuscripts Collection, Manuscripts Division].

Zach and Johann Gottfried Köhler. Throughout his life, Humboldt would meet and correspond with an unprecedented number of important figures in a wide range of disciplines.

In 1792, Humboldt received his first official employment as assessor of mines for the Prussian Ministry of Industry and Mines. This service to the state he viewed as an apprenticeship only, but he performed it so diligently—his first report, which weighed in at 150 pages, won him an immediate promotion to chief inspector—that he probably would have become superintendent. Yet, though he seemed to enjoy dashing around the country on official business, improving mining conditions and output, and even setting up the country's first workers' training school, the bureaucrat continued to fan the scientific flame. He could not be deterred from conducting muscle-electricity experiments and publishing a botanical book, activities that ultimately brought him into the Weimar circle of German literary giants Johann Wolfgang von Goethe and Friedrich Schiller, whose interests included natural science. When his mother died in the fall of 1796, Humboldt was finally freed from family career expectations, and he had suddenly through inheritance become a millionaire. So, in February 1797, he resigned from his mining job and began calculating his next move. What opportunity would present itself?

✺ ✺ ✺

In short order he was living in his brother's house in Paris, where Wilhelm was taking a sojourn of his own to follow his cultural interests and indulging himself

{19}

in the intellectual and social life of the city, which had become an international meeting-ground of top-flight thinkers. While visiting Louis Antoine de Bougainville, France's first circumnavigator, Humboldt learned of the government's plans for a new, five-year scientific expedition round the world on land and sea. The venerable explorer was in charge and invited Humboldt to join its staff. But the news was too good to last, for a new war soon was breaking out and the expedition plans were shelved.

Disappointed but still desiring to do something stimulating and challenging, Humboldt joined forces with Aimé Bonpland (1773–1858), the now-defunct expedition's first-rate botanist, and the two ultimately walked from the Pyrenees to Madrid on a six-week journey of their own. Bonpland would prove to be the perfect companion (then and later)—always positive, level-headed, healthy, and humorous. During the trek Humboldt assiduously took scientific readings (astronomical and barometric) with his instruments, and his resulting topographic profile of the peninsula, the first of its kind, proved that central Spain was a high plateau.

In Madrid, his connections got him an introduction to the king and queen at court, where he explained his desire to visit Spanish-American colonies and the possible benefits that might result. Indeed, King Carlos IV thought a good geologist in New Spain might discover rich mineral deposits and readily agreed to lend his support: Humboldt and Bonpland were given unlimited permission to explore Spanish territory and passports that would open any door they encountered. Humboldt could not believe his sudden good fortune. One of the largest territories on the earth, stretching from Cape Horn to California, including most of the West Indies and all of Central America, as well as one-third of what is now the continental United States, was offered up for his scientific exploration! Most of that terrain was terra incognita, and no foreign scientist had been given such free rein there. He was determined to make the most of this unique opportunity, which he would finance from his own pocket.

* * *

The resulting five-year expedition (1799–1804) to the Americas that Humboldt undertook with Bonpland took virtually the rest of his life to fully digest and describe. The two men would cover six thousand miles, from 52° N to 12° S, and bring back forty-five cases of specimens (sixty thousand items!), as well as a mass of astronomical, geological, meteorological, botanical, and oceanographic data. The expedition would lay the groundwork for a new direction in geography.

On June 5, 1799, the two men left the Spanish port of Corunna, bound for Havana aboard a packet-boat named *Pizarro*. Stocked with the most advanced scientific instruments he could acquire, Humboldt planned to measure and observe everything, including atmospheric temperature and pressure, ocean temperature and currents, terrestrial magnetism, the distribution of plants and animals, rocks and strata, humidity and other climatic conditions. The ship put in for a few days at Tenerife in the Canary Islands so the men could explore the volcano Pico de Teide, which had recently been active. (See Humboldt's profile of the mountain, opposite.) During the Atlantic crossing, the ship's crew and passengers suffered from a serious outbreak of typhoid fever, and so they changed course to land at the first South American port they could find. That was Cumaná, Venezuela, where they anchored on July 16. It was a serendipitous altering of plans for Humboldt and Bonpland, who had miraculously escaped the epidemic: they would begin their explorations in South America.

For the next two-and-a-half years (to February 1803), Humboldt and Bonpland's itinerary took them through what is now Venezuela, Colombia, Ecuador, and Peru. Their interior route also took them through different stages of human civilization—from the coastal towns with eighteenth-century amenities to remote regions where tribes lived in extremely primitive states, unchanged since Columbus's first footsteps on the continent and ruled by a small number of Franciscan missionaries. In a 1,500-mile exploratory loop, they canoed past the cataracts of the Upper Orinoco River and confirmed the existence of the Casiquare Canal, the world's only natural waterway connecting two huge river systems (Orinoco and Amazon). (See Humboldt's map of the province of Verina, overleaf.)

In 1801, they journeyed overland from Cartagena to Bogotá and then, crossing the Andes at almost twelve thousand feet, to Quito, where Humboldt spent

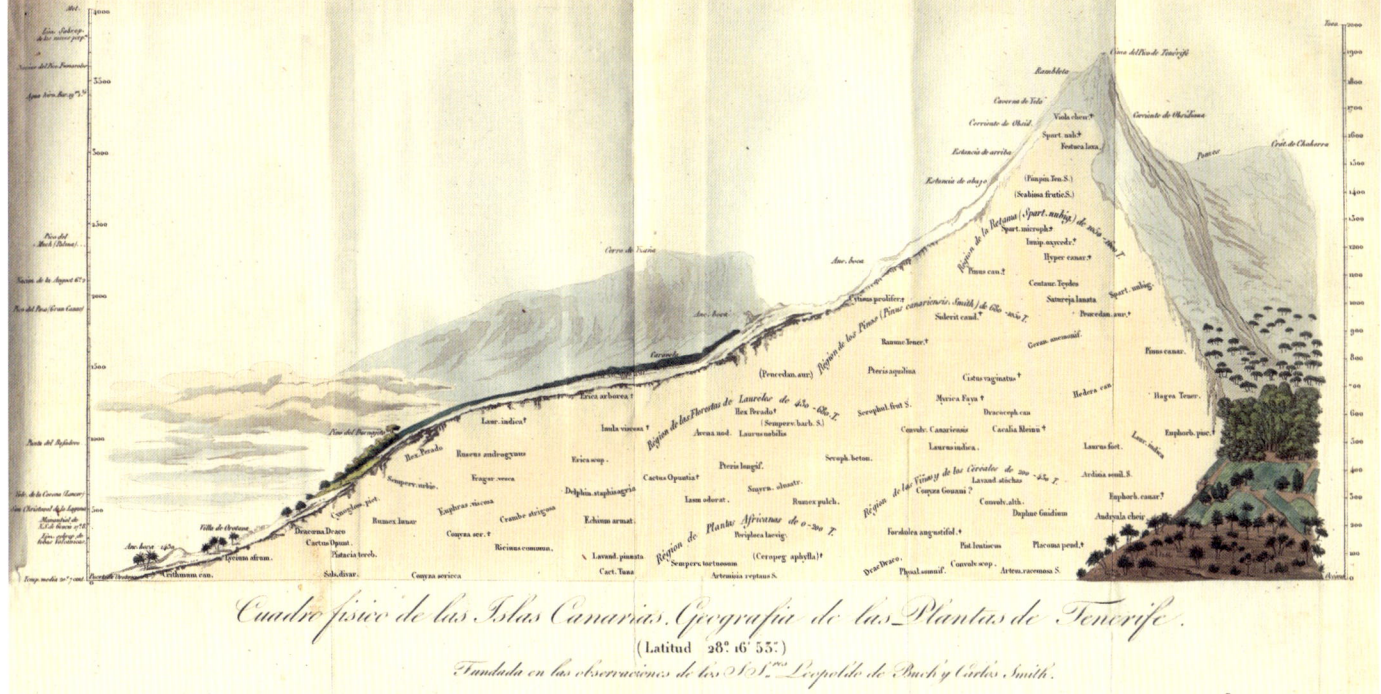

half a year examining the major volcanoes. He was at the physical peak of his life and earned universal fame by climbing Chimborazo, which was considered the highest mountain in the world at the time. By his own instrument's reading, he estimated that he reached an altitude of 19,286 feet before an impassable ravine forced them—Humboldt, Bonpland, and local friend Carlos Montúfar—to turn back. (See Humboldt's landmark profile of the mountain, overleaf.) Today, Chimborazo's height is given as 20,565 feet. In his old age, this climb still ranked among Humboldt's proudest achievements. Interestingly, because of Chimborazo's height and location near the equator, its summit is the furthest point from the earth's center.

While traveling through Peru, the group crossed the

✻ [*Above*] "Cuadro fisico de las Islas Canarias. Geografia de las Plantas de Tenerife." Copperplate profile chart, with added color, 17.5 × 39.4 cm. From vol. 1 of Humboldt's *Viage á las regiones equinocciales del nuevo continente: Hecho en 1799 hasta 1804, por Al. de Humboldt y A. Bonpland* (Paris: En Casa de Rosa, 1826) [Rare Books Division].

Leopold von Buch (1774–1853) studied with Humboldt and published a multivolume description of the Canary Islands in 1825, which included an atlas. Note that Humboldt credits Buch's observations in the caption to the chart.

✻ [*Overleaf*] "Map of the Eastern Part of the Province of Verina, between the Oronooko the Abura & the Rio Meta Compiled from Astronomical Observations & Materials Collected on the Spot by Alexander Humboldt." Copperplate map, 16.8 × 26 cm. From vol. 3 of Humboldt's *Personal Narrative of Travels to the Equinoctial Regions of the New Continent, during the Years 1799–1804*, trans. from the French by Helen Maria Williams (London: Longman, Hurst, Rees, Orme, and Brown, 1818) [Rare Books Division].

Humboldt's map of some of the remote areas in Venezuela that he and Bonpland explored at the beginning of their five-year expedition.

✻ [*Overleaf*] "Journey towards the Summit of Chimborazo, Attempted on the 23rd June 1802. By Alexander de Humboldt, Aimé Bonpland & Carlos Montúfar." Copperplate profile chart, 24 × 37.4 cm. From vol. 6, pt. 2 of Humboldt's *Personal Narrative of Travels to the Equinoctial Regions of the New Continent, during the Years 1799–1804*, trans. from the French by Helen Maria Williams (London: Longman, Rees, Orme, Brown, and Green, 1826) [Rare Books Division].

One of the most famous of Humboldt's charts and maps, a landmark linking of plant life to altitude.

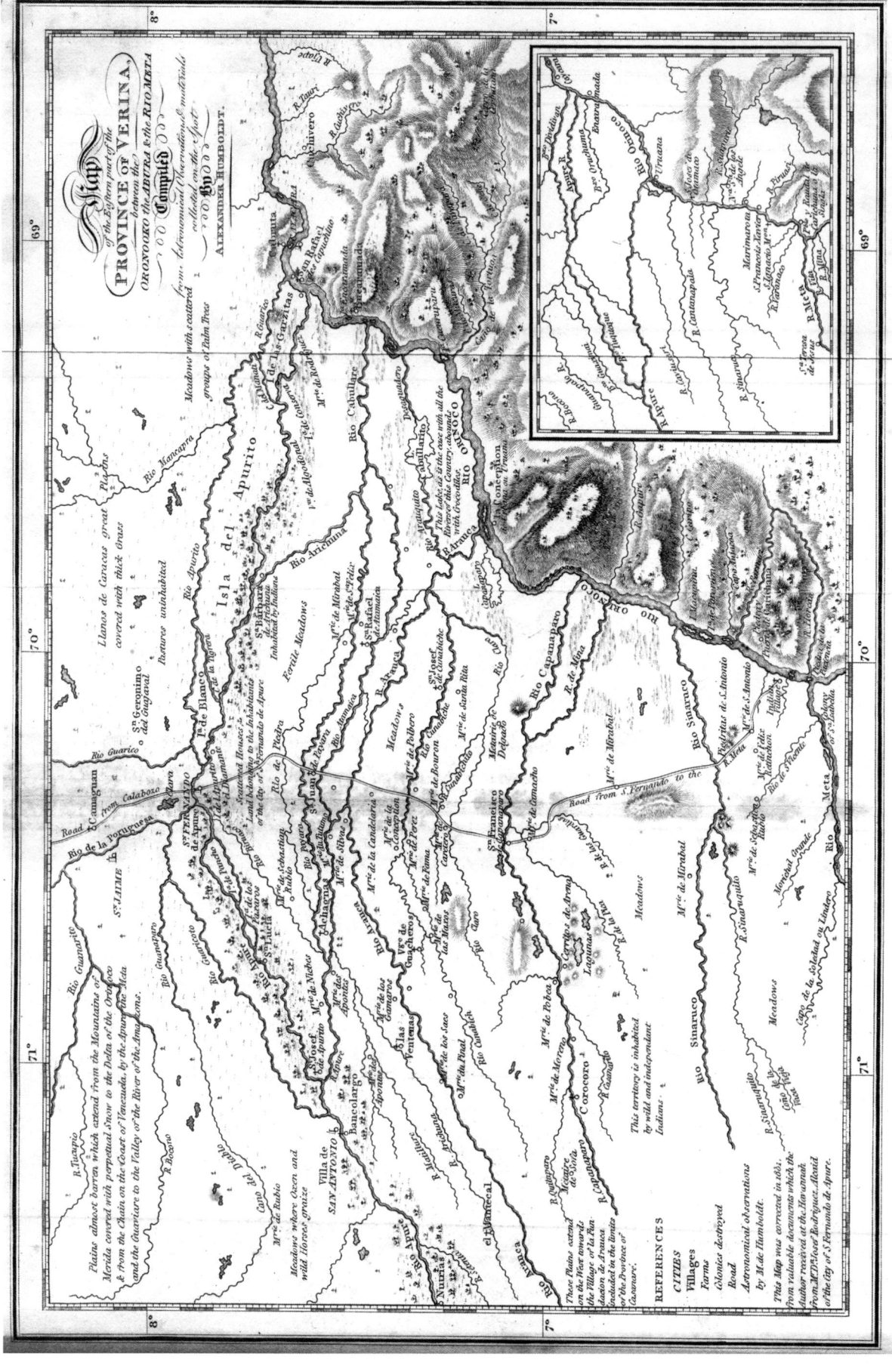

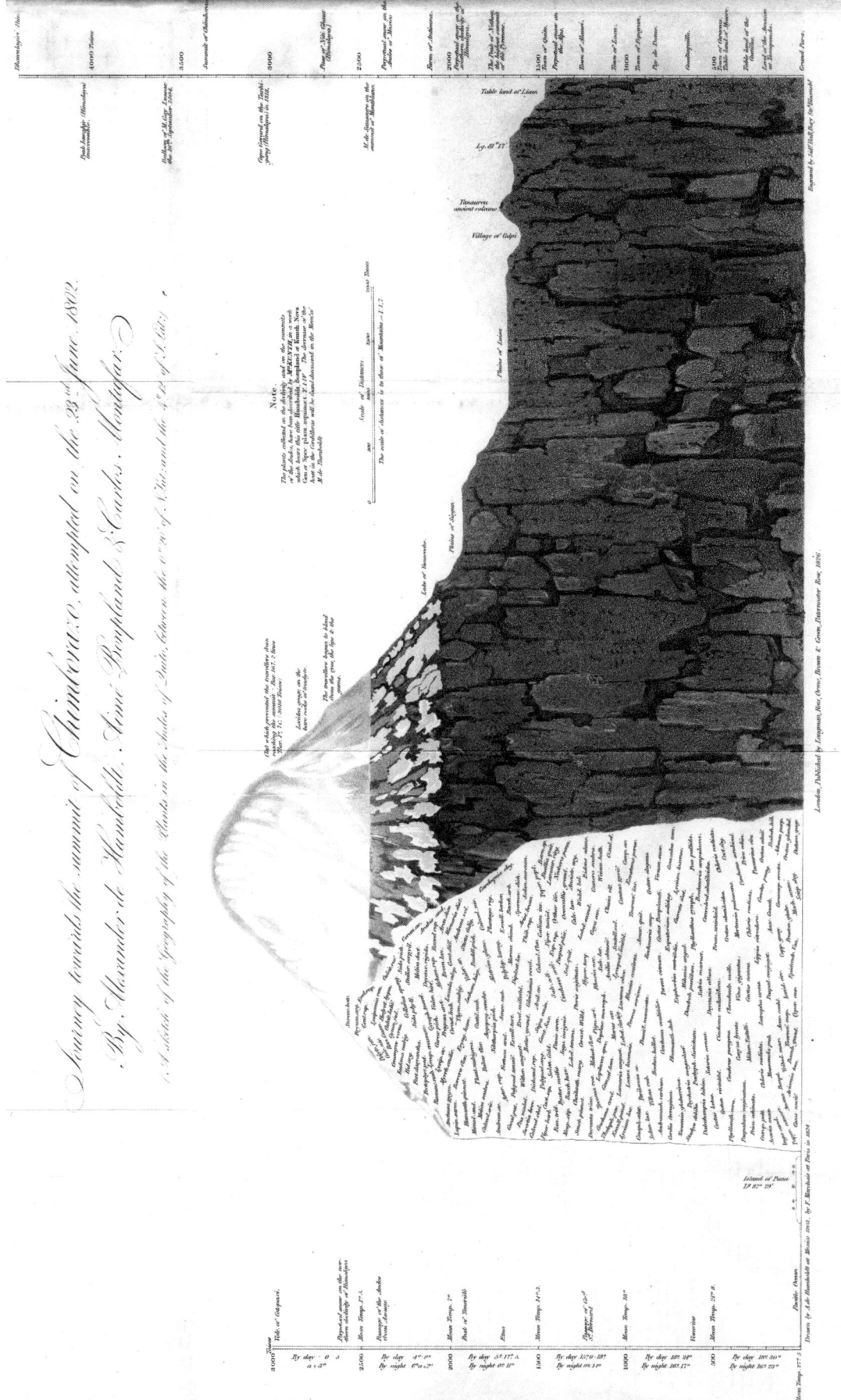

magnetic equator, where the compass needle balances between north and south; Humboldt's measurement of the spot's magnetic intensity would become a standard reference for future geomagnetic readings. From Lima, in the fall of 1802, he sent home samples of guano for analysis. Peruvian farmers had known of its great fertilizing properties for centuries, but Humboldt was the first to draw European attention to its value. On Christmas Eve, they embarked for Guayaquil from Callao, and during the voyage the ever-observant scientist measured the temperature and flow of the current they followed north. Though Humboldt did not discover it, the Humboldt Current, still shown on modern maps, is his most lasting legacy.

Reaching Acapulco in March 1803, the men spent the next year exploring Mexico. Based in Mexico City, Humboldt spent much of his time doing research in government offices, archives, and libraries as background for the first regional geographic essay ever written, his *Essai politique sur le Royaume de la Nouvelle-Espagne* (Political Essay on the Kingdom of New Spain, 2 vols., 1811). (See his thematic map of the worldwide flow of precious metals, opposite.) He made journeys to climb or measure the surrounding volcanoes, explored silver mines, corrected numerous latitude and longitude errors on maps, and even studied Aztec artifacts. In March 1804, the three men—Montúfar had become an inseparable companion—were in Havana to pick up scientific collections sent there for safe-keeping, and they then boarded a Spanish frigate bound for Philadelphia. Humboldt was reluctant to depart from the New World without meeting Thomas Jefferson, a man whose promotion of liberty he admired, and learning of his plans for exploring the West of North America which the country had just acquired from France in the Louisiana Purchase.

While waiting for a formal invitation from the president, Humboldt became the toast of the American Philosophical Society, founded by Benjamin Franklin, the U.S. version of London's Royal Society. In a Philadelphia news item, he learned of the arrival of some of his manuscripts and collections at his brother's house in Paris, which he had sent three years earlier! During his stay in Washington, D.C. (June 1–13), Humboldt was invited everywhere by everyone, including Secretary of State James Madison and Secretary of the Treasury Albert Gallatin. He lunched with Jefferson at his unfinished Executive Mansion on his second day, and the two got on so well that Jefferson offered Humboldt free use of his personal residence and invited him to Monticello. Having already dispatched Lewis and Clark on their epic western journey, Jefferson sought from Humboldt the latest cartographic and statistical information he had developed on New Spain, now the country's newest neighbor. The scientist was happy to oblige: he had fallen in love with the young country.

On June 30, 1804, Humboldt and Bonpland, with Montúfar, boarded the French frigate *La Favorite* in Philadelphia for the return to Europe, arriving in the Garonne River off Bordeaux on August 1. After a five-years' absence, Humboldt was soon back in Paris, having spent approximately a third of his fortune on one of history's most extraordinary and defining scientific expeditions.

✶ [*Opposite*] "Map of the Different Channels by Which the Precious Metals Flow from the One Continent to the Other." Copperplate map, 15 × 28.7 cm. From vol. 4 of Humboldt's *Political Essay on the Kingdom of New Spain*, trans. from the French by John Black (London: Longman, Hurst, Rees, Orme, and Brown, 1811) [Rare Books Division].

Because of his own mining experience, Humboldt showed particular interest in raw materials of the New World and devoted a large part of his examination of statistical records to the subject of precious metals. He provides numerous tables of data in the work, and one of the amazing numbers he calculates is the sum value of all the gold and silver shipped to Europe from America since the time of Christopher Columbus:

> Taking also the 186,000 marcs of gold, which have passed as spoil into the hands of the conquerors at 25 millions, it follows that the quantity of gold and silver imported into Europe from America, between 1492 and 1803, amounts to *five thousand four hundred and forty-five millions of piastres, or to twenty eight thousand five hundred and eighty-six millions of livres tournois*.*

* £1,166,775,322 Sterling [vol. 3, pp. 431–32; his emphasis].

I

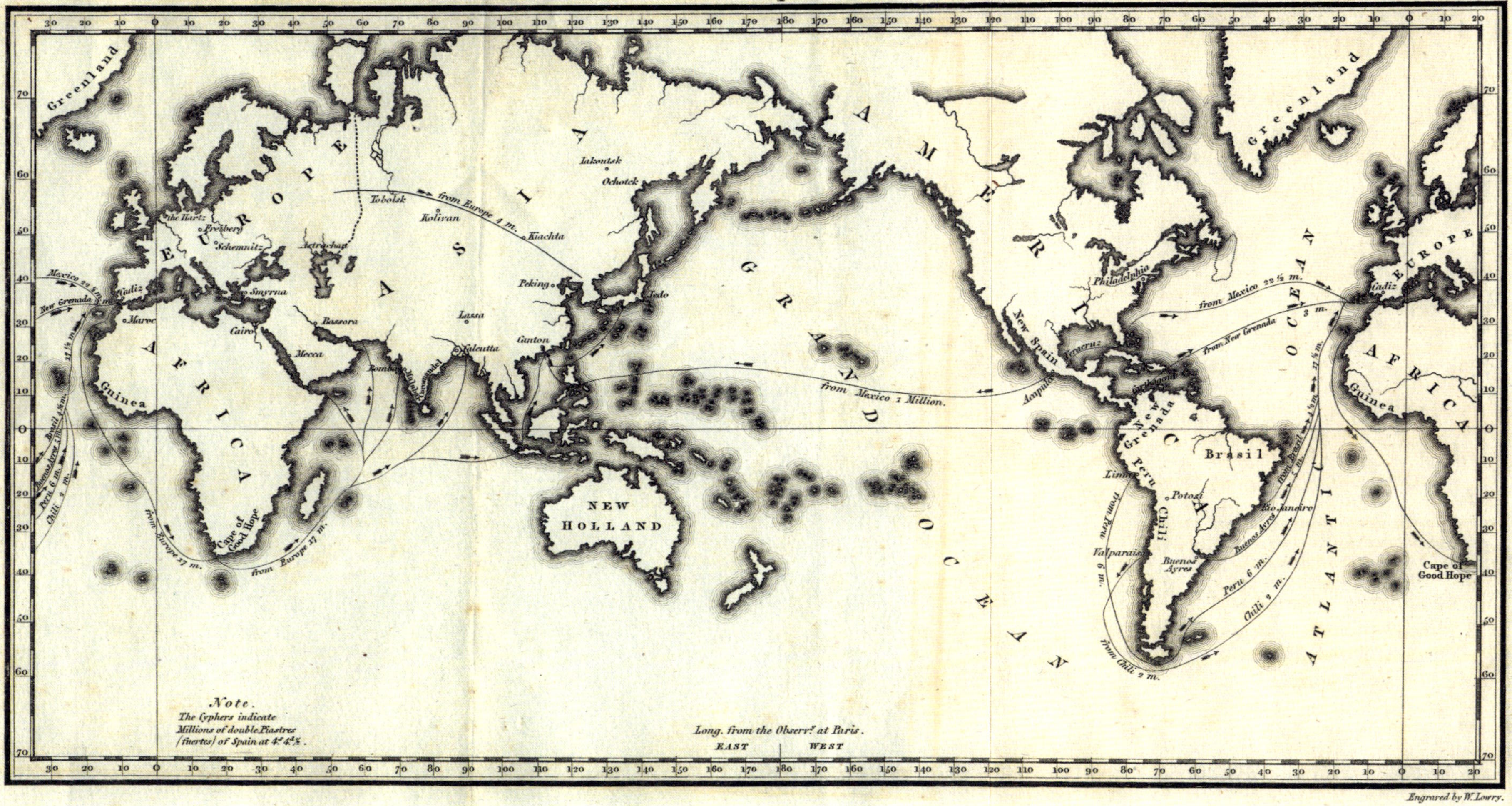

Engraved by W. Lowry.

* * *

In thirty volumes, published over the next thirty years (1805–1834), Humboldt would exhaust most of the rest of his fortune to mine his epic story for all of its ramifications. There were three main categories of publications that fell under the general umbrella title of *Voyage aux regions équinoxiales du Nouveau Continent fait en 1799, 1800, 1801, 1802, 1803 et 1804, par A. Humboldt et A. Bonpland*: (1) scientific works containing botanical, zoological, astronomical, geological, and meteorological data, with two atlases; (2) treatises on the economy and geography of Mexico and Cuba; (3) miscellaneous, more "popular" volumes, including an incomplete narrative of his travels (1799–1801) and *Vues des Cordillères*, which was a strange hodgepodge of Aztec art and descriptions/illustrations of mountains. For titles in the first category, Humboldt sought scientific collaboration with contemporary experts in these subjects; he wrote all the volumes in the other two groups himself, in French.

As stated in the preface to his travel narrative, Humboldt's general purpose was "to collect such facts as are fitted to elucidate a science, of which we have possessed scarcely the outline, and which has been vaguely denominated *natural history of the world, theory of the Earth, or physical geography*" [his emphasis, vol. 1 (1814), p. iii of the Helen Maria Williams translation]. He noted that maritime voyages and circumnavigations had been in vogue, but they did little to promote scientific knowledge of the earth sciences. Widely translated, *Aspects* [or *Views*] *of Nature* (1808) was his most popular work. He was sixty-five when the final volume of the great opus appeared. (Bonpland, for all his trusted abilities during the long trip, proved unhelpful on the writing end. He returned to South America in 1816, initially as a professor in Argentina. But life went downhill for him, and he died in 1858 in a remote village now called Bonpland, where he had been living in a mud hut surrounded by his beloved plants.)

Lionized when he returned, Humboldt settled down in Paris. For fifteen years, he held to a schedule of morning work and evening salon hopping. Apparently, he needed only three or four hours of sleep per day. He maintained a prodigious correspondence (wrote between one thousand and two thousand letters each year, but in an appalling scribble); was a great, often sarcastic conversationalist—more like a noisy lecturer—and knew every scientist and socialite of note. Moreover, as a living legend, Humboldt began to see his role as an inspirer and supporter of young scientific talent. Among those he championed then, and later, were geographer Heinrich Berghaus (1797–1884), organic chemist Justus Liebig (1803–1873), geologist Charles Lyell (1797–1875), and naturalist Louis Agassiz (1807–1873). A planned expedition to Russia was stymied by Napoleon's wars; another, to India, by the British East India Company. But the adventurous Humboldt still managed to climb Mount Vesuvius in 1822, and in April 1827, he spent forty minutes at the bottom of the Thames River in the diving bell used by the British civil engineer Isambard Kingdom Brunel during the construction of the Thames Tunnel.

* * *

The last phase of Humboldt's life began when he moved permanently to Berlin in 1827 and took up residence in a first-floor apartment at 67 Oranienburger Strasse. (See the illustration of his library on the cover.) At that time, Prussia was a repressive police state. A close friendship with King Frederick William III protected Humboldt from conservative enemies at court. But he had many friends outside of government. From the fall of 1827 through April 1828, he delivered sixty-one lectures on physical geography at the University of Berlin, which his brother had founded in 1810. With echoes of Sir Francis Bacon, Humboldt argued that knowledge had to be derived from verifiable experience, but that scientific facts (data) could also appeal to the imagination. Delivered in fluent German, from bare outlines without notes, the lectures were hugely popular with the public. They became the basis of his final great work, *Kosmos*.

In April 1829, Humboldt used a sudden invitation to go to Russia to consult about the new metal called platinum as an opportunity to realize his other grand dream: an expedition through Asia. But he was now thirty years older than when he toured New Spain, and exceedingly famous; he could not travel incognito or in peace. In St. Petersburg, he was treated as a personal guest of Czar Nicholas I, and, as an unfortu-

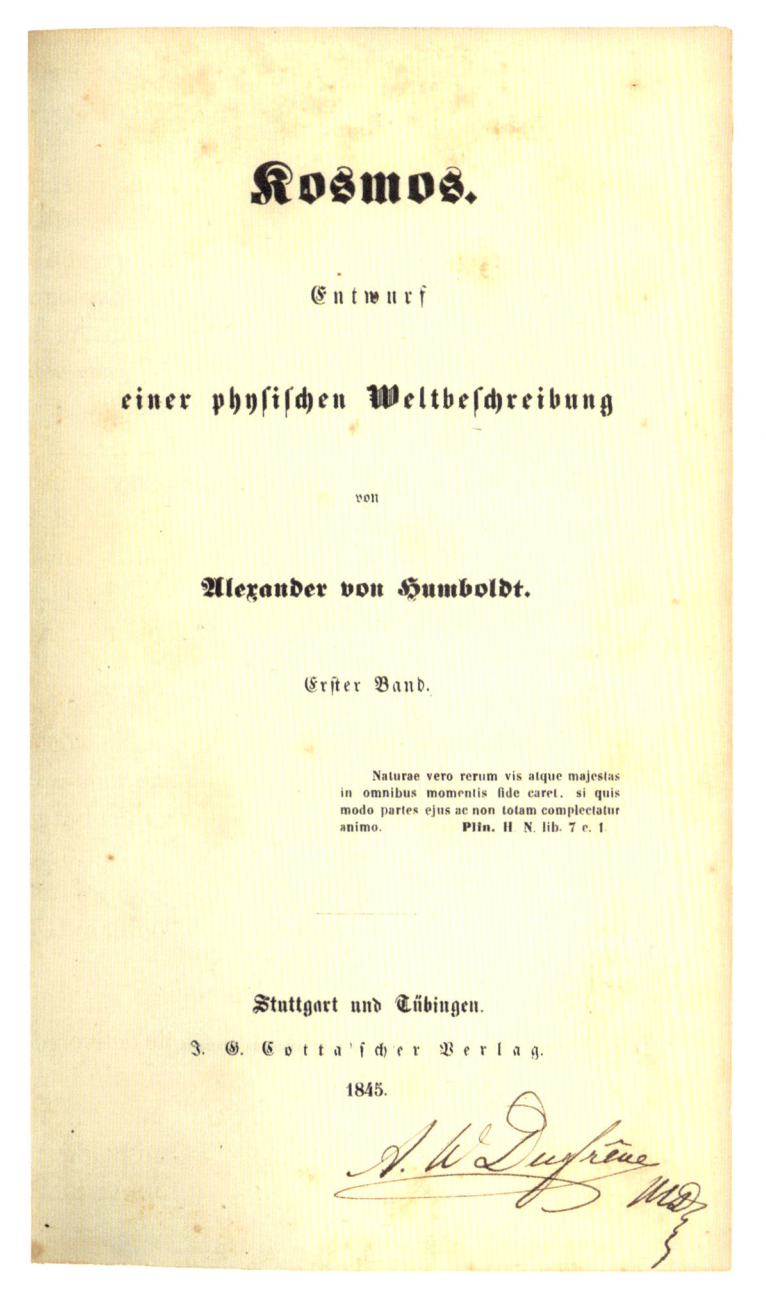

✳ Title page of vol. 1 of Humboldt's master work, *Kosmos: Entwurf einer physischen Weltbeschreibung von Alexander von Humboldt…*, 5 vols. (Stuttgart and Tübingen: Cotta, 1845–1862) [Rare Books Division].

nate result, his expedition became more of a traveling circus with its entourage of officials. In a whirlwind of about six months' duration, the party covered approximately 9,700 miles (some by river), passed through 658 post-stations, and used more than 12,000 post-horses! Knowing the geology of the Ural Mountains, Humboldt predicted that diamonds would be found there, and shortly afterward they were, the first outside of the tropics. He was back in Berlin just after Christmas. The net achievement of the trip was not a publication—Humboldt's modest work about it would not appear for many years—but impetus for establishing a chain of geomagnetic observation stations around the world to develop international scientific collaboration. Gradually, in pieces, this would be accomplished, particularly with the support of the British government, which eventually equipped stations across its vast empire.

After his brother died in 1835, leaving him deeply bereft, Humboldt devoted himself to his master work about the entire material world, titled (in its English translation) *Cosmos: A Sketch of a Physical Description of the World*. His goal, of course, was to stimulate further scientific inquiry, but he also hoped to promote the enjoyment of nature using a vivid, accessible style—in short, to communicate intellectual excitement. The first volume appeared in 1845 when he was seventy-six, the second when he was seventy-eight, the third at eighty-one, and the fourth at the age of eighty-nine! The fifth volume, unfinished at his death, was published from Humboldt's notes and with a lengthy index in 1862. Humboldt viewed nature as a unified whole of which humanity was part, and he thought that scientific knowledge was part of a country's wealth, a natural resource that needed support and development. Called the last great work of the last universal man, *Cosmos* was spectacularly received.

Fate was not so kind. Having known, literally, all the great men of his time—even having become one himself—Humboldt died penniless and possession-less: he had to deed everything he owned to his valet to pay his back wages.

✳ ✳ ✳

If he were alive today, Humboldt would be a strong supporter of the environment, urging global ecological studies, for he saw clearly the interrelationship of humankind and nature. In the preface to the first edition of *Views of Nature*, he wrote: "Everywhere the reader's attention is directed to the perpetual influence which physical nature exercises on the moral condition and on the destiny of man" (p. x of the 1850 London edition, translated from the German by E. C. Otté and Henry G. Bohn). Thematic maps now play an important role in such studies. In fact, though Humboldt may not have understood it then, thematic maps have continued to do his work.

✽ [*Opposite*] "Vulkanischen erscheinungen der Erdoberfläche" (plate 12). Lithograph map, with added color, 20.2 × 28 cm. From Traugott Bromme's *Atlas zu Alex. v. Humboldt's Kosmos in zweiundvierzig tafeln mit erläuterndem texte* (Stuttgart: Krais & Hoffmann, [1851]) [Rare Books Division].

The atlas was published as a companion volume to Humboldt's *Kosmos*, with forty-two thematic maps and plates by Bromme and explanatory text drawn from Humboldt and others. This map focuses on volcanic activity around the world: eruptions (red dots), regions (green circles), and ranges (colored lines)—most seem familiar to us today. Inset maps highlight Italy/Sicily, Java, and Iceland. The catastrophic eruption (1881) of Krakatoa in Indonesia is thirty years away, but the large yellow circle around Indonesia and part of Australia shows the destructive reach of Mount Tambora's explosive eruption on April 11, 1815. Its magnitude has been given a 7 on today's Volcanic Explosivity Index, the highest rating of any volcanic eruption since the Lake Taupo (New Zealand) eruption circa A.D. 180.

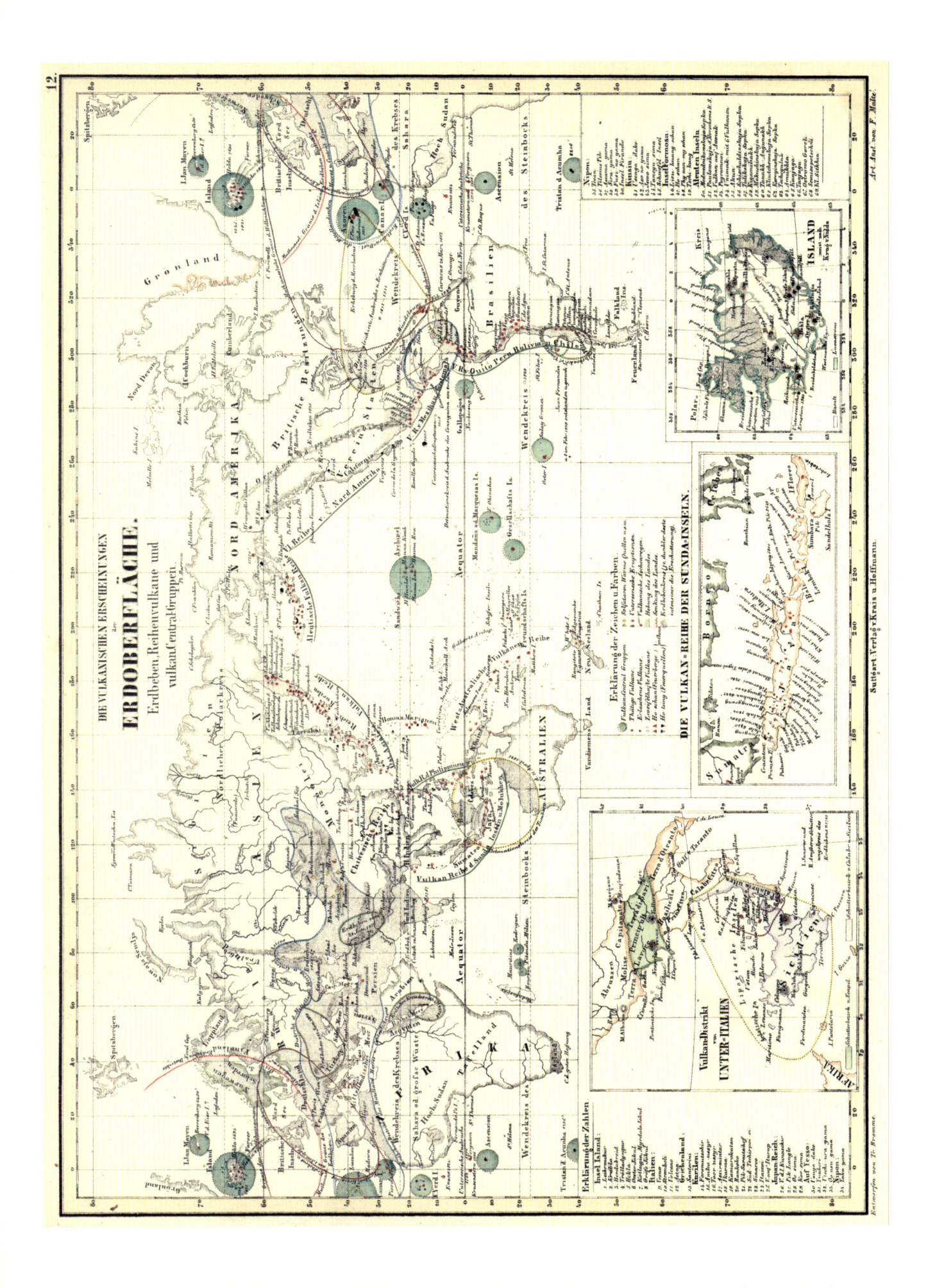

DIE VULKANISCHEN ERSCHEINUNGEN der ERDOBERFLÄCHE.
Erdbeben, Reihenvulkane und vulkan. Central-Gruppen.

Explanation:

The total number of INSANE in each State as reported in the Census is reduced to thousandths, and the number of thousandths of each sex, in each decade of life, is represented by the distance measured on the horizontal lines, severally, from the perpendicular base line.

The males are on the left of the base line, and the females on the right.

The lowest horizontal line represents the first decade, under ten years of age, and the highest over one hundred years.

The sex which preponderates is shaded.

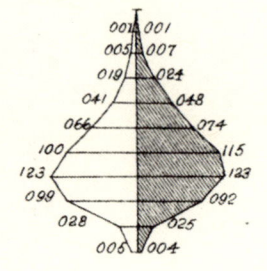

UNITED STATES

✼ Key to Francis Amasa Walker's "Chart Showing the Distribution by Age and Sex of Insanity" (1874).

LANDMARK THEMATIC ATLASES

THIS SECTION reads as would a biblical genealogy of sorts: Alexander von Humboldt taught Heinrich Berghaus and influenced Alexander Keith Johnston; Berghaus taught August Petermann; and Petermann collaborated with Berghaus and Johnston. More accurately, it reflects the passing on of the thematic torch lit by Humboldt. There were isolated "ignitions" throughout Europe before him—he, of course, was not the first to construct a thematic map or even to think of how one might do it—but every new direction needs a leader. More than anyone who preceded him, Humboldt provided that role.

N. M. MAIRE, *fl.* 1820s

DEVELOPMENTS in urban cartography naturally embraced thematic mapping, for city administrations needed to understand, identify, and deliver services throughout their jurisdictions. Maps provided the visual aids. (See also Urban Planning in the Qualitative Thematic Maps section.)

Little is known about N. M. Maire, but he certainly had contacts in Paris's 1820s government. In 1808, he self-published *La topographie de Paris, ou, Plan détaillé de la ville de Paris et de ses faubourgs*, a small city atlas containing twenty maps and 104 pages of alphabetical listings of streets and the addresses of public offices, hotels, hospitals, and other establishments of interest. According to his preface, a number of changes to street names followed an imperial decree of May 1806 (probably Napoleon's demand for fifteen new public fountains and related construction projects)—hence, the need for such an updated work. Each of Paris's twenty *arrondissements* (districts) has its own map in this atlas, but they are designed as individual parts of a larger city map. A key map, showing how the pieces fit together, is provided. Obviously, Maire was someone with cartographic experience who had good access to government information by the time he published his urban thematic atlas approximately a dozen years later.

✻ [*Pages following*] *Atlas administratif de Paris*. Seventeen copperplate maps, fourteen with added color, each 35.3 × 46.8 cm ([Paris: Lottin de St-Germain, 1828?]) [Marquand Art Library]. Each map was printed with a blank round title cartouche in the upper right, to be pasted over with a different engraved title label. The first edition appeared in 1821, and only about a dozen copies of that have been catalogued in national databases.

First urban thematic atlas. It consists of fourteen copies of the same map of Paris, each devoted to a specific subject identified in the title cartouche (such as lighting districts, sewers, markets, firefighting districts); hand-coloring adds the visual thematic layer. Princeton's copy also includes three blank, uncolored copies of the map bound in the back—reserved, presumably, for future topics.

The title page, lacking in Princeton's copy, carries a dedication to the "le comte Anglès, ministre d'état, préfet de police" (Jules-Jean-Baptiste Anglès, comte, 1778–1828, French politician). The brief prefatory text acknowledges that several of the maps may be "aussi curieux pour l'amateur, que nécessaires pour l'administrateur": essentially, the atlas is intended as a bureaucratic tool. Maire says, for example, that it is important to know where the sewer lines run before initiating construction projects.

✻ [*Overleaf*] Untitled map of Paris. Copperplate map, 35.3 × 46.8 cm. From *Atlas administratif de Paris*. The template for the maps.

✻ [*Overleaf*] "Plan lavé topographiquement de la ville de Paris." Copperplate map, 35.3 × 46.8 cm, with added color. From *Atlas administratif de Paris*.

The four colors (besides the blue for water) indicate public edifices (gray, slanted lines), housing areas (pink), remarkable gardens (green), and promenades (pale orange).

✻ [*Overleaf*] "Tracé des conduites d'eaux qui alimentent les fontaines de Paris." Copperplate map, 35.3 ×

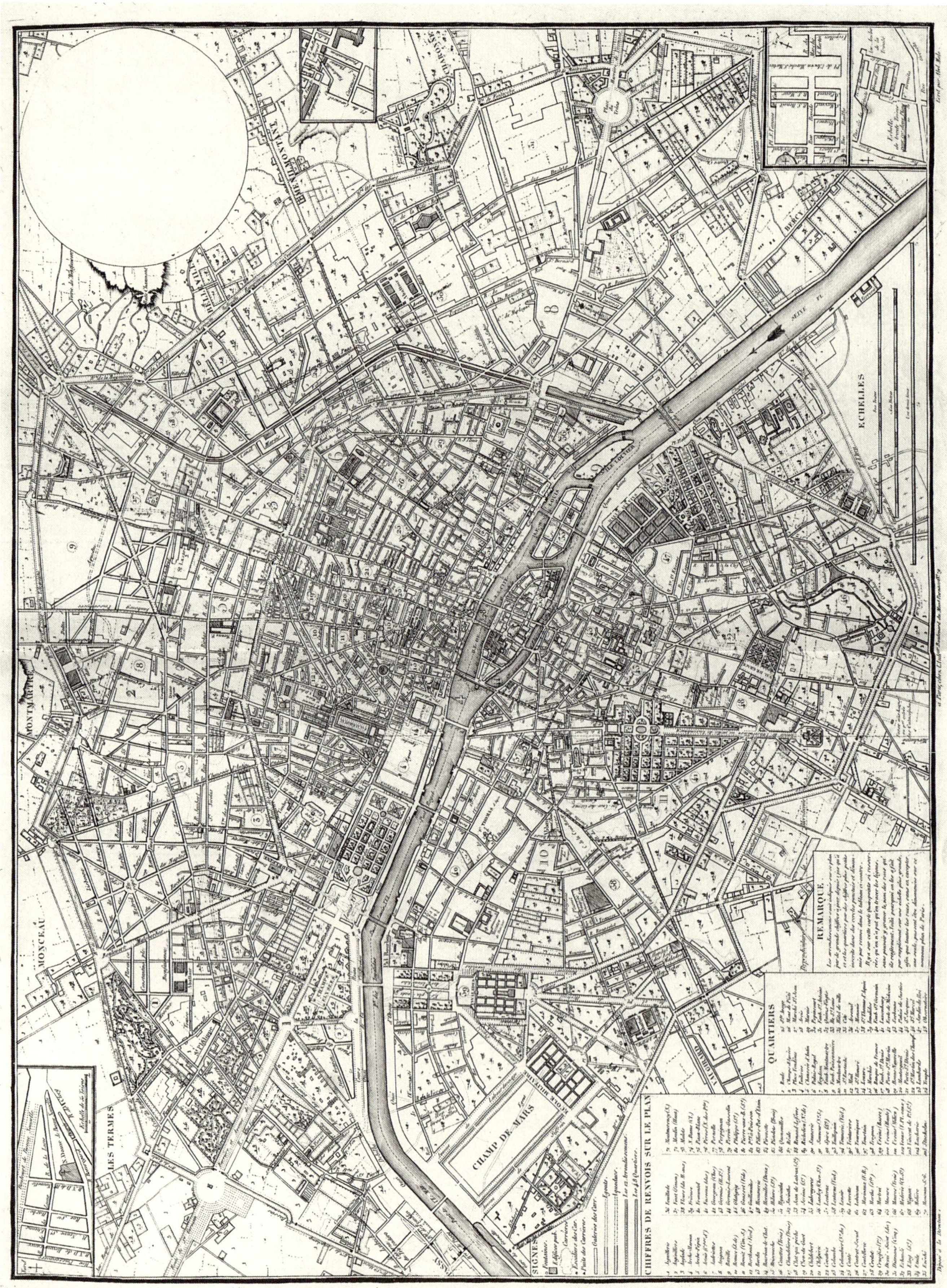

CHAMP DE MARS
ECHELLES
MONCEAU
LES TERMES
MONTMARTRE
REMARQUE
QUARTIERS
CHIFFRES DE RENVOIS SUR LE PLAN

PLAN
LEVÉ TOPOGRAPHIQUEMENT
DE LA
VILLE DE PARIS
Par MAIRE Géog.

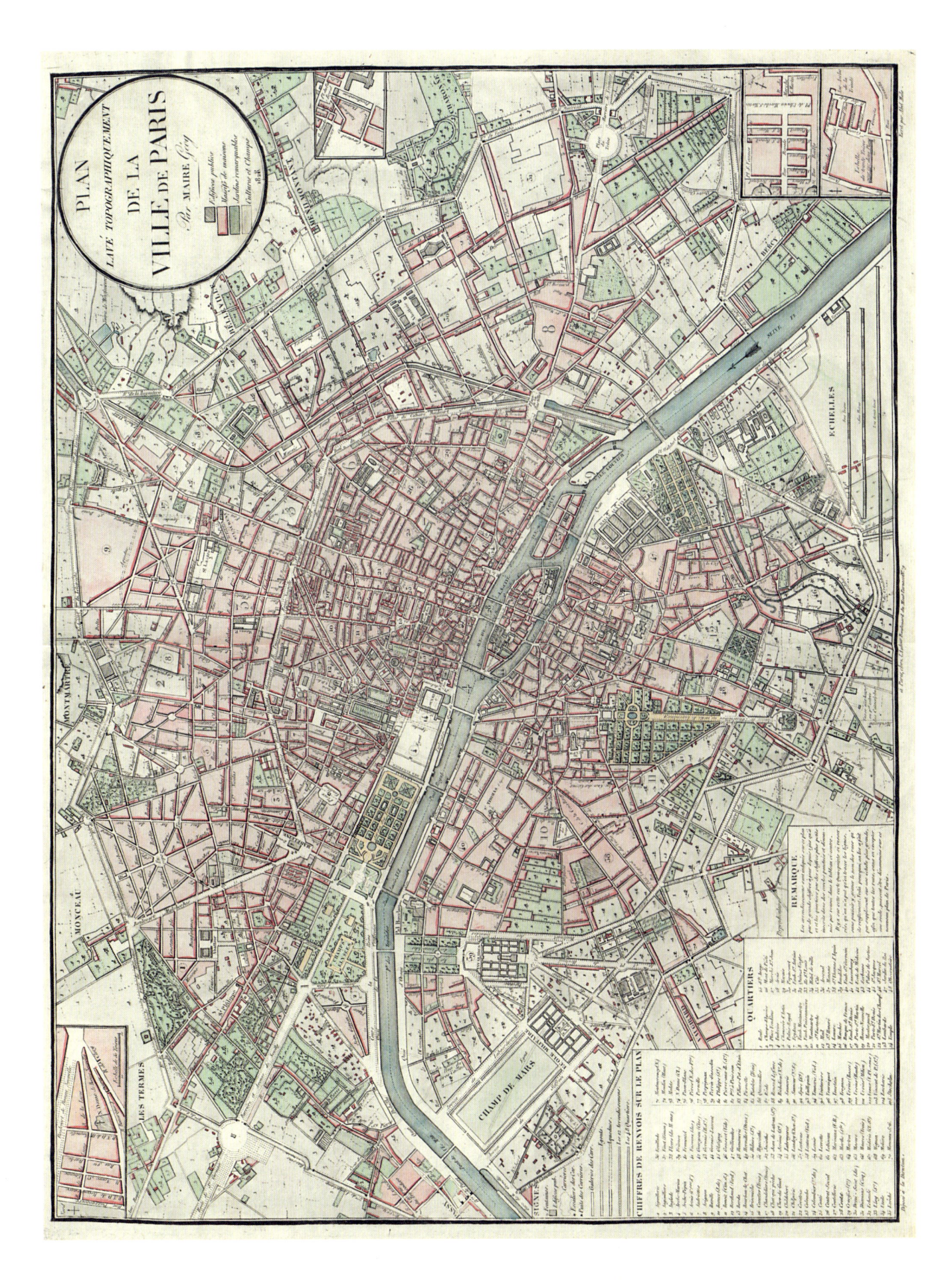

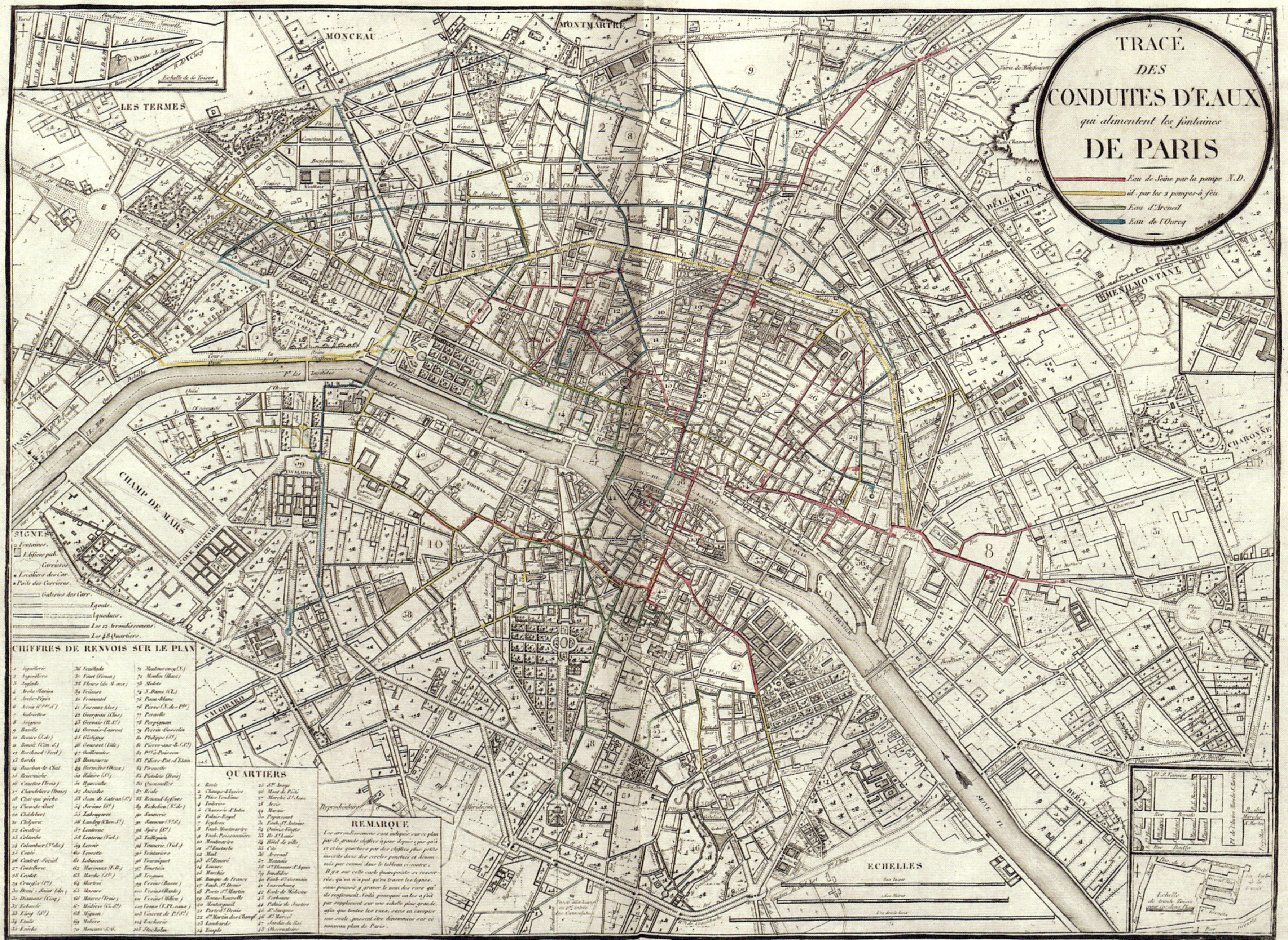
TRACÉ
DES
CONDUITES D'EAUX
qui alimentent les fontaines
DE PARIS
Eau de Seine par la pompe N.D.
id. par les 2 pompes-à-feu
Eau d'Arcueil
Eau de l'Ourcq
MONCEAU
MONTMARTRE
LES TERMES
CHAMP DE MARS
SIGNES
CHIFFRES DE RENVOIS SUR LE PLAN
QUARTIERS
REMARQUE
ECHELLES
CHARONNE
BERCY

46.8 cm, with outline color. From *Atlas administratif de Paris*.

The map traces the routes of water pipes that feed the various fountains in Paris. Four colors are used to indicate different water sources: Seine (via two pumping systems), Arcueil, and Ourcq.

HEINRICH KARL WILHELM BERGHAUS
1797–1884

Heinrich Karl Wilhelm Berghaus was born in the Prussian city of Kleve and was educated as a surveyor. He served in the Prussian army, became a geographical engineer employed in the War Department, and was assigned in 1816 to help conduct a trigonometrical field survey of the country. In 1821, he assumed an applied mathematics (surveying and geodesy) teaching post at a school in Berlin, which he held until 1854. Some of his first maps appeared in *Hertha*, a geographical journal that Berghaus cofounded and coedited, beginning in 1825. With the help of Alexander von Humboldt he established a geographical school (Geographische Kunstschule) in Potsdam in 1836. Future important mapmaker August Petermann (see his entry in this Landmark Thematic Atlases section) was one of his students.

Berghaus's greatest achievement, originally intended to supplement Humboldt's last work, *Cosmos*, was his *Physikalischer Atlas* (1845–1848). For the first time in an atlas, different physical aspects of Earth were represented graphically in maps, supported with tables of observed data. Throughout his life, Berghaus also published a number of scholarly texts on geographical subjects and was associated with several geographical journals. His lengthy correspondence (1825–1858) with Humboldt was published in three volumes in 1863. Berghaus died in Stettin, today's Szczecin in Poland, in 1884.

✻ Portrait of Heinrich Karl Wilhelm Berghaus. From Friedrich Beck and Eckart Henning's *Brandenburgisches Biographisches Lexikon* (Potsdam: Verlag für Berlin-Brandenburg, 2002) [courtesy of Verlag für Berlin-Brandenburg].

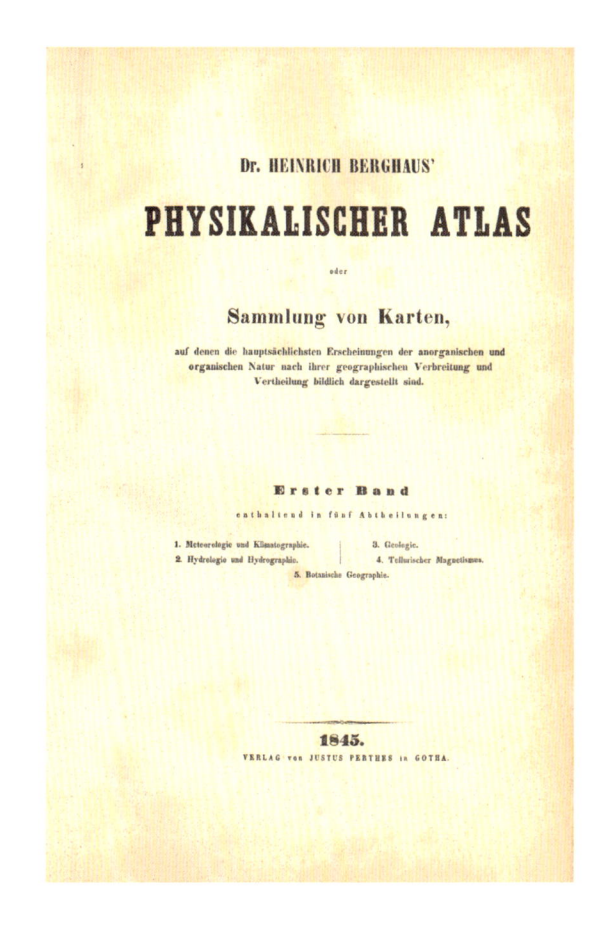

✻ Title page of Berghaus's *Dr. Heinrich Berghaus' Physikalischer Atlas: oder, Sammlung von Karten, auf denen die hauptsächlichsten Erscheinungen der anorganischen und organischen Natur nach ihrer geographischen Verbreitung und Vertheilung bildlich dargestellt sind*, 2 vols. (Gotha: J. Perthes, 1845–1848[–1849]) [Historic Maps Collection].

DIE ISOTHERMKURVEN DER NÖRDLICHEN HALBKUGEL

POLAR-PROJECTION

The first great scientific physical atlas, which created a new genre of thematic atlases. This work represents the culmination of all the innovations in the different ways that people had looked at the geographic landscape of the world, and the evolving techniques that had developed to display those views, since the time of Francis Bacon. Issued gradually in eighteen installments over a dozen years (1837–1848), the first edition of the bound atlas consists of ninety maps in two volumes, dated 1845 and 1848, with individual maps dated from 1837 to 1848. Princeton's bibliographically complicated copy appears to substitute some maps and text from the enlarged second edition (1849–1852). There are eight sections—meteorology and climatology, hydrology and hydrography, geology, terrestrial magnetism, botany, zoology, anthropology, and ethnography—representing both "hard" and "soft" sciences.

✷ [*Opposite*] "Die Isothurmkurven der Nördlichen Halbkugel." Lithograph map, with added color, diameter of 27.5 cm, on sheet 37 × 45.4 cm. From vol. 1 of Berghaus's *Physikalischer Atlas* [Historic Maps Collection].

This is the second map of the first section of the atlas, devoted to meteorology. The subject is the mean temperature in the northern hemisphere, shown in a polar projection and circled with isotherms at 5° C intervals.

✷ [*Overleaf*] "Geographische Verbreitung der Menschen-Rassen." Lithograph map, 16.7 × 28.3 cm, within larger border, on sheet 37 × 46 cm. From vol. 2 of Berghaus's *Physikalischer Atlas* [Historic Maps Collection].

This is the first map of the seventh section of the atlas, devoted to anthropology. The design of the sheet, with surrounding head-portraits of men and women representing different human races, harkens back to the beautiful carte-à-figures maps of the Dutch golden age of mapmaking. However, a glimpse of the charts at the bottom confirm its scientific foundation.

ALEXANDER KEITH JOHNSTON
1804–1871

THE SCOTTISH NOVELIST Sir Walter Scott described the Johnston clan as "a race of uncommon hardihood, much attached to each other and their

✷ Portrait of Alexander Keith Johnston. From *One Hundred Years of Map Making: The Story of W. & A. K. Johnston* (Edinburgh: W. & A. K. Johnston, 1925) [Historic Maps Collection].

chieftain" (*Tales of a Grandfather: Being Stories Taken from Scottish History*, 2nd ser., 1829). Their crest was a flying spur and their motto was "Ready Aye Ready." Both were adopted by the Edinburgh publishing firm W. & A. K. Johnston, when it was formed in 1826 by the two Johnston brothers William and Alexander Keith. (William had started his own steel and copperplate printing business the previous year.)

Alexander Keith Johnston was educated at the Royal High School, Scott's alma mater, and the University of Edinburgh. Though he originally intended to go into medicine, an early fascination with geography led him to an apprenticeship with the local engraving firm of James Kirkwood & Sons, where he had been preceded in that capacity by his brother. During hikes in the West Highlands in 1830, he found so many inaccuracies in the best maps of Scotland that he was eager for the Johnston brothers to make high-quality mapmaking their central business focus. In 1834, the firm was appointed as engravers to King William IV,

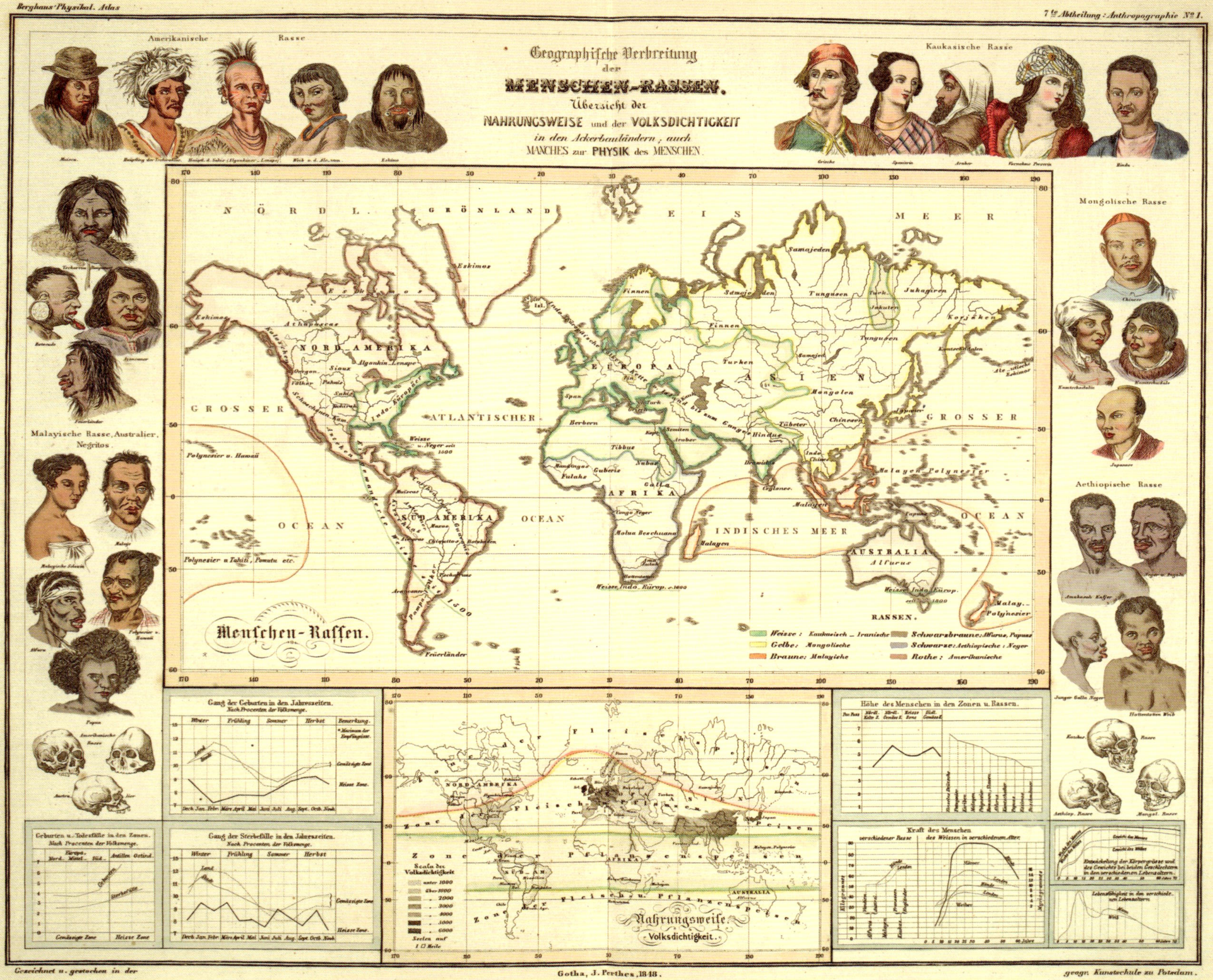
Berghaus' Physikal. Atlas
7te Abtheilung: Anthropographie No 1.
Geographische Verbreitung der
MENSCHEN-RASSEN.
Übersicht der
NAHRUNGSWEISE und der VOLKSDICHTIGKEIT
in den Ackerbauländern; auch
MANCHES zur PHYSIK des MENSCHEN.
Amerikanische Rasse
Kaukasische Rasse
Mongolische Rasse
Aethiopische Rasse
Malayische Rasse, Australier, Negritos.
Menschen-Rassen.
RASSEN.
Weisse: Kaukasisch - Iranische
Gelbe: Mongolische
Braune: Malayische
Schwarzbraune: Alfurus, Papuas
Schwarze: Aethiopische: Neger
Rothe: Amerikanische
Gang der Geburten in den Jahreszeiten.
Gang der Sterbefälle in den Jahreszeiten.
Geburten u. Todesfälle in den Zonen.
Höhe des Menschen in den Zonen u. Rassen.
Kraft des Menschen
Nahrungsweise
Volksdichtigkeit.
Gezeichnet u. gestochen in der
Gotha, J. Perthes, 1848.
geogr. Kunstschule zu Potsdam.

an honor continued under Queen Victoria. With the publication of Alexander's important *National Atlas of Historical, Commercial, and Political Geography: Constructed from the Most Recent and Authentic Sources* (1843), most of which maps he had personally engraved, the firm became "Geographers to the Queen."

The work of Alexander von Humboldt introduced Alexander to the importance of physical geography. In 1848, with the assistance of August Petermann (see Petermann's entry in this Landmark Thematic Atlases section), he produced the very substantial *Physical Atlas*, engraved and printed by the Johnston firm and published by William Blackwood & Sons. This was the pioneer work in English in this genre. The first edition was printed from a hand press and the second (1856) by means of lithography, though the plates were still hand-colored. His *Royal Atlas* (1861), containing forty-eight large maps (19.25 × 24 inches), became the standard-bearer of the firm and went through numerous revised editions.

William Johnston became lord provost of Edinburgh (1848–1851) and was knighted by Queen Victoria at the end of his term. He retired from the business in 1867. Alexander's son, Keith Johnston (1844–1879), was a well-trained draughtsman and authored a number of geographical works, but he met an untimely death leading the Royal Geographical Society's exploring expedition to Lake Nyasa in Africa.

✱ Title page of Johnston's *The Physical Atlas: A Series of Maps & Illustrations of the Geographical Distribution of Natural Phenomena, Embracing: I. Geology. II. Hydrography. III. Meteorology. IV. Natural History. By Alexander Keith Johnston … with the Co-operation of Men Eminent in the Different Departments of Science* (Edinburgh: W. Blackwood & Sons, 1849) [Historic Maps Collection]. The first printing of the atlas appeared in the previous year. Princeton's copy is inscribed: "To the College of New Jersey who lately conferred the Degree in Divinity on the Revd John Somerville this volume is presented by a few of his friends in Glasgow January 1st 1856."

First English atlas devoted to thematic maps, based on Heinrich Berghaus's *Physikalischer Atlas* and dedicated to Alexander von Humboldt. Of the thirty maps, fifteen were designed by Berghaus but enlarged and revised by Johnston; the rest are Johnston's original maps reflecting the latest work of scientific authorities. Preceding each double-page sheet are several pages of explanatory text and supporting tables of data.

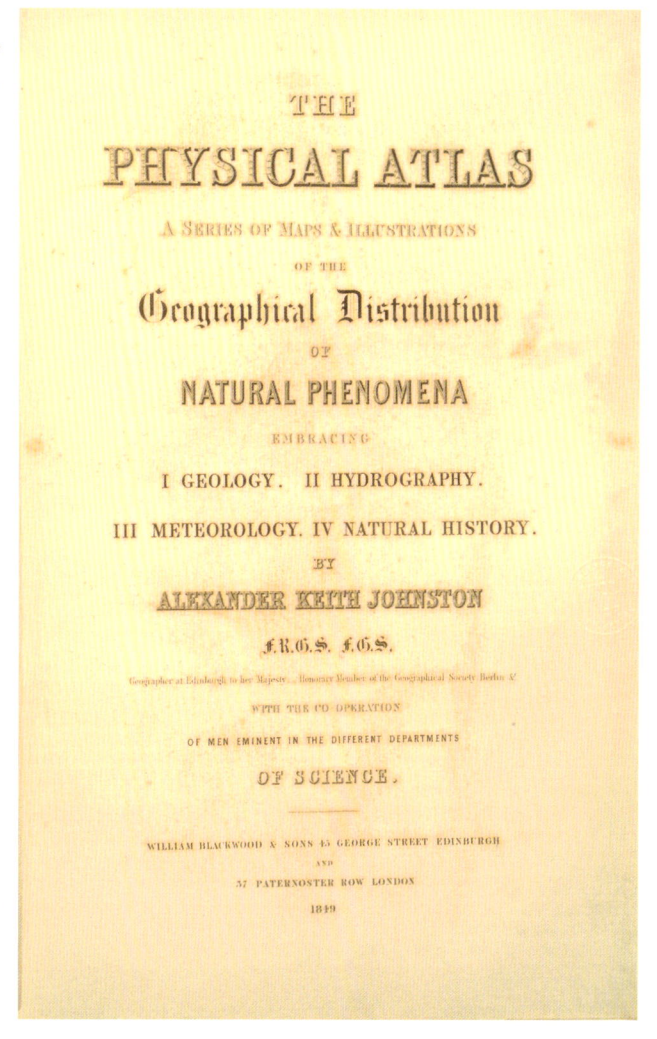

✱ [*Overleaf*] "Outlines of Botanical Geography" and "The Geographical Distribution of Plants." Engraved map and illustrations within one border, 47 × 55.2 cm, with added color. From Johnston's *The Physical Atlas* (1849) [Historic Maps Collection]. On this sheet, Johnston incorporated and expanded data from both Humboldt and Berghaus.

✱ [*Overleaf*] "Geographical Division and Distribution of Aves (Birds) over the World" and "Geographical Division and Distribution of the Birds of Europe." Engraved maps and illustrations within one border,

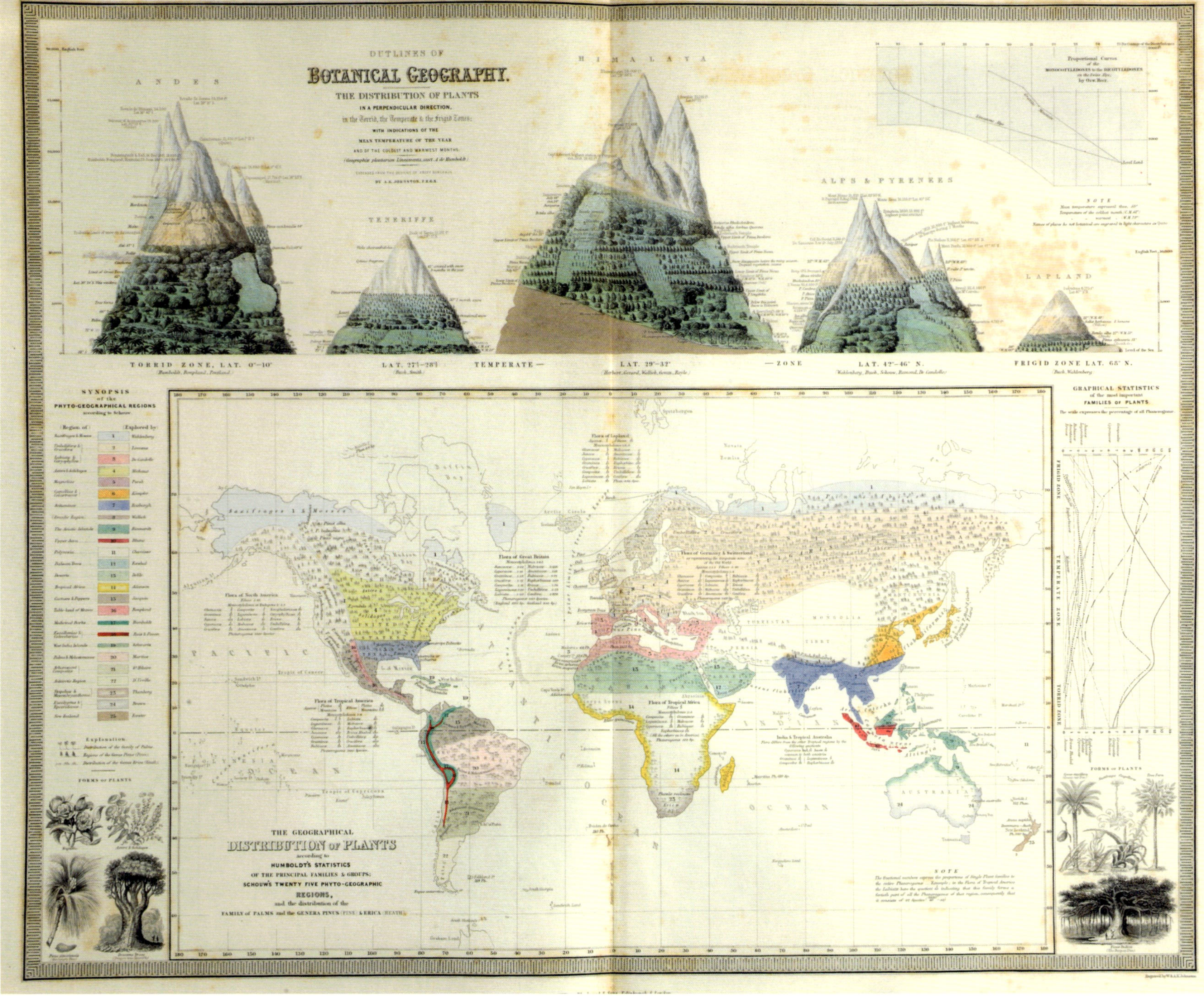
OUTLINES OF
BOTANICAL GEOGRAPHY.
THE DISTRIBUTION OF PLANTS
IN A PERPENDICULAR DIRECTION,
in the Torrid, the Temperate & the Frigid Zones;
WITH INDICATIONS OF THE
MEAN TEMPERATURE OF THE YEAR
AND OF THE COLDEST AND WARMEST MONTHS.
(Geographiæ plantarum Lineamenta, auct. A. de Humboldt.)
BY A.K. JOHNSTON, F.R.G.S.
ANDES
TENERIFFE
HIMALAYA
ALPS & PYRENEES
LAPLAND
TORRID ZONE, LAT. 0°–10°
LAT. 27½–28½
TEMPERATE —
LAT. 29°–32°
— ZONE
LAT. 42°–46° N.
FRIGID ZONE LAT. 68° N.
SYNOPSIS
of the
PHYTO-GEOGRAPHICAL REGIONS
according to Schouw.
GRAPHICAL STATISTICS
of the most important
FAMILIES OF PLANTS.
FRIGID ZONE
TEMPERATE ZONE
TORRID ZONE
FORMS OF PLANTS
Explanation
NOTE
PACIFIC
OCEAN
INDIAN
AUSTRALIA
Flora of Great Britain
Flora of Lapland
Flora of Germany & Switzerland
Flora of North America
Flora of Tropical America
Flora of Tropical Africa
India & Tropical Australia
THE GEOGRAPHICAL
DISTRIBUTION OF PLANTS
according to
HUMBOLDT'S STATISTICS
OF THE PRINCIPAL FAMILIES & GROUPS;
SCHOUW'S TWENTY FIVE PHYTO-GEOGRAPHIC
REGIONS,
and the distribution of the
FAMILY of PALMS and the GENERA PINUS (PINE) & ERICA (HEATH).

ZOOLOGICAL GEOGRAPHY

TYPES OF THE BIRDS OF THE OLD WORLD

GEOGRAPHICAL DIVISION AND DISTRIBUTION OF AVES BIRDS OVER THE WORLD

GEOGRAPHICAL DIVISION AND DISTRIBUTION OF THE BIRDS OF EUROPE FROM THE LATEST AUTHORITIES BY A.K. JOHNSTON, F.R.G.S.

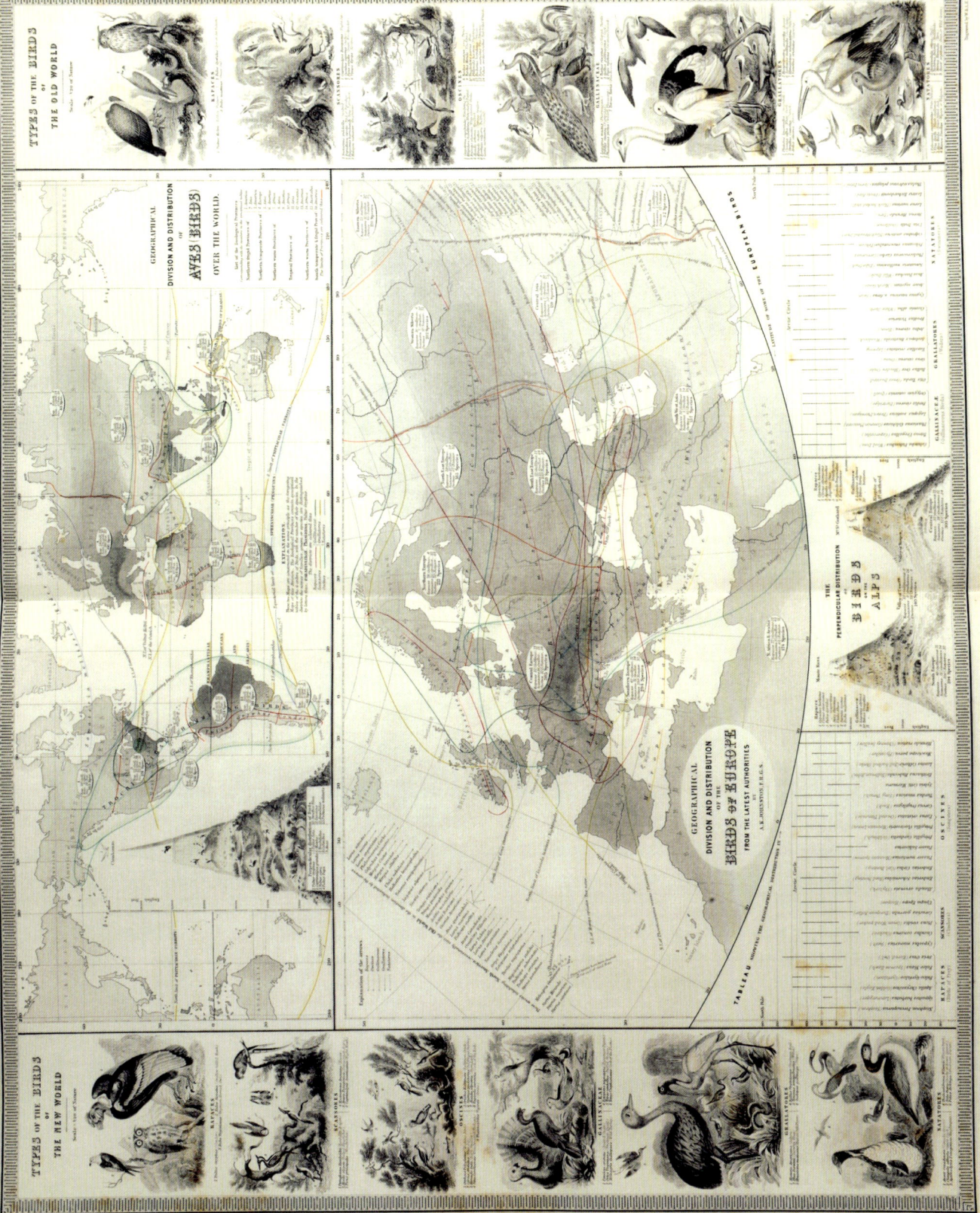

THE PERPENDICULAR DISTRIBUTION OF THE BIRDS OF THE ALPS

TYPES OF THE BIRDS OF THE NEW WORLD

46.5 × 57.7 cm, with added color. From Johnston's *The Physical Atlas* (1849) [Historic Maps Collection]. One of Johnston's original thematic works.

AUGUST PETERMANN
1822–1878

BORN IN THE Prussian province of Saxony, August Petermann was destined for the ministry by his parents. However, proving at an early age to enjoy and excel in geography, particularly in drawing maps, he was admitted to the Geographische Kunstschule (School of Geographical Art) at Potsdam in 1839. The school had been started by Heinrich Berghaus, with the support of Alexander von Humboldt, just three years earlier, and Berghaus was Petermann's instructor. Here, over the course of six years, he studied mathematical, physical, and political geography, ultimately becoming Berghaus's assistant and collaborating on his mentor's great *Physikalischer Atlas*.

For two years (1845–1847), Petermann lived in Edinburgh, where he had gone to assist Alexander Keith Johnston in producing an English adaptation of Berghaus's atlas. *The Physical Atlas: A Series of Maps & Notes Illustrating the Geographical Distribution of Natural Phenomena* appeared in 1848. Then Petermann was drawn to London. During his seven-years' sojourn in the city, he was elected to the Royal Geographical Society, wrote weekly geographical articles, helped Reverend Thomas Milner prepare the popular *Atlas of Physical Geography* (1850), and published a number of separate maps. In addition, he pressured for more government sponsorship of exploration, successfully getting German explorer Heinrich Barth appointed to join James Richardson on an expedition into central Africa. (Petermann's maps later illustrated Barth's published narrative.) Africa and the Arctic would become Petermann's major geographic interests.

In 1854, he moved to Gotha, Germany, to work for Justus Perthes's Geographical Institute, the most extensive map-publishing concern in the world. Here Petermann assumed editorship of a new geographical journal, *Mittheilungen aus Justus Perthes' geographischer Anstalt über wichtige neue Erforschungen auf dem Gesammtgebiete der Geographie von Dr. A. Petermann* [Communications from

✱ Portrait of August Petermann. Frontispiece to *The Popular Science Monthly* 14, no. 2 (December 1878) [General Library Collection].

the Justus Perthes Geographical Institute concerning important new studies in the whole field of geography, by Dr. A. Petermann] or *PGM*, a position he held until his death. His strengths were in the evaluation and analysis of cartographic information sources—not just blindly copying what others had produced—and he drew most of the maps for the first years of the journal.

Beyond their up-to-date geography, "Petermann school" (or "Gotha school") maps were known for their precise lettering and drawing, use of elevation figures, and attractive coloring (many of their lithographed maps were hand-colored). In thematic maps, Petermann also encouraged his pupils to provide the underlying physical characteristics of the terrain. With its Petermann edition (the 6th, 1871–1875), the popular German world atlas *Stielers Handatlas* reached an unparalleled level of scientific achievement and world renown. Sadly, aggravating family and mental health issues caused Petermann to take his own life in 1878.

As his eminent career demonstrates, Petermann deserves to hold an important position in the history of cartography, not just in thematic maps.

✻ Title page of the first issue of Petermann's *PGM* (Gotha: Justus Perthes, 1855) [General Library Collection].

In his preface to the first issue, Petermann famously wrote: "Nie wird deshalb eine Nummer unserer Schrift ausgegeben warden, ohne eine oder mehrere Karten-Beilagen" ("No issue of our publication will ever appear without one or more map supplements"). Known as *Petermanns geographischer Mittheilungen* (*PGM*), the journal ceased publication in 2004. For perspective, consider that the Royal Geographical Society's *The Geographical Journal* began in 1831 under the name of *The Journal of the Royal Geographical Society* and assumed its current title in 1893. The first issue of *National Geographic* appeared in October 1888.

✻ Initial subscription blank for *Petermanns geographischer Mittheilungen*, 1855 [Historic Maps Collection].

✻ [*Overleaf*] "Tafel 1" and "Tafel 2." Lithographed maps, with added color, from *PGM*, issue no. 1 (February 1855) [Historic Maps Collection].

These first maps from the first issue of the periodical, signed "A. Petermann," show some of explorer Heinrich Barth's travels in central Africa, including his trip to Tombouctou in September 1853. They supplement his article "Die Expedition nach Central-Afrika: I. Dr. H. Barth's Reise von Kuka nach Timbuktu" on pages 3–14.

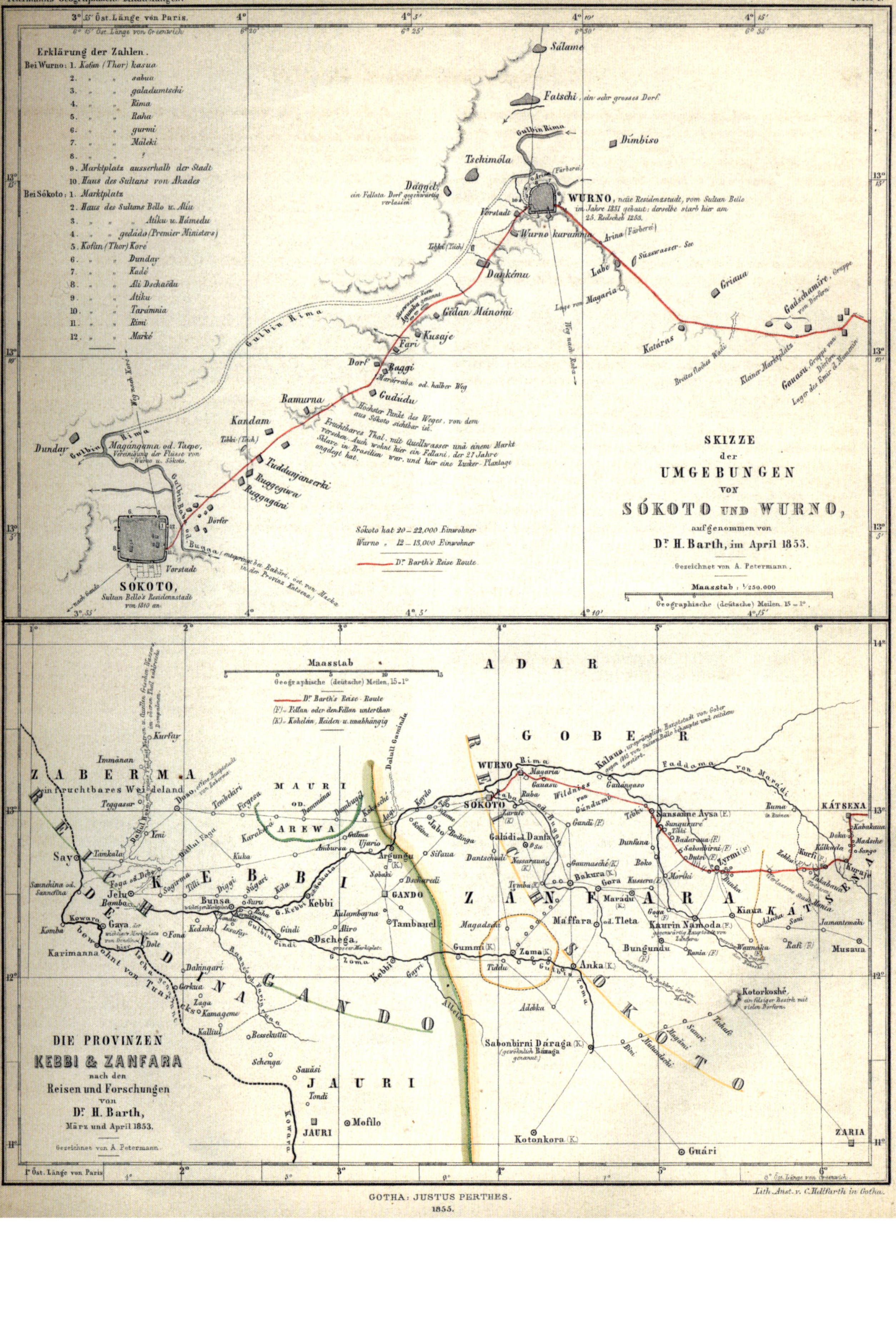

GOTHA: JUSTUS PERTHES.
1855.
Lith. Anst. v. C. Hellfarth in Gotha.

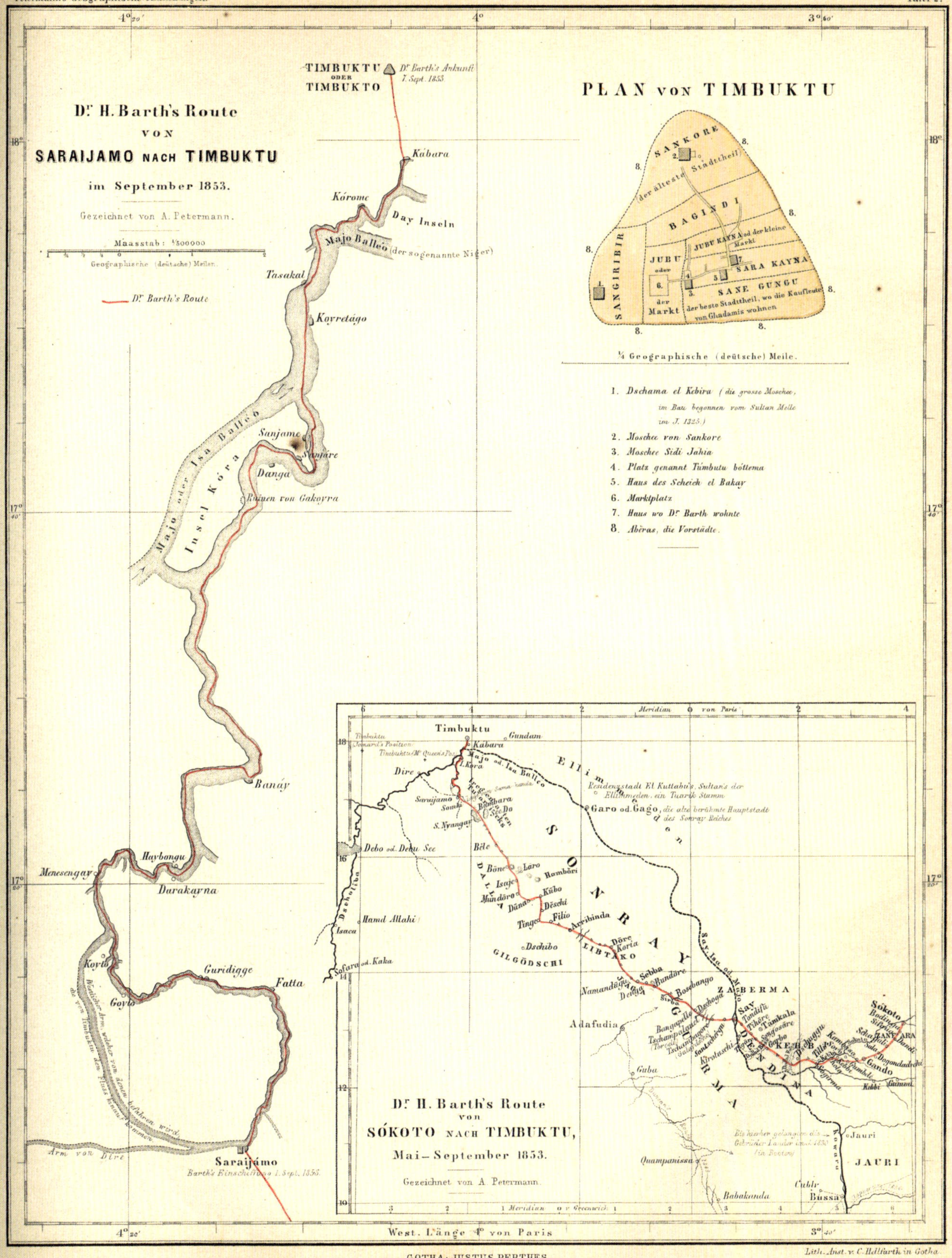

GOTHA: JUSTUS PERTHES.
1855.
Lith. Anst. v. C. Hellfarth in Gotha.

FRANCIS AMASA WALKER
1840–1897

SON OF AN ECONOMIST, Francis Amasa Walker was born into a prominent Boston family and followed its well-worn path of public service. After graduation from Amherst College, he volunteered in a Massachusetts regiment to fight for the North in the Civil War. He rose quickly to the rank of assistant adjutant general but was captured by Confederate forces after the Richmond-Petersburg campaign and served time in Richmond's infamous Libby Prison. Brevetted brigadier general after the war, Walker earned the contemporary appellation "General Walker." (Medical men of the period attributed Walker's early death to the strains and wounds of his military life and the miseries he experienced in the prison.)

Seeming recovery from the war took several years, during which time Walker assisted his father by taking over some of his lecturing duties at Amherst. He got married, started teaching at Williston Academy (Latin, Greek, mathematics), and studied economics in his spare time. In 1868, he joined the editorial staff of the *Springfield Republican* and was determined to follow a career in journalism. However, his family's extensive network of contacts easily secured for him a federal appointment as chief of the Bureau of Statistics (1869–1870), where he became superintendent of the 1870 census.

Overcoming special difficulties caused by the disruption of the war—the demoralization of the South and the new status of blacks—the now-talented statistician created a landmark (for the United States) in the visualization of census data: the *Statistical Atlas of the United States* (1874). Afterward, he joined Yale's economics faculty. In 1881, Walker accepted the presidency of the Massachusetts Institute of Technology, a position he held until his death. During that period, he was also president of the American Statistical Association (1882–1897), the first president of the American Economic Association (1885–1892), and vice president of the National Academy of Sciences (1891–1897).

Walker was a prolific author and made numerous contributions to economic theory. In recognition of his work, the American Economic Association, beginning in 1947, instituted the Francis A. Walker Medal for the lifetime achievement of an individual economist. This award was discontinued in 1982, having been overshadowed by the Nobel Prize for Economics.

✻ Portrait of Francis Amasa Walker as president of the Massachusetts Institute of Technology. From James Phinney Munroe's *A Life of Francis Amasa Walker* (New York: Henry Holt, 1923) [General Library Collection].

✻ [*Opposite*] Title page of the *Statistical Atlas of the United States Based on the Results of the Ninth Census 1870: With Contributions from Many Eminent Men of Science and Several Departments of the Government*, compiled under the authority of Congress by Francis A. Walker ([New York]: Julius Bien, 1874) [Historic Maps Collection].

First U.S. statistical atlas, hence, first real national atlas of the United States, where many important demographics are mapped for the first time. It consists of three sections: I. Physical Features of the United States; II. Population, Social and Industrial Statistics; III. Vital Statistics. Included in the last part are charts devoted to "the Afflicted Classes," referring in the jargon of the period to the "blind, deaf mutes, insane, idiots." In addition, the atlas contains essays on various subjects covered by the visual data—such as woodlands and forest systems, mines and mining in the West, political divisions, population, relation of race and nationality to mortality—authored by, as the title states, "eminent men of science." There are sixty full-page plates, though double-page maps are counted as two plates. Many of the maps cover only the region of the country that is east of the Mississippi River, for there were only thirty-seven states in 1870. Congress authorized an edition of five thousand copies, to be distributed to public libraries, learned societies, colleges, and academies to promulgate the study of political and social statistics. The atlas was awarded a first-class medal at the 1875 International Geographical Congress in Paris.

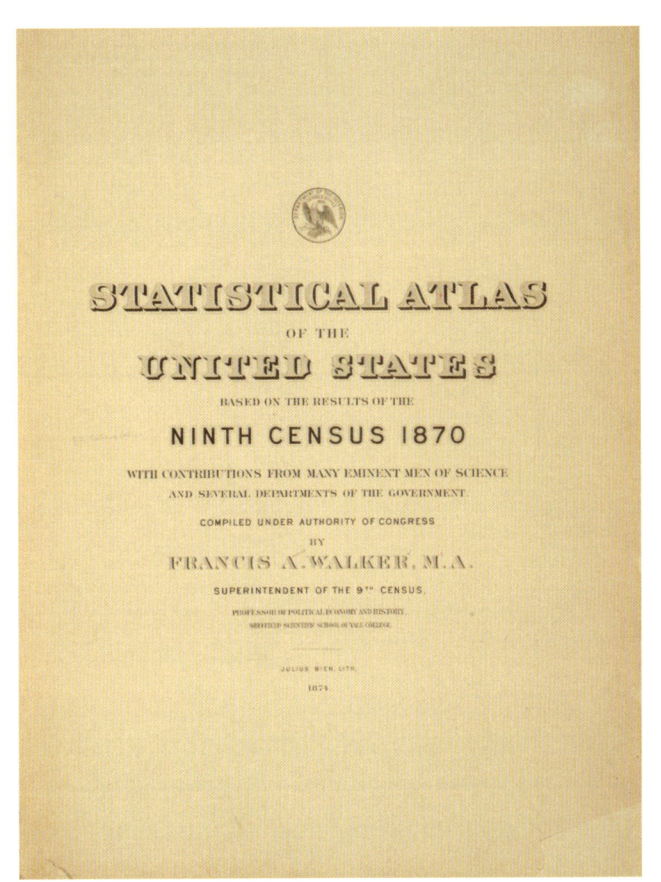

✻ [*Overleaf*] "Geological Map of the United States Compiled by C. H. Hitchcock and W. P. Blake." Lithograph map, 48.5 × 70.5 cm, comprising plates XIII and XIV of the *Statistical Atlas* (1874). (Compare to the William Maclure map of 1817 in the Geology section.)

✻ [*Overleaf*] "Map Showing the Proportion of the Colored to the Aggregate Population. Compiled from the Returns of Population at the Ninth Census of the United States 1870. By Francis A. Walker." Lithograph map, 49 × 36.5 cm. Plate XXII of the *Statistical Atlas* (1874).

This thematic map recognizes six levels of black population density (in number of inhabitants per square mile): less than 1, 1–7, 7–17, 17–35, 35–60, 60+. Dark blue lines indicate the boundaries of groups of population where the number of black inhabitants per square mile is expressed in ranges: 2–18, 18–45, 45+. The shaded blue lines indicate boundaries beyond which the population density is less than two inhabitants per square mile. The 1870 census was the first survey in which emancipated African Americans were fully counted.

✻ [*Overleaves*] "Chart Showing the Ratio of Church Accommodation to the Total Population over 10 Years of Age with the Proportion of Such Church Accommodation Furnished by Each of the Largest Four Denominations within Each State and by Each of the Largest Eight Denominations within the United States. Compiled from the Social Statistics of the Ninth Census 1870 by Francis A. Walker." Lithograph chart, plate size 50.4 × 37.7 cm. Plate XXXI of the *Statistical Atlas* (1874).

For the purposes of comparison here, each state's square is the same size. Nationally, in order of predominance, the named denominations are Methodist, Baptist, Presbyterian, Roman Catholic, Congregationalist, Episcopal, Lutheran, Christian, Dutch Reformed, Universalist, and Mormon. The size of the gray border of each square represents that proportion of the state's over-age-ten population that is not affiliated with any church. The squares for Ohio and Vermont, having no such border, suggest an accommodation of 100 percent—meaning, apparently, that everyone over the age of ten went to church in those states.

✻ [*Overleaves*] "Fiscal Chart of the United States Showing the Course of the Public Debt by Years 1789 to 1870. Together with the Proportion of the Total Receipts from Each Principal Source of Revenue and the Proportion of Total Expenditures for Each Principal

Pl. XIII. Pl. XIV.

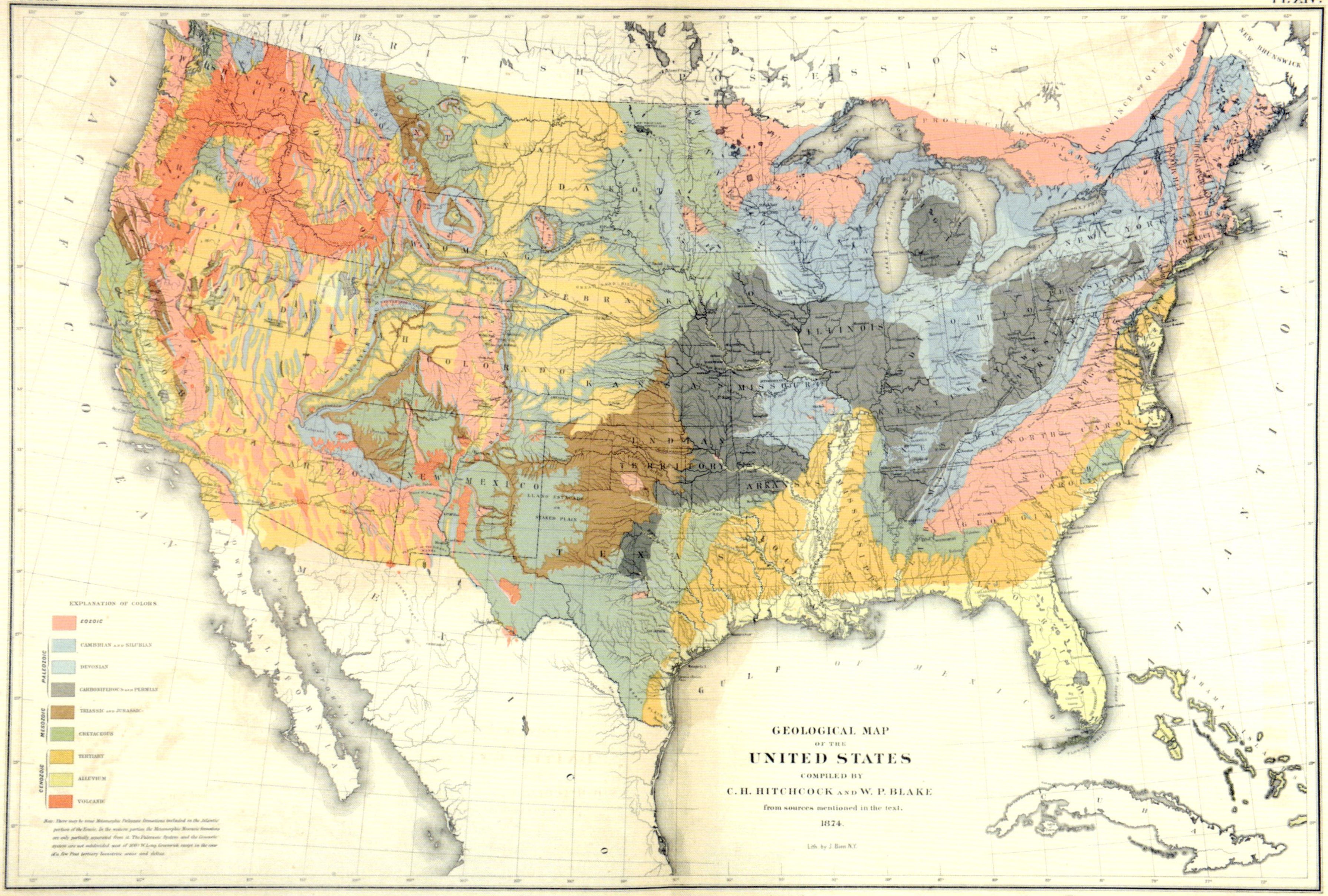

MAP
SHOWING THE PROPORTION OF THE
COLORED
TO THE AGGREGATE POPULATION.
Compiled from the Returns of Population at the Ninth Census
OF THE UNITED STATES 1870.
BY
FRANCIS A. WALKER.

CHART
SHOWING THE RATIO OF
CHURCH ACCOMMODATION
TO THE TOTAL POPULATION OVER 10 YEARS OF AGE
WITH THE PROPORTION OF SUCH CHURCH ACCOMMODATION FURNISHED BY EACH OF
THE LARGEST FOUR DENOMINATIONS WITHIN EACH STATE AND BY EACH OF
THE LARGEST EIGHT DENOMINATIONS WITHIN THE UNITED STATES.
Compiled from the Social Statistics of the Ninth Census 1870
BY
FRANCIS A. WALKER.

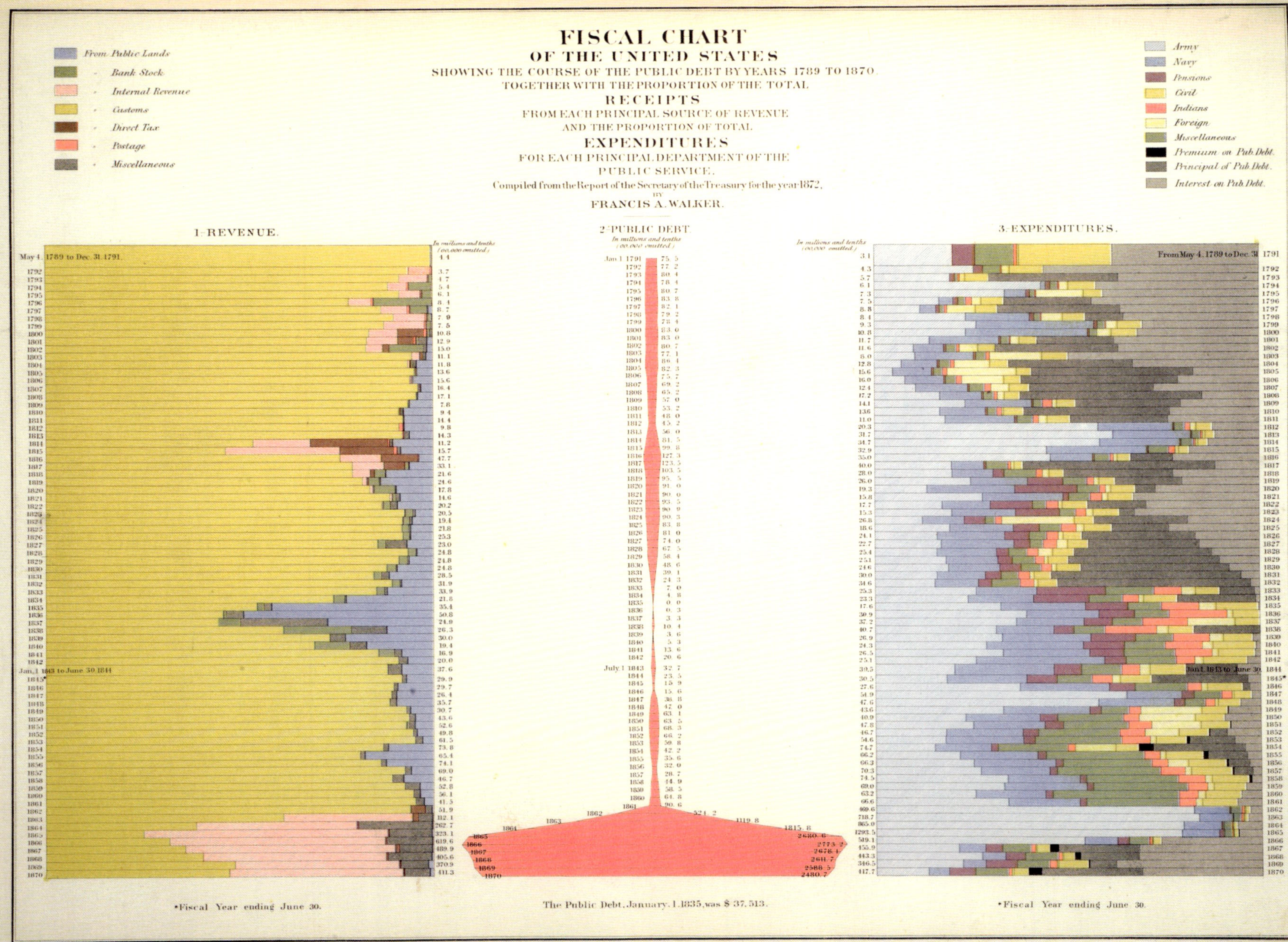
FISCAL CHART
OF THE UNITED STATES
SHOWING THE COURSE OF THE PUBLIC DEBT BY YEARS 1789 TO 1870,
TOGETHER WITH THE PROPORTION OF THE TOTAL
RECEIPTS
FROM EACH PRINCIPAL SOURCE OF REVENUE
AND THE PROPORTION OF TOTAL
EXPENDITURES
FOR EACH PRINCIPAL DEPARTMENT OF THE
PUBLIC SERVICE.
Compiled from the Report of the Secretary of the Treasury for the year 1872,
BY
FRANCIS A. WALKER.
From Public Lands
Bank Stock
Internal Revenue
Customs
Direct Tax
Postage
Miscellaneous
Army
Navy
Pensions
Civil
Indians
Foreign
Miscellaneous
Premium on Pub. Debt.
Principal of Pub. Debt.
Interest on Pub. Debt.
1. REVENUE.
2. PUBLIC DEBT.
3. EXPENDITURES.
In millions and tenths (00,000 omitted.)
May 4. 1789 to Dec. 31. 1791.
Jan. 1 1843 to June 30 1844
Jan. 1 1791
July 1 1843
From May 4. 1789 to Dec. 31 1791
Jan. 1 1843 to June 30
*Fiscal Year ending June 30.
The Public Debt, January 1. 1835, was $ 37.513.
*Fiscal Year ending June 30.

Department of the Public Service. Compiled from the Report of the Secretary of the Treasury for the Year 1872, by Francis A. Walker." Lithograph chart, plate size 37.7 × 50.2 cm. Plate XXXV of the *Statistical Atlas* (1874). (Compare to William Playfair's chart of England's debt in the Sociology and Economics section.)

Walker chose to contrast receipts to expenditures by treating each year's inflow and outflow as the same in order to emphasize (with color) specific aspects rather than absolutes. In 1866, for example, receipts were 170 times those for 1789, but they are visually represented as equal. Some of the more obvious conclusions one can draw from the three parts of this chart:

REVENUE: reliance on customs (trade) dollars until the rise of internal revenue sources in 1862, when President Abraham Lincoln and Congress created an income tax to pay for war costs.

EXPENDITURES: military expenses loom large, expanding during the Civil War, then competing with the rising interest costs of the national debt.

PUBLIC DEBT: a visual "drip" grows into a huge "pool." The year of least debt (narrowest point) was 1835, when the total amount had shrunk to $37,513!

✻ [*Opposite*] "Chart Showing the Distribution by Age and Sex of Insanity" and "Chart Showing the Distribution by Age and Sex of Idiocy." Both prepared by Fred H. Wines, secretary of the Illinois Board of Charities, from the Ninth Census 1870. Lithograph charts, each plate 20.8 × 37 cm. Top halves of Plates XLIX and L of the *Statistical Atlas*.

These innovative graphic figures split the reporting population in half, with males on the left and females on the right. Each decade is represented by a horizontal line, and its length outward from the center indicates the relative number of the subjects in question. The sex that predominates is shaded. Accordingly, in 1870, there were more "insane" females than males, but more "idiotic" men than women; the atlas does not define this terminology.

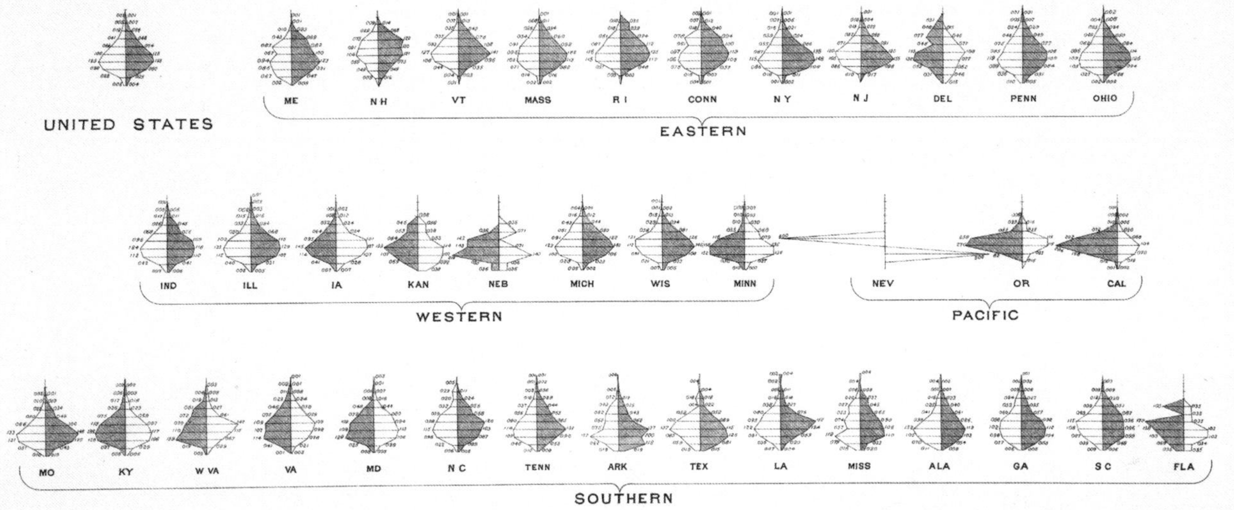

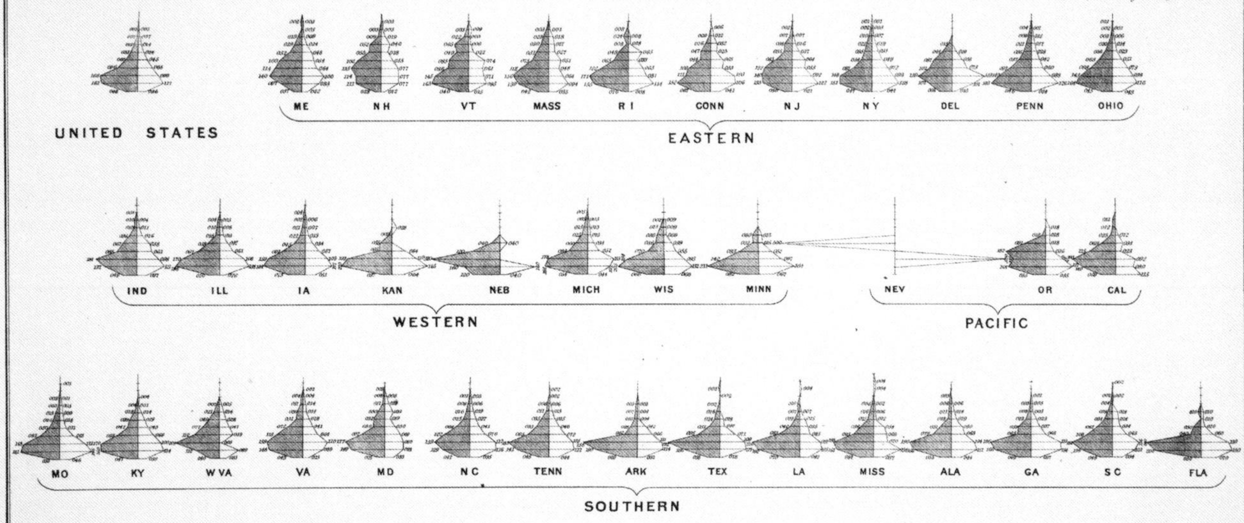

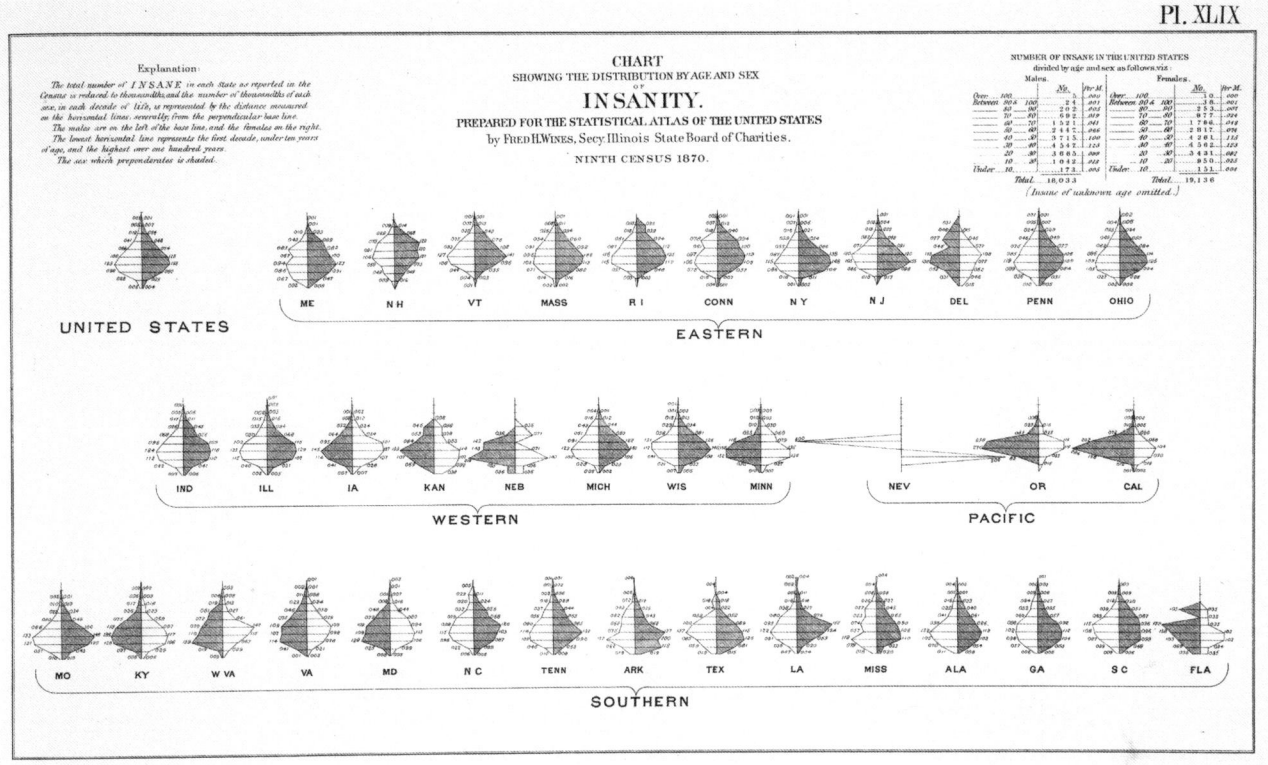

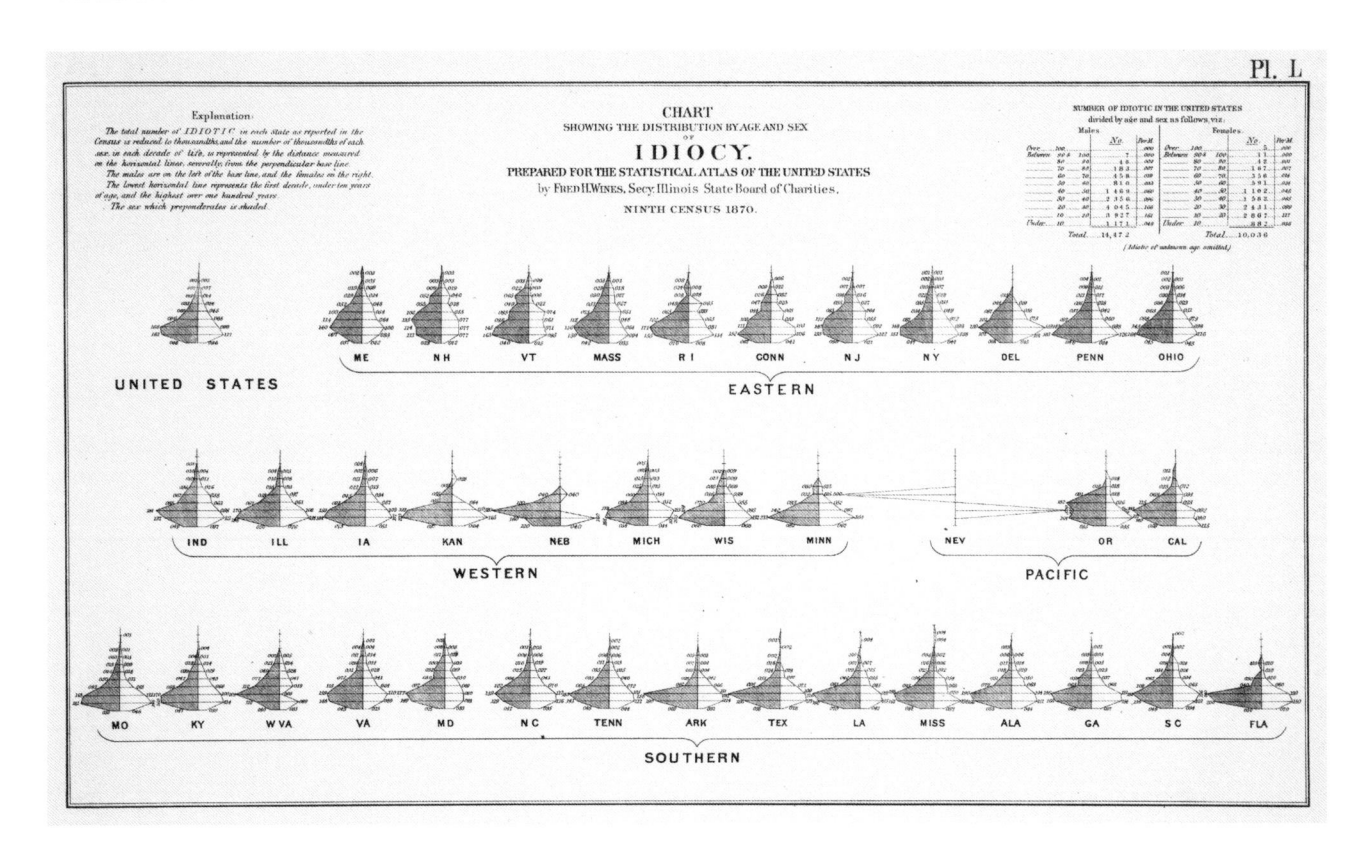

The Curve Lines which are drawn over the Seas in this Chart do shew at one View all the places where the Variation of the Compass is the same: The Numbers to them shew how many degrees the Needle declines either Eastward or Westward from the true North: and the Double Line passing near Bermudas and the Cape de Verde Isles is that where the Needle stands true without Variation

Quantitative Thematic Maps

✸

BASED ON quantifiable, empirical data, these were the first type of thematic maps to appear. They are often associated with the "hard" sciences, but some "softer," statistically dependent disciplines, such as sociology and economics, have made significant use of them. Depending on the nature of the data and the audience for the map, only certain basic features of the underlying reference map are shown so that the thematic layer(s) is/are prominent.

✸ Detail and legend from Edmond Halley's "A New and Correct Chart Shewing the Variations of the Compass in the Western & Southern Oceans as Observed in ye Year 1700 by … Edm Halley" (1701).

EXPLANATIONS.

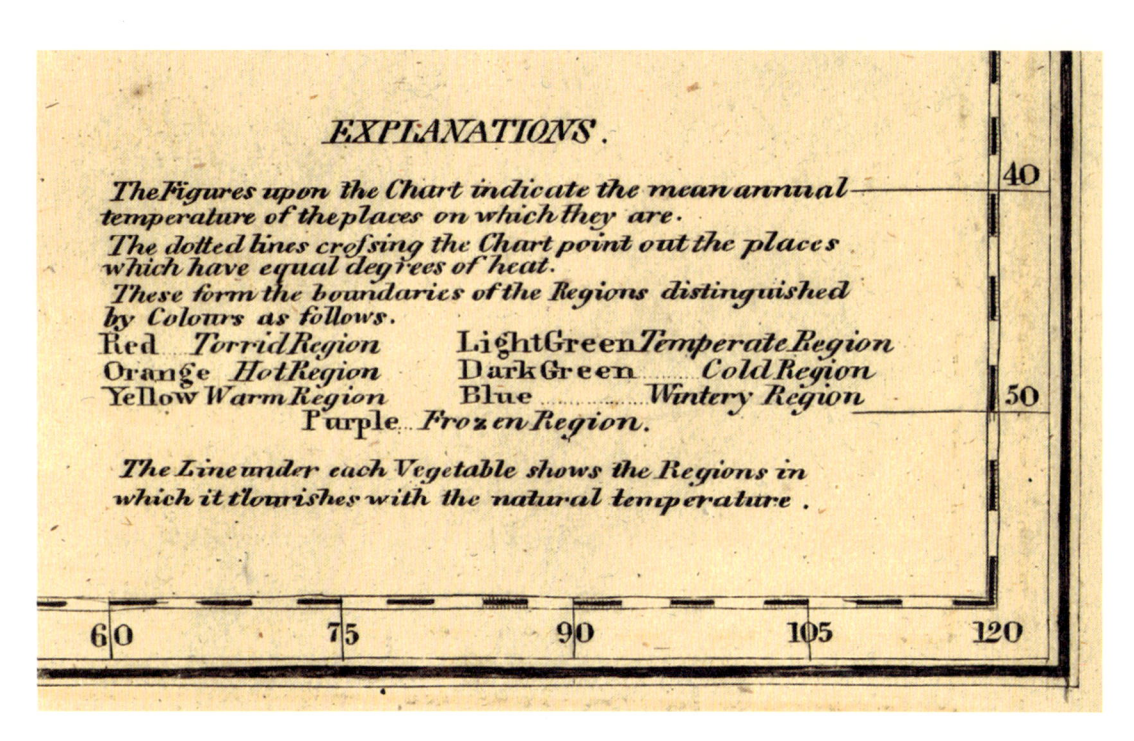

The Figures upon the Chart indicate the mean annual temperature of the places on which they are.

The dotted lines crossing the Chart point out the places which have equal degrees of heat.

These form the boundaries of the Regions distinguished by Colours as follows.

Red — Torrid Region   Light Green — Temperate Region
Orange — Hot Region   Dark Green — Cold Region
Yellow — Warm Region   Blue — Wintery Region
Purple — Frozen Region.

The Line under each Vegetable shows the Regions in which it flourishes with the natural temperature.

✻ Key to William C. Woodbridge's "Isothermal Chart…" (1823).

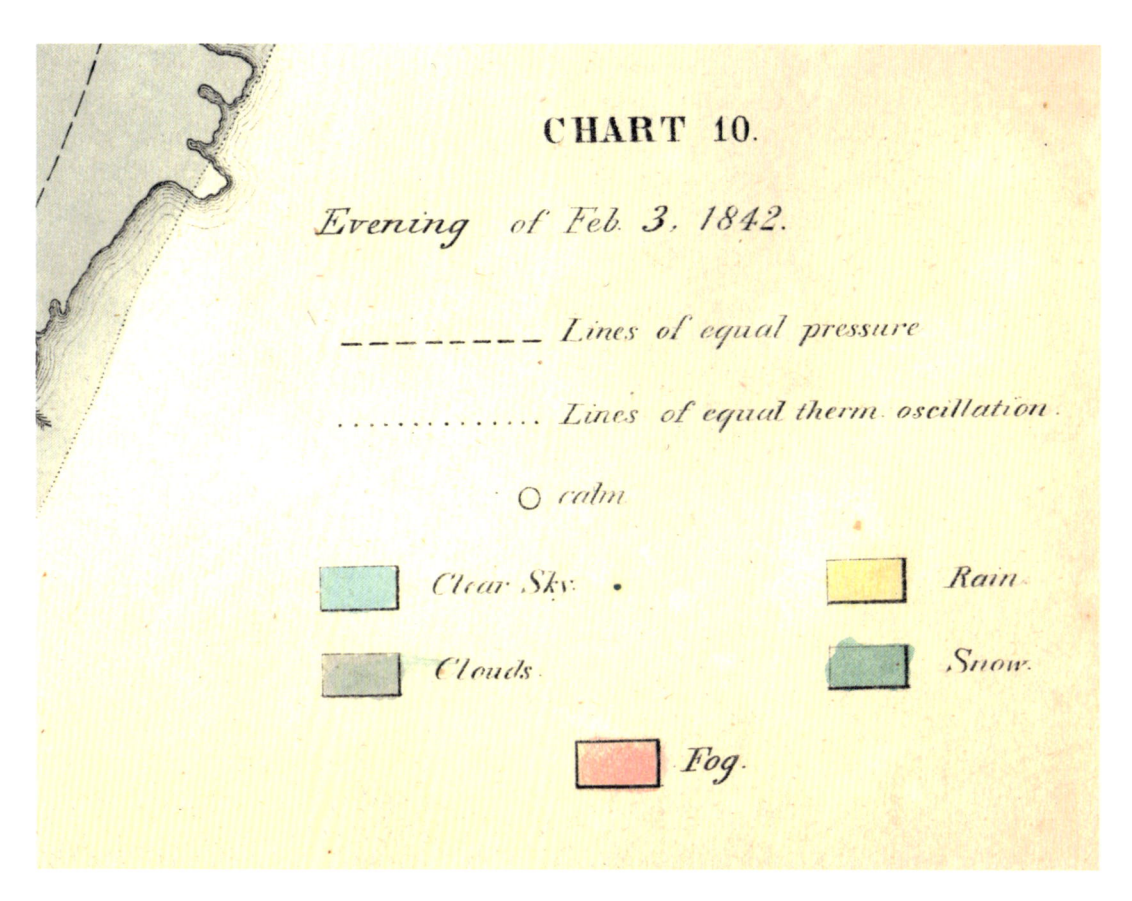

CHART 10.

Evening of Feb. 3, 1842.

———— Lines of equal pressure

············ Lines of equal therm. oscillation

○ calm

▢ Clear Sky   ▢ Rain

▢ Clouds   ▢ Snow

▢ Fog

✻ Key to Elias Loomis's "Chart 10" (1845).

METEOROLOGY

WEATHER is a moving phenomenon. Obtaining useful data about it requires collecting observations taken over wide ranges of territory. Determining what to measure and how to gather the measurements reliably and consistently were major challenges during the infancy of this science—even as researchers began interpreting the data. Maps became essential tools in the analysis.

EDMOND HALLEY
1656–1742

BEST KNOWN for the comet bearing his name, English astronomer Edmond Halley applied his scientific talents in many other fields, including meteorology, geophysics, and mathematics. As an undergraduate at Oxford, he published papers on the solar system and sunspots. In 1679, his publication *Catalogus stellarum australium*, providing details on almost 350 southern hemisphere stars, earned him election to the Royal Society. Subsequently, he studied trade winds and monsoons, established the relationship between barometric pressure and elevation, designed and demonstrated the use of a diving bell in the Thames River, and published an article (1693) on life annuities that helped foster the development of actuarial science. In *Astronomiæ cometicæ synopsis* (1705), he postulated that the comet sightings of 1456, 1531, 1607, and 1682 related to the same comet, and extrapolated its return in 1758. But Halley did not live to witness the truth of his prediction.

In map circles, Halley is usually considered to be the first thematic cartographer.

✻ [*Overleaf*] An untitled, copperplate world map, 14.8 × 48 cm. French version of Halley's map, accompanying a French translation of his article "An Historical Account of the Trade Winds, and Monsoons, Observable in the Seas between and near the Tropicks, with an Attempt to Assign the Phisical Cause of the Said Wind," which had appeared several months earlier in

✻ Portrait of Edmond Halley, at age eighty. From vol. 1 (1833) of *The Gallery of Portraits: With Memoirs* (London: C. Knight, 1833–1837) [General Library Collection].

issue no. 183 (1686) of the *Philosophical Transactions* of the Royal Society. From *Bibliothèque universelle et historique* 4 (1687): 66–93 [Rare Books Division].

First meteorological map, charting the directions of trade winds and monsoons. Having collected information from navigators familiar with ocean transits, and also from his own tropical experience on St. Helena (1677–1678), Halley sought to rectify the work of earlier writers on the subject. He attributes the circulation of prevailing winds to the solar heating of volumes of atmosphere as the earth revolves, which thus draw air after them, forming a generally easterly wind; as the sun departs, the air reverses direction to establish equilibrium. He argues that the effects of continents (and other landmasses) and latitudes complicate but do not compromise the basic principle. (Today, of course, solar heating is viewed as only a piece in the puzzle of winds; ocean currents would be another. Adding Halley's wind map data to Eberhard Happel's 1675 map of ocean currents [see his entry in the Hydrography section] would make an interesting thematic map.) Elsewhere in the article, Halley correctly identifies the West Indies as the source of hurricanes in the Atlantic.

On the map, rows of brief lines show the course of the winds; the sharp ends of those lines point to wind sources. Where winds go back and forth, notably in the monsoon-prone area of the Indian Ocean, the lines are thicker than elsewhere and point both ways. Halley's statement from *Philosophical Transactions* about his map is a very early affirmation of thematic cartography:

To help the conception of the reader in a manner of so much difficulty, I believed it necessary to adjoyn a Scheme, shewing at one view all the various Tracts and Courses of these Winds; whereby 'tis possible the thing may be better understood, than by any verbal description whatsoever [vol. 16, pp. 162–163].

✳ [*Overleaf*] "A New and Correct Chart Shewing the Variations of the Compass in the Western & Southern Oceans as Observed in ye Year 1700 by ... Edm Halley" [London: s.n., 1701?] Copperplate map, with added color, 56 × 48 cm [Historic Maps Collection]. Princeton's copy is an unrecorded state.

In 1698–1700, Halley's explorations in the Atlantic Ocean aboard the fifty-two-foot *Paramore*, from about 52° N to 52° S, led to this printed map, the first of its kind and the first to use isogonic lines, showing equal declinations of the magnetic compass. It became a

Meteorology 59

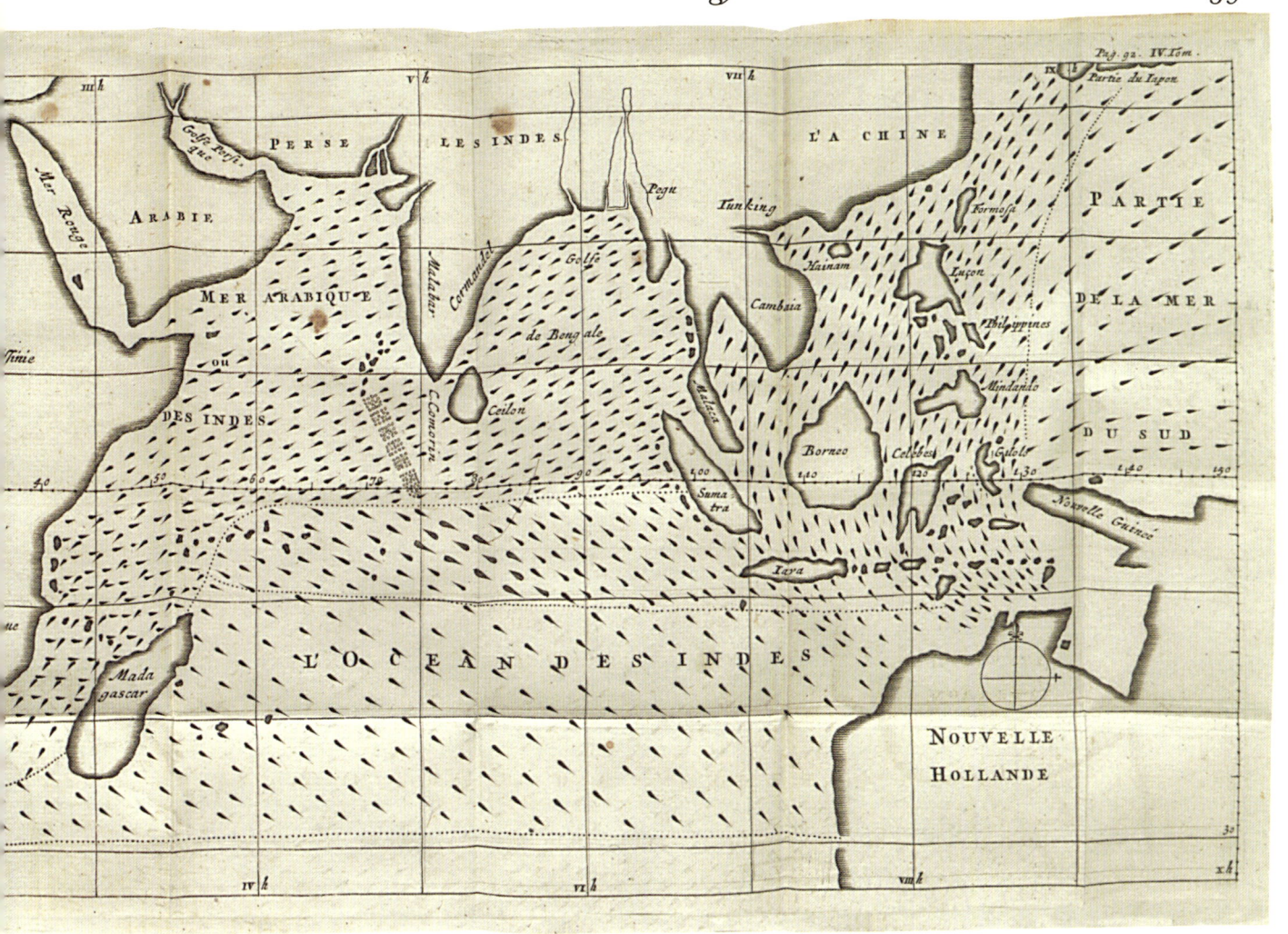

model for how to show geographical observations and is recognized as one of the most important maps in the history of cartography. Halley and others felt that data maps like these might solve the longitude problem for seamen, as they could look up their locations by comparing their compass readings to those on the map. Unfortunately, such readings are not stable over time because the earth's magnetic pole shifts. And Halley's own longitude readings were unreliable.

ALEXANDER VON HUMBOLDT
1769–1859

✻ Portrait of Alexander von Humboldt. Undated steel engraving: artist, F. Kreuger, engraver, Alexander Szchokke [Graphic Arts Collection]. (For more

A New and Correct CHART Shewing the VARIATIONS of the COMPASS in the WESTERN & SOUTHERN OCEANS as Observed in y Year 1700 by his Maty's Command by Edm. Halley
Majestati semper Augustæ GULIELMI III DG MAGNÆ BRITANNIÆ FRA&HIB Regis Invictissimi Tabula hæc Hydrographica VARIATIONUM MAGNETICARUM INDEX Devotissime Consecratur a Subdito Humillimo Edm. Halley
The Curve Lines which are drawn over the Seas in this Chart do shew at one View all the places where the Variation of the Compass is the same; The Numbers to them shew how many degrees the Needle declines either Eastward or Westward from the true North; and the Double Line passing near Bermudas and the Cape de Virde Isles is that where the Needle stands true without Variation
NORTH AMERICA
SOUTH AMERICA
HUDSONS BAY
TERRA DE LABORADOR OR NOVA BRITANNIA
CANADA NEW FRANCE
NOVA SCOTIA
NEW ENGLAND
NEW YORK
PENSYLVANIA
MARY LAND
VIRGINIA
CAROLINA
FLORIDA
GOLFE de MEXICO
BAHAMA ISLES
CUBA
HISPANIOLA
CARIBBE ISLANDS
HONDURAS
VENEZUELA
PERU
BRASILE
PARAGUAY
CHILI
PATAGONIA
TERRA DEL FUEGO
C Horn
THE PACIFICK SEA
THE WESTERN OCEAN
THE SOUTHERN OCEAN
West Variation
East Variation
The Line of no Variation
Tropick of Cancer
Tropick of Capricorn
The Equinoctiall
The Meridian of London
AZORES or WESTERN ISLES
CANARI ISLES
CAPE DE VIRDE
EUROPE
FRANCE
SPAIN
BAY OF BISCAY
HOLLAND
FLANDERS
ITALY
MEDITERRANEAN SEA
BARBARY
GUALATA
ARGUIN
AFRICA
GUINEA
BINNI
BIAFARA
GABON
LOANGO
CONGO
ANGOLA
MATAMAN
THE ICEY SEA
DEGREES of Variation
EAST WEST

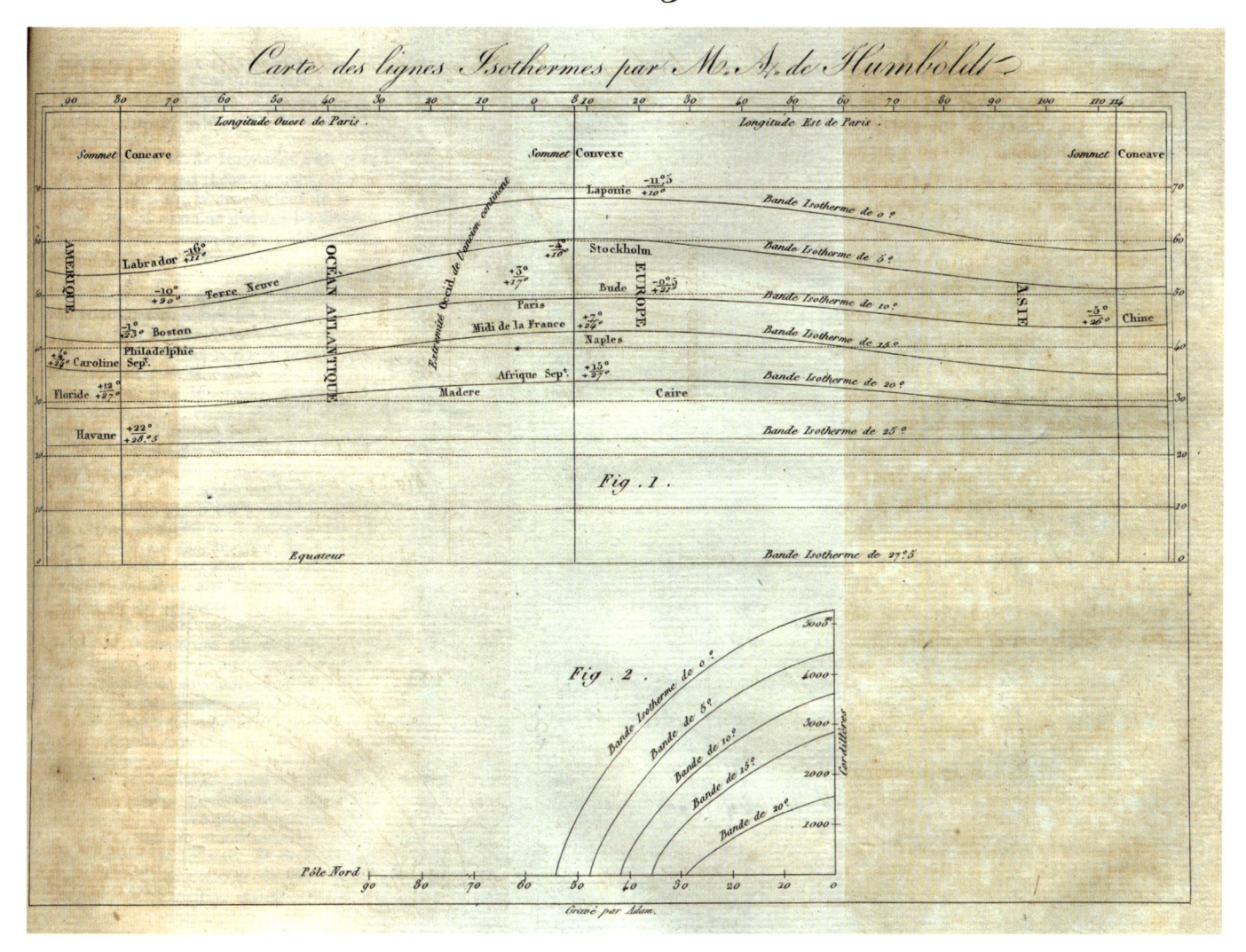

[Above] "Carte des lignes isothermes." Copperplate chart, 14.3 × 21.9 cm, accompanying Humboldt's article "Sur les lignes isothermes." From *Annales de Chimie et de Physique* 5 (1817): 102–112 [Historic Maps Collection].

Humboldt "raises the bar," literally: this is the first map to show the use of *isotherms*, a term Humboldt coined for lines of equal temperature. The graph in the bottom right shows the relationship between temperature and latitude/altitude. Despite its pictorial simplicity, the map revolutionized physical geography and all future thematic mapping.

WILLIAM CHANNING WOODBRIDGE
1794–1845

SON OF A MINISTER who pioneered female education, William C. Woodbridge became a strong voice for American educational reform, particularly in geography. He graduated from Yale in 1811 at the age of sixteen, intending to become a missionary, but ill health (he suffered from scrofula throughout his life) led him to teaching. Ultimately, he became an instructor at the Asylum for the Deaf and Dumb in Hartford, Connecticut, with Thomas Hopkins Gallaudet. Working with the deaf and disabled helped Woodbridge discover the power of visualizing information, and this approach accounted for much of the success of his geographies, many of which he coauthored with Emma Willard

✱ Portrait of William C. Woodbridge. From vol. 1 of Henry Barnard's *Educational Biography: Memoirs of Teachers, Educators, and Promoters and Benefactors of Education, Literature, and Science, Reprinted from the American Journal of Education* (New York: F. C. Brownell, 1859) [Rare Books Division].

(1787–1870), founder of the first women's school of higher education.

Woodbridge traveled to Europe several times, becoming a member of the geographical societies of Paris, Berlin, and Frankfurt, and meeting the influential geographer Alexander von Humboldt, who showed how a physical map could be the foundation for a broad range of themes. Back home, he sought to introduce European geographical concepts into American textbooks, preaching against rote memorization and promoting an understanding of unifying ideas. He wanted more and better maps in classrooms and books. In 1831, Woodbridge purchased the *American Journal of Education*, renamed it the *Annals of Education*, and with William A. Alcott (1798–1859) turned the Boston publication into the leading American educational periodical.

But innovative maps and textbooks with a strong Christian tone were clearly the educator's passion, as evident in the title of his first work (1821): *Rudiments of Geography: On a New Plan: Designed to Assist the Memory by Comparison and Classification: With Numerous Engravings of Manners, Customs, and Curiosities: Accompanied with an Atlas, Exhibiting the Prevailing Religions, Forms of Government, Degrees of Civilization, and the Comparative Size of Towns, Rivers, and Mountains*. He constantly revised, updated, and expanded his geographies but benefited little economically from their success, as he was always helping others. For health reasons, Woodbridge spent the last three winters of his life in St. Croix, now part of the American Virgin Islands (see the frontispiece foldout).

✱ [*Opposite*] "Isothermal Chart, or View of Climates & Production, Drawn from the Accounts of Humboldt & Others," dated January 13, 1823. Engraved map, with added color, 20.3 × 28.2 cm. From Woodbridge's *School Atlas to Accompany Woodbridge's Rudiments of Geography: Atlas on a New Plan* ... (Hartford, Conn.: Oliver D. Cooke & Co., [1823]) [Graphic Arts Collection].

First world isothermal chart. Woodbridge was quick to incorporate the latest scientific and educational ideas, here expanding on Humboldt's concept of isotherms to show the relationship of mean annual temperatures to world climates and crops. (For Humboldt's isothermal map, see his entry in this Meteorology section.) In his 1833 lecture "On the Best Method of Teaching Geography," Woodbridge argued:

> The foundation of geographical knowledge must be laid in a knowledge of the relative situation of places, and this, the pupils of our schools must acquire chiefly through the medium of *maps*.... Indeed, it is only by this process of comparison, that the great objects of geography—the expansion of the mind, and the discipline of the reflective powers—can be attained [*The Introductory Discourse and the Lectures Delivered before the American Institute of Instruction, in Boston, August, 1833* ... (Boston: Carter, Hendee and Co., 1834), 212, 231].

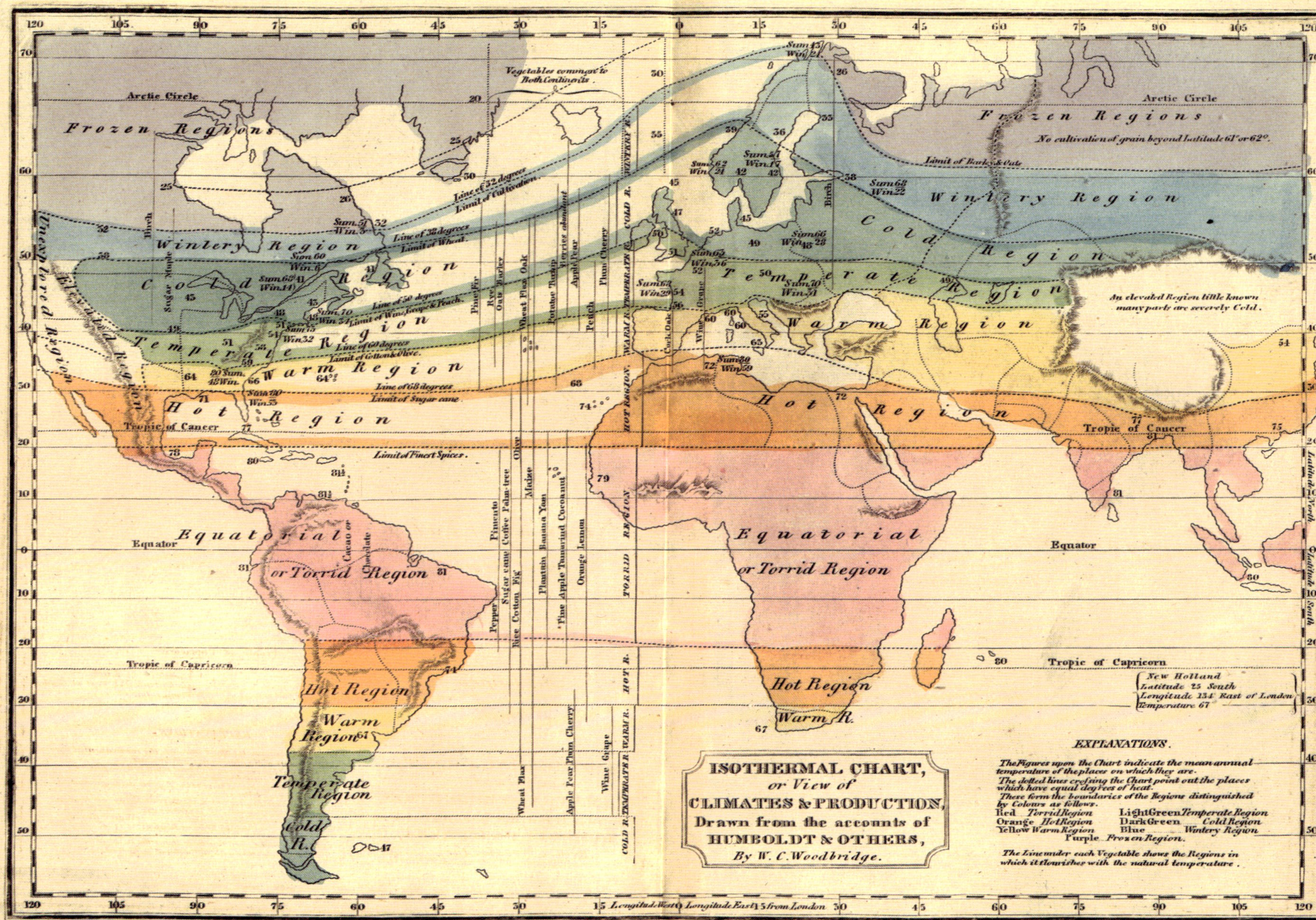
ISOTHERMAL CHART,
or View of
CLIMATES & PRODUCTIONS,
Drawn from the accounts of
HUMBOLDT & OTHERS,
By W. C. Woodbridge.
EXPLANATIONS.
The Figures upon the Chart indicate the mean annual temperature of the places on which they are.
The dotted lines crossing the Chart point out the places which have equal degrees of heat.
These form the boundaries of the Regions distinguished by Colours as follows.
Red Torrid Region
Orange Hot Region
Yellow Warm Region
Light Green Temperate Region
Dark Green Cold Region
Blue Wintery Region
Purple Frozen Region.
The Line under each Vegetable shows the Regions in which it flourishes with the natural temperature.
New Holland
Latitude 25 South
Longitude 134 East of London
Temperature 67
Frozen Regions
Wintery Region
Cold Region
Temperate Region
Warm Region
Hot Region
Equatorial or Torrid Region
Arctic Circle
Tropic of Cancer
Equator
Tropic of Capricorn
No cultivation of grain beyond Latitude 61° or 62°.
Limit of Barley & Oats
An elevated Region little known many parts are severely Cold.
Vegetables common to Both Continents
Line of 32 degrees Limit of Cultivation
Line of 38 degrees Limit of Wheat.
Line of 50 degrees Limit of Wine, Grape & Peach
Line of 60 degrees Limit of Cotton & Olive.
Line of 68 degrees Limit of Sugar cane
Limit of Finest Spices.
Unexplored Region
Elevated Region
Longitude West
Longitude East from London
Latitude North
Latitude South

JAMES POLLARD ESPY
1785–1860

THE YOUNGEST of ten children, James P. Espy was born in Washington County, Pennsylvania. His father was a pioneer farmer. After studying law with his uncle, Espy practiced the profession in Xenia, Ohio, from 1814 to 1817, when he moved to Philadelphia and began teaching mathematics and classics. Some of his classes were at the Franklin Institute, beginning a more than twenty-year association with that important American scientific organization. In the 1830s, his interests turned to meteorology, and he found a scholarly outlet in the Institute's journal. During this time he also established a committee on meteorological observations and persuaded the state to create a network of county weather observers supplied with basic instruments to complement his volunteer national system.

From 1839 to 1841, Espy lectured widely in the United States and abroad, earning him the nickname of Storm King. His work *The Philosophy of Storms* (1841) espoused his thermal theory, whereby all atmospheric disturbances involved the movement of heated air and its ultimate caloric release. The next year he moved to Washington, D.C., working for the government, first as a mathematics teacher in the navy and then as meteorologist for the Army Medical Department. For ten years (1847–1857), he was assigned to the navy and issued several of his important meteorological reports as U.S. Senate documents. Espy also had a prominent role in establishing the Smithsonian meteorological system of weather observers (see also Elias Loomis in this Meteorology section), which became the basis of a national system.

✴ [*Opposite*] "Map Embodying the Information Received by the Committee on Meteorology of the Franklin Institute of the State of Pennsylvania in Relation to the Storm of March, 16th, 17th, & 18th, 1838, Illustrating the Report of the Meteorologist." Lithograph map, 23 × 27 cm. From Espy's "Report of the Committee on Meteorology" in *Journal of the Franklin Institute of the State of Pennsylvania and Mechanics' Register. Devoted to Mechanical and Physical Science, Civil Engineering, the Arts and Manufactures and the Recording of American and Other Patented Inventions*, n.s., 22 (1838): 161–175 [Historic Maps Collection].

✴ Portrait of James P. Espy. From the National Oceanic and Atmospheric Administration (NOAA) Photo Library.

First U.S. weather map. In his accompanying report, Espy states that the committee received back 50 responses from the 250 circulars it sent out to different parts of the United States and Canada regarding this notable storm. The map represents the assembled data, with reporting stations numbered from 1 to 50, roughly in order from south to north and from west to east as the storm was tracked. Among them were Franklin (La., 1), U.S. Frigate *Constellation* (Pensacola Bay, Fla., 5), Nashville (Tenn., 7), Warren Court House (Ill., 9), Springfield (Ohio, 14), Western Reserve College (Hudson, Ohio, 17), Charleston (S.C., 19), Capitol Hill (Washington, D.C., 23), Gettysburg (Pa., 25), Bucks County Academy (Pa., 32), Philadelphia (Pa., 34, by Espy himself), University of Vermont (Burlington, Vt., 40), Newport (R.I., 44), Brown University (Providence, R.I., 45), Williams College (Mass., part of 47), Concord (N.H., 48), and Portland (Maine, 50). Reports published in newspapers were also consulted.

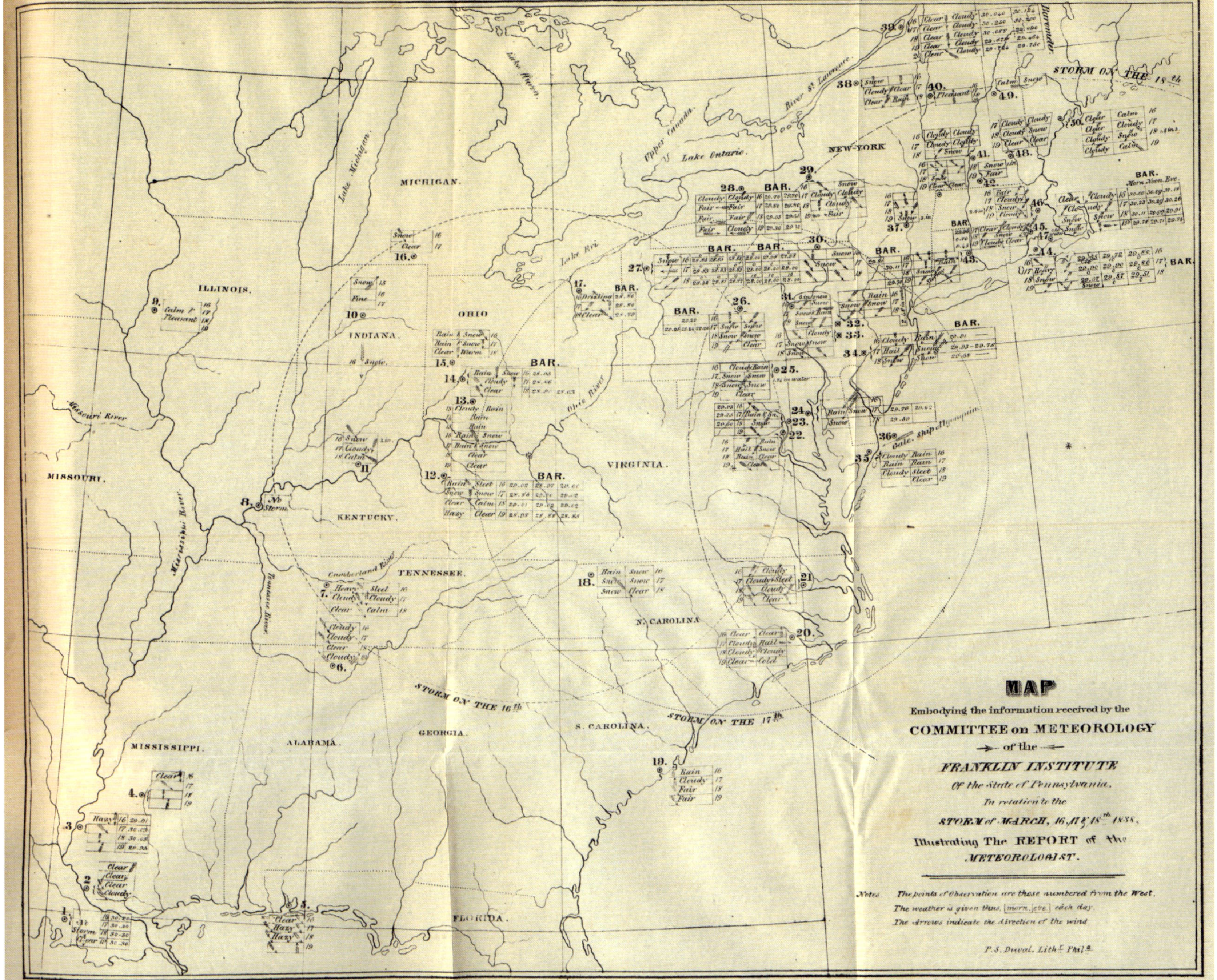
MAP
Embodying the information received by the
COMMITTEE on METEOROLOGY
of the
FRANKLIN INSTITUTE
Of the State of Pennsylvania,
In relation to the
STORM of MARCH, 16, 17 & 18th 1838,
Illustrating The REPORT of the
METEOROLOGIST.
Notes. The points of Observation are those numbered from the West.
The weather is given thus, morn. eve. each day.
The Arrows indicate the direction of the wind
P. S. Duval, Lith. Phil.
STORM ON THE 16th
STORM ON THE 17th
STORM ON THE 18th
MICHIGAN.
ILLINOIS.
INDIANA.
OHIO
MISSOURI.
KENTUCKY.
TENNESSEE.
VIRGINIA.
N. CAROLINA
S. CAROLINA.
GEORGIA.
ALABAMA.
MISSISSIPPI.
FLORIDA.
NEW-YORK
Lake Michigan.
Lake Huron.
Lake Erie
Lake Ontario.
Upper Canada.
River St Lawrence.
Missouri River
Mississippi River
Ohio River
Cumberland River
Tennessee River.
Barometer.
BAR.

The three large circles show the eastern progress of the storm over the three days. Readings of barometric pressure, arrows for wind direction and relative strength, and descriptive words for precipitation/sky (rain/sleet/hail/snow, clear/fair/cloudy/heavy) are provided in the cells of small tables (three or four rows by two or three columns) printed next to each station number; moreover, morning and evening results, if given, appear in adjacent cells of a row, and each row represents a different day (March 16, 17, 18, and sometimes 19). Like a time-delay photograph, the map nicely traces the regional movement of the storm, but graphic methods (shading, color, use of symbols) have not been developed yet to replace Espy's data tables. Hence, his thematic map is not as visually effective as future ones would be. (For example, see Elias Loomis's map in this Meteorology section.)

✳ [*Opposite*] First two weather maps ("April 1st 1843. 3 P.M." and "April 2nd 1843. 3 P.M.") from Espy's *Second [-Third] Report on Meteorology* (Washington, D.C., 1849–1851) [Historic Maps Collection].

In his second report, Espy provides the names and city/state locations of all of the "meteorological correspondents" who provided the data exhibited in his charts. Then he turns to their contents.

> By casting your eye on one of the charts, you will see how easy it is to comprehend all the principal phases of a storm at once; the *position* and extent of a storm at a particular moment by the red figures, indicating the quantity of rain or snow that fell in it; the *locality* of the minimum barometer indicated by a red line, and its maximum by a black line; the *direction* and *force* of the wind, by arrows of different lengths; and by turning to the map of the next day, the change of position of the storm will also be seen [pp. 4–5; Espy's emphasis].

The black numbers standing by themselves, with + or − signs appended, indicate the high and low fluctuations of temperature; when *max* is added, it means the highest temperature of the month, *min*, the lowest. Since the earlier map of 1838, Espy has achieved a simplification that improves visualization of the weather data, but the results are not yet intuitive.

ELIAS LOOMIS
1811–1889

ELIAS LOOMIS was a professor of mathematics and natural philosophy (Western Reserve, New York University, Yale). Although he became an author of a best-selling series of textbooks on mathematics and an introduction to astronomy, his research interests—and contributions to science—were more meteorological. In the United States in the early 1840s, two basic theories of winds in storms found support but reached no verdict: do winds blow in circular whirls, or do they blow in toward a center? William C. Redfield (1789–1857), first president of the American Association for the Advancement of Science, presented facts that winds blew counterclockwise around a center that advanced in the direction of the prevalent winds. James P. Espy (1785–1860), appointed the first meteorologist of the U.S. government and popularly known as the Storm King from his extensive lecturing, observed a centripetal motion of the winds toward a center and theorized that there was an upward motion of air at that center. To provide an answer, Loomis determined to make a thorough examination of a violent storm.

In February 1842, he investigated the paths of two large storms moving across the eastern half of the United States. His published observations were not definitive, in that they supported features of both rival wind theories—but his more important contributions were in his methodology and mapping. By tracking the storms over a wide area for several days, he was able to accurately chart the storms' courses and show their meteorological changes. In two series of sequential maps (dated morning/evening, day), he drew lines of equal deviations in barometric pressure and equal oscillations in temperature, and assigned colors to areas of clear sky, clouds, rain, snow, and even fog. In addition, Loomis used arrows of varying length to indicate wind direction and intensity. In fact, he was anticipating common characteristics of the modern weather map: when the Signal Service's weather maps began appearing in 1871, they were constructed on Loomis's model.

✳ [*Overleaf*] "Chart 10." Printed map, with added color, on sheet 23.5 × 30.5 cm. One of thirteen charts

April 1st 1843. 3. P. M.

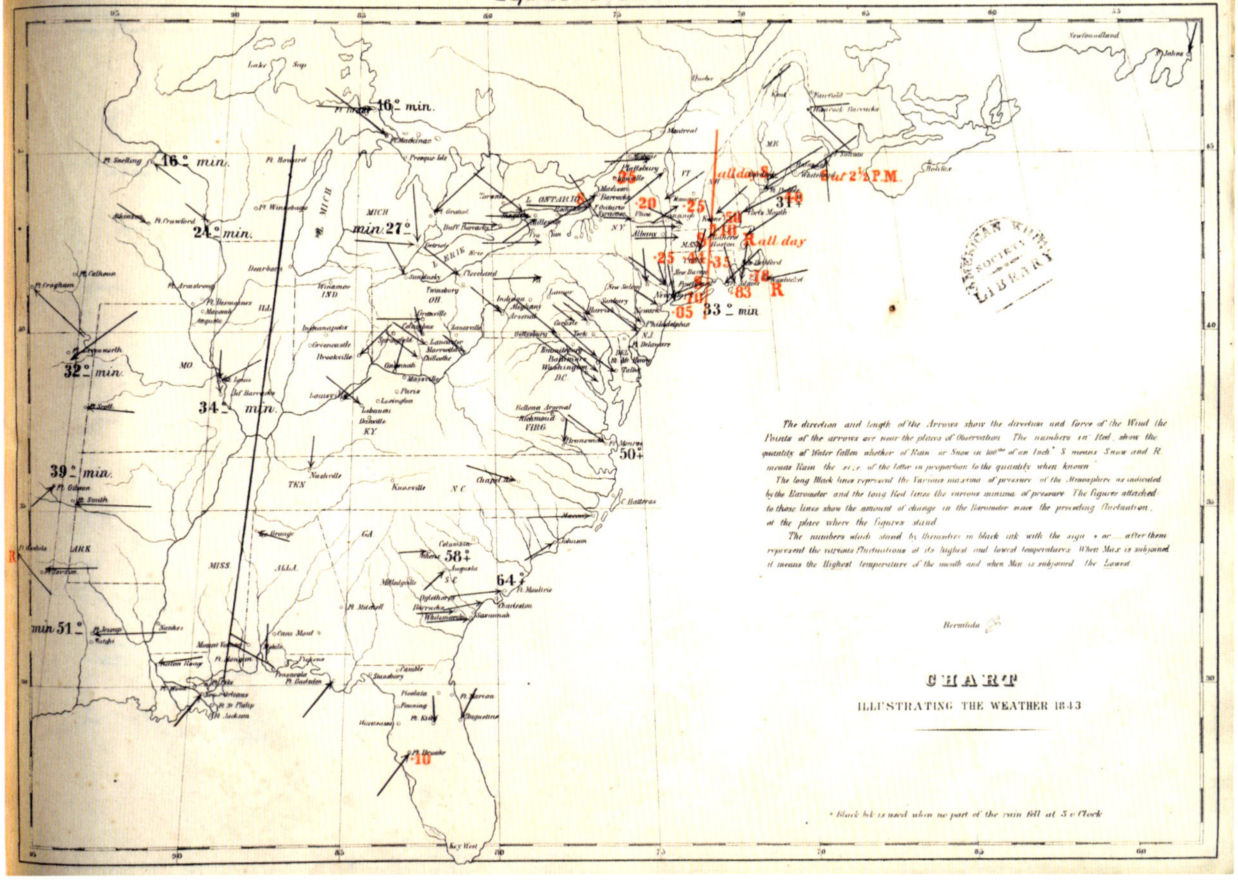

April 2d 1843 3 P. M.

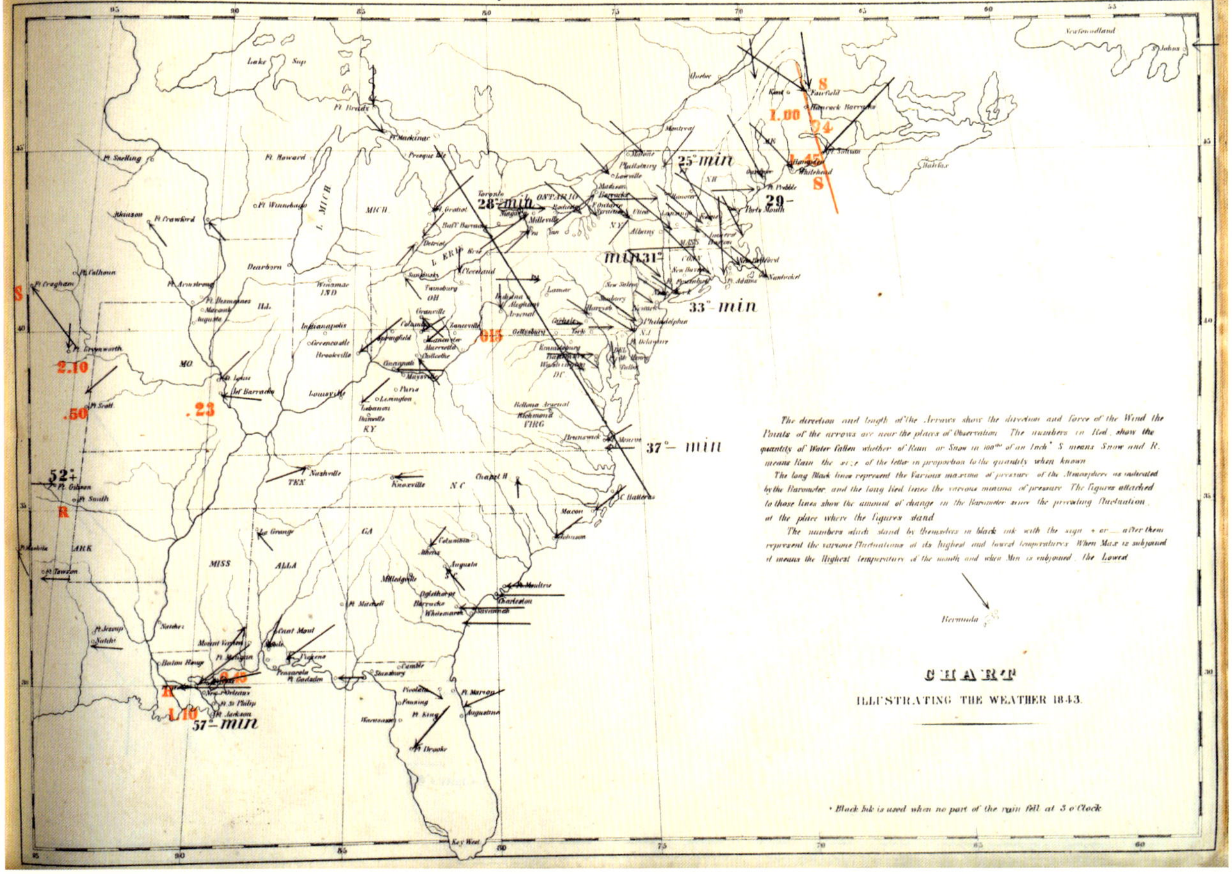

✸ Portrait of Elias Loomis. From H. A. Newton's *Elias Loomis, LL. D., 1811–1889* (New Haven, Conn.: Tuttle, Morehouse & Taylor, 1890) [General Library Collection].

---

accompanying Loomis's article "On Two Storms Which Were Experienced throughout the United States, in the Month of February, 1842." From *Transactions of the American Philosophical Society*, 9 (1845): 161–184 [Historic Maps Collection]. Charts 1–5 cover the storm of February 16; charts 6–13 cover the storm of February 3.

First U.S. synoptic weather maps. In the conclusion of his lengthy study of these storms, Loomis makes some suggestions that will have a major effect on the study of meteorology:

> If we could be furnished with two meteorological charts of the United States, daily, for one year, charts showing the state of the barometer, thermometer, winds, sky, &c., for every part of the country, it would settle for ever the laws of storms…. Such a set of maps would be worth more than all which has been hitherto done in meteorology…. A well arranged system of observations spread over the course of the country, would accomplish more in one year, than observations at a few isolated posts, however accurate and complete, to the end of time…. We need observers spread over the entire country at distances from each other not less than fifty miles. This would require five or six hundred observers for the United States [pp. 183–184].

He later developed a plan for Joseph Henry, secretary of the Smithsonian Institution, but only a fragmentary implementation resulted. Ultimately, Loomis's proposal for a system of observers across the United States and for daily weather maps was realized in Congress's creation of the Weather Bureau of the United States Signal Service in 1870. This became the National Weather Service we know today.

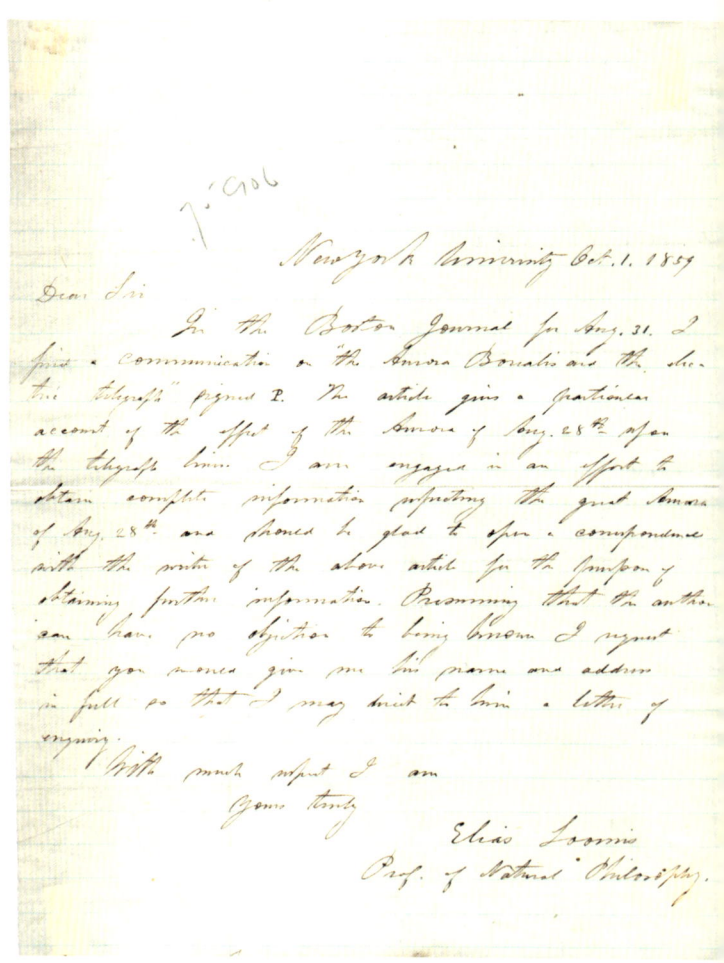

✸ [*Above*] One-page autograph letter by Loomis, addressed to the *Boston Journal* and dated 1 October 1859 [Moore Autograph Collection of Princetonians, Manuscripts Division].

Meteorology 69

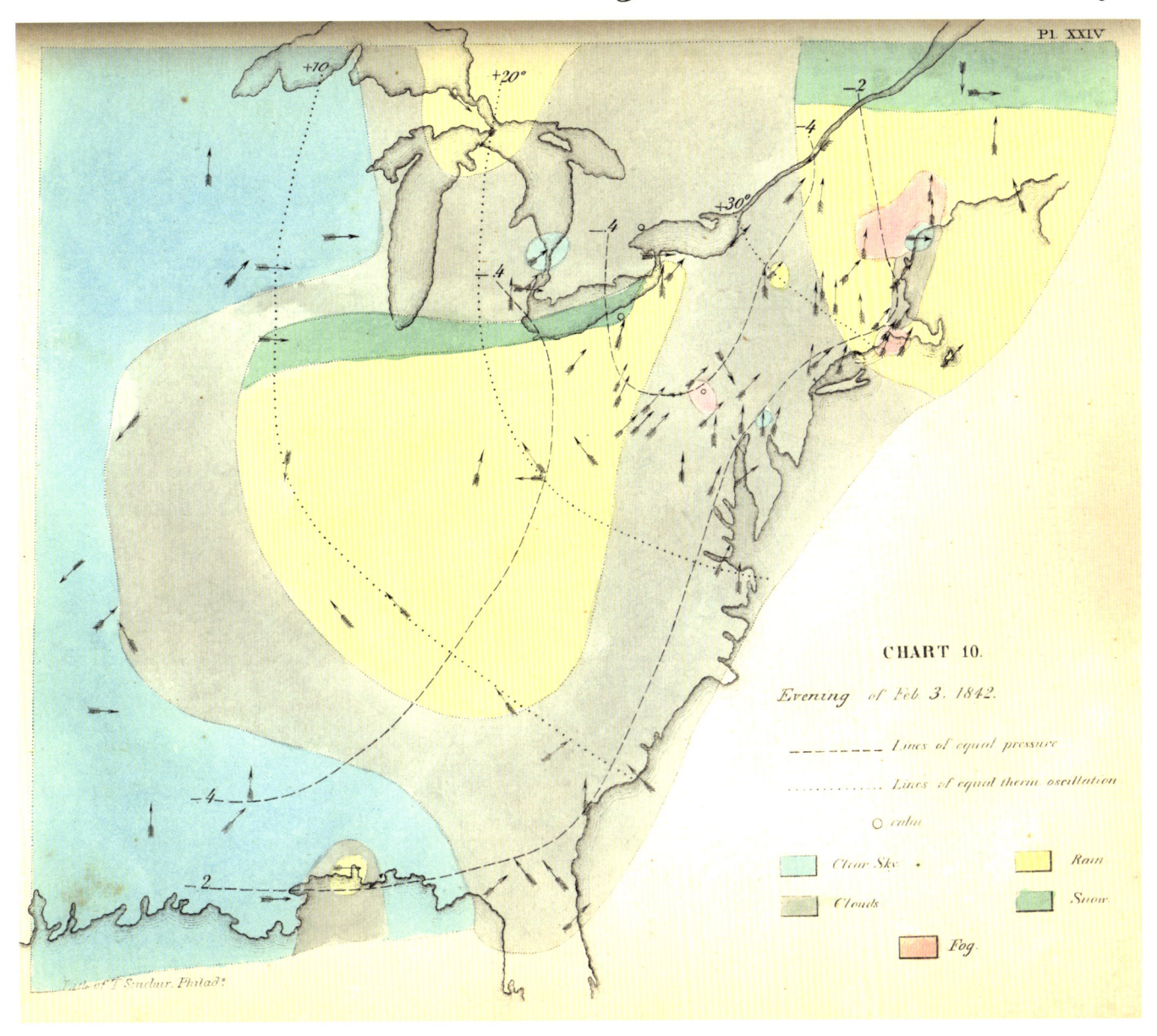

CHART 10.

Evening of Feb 3. 1842.

– – – – – Lines of equal pressure
.... Lines of equal therm. oscillation
○ calm

Clear Sky   Rain
Clouds   Snow
Fog

Loomis's letter reflects the laborious work of a mid-nineteenth-century meteorologist trying to track down and collect data from distant sources. The subject of the letter is the extraordinary aurora borealis display that occurred throughout the United States, Europe, Japan, and Australia, from August 28 through September 4, 1859, which is considered to be the most spectacular of recorded history. Loomis would publish nine scientific papers on the Great Auroral Exhibition of 1859 from the data he collected.

LÉON LALANNE, 1811–1892

A GRADUATE of France's École Nationale des Ponts et Chaussées (National School of Bridges and Roads), the world's oldest civil engineering school, Léon Lalanne had a successful career managing public works in Romania, constructing railroads in Switzerland and Spain, and eventually directing his alma mater. In 1837, Lalanne was one of a team of mostly French scholars, scientists, and artists that were invited on a scientific expedition to southern Russia and the Crimean Peninsula, organized by the Russian mining industrialist Anatolii Demidov. When Lalanne retired from the ENPC, he entered politics and was elected senator for life in 1883. His strength in mathematics led to a number of important graphical contributions, including the very first log-log plot or logarithmic grid, a "universal calculator" that allowed one to read off the product of more than sixty functions of arithmetic, geometry, and trigonometry—essentially a one-sheet graphical slide rule.

✻ [*Opposite*] "Abaque ou Compteur Universel...." Lithograph chart, 20 × 20 cm, with explanatory text, "approuvé par l'Académie des Sciences" on 11 September 1843. From *Bulletin de la Société d'encouragement pour l'industrie nationale* 45, no. 502 (April 1846) [General Library Collection].

Lalanne's ingenious graphic calculator (abacus).

✻ Title page of Ludwig Friedrich Kämtz's *Cours complet de météorologie*, trans. and annotated by Ch. Martins, with an appendix by L. Lalanne (Paris: Paulin, 1843) [Historic Maps Collection].

An early, very influential book on meteorology by German meteorologist Kämtz. Translated into numerous languages, the work is considered a landmark in the history of science. Lalanne's contribution to the volume, "Appendice sur la représentation graphique des tableaux météorologiques et des lois naturelles en général," consists of forty-two meteorological graphs with explanatory notes.

✻ [*Overleaf*] Lalanne's "Appendix Plate 1." From the English edition of Kämtz's book, *A Complete Course of Meteorology*, trans. C. V. Walker (London: Hippolyte Baillière, 1845) [courtesy of John Delaney].

Figure 1 is the first contour map of a three-variable (x, y, z) table of data—here, showing the mean temperature of Halle, Germany, by hour and month—using the data supplied by Kämtz on page 15. The advantage of the map over tabular data is clear:

> Whatever be the plan, we are convinced that the graphic representation of natural or mathematical laws with three variables, that the substitution of indexed planes for numerical tables with a double entry is a fertile idea, that will not fail in bearing fruit. When meteorologists, philosophers, and engineers, shall become familiar with the employment of this process, they will be in a better condition for discussing the results of their experiments, of directing their researches, of simplifying their calculations, than if they operate directly on numbers ... [p. 511].

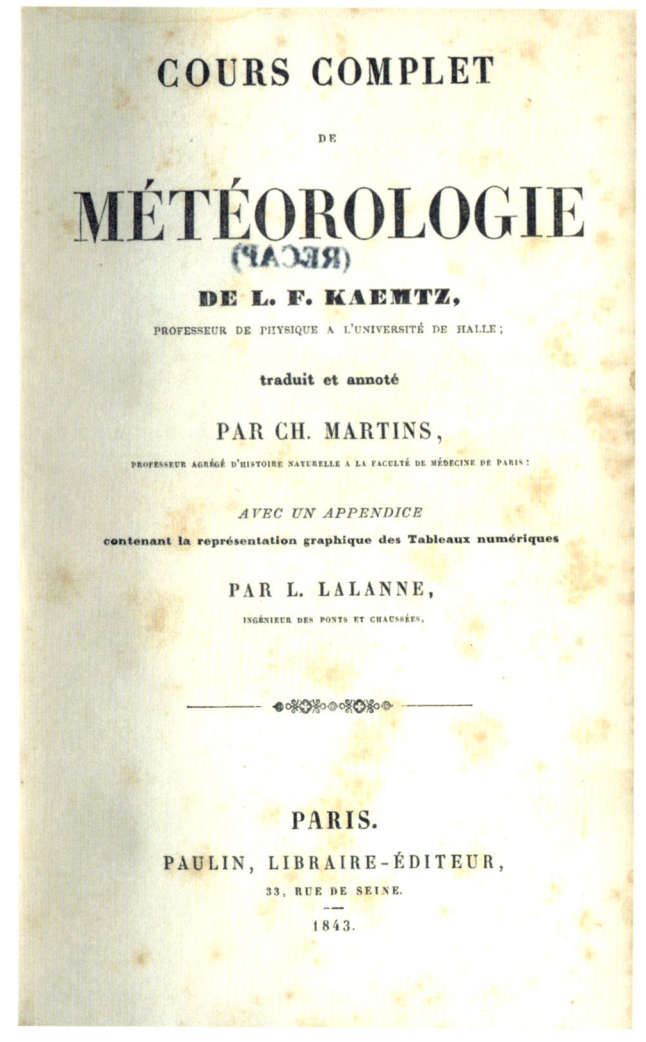

Other good examples of Lalanne's mapping techniques, using Kämtz's meteorological data, are figures 4, 4bis, and 4ter. They graph the frequency, duration, and direction of winds (monsoons) over the months of the year at Dum-Dum, near Calcutta, India. Lalanne credits Humboldt with the basic idea:

> M. de Humboldt was then the first who thought of uniting on the surface of the globe, by continuous curves, other points than those that are found at the same level above the ocean. The analogy of his *isothermals*, with the application that we make to meteorological laws, is manifest. The difference consists merely in that the isothermals are applied to points, the existence of which on the surface of

ABAQUE ou COMPTEUR UNIVERSEL,

donnant à vue, à moins de $\frac{1}{200}$ près, les résultats de tous les calculs d'Arithmétique, de Géométrie et de Mécanique pratique, &c.

par Léon Lalanne, ancien élève de l'Ecole Polytechnique, ingénieur des Ponts et Chaussées.

Cet Abaque a été approuvé par l'Académie des Sciences le 11 Septembre 1843.

(MODÈLE N°1. — Déposé à la Direction).

INSTRUCTION ABRÉGÉE POUR L'USAGE DE L'ABAQUE.

Lecture des nombres sur l'Abaque. *Le nombre correspondant à un point, soit sur les bords du cadre, soit sur une des droites inclinées de l'intérieur de la figure, s'obtiendra facilement en considérant les chiffres 1, 2, 3, 4.... 10, 20, 30.... 100 placés sur ces bords, comme représentant à volonté des unités entières ou décimales d'un ordre quelconque.*

Ainsi le 5ᵉ point de division entre 2 et 3 peut représenter à volonté les nombres 2,5, 25, 250 &c. et 0,25, 0,025 &c.

Mais sur les lignes inclinées transversalement qui portent les désignations de **carrés**, *et de* **surface du cercle** *on ne devra lire que les nombres qui y sont inscrits et leurs multiples ou sous-multiples par 100, 10 000, 1 000 000, &c.; sur celles qui sont relatives au* **volume de la sphère** *et aux* **cubes**, *on ne lira que les nombres inscrits et leurs multiples ou sous-multiples par 1 000, 1 000 000, &c......*

Principe général de l'Abaque. *Le produit de deux nombres se trouve absolument comme dans la table attribuée vulgairement à Pythagore, par la lecture du nombre de la ligne inclinée dans ce sens* \ *qui est à la rencontre des deux droites l'une verticale, l'autre horizontale, correspondant aux deux facteurs.*

Ainsi le produit de 2 par 3 se trouve sur la droite inclinée portant le chiffre 6; celui de 13 par 2,5 tombant entre les lignes 3,2 et 3,3, on prendra 325 pour la valeur absolue du produit, qui est réellement 32,5 en plaçant convenablement la virgule.

Réciproquement on fera la division de 32,5 par 13 en partant du point de rencontre de la droite inclinée 325 avec la verticale 13 et en suivant une horizontale jusqu'à la division 2,5 du bord vertical du cadre.

Rien n'est donc plus facile que d'obtenir le résultat de la multiplication et de la division d'un nombre quelconque de quantités et notamment le quatrième terme d'une proportion.

Puissances et racines. *Les* **carrés** *et les* **cubes** *se trouvent sur les lignes transversales qui portent ces désignations, en partant des nombres comptés sur le bas du cadre; et réciproquement, les* **racines carrées** *et* **cubiques** *s'obtiennent en partant des lignes des carrés et des cubes et en descendant sur les lignes du bas du cadre.*

*Pour les puissances $\frac{3}{2}$ qui se présentent dans diverses questions d'***hydraulique***, il faut partir du bord vertical du cadre, et faire la lecture sur la ligne des cubes la plus proche.*

Exemples: $\sqrt{2} = 1{,}41$; $\sqrt[3]{1318} = 11{,}0$; $4{,}5^{\frac{3}{2}} = \sqrt{(4{,}5)^3} = 9{,}54$.

Pour obtenir une puissance du 4ᵉ, du 5ᵉ.... du nᵉ degré, ce qui est utile dans les **règles d'intérêt** *composé, il suffit de tracer sur l'Abaque des transversales inclinées à 1 de base pour 3, 4 .... n−1 de hauteur; la première partant du point 1, et les autres se succédant mutuellement comme les lignes des cubes.*

Circonférence, cercle, sphère. *On se sert des transversales inclinées qui portent ces dénominations pour obtenir la longueur d'une circonférence, la superficie d'un cercle et le volume d'une sphère, le rayon étant compté sur le bord inférieur du cadre.*

Ainsi le rayon étant 5, la circonférence 31,4, le cercle est 78,6 et la sphère 527. Les questions inverses se résolvent aussi facilement.

Conversions des poids et mesures. *Les hauteurs comprises sur le bord à gauche du cadre entre le point de départ 1 et les petits traits correspondant aux conversions des poids et mesures, serviront de multiplicateurs pour changer des mesures anciennes en nouvelles; et elles serviront de diviseurs pour le problème inverse.*

Poids des volumes de diverses substances. *De même, aux noms des diverses substances placés à côté du bord à droite, correspondent des multiplicateurs ou des diviseurs, suivant la nature de la question à résoudre.*

Pesanteur. *Les questions relatives à la chûte des corps dans le vide, au pendule, à l'écoulement des liquides, se résoudront facilement à l'aide des nombres correspondant à g, à $\frac{1}{2}g$, à $\sqrt{2g}$, $\sqrt{g}$, à 2g, lesquels ont été marqués sur le bord à droite du cadre.*

Polygones réguliers. *On obtiendra l'aire d'un de ces Polygones en divisant le carré de son côté par un nombre correspondant marqué sur le bord à droite du cadre avec la lettre A.*

N.B. *Pour plus amples détails, voir l'***instruction** *imprimée qui se trouve chez les mêmes dépositaires, ainsi que les autres modèles d'Abaque.*

A Paris, chez J.J.Dubochet, Le Chevalier *et Cⁱᵉ Editeurs, Rue Richelieu, 60.*

Gravé par Lemaitre. Écrit par Martin. Imp. par Lemercier.

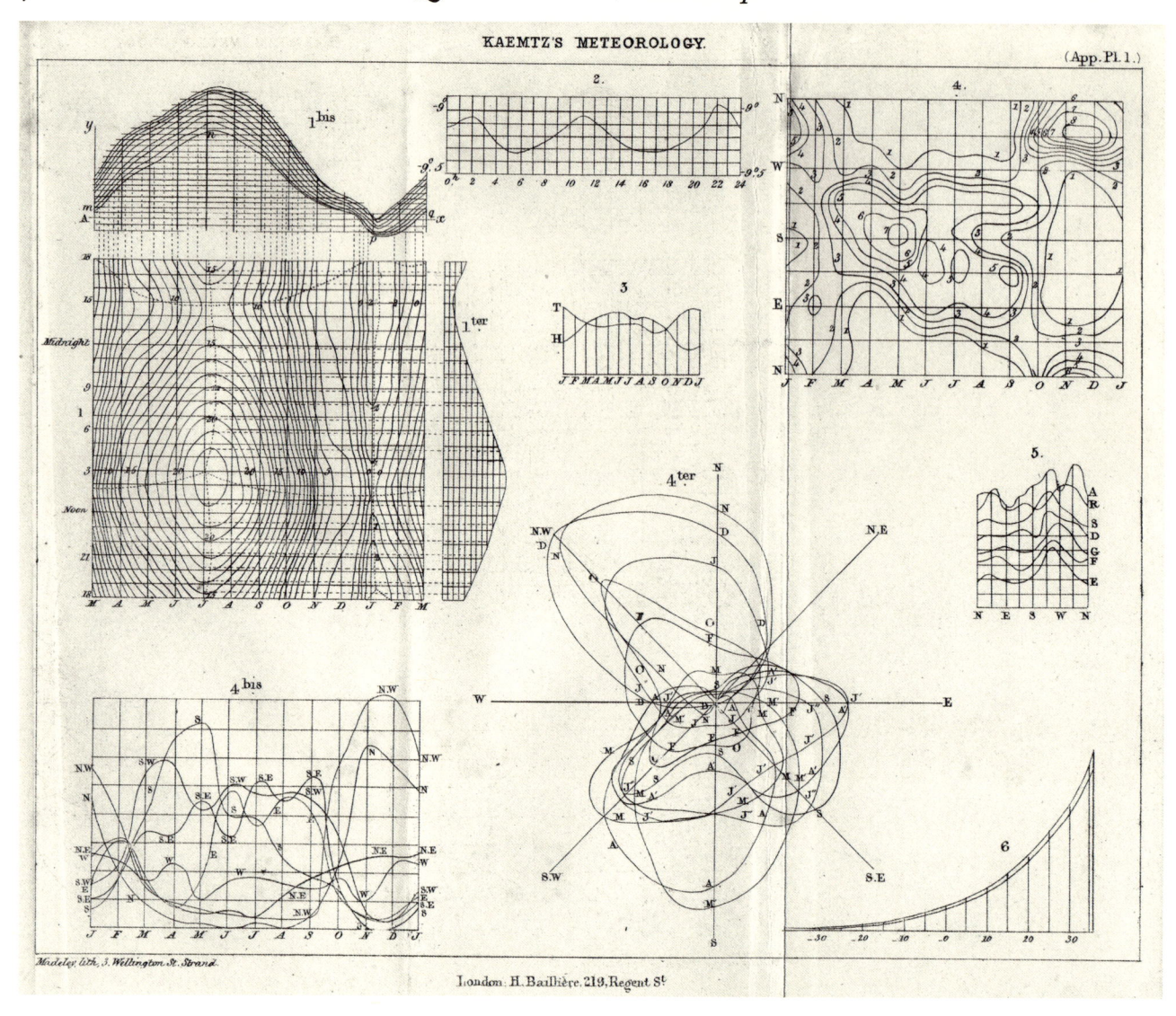

the terrestrial globe is real; whilst the curves of the equal duration of the winds in the same place, during the different seasons of the year, are applied to points, whose position on a plane, or a sphere, or a cone, has been determined by pure convention, by a particular choice of co-ordinates to represent two variable elements [p. 514].

JOHN CHAPPELSMITH
1807?–1885?

NOT MUCH is known about John Chappelsmith except that he was one of the best painters on founder Robert Owen's staff at the idealistic community of New Harmony, Indiana. The wealthy English artist and his wife were among Owen's scientists and educators who descended the Ohio River in the winter of 1825–1826 aboard the *Philanthropist*, symbolically representing a "boatload of knowledge." Apparently, he spent most of his time making scientific drawings of fossils for government geological reports. He lived in New Harmony until his wife's death in 1883, then returned to England, where he died several years later.

✷ [*Opposite*] "Map of the Track of the Tornado of April 30th 1852. From Golconda Illinois, to Wabash River across Indiana & the Ohio River to Georgetown Kentucky, U.S. With a Survey on an Enlarged Scale of the Prostrated Trees on Those Portions of the Track That Intersect the New Harmony Plank Road,

Meteorology

the Springfield, Evansville & Cynthiana Roads, with Sketches of Individual Trees and Diagrams Illustrative of the Redfield and Espy Theories of the Cause of the Phenomena. By John Chappelsmith. 1852." Sheet size 55 × 74 cm. Accompanying his article "Account of a Tornado near New Harmony, Ind., April 30, 1852, with a Map of the Track, &c." in *Smithsonian Contributions to Knowledge* (Washington, D.C.) 7 (1855): 1–13 [Historic Maps Collection].

First scientific study of a tornado's path and the first conclusive proof that tornadoes are an inward, upward, and onward moving column of air. In his article, Chappelsmith notes that people living five miles north of the storm continued to plough their fields during the whole time. The tornado's track was one mile wide and sped from New Harmony to Leavenworth in 1.5 hours, averaging sixty miles per hour and toppling trees at the rate of seven thousand per minute. Primarily based on his detailed examination of these prostrated trees left in the storm's wake, he concludes that the "phenomena are incompatible with the rotary hypothesis…. I am inclined to believe in Professor Espy's idea of an ascensional column …" [pp. 10–11].

✻ [*Overleaf*] Engraving of "Group of Trees Prostrated by the New Harmony Tornado" that accompanied Chappelsmith's Smithsonian article.

In his explanation of the plate, Chappelsmith states that it is another view of the group represented in figure 8 of the map, "about three hundred yards a little west of south of the five mile post on the New Harmony Plank Road" [p. 12].

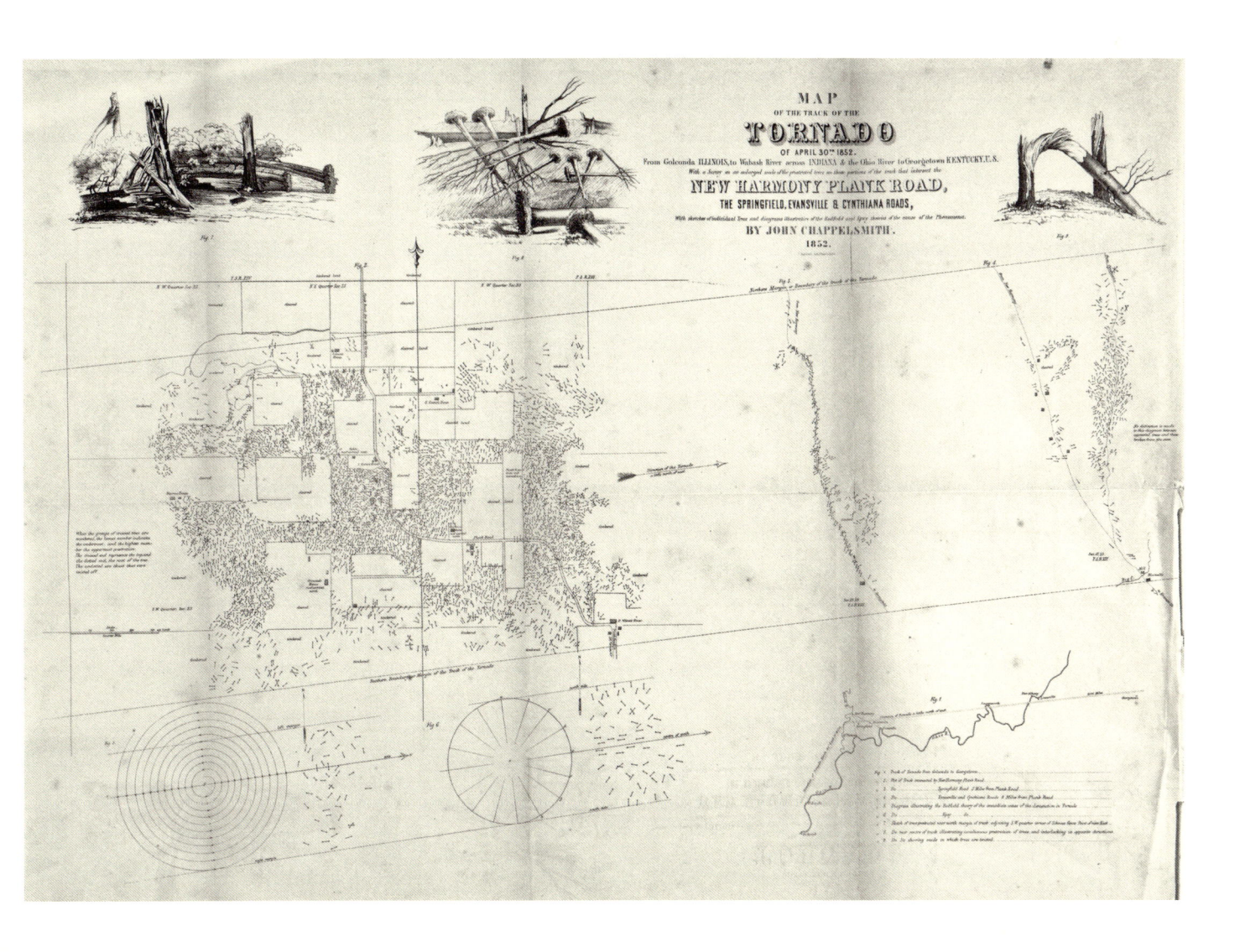

FRANCIS GALTON
1822–1911

KNIGHTED IN 1909, Francis Galton was a Victorian polymath whose legacy in numerous scientific fields is extraordinary. (He was a relative of naturalist Charles Darwin.) Much of it derived from his interest in numerical data and statistical analysis. During his lifetime, he published almost 350 papers and books. The following are some of his contributions:

METEOROLOGY (see below).

GEOGRAPHY: Galton financed and led a difficult exploring expedition (1850–1852) into relatively uncharted southwestern Africa (now Namibia), which won him a gold medal from the Royal Geographical Society.

STATISTICS: Galton created the concept of correlation and popularized the notion of regression toward the mean.

HEREDITY AND EVOLUTION: He coined the word "eugenics" and the phrase "nature and nurture," influenced by his half-cousin Charles Darwin's theory of natural selection.

PSYCHOLOGY: He founded psychometrics, the science of mental measurement (knowledge, abilities, attitudes, personality traits). He also introduced the methodology of surveys and questionnaires of human communities.

PHOTOGRAPHY: He developed a method to form a composite portrait from photographs of several persons, with implications for shared features.

FORENSICS: His detailed statistical analysis of fin-

✳︎ Portrait of Sir Francis Galton. From his *Memories of My Life* (London: Methuen & Co., 1909) [General Library Collection].

gerprints showed that the chance of two persons sharing the same characteristics was about 1 in 64 billion; hence, he greatly encouraged the use of fingerprints in criminology. His classification system survives today.

✳︎ [*Overleaf*] "English Weather Data, Feb. 9, 1861, 9h a.m." Printed map, 24.5 × 16.5 cm, accompanying Galton's piece on "Meteorological Charts." From *Philosophical Magazine* 22 (1861): 34–35 [General Library Collection].

First European weather map for an actual time and place. In this brief article, Galton decries contemporary meteorological reports that are printed in columns in newspapers. Meteorologists require charts, he argues, upon which they can present detailed information in easy-to-understand fashion. Hence, he offers this map, printed with moveable type, as a possible solution. In discussing the map, which utilizes real data acquired from the time, date, and region in its title, Galton proposes a number of symbols that meteorologists might use to show aspects of weather. For example, he uses a horseshoe to represent wind and to indicate its direction, and the dot, minus and plus signs within it signify whether the wind is gentle, moderate, or strong; an empty horseshoe means that the force of that wind is unknown. Though Galton's specific symbols were not adopted, his idea gained widespread support. Compare to the standardized weather maps in today's newspapers.

✳︎ [*Overleaf*] "European Weather-Charts for December 1861." Brief report summary from p. 30 of the "Notices and Abstracts of Miscellaneous Communications to the Sections" in *Report of the Thirty-Second Meeting of the British Association for the Advancement of Science, Held at Cambridge in October 1862* (London: John Murray, 1863) [General Library Collection].

The maps alluded to here ultimately appeared in a separate publication by Galton: *Meteorographica...*, a landmark meteorological publication (see below). The work represents the study of weather across Europe, an area stretching 1,500 miles east to west and 1,200 miles north to south, during the thirty-one days of December 1861. Galton collected data from several hundred observers distributed over the region; included were thrice-daily measurements of temperature, barometric pressure, wind direction and strength, and cloud conditions. The results were reported on ninety-three (31 days × 3 times) maps.

✳︎ [*Overleaf*] Untitled section of the page for December 30, 1861, from Galton's *Meteorographica, or Methods of Mapping the Weather; Illustrated by Upwards of 600 Printed and Lithographed Diagrams Referring to the Weather of a Large Part of Europe, during the Month of December 1861* (London: Macmillan and Co., 1863). Reprint by Archival Reprint Co., no. 32 of eighty-five copies [Historic Maps Collection].

These sample charts and map of the British Isles illustrate the two-step process of mapping weather that Galton describes below:

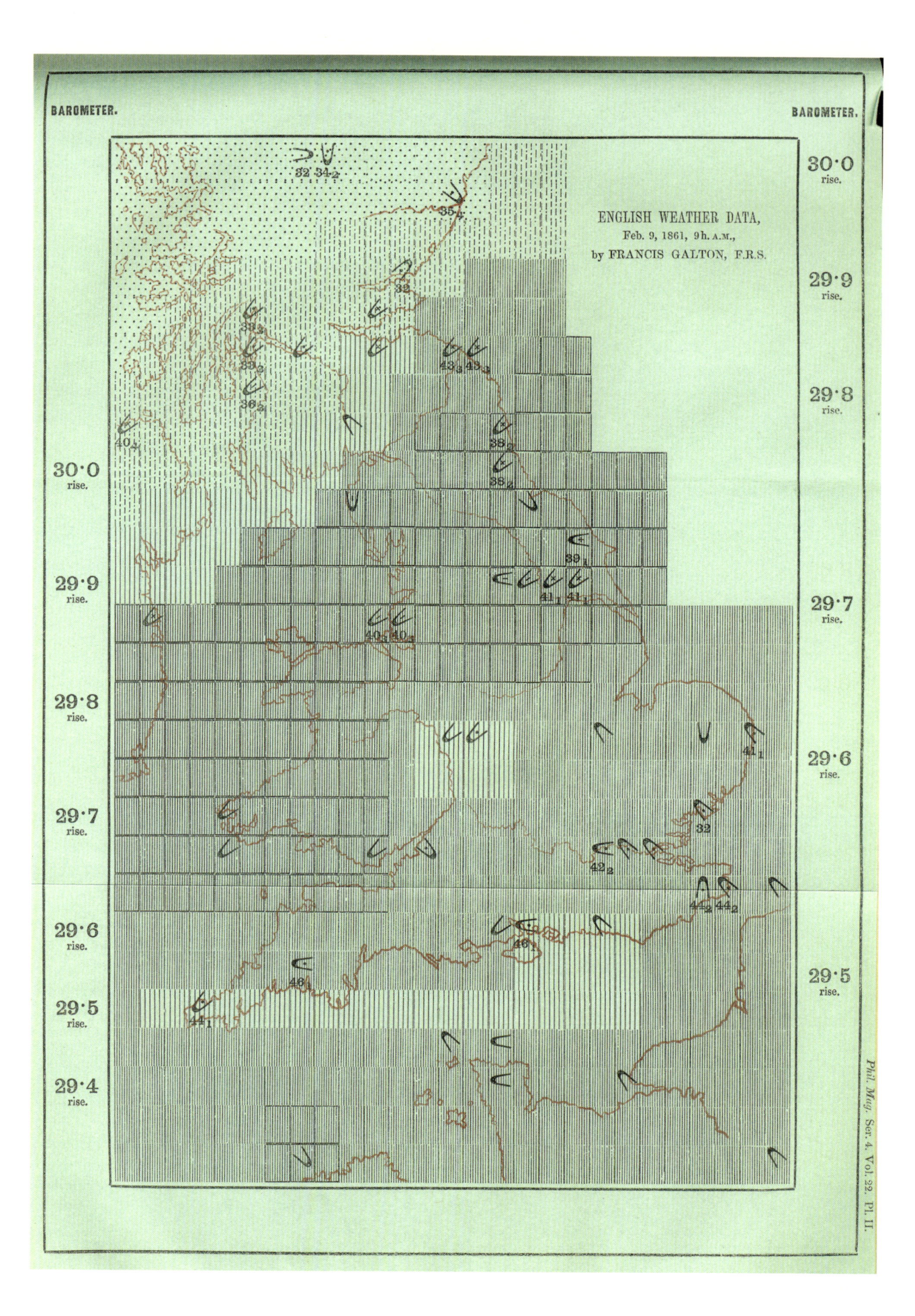

ENGLISH WEATHER DATA,
Feb. 9, 1861, 9h. A.M.,
by FRANCIS GALTON, F.R.S.

Meteorology

European Weather-Charts for December 1861. By F. GALTON, *F.R.S., F.R.G.S.*

The author submitted for examination a series of printed and stereotyped charts, compiled by himself, that contained the usual meteorological observations made at eighty stations in Europe, on the morning, afternoon, and evening of each day of December 1861. They were printed partly in symbols and partly in figures, in such a form that each separate group of observations occupies a small label, whose centre coincides with the geographical position of the station where the observations were made. The amount of cloud is expressed by shaded types, the direction of the wind by an equivalent to an arrow, and its force by a symbolical mark. The temperature of the wet and dry thermometers, and the barometric readings (reduced to zero and sea-level) are given in figures. As the charts had been too recently printed to admit of a thorough examination, and as they were ultimately to appear as a separate publication, the author abstained from other deductions than those that were obvious on inspection. Among these, the enormous range and the simultaneity of the wind-changes, testifying to the remarkable mobility of the air, were exceedingly conspicuous.

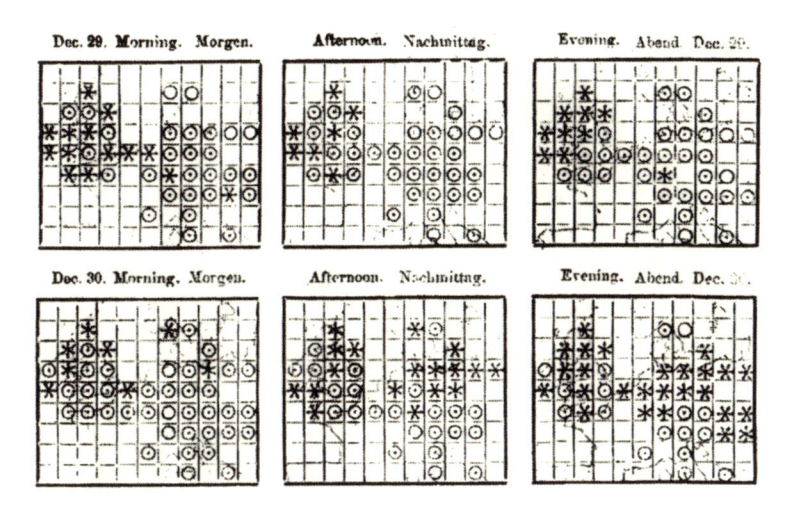

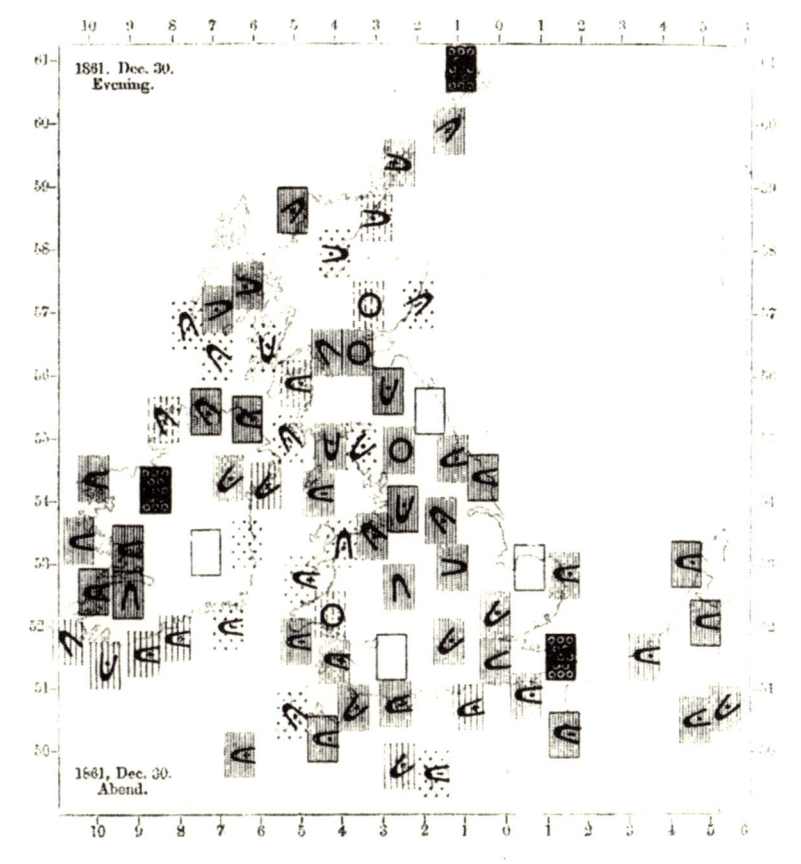

The accompanying Charts and Maps are contributions to a branch of Meteorology which is theoretically divisible into two separate portions, though they may be more or less united in practice, and it is convenient to class them under a single term,—Meteorography. I mean by that phrase, 1st, the art and practice of tabulating Observations which have been made simultaneously at numerous stations, each record being inscribed in the geographical position of the place where it was made; and, 2ndly, the subsequent step of delineating the General Results of the Observations in a pictorial form. The necessity and character of the double process I have described, may be illustrated by the well-known methods employed in Geography [p. 3].

Galton admitted, however, that it was impossible "at the present time" to scientifically study weather on a "worthy scale," for want of accessible data.

The three pairs of charts show barometric readings for the morning, afternoon, and evening of December 29 and 30. An empty circle, a circle with a dot, a star, and a black circle are symbols Galton used to indicate specific ranges of increasing barometric pressure. In the map for the evening of December 30, the U-shaped symbol shows the direction of the wind (its fill, the wind's strength), and the O's represent areas of calm. The symbols' rectangular background panels refer to rain and cloud cover.

✳ Key to Jean Etienne Guettard's "Carte minéralogique, où l'on voit la nature des terreins du Canada et de la Louisane … 1752" (1756).

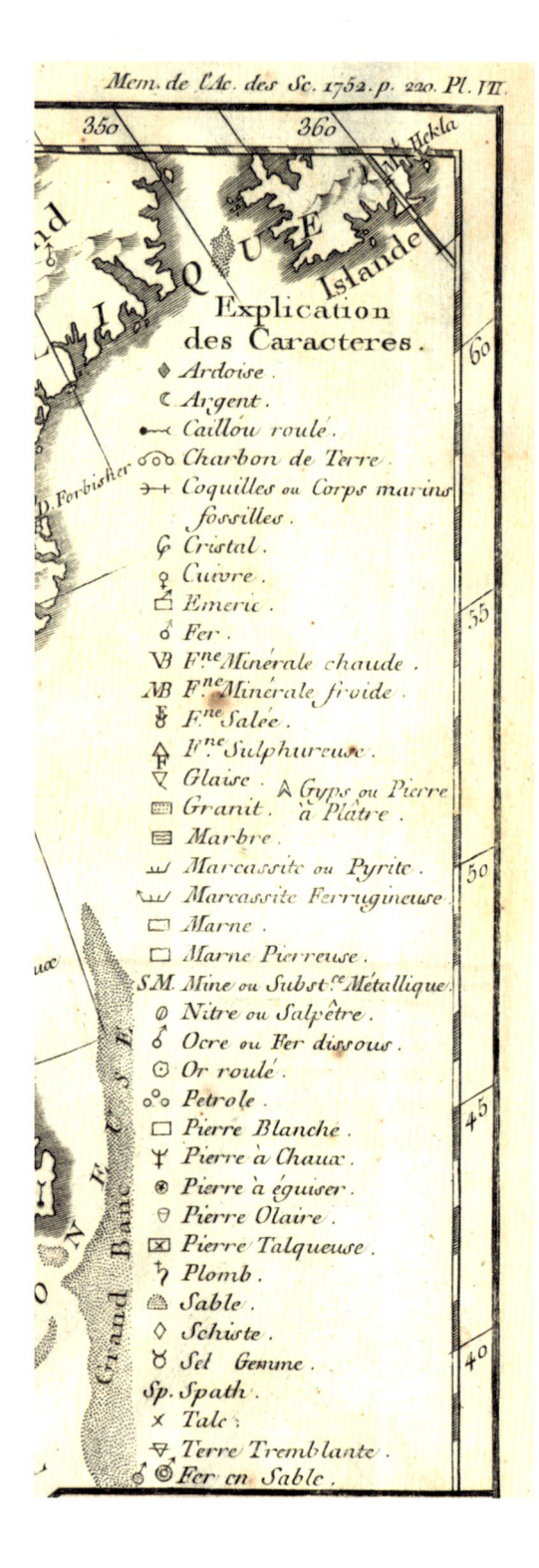

GEOLOGY

GEOLOGICAL MAPS began with the examination of land surfaces and then literally went underground in portraying the underlying stratification of geologic layers.

MARTIN LISTER
1638?–1712

AN ENGLISH naturalist and physician, Lister did not subscribe to fellow countryman William Gilbert's influential theory that the interior of the earth was composed primarily of iron; rather, he felt that top soils and clays were indicative of underlayers of different minerals. His proposal (1683) for a "Soil or Mineral Map" first launched the idea of geological mapping. To a general map of England, divided into sections and showing basic rivers and towns, he suggested adding soil data, such as he had been collecting for many years:

> The *Soil* might either be coloured, by variety of *Lines*, or *Etchings*; but the great care must be, very exactly to note upon the *Map*, where such and such *Soiles* are bounded.... Now if it were noted, how far these extended, and the limits of each Soil appeared upon a *Map*, something more might be comprehended from the whole, and from every part, then I can possibly foresee, which would make such a labour very well worth the pains. For I am of the opinion, such upper *Soiles*, if natural, infallibly produce such *under Minerals*, and for the most part in such order. But I leave this to the industry of future times [pp. 739–740; Lister's emphasis].

Latent in his message is the concept of geological stratification, which would be championed by William Smith in the early nineteenth century. (See his entry in this Geology section.) Apparently, Lister's call fell upon deaf ears, for more than a half-century would pass before any geological maps appeared.

✻ [*Overleaf*] First page of Lister's "An Ingenious Proposal for a New Sort of Maps of Countrys, together with Tables of Sands and Clays, Such Chiefly as Are

✻ Portrait of Martin Lister [*Wikipedia*].

Found in the North Parts of England, Drawn Up about 10 Years Since, and Delivered to the Royal Society Mar. 12. 1683." From *Philosophical Transactions* 14, no. 164 (October 20, 1685): 739–746 [Rare Books Division]. Includes tables of sands/clays he found in northern England.

JEAN ETIENNE GUETTARD
1715–1786

JEAN ETIENNE GUETTARD's grandfather was an apothecary and physician who taught him about plants at a young age. In Paris, he pursued botanical and medical studies and by his early thirties had

[739]

An Ingenious proposal for a new sort of Maps of Countrys, together with Tables of Sands and Clays, such chiefly as are found in the North parts of England, drawn up about 10 years since, and delivered to the Royal Society Mar. 12. 1683. by the Learned Martin Lister M. D.

WE shall then be better able to judge of the make of the *Earth*, and of many *Phænomena* belonging thereto, when we have well and duely examined it, as far as human art can possibly reach, beginning from the *outside* downwards. As for the more *inward* and *Central* parts thereof, I think we shall never be able to confute *Gilbert's* opinion thereof, who will, not without Reason, have it altogether *Iron**. And for this purpose it were advisable, that a *Soil* or *Mineral Map*, as I may call it, were devised. The same *Map* of *England* may, for want of a better, at present serve the Turn. It might be distinguisht into *Countries*, with the *River* and some of the noted *Towns* put in. The *Soil* might either be coloured, by variety of *Lines*, or *Etchings*; but the great care must be, very exactly to note upon the *Map*, where such and such *Soiles* are bounded. As for example in *Yorkshire* (1.) The *Woolds*, Chaulk, Flint, and Pyrites, &c. (2.) *Black moore*; Moores, Sandstone, &c. (3.) *Holderness*; Boggy, Turf, Clay, Sand, &c. (4.) *Western Mountains*; Moores, Sand-stone, Coal, Iron-stone, Lead Ore, Sand, Clay, &c. *Nottinghamshire*, mostly Gravel Pebble, Clay, Sand-stone, Half-playster, or *Gypsum*, &c. Now if it were noted, how far these extended, and the limits of each Soil appeared upon a *Map*, something more might

* *De Magn.* Lib. 1. Cap. 17. *Tellus in interioribus partibus magneticam homogeneicam naturam habet.*

※ Portrait of Jean Etienne Guettard [*Wikipedia*].

become *médecin botaniste* to Louis, the duke of Orléans. After the duke's death in 1752, Guettard continued to enjoy the support of the duke's son, Louis-Philippe, with rooms in the Palais-Royal, a laboratory, and guaranteed income. By this time, he was devoted to geological study, having become intrigued with the distribution of rocks and minerals during his wide travels in France while gathering data for a national geological survey. He was the first to recognize the volcanic nature of the district of Auvergne. With Antoine Grimoald Monnet, Guettard created the first geological atlas, *Atlas et description minéralogiques de la France* (1780).

※ [*Opposite*] "Carte minéralogique où l'on quoit la nature et la situation des terrains qui traversent la France et l'Angleterre … 1746." Copperplate map, 30.6 × 26 cm, one of two maps accompanying Guettard's "Mémoire et carte minéralogique sur la nature & la situation des terrains qui traversent la France & l'Angleterre," dated February 19, 1746. From *Histoire de l'Académie Royale des Sciences* (1751): 363–392 [Rare Books Division]. Both maps were engraved by Philippe Buache (1700–1773), a leading French geographer and mapmaker.

First maps to show bands or zones of surface geological similarity. (This map is simply an enlargement of the central section of the other.) Guettard utilizes almost fifty symbols to identify the locations of different rocks and minerals, but the main foci of the map are the three bands shown by dotted lines and shaded areas: "Bande sabloneuse" (sandy zone), which includes Paris; "Bande marneus" (marly zone), which he hypothesizes continues under the English Channel to join a similar band in England; and "Bande schiteuse ou metallique" (metalliferous zone). Guettard states his work's raison d'être at the very beginning of his article (which I have translated loosely):

Nothing can contribute better to a general and physical theory of the earth than collecting diverse observations of minerals and rocks, and the fossils they

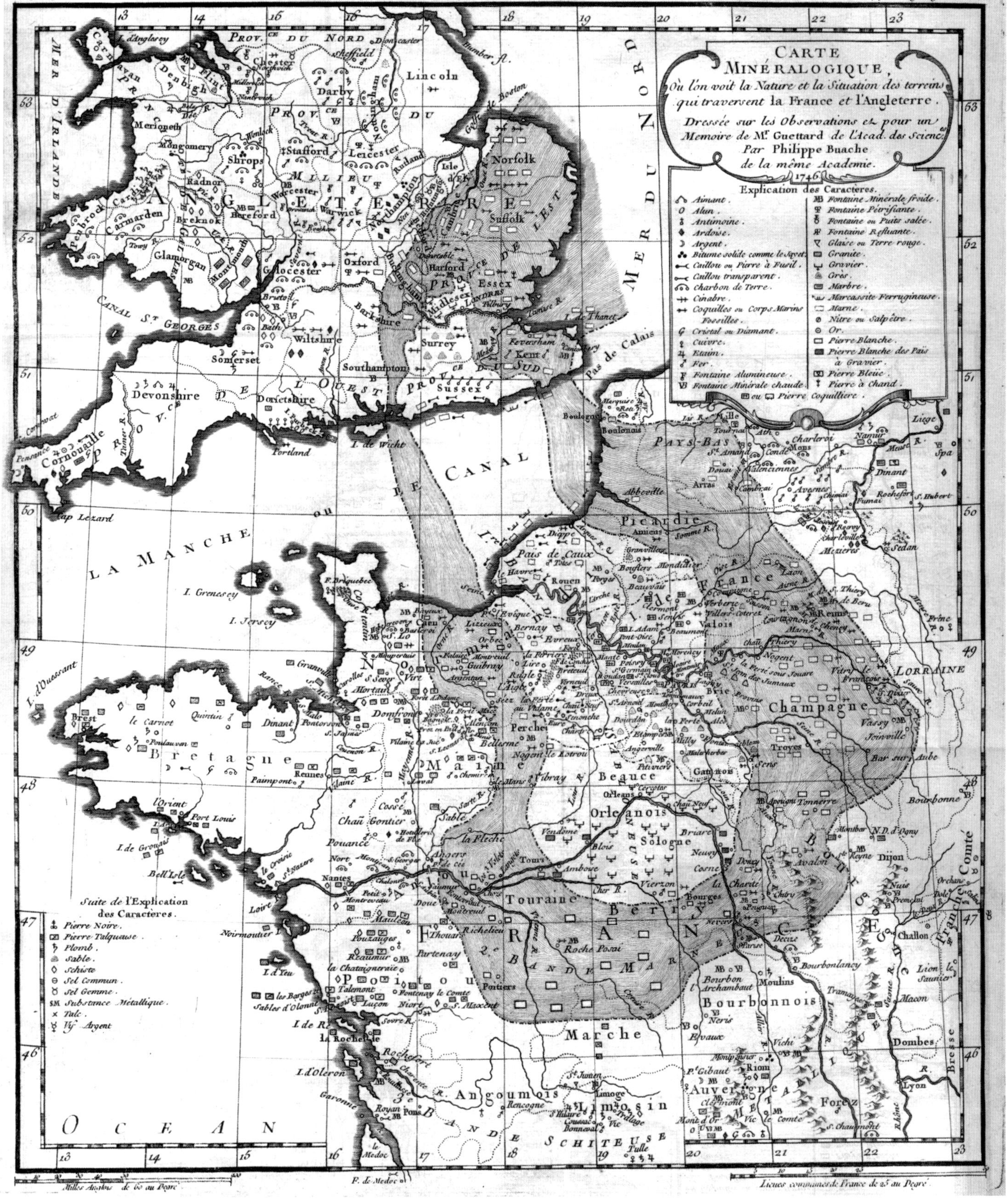

CARTE MINÉRALOGIQUE,
Où l'on voit la Nature et la Situation des terreins qui traversent la France et l'Angleterre.
Dressée sur les Observations et pour un Memoire de Mr. Guettard de l'Acad. des Sciences
Par Philippe Buache de la même Academie.
1746.
Explication des Caracteres.
Aimant.
Alun.
Antimoine.
Ardoise.
Argent.
Bitume solide comme le Jayet.
Caillou ou Pierre à Fusil.
Caillou transparent.
Charbon de Terre.
Cinabre.
Coquilles ou Corps Marins Fossilles.
Cristal ou Diamant.
Cuivre.
Etaim.
Fer.
Fontaine Alumineuse.
Fontaine Minérale chaude.
Fontaine Minérale froide.
Fontaine Pétrifiante.
Fontaine ou Puits salée.
Fontaine Refluante.
Glaise ou Terre rouge.
Granite.
Gravier.
Grès.
Marbre.
Marcassite Ferrugineuse.
Marne.
Nitre ou Salpêtre.
Or.
Pierre Blanche.
Pierre Blanche des Païs à Gravier.
Pierre Bleüe.
Pierre à Chaud.
ou Pierre Coquilliere.
Suite de l'Explication des Caracteres.
Pierre Noire.
Pierre Talqueuse.
Plomb.
Sable.
Schiste
Sel Commun.
Sel Gemme.
SM Substance Métallique.
Talc.
Vif Argent
LA MANCHE ou LE CANAL
CANAL ST. GEORGES
MER DU NORD
OCEAN
ANGLETERRE
FRANCE
Milles Anglois de 60 au Degré
Lieues communes de France de 25 au Degré

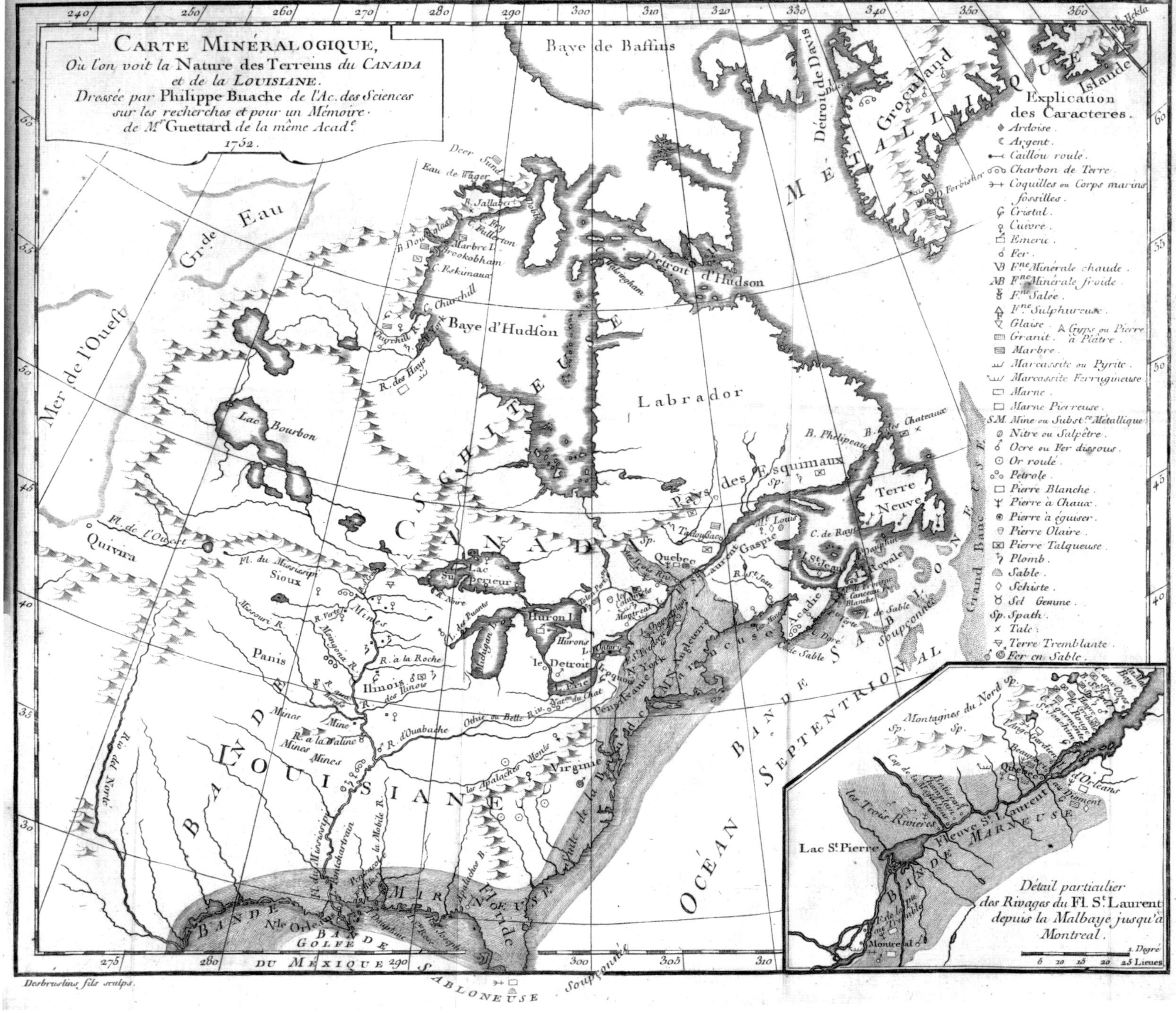
Carte Minéralogique,
Où l'on voit la Nature des Terreins du Canada et de la Louisiane.
Dressée par Philippe Buache de l'Ac. des Sciences sur les recherches et pour un Mémoire de Mr. Guettard de la même Acad.e
1752.
Explication des Caracteres.
Ardoise.
Argent.
Caillou roulé.
Charbon de Terre.
Coquilles ou Corps marins fossilles.
Cristal.
Cuivre.
Emeri.
Fer.
F.ne Minérale chaude.
F.ne Minérale froide.
F.ne Salée.
F.ne Sulphureuse.
Glaise.
Granit.
Gyps ou Pierre à Plâtre.
Marbre.
Marcassite ou Pyrite.
Marcassite Ferrugineuse.
Marne.
Marne Pierreuse.
S.M. Mine ou Subst.ce Métallique.
Nitre ou Salpêtre.
Ocre ou Fer dissous.
Or roulé.
Petrole.
Pierre Blanche.
Pierre à Chaux.
Pierre à éguiser.
Pierre Olaire.
Pierre Talqueuse.
Plomb.
Sable.
Schiste.
Sel Gemme.
Sp. Spath.
Talc.
Terre Tremblante.
Fer en Sable.
Détail particulier des Rivages du Fl. St. Laurent depuis la Malbaye jusqu'à Montreal.
1 Degré
25 Lieues
Lac St. Pierre
les Trois Rivieres
Fleuve St. Laurent
Quebec
Montreal
Montagnes du Nord
Baye de Baffins
Détroit de Davis
Groenland
Islande
Détroit d'Hudson
Baye d'Hudson
Labrador
Terre Neuve
Grand Banc
Pays des Esquimaux
Canada
Louisiane
Lac Bourbon
Mer de l'Ouest
Gr.de Eau
Quivira
Sioux
Panis
Ilinois
Virginie
Floride
Océan Septentrional
Golfe du Mexique
Rio del Norte
Desbruslins fils sculps.

Geology

contain, and presenting them all at one glance [*sous un coup d'oeil*] in mineralogical maps [p. 363].

By viewing the maps, he argues, one can see a regularity in the distribution of certain rocks and metals and thus can extrapolate from these patterns the conclusions he has drawn about the bands.

✳ [*Opposite*] "Carte minéralogique, où l'on voit la nature des terreins du Canada et de la Louisane ... 1752." Copperplate map, 25.5 × 29.6 cm, one of two maps accompanying Guettard's "Mémoire dans lequel on compare le Canada à la Suisse, par rapport à ses minéraux," dated June 7, 1752. From *Histoire de l'Académie Royale des Sciences* (1756): 189–220, 323–360 [Rare Books Division]. Both maps were engraved by Philippe Buache.

First geological map of North America. Never having traveled to New France, Guettard examined sample rocks that had been sent back to France and also drew from the firsthand observations of other countrymen, particularly those in the landmark *Histoire et description générale de la Nouvelle-France* (1744) of the French Jesuit Pierre-François-Xavier de Charlevoix (1682–1761) and a memoir by Quebec physician J. F. Gautier. He found enough parallels with Europe to apply his system of three mineralogical bands to the new continent.

✳ Portrait of William Smith, aged 69. From Horace B. Woodward's The History of the Geological Society of London (London: Geological Society, 1907) [General Library Collection].

WILLIAM SMITH
1769–1839

CONSIDERED NOW the father of English geology, William Smith waited for most of his life to get the recognition he deserved. Raised by his uncle, Smith found work in 1787 as a surveyor's assistant; later, he worked for an extended period for the Somerset Coal Canal Company. At the Mearns Pit in High Littleton, he first observed a predictable pattern of layers or strata in the vertical rock and a consistent order among them. Moreover, he noticed that each layer could be identified by its fossils and that a succession of fossil groups, from older to younger, paralleled the changes in rock strata. This principle, which he termed faunal succession, became his operative hypothesis, the consistency of which he spent years in testing around England and Wales by collecting fossil samples and mapping locations of their related strata. In time, he was known as "Strata Smith."

Drawing on his growing collection of fossils, Smith began publishing these findings; important titles were *Geological Table of British Organized Fossils* (1815) and *Strata Identified by Organized Fossils* (1816). In 1815, Smith also released his large-scale (five miles to the inch!) geological map of Great Britain, "A Delineation of the Strata of England and Wales with a Part of Scotland," the first national geological map, which, in a recent biographer's words, "changed the world."

But Smith's works were quickly plagiarized; he became bankrupt and was thrown into debtor's prison. When he emerged in 1819, he found that his home and property had been repossessed. For a number of years Smith resorted to working as an itinerant surveyor and gave lectures before his achievements began to be fully

GENERAL MAP.

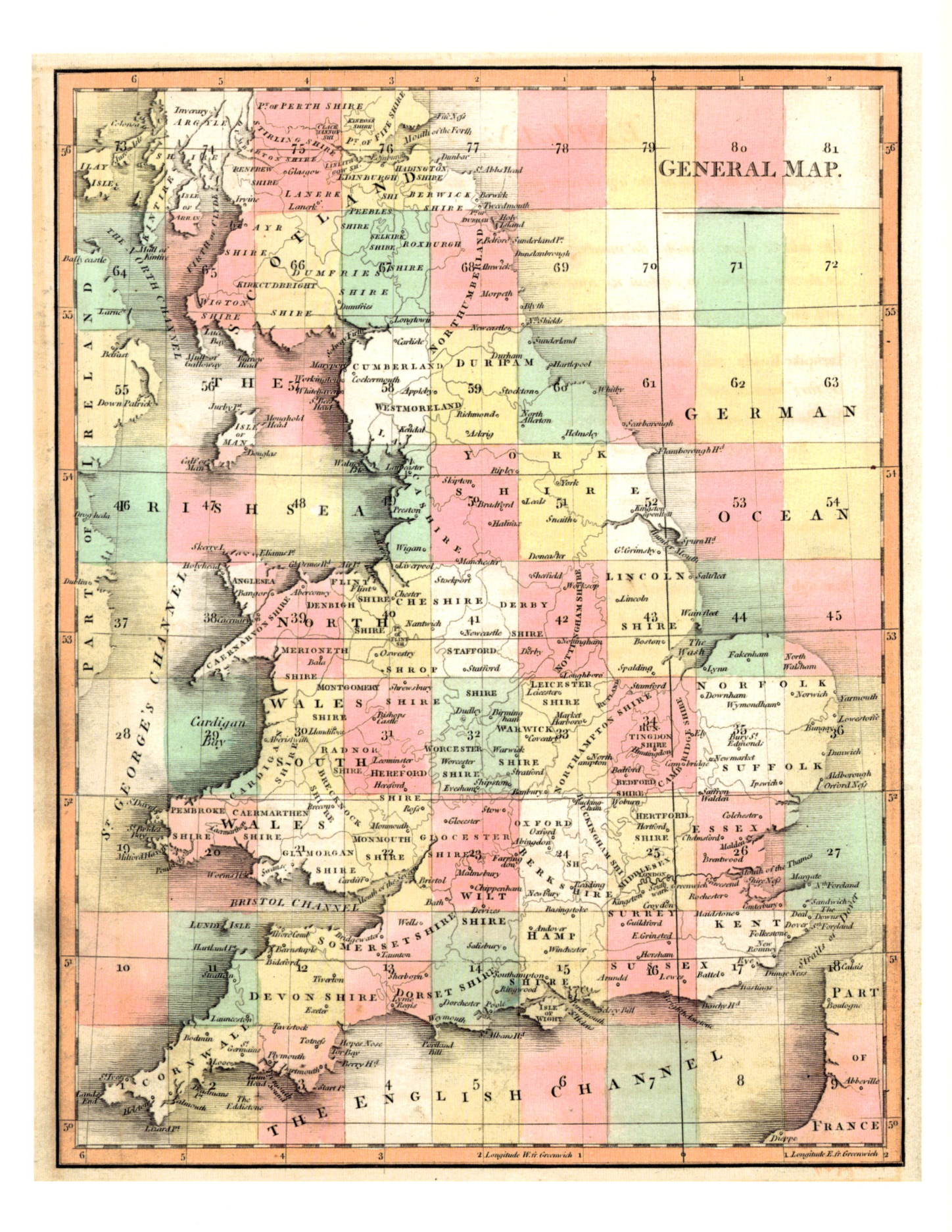

Geology

recognized and appreciated. In Scarborough, he raised money to build a rotunda-shaped museum to display fossils in their proper chronological order; today, it is called the William Smith Museum of Geology.

In 1831, the Geological Society of London bestowed on him the first Wollaston Medal, its highest award; the following year, the British government honored him with a pension of 100 £ per year. With several others, Smith was appointed by the government to make a tour (1837–1838) through England and Wales to select suitable stone for the building of the Houses of Parliament. Sand-colored magnesium limestone, from Bolsover Moor, Derbyshire, was ultimately chosen—this project was his last scientific engagement.

Great Britain's modern geological map is still based on Smith's landmark 1815 work, the original of which is protected behind a blue curtain beside the main staircase at the Geological Society's London office.

✳ [*Opposite*] "General Map." Copperplate map, with added color, 23.8 × 18.8 cm. The index map for John Cary's *Cary's New Map of England and Wales* ... (London: J. Cary, 1794) [Rare Books Division]. This is the first published map to use Greenwich as the prime meridian (0°).

Smith chose this as his base map when he began to color in the extents of geological formations that he had developed from his notes—the beginning of his pioneer attempt to map the entire country. The resulting small-scale map, titled "General Map of Strata in England and Wales," simply expanding on Cary's title, was finished in 1801.

✳ [*Overleaf*] "A Delineation of the Strata of England and Wales with a Part of Scotland, Exhibiting the Collieries and Mines, the Marshes and Fen Lands Originally Overflowed by the Sea, and the Varieties of Soil According to the Variations in the Substrata, Illustrated by the Most Descriptive Names" (London: J. Cary, August 1, 1815). Reduced facsimile copy (2003) of Smith's copperplate map, 127 by 88 cm [Map Library].

Smith's landmark map. Four hundred copies of the original were printed, numbered, and signed; only about forty are known to be extant. It was dedicated to the noted English naturalist and botanist Sir Joseph Banks (1743–1820), who had been Smith's supporter and first subscriber. Among other things, the map changed the human concept of geological time.

The map is so large—this copy is half the size of the original—that one easily can lose sight of the detailed and extensive information that Smith has provided. The coal-bearing regions are appropriately colored charcoal, and the locations of the collieries are marked with plus signs (+). Lead, copper, and tin mines are also identified.

✳ [*Below*] "Sketch of the Succession of STRATA and Their Relative Altitudes." Inset taken from Smith's 1815 map.

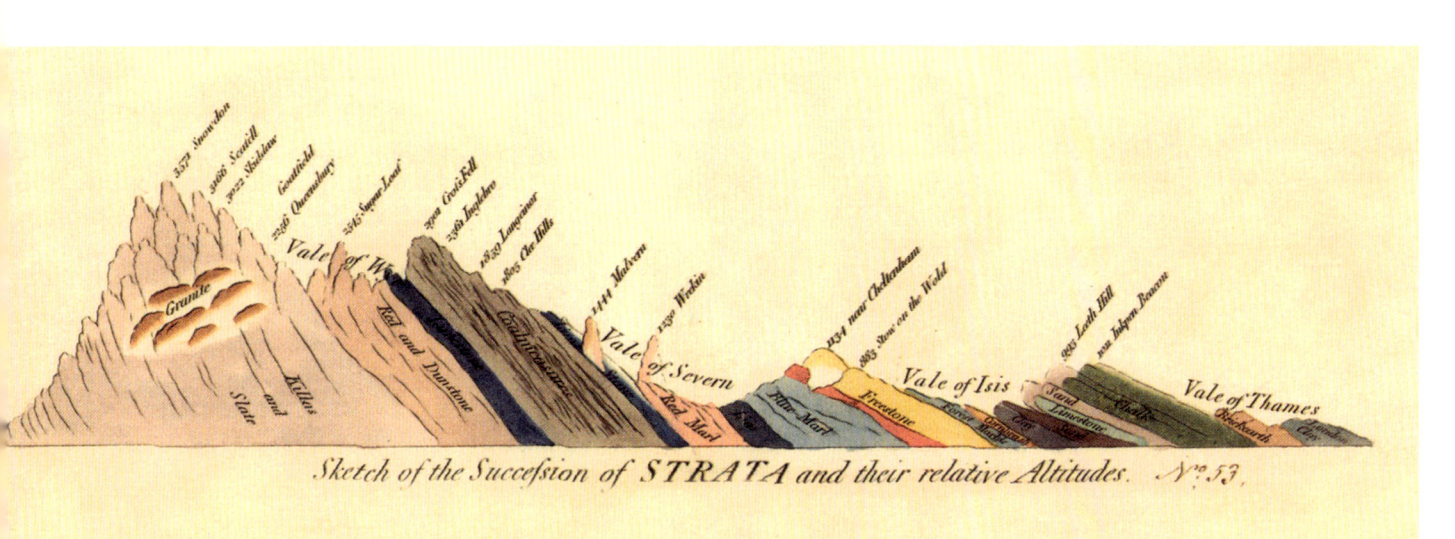

Sketch of the Succession of STRATA and their relative Altitudes. Nº 53.

A DELINEATION OF THE STRATA OF ENGLAND AND WALES, WITH PART OF SCOTLAND; EXHIBITING THE COLLIERIES AND MINES, THE MARSHES AND FEN LANDS ORIGINALLY OVERFLOWED BY THE SEA, AND THE VARIETIES OF SOIL ACCORDING TO THE VARIATIONS IN THE SUBSTRATA, ILLUSTRATED BY THE MOST DESCRIPTIVE NAMES BY W. SMITH

CARDIGAN BAY
ST GEORGE
EXPLANATION
BRISTOL CHANNEL
MOUTH of the THAMES
STRAITS of DOVER
THE ENGLISH CHANNEL

GEORGES CUVIER, 1769–1832
ALEXANDRE BRONGNIART, 1770–1847

Born in Montbéliard, France, Georges Cuvier was a precocious youth who was drawn to natural history at the age of ten and acquired the animal knowledge of a first-rate naturalist by twelve. In his early twenties, he began comparing fossils with extant forms, leading, in 1796, to his presentation of two landmark papers. One, by providing his analysis of the fossils of elephants, mammoths, and other skeletal remains that he later named "mastodon," proved that all were distinct species and, therefore, that mammoths and mastodons must be extinct. Moreover, he concluded that some kind of catastrophe had precipitated the demise of these extinct species. The other paper argued similarly about the skeleton of a large animal found in Paraguay that was related to, but different from, living sloths: here was another extinct species. As a result, Cuvier is credited with ending the debate about the extinction of species—most fossils were "extinct" evidence—and became a proponent of the concept of catastrophism, which claimed that past dramatic events could explain changes in geological features and the extinction of species. (Interestingly, while believing in extinct species, Cuvier rejected the idea of evolution.)

The son of an architect, Alexandre Brongniart became a chemist and mineralogist, a combination that suited him well for a later career in ceramics. (From 1800 until his death, he directed the internationally famous Sèvres porcelain factory and founded the Musée National de Céramique-Sèvres, the national museum of ceramics.) In earlier years, he taught mineralogy in Paris, introduced a new classification scheme for reptiles, made the first arrangement of Tertiary Period geological formations, and contributed the first thorough study of trilobites, extinct arthropods that would prove useful in date-marking Paleozoic strata. In 1804, he began studying the fossil-bearing terrain of the region around Paris with Cuvier. The final version of their findings was published in 1811.

✻ [*Opposite*] "Carte géognostique des environs de Paris ... 1810." Copperplate map, with added color, in twelve sections backed on linen, 61.4 × 71.4 cm. From Cuvier

✻ Portrait of Baron Georges Cuvier. From vol. 2 (1833) of *The Gallery of Portraits: With Memoirs* (London: C. Knight, 1833–1837) [General Library Collection]. For his work, Cuvier was honored with the title of baron in 1819.

✻ Portrait of Alexandre Brongniart. From Jules Pizzetta's *Galerie des naturalistes: Histoire des sciences naturelles depuis leur origine jusqu'a nos jours* (Paris: A. Hennuyer, 1891) [General Library Collection].

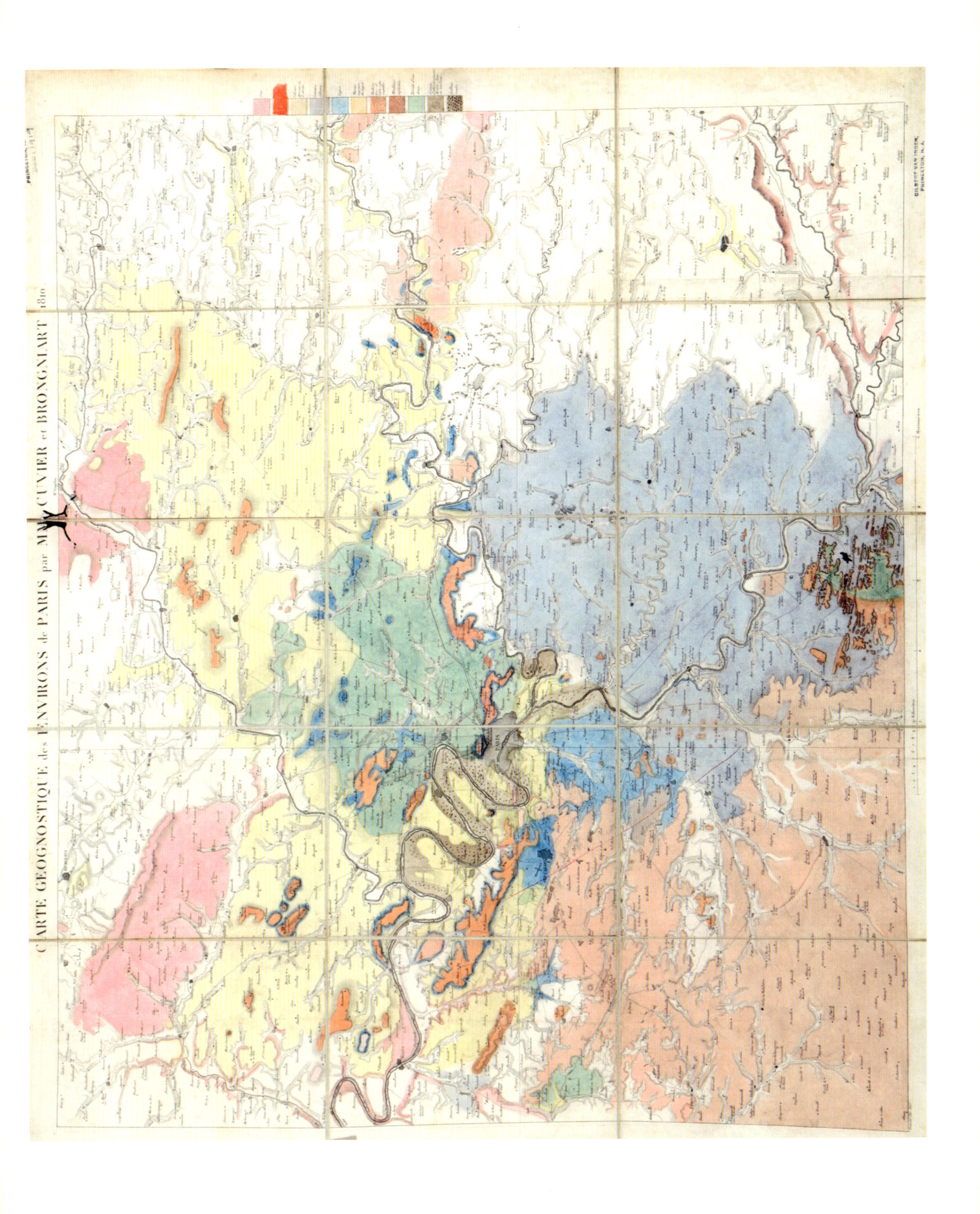

CARTE GEOGNOSTIQUE des ENVIRONS de PARIS par MM. CUVIER et BRONGNIART 1810

and Brongniart's *Essai sur la géographie minéralogique des environs de Paris, avec une carte géognostique, et des coupes de terrain*, 2 vols. (Paris: Baudouin, 1811) [Historic Maps Collection].

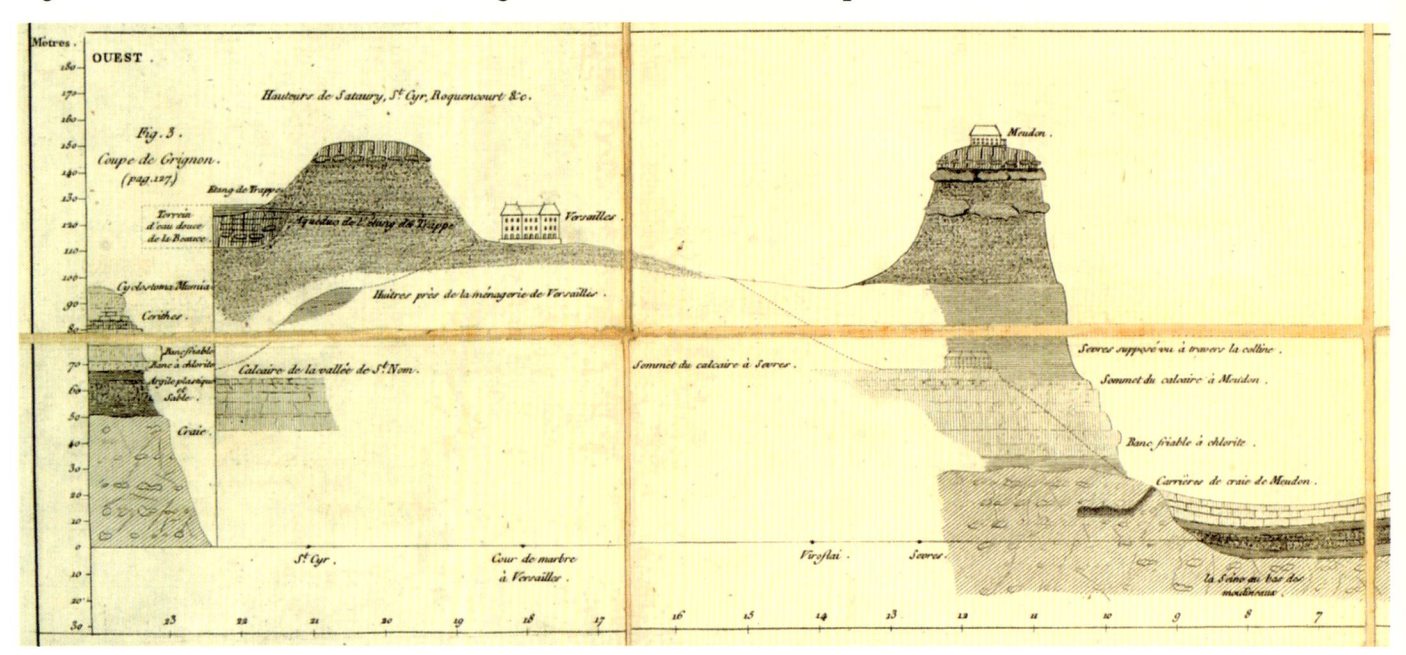

Landmark geological map that helped establish paleontological stratigraphy, the idea that distinctive fossils found in various sedimentary strata can be used to date the rock layers. (See also William Smith in this Geology section.) Cuvier and Brongniart's discoveries proved that the strata formations in the Paris basin had been laid down under alternating fresh and saltwater conditions—hence, there had been inland seas at various times in the remote history of the region. Dotted lines indicate the men's travels, identifying the areas that they observed directly. Intermediate regions were characterized from accounts of others accumulated over time and from information available from architectural sites and quarries. The men had no data precise enough to label regions shown uncolored on the map. Strata identified by the colors include limestone ("craie") in pink, gypsum ("gypse") in blue, and marine gypsum marls ("marnes marines de gypse") in yellow. The green areas are labeled freshwater terrain ("terrein d'eau douce").

✱ [*Above*] "Figure 3" from the large, untitled plate containing numerous cross-section views of stratified rock, 38.3 × 74.9 cm. From Cuvier and Brongniart's *Essai sur la géographie minéralogique des environs de Paris ...* (1811) [Historic Maps Collection].

A cross section (height in meters, distance in kilometers) of the terrain in the Versailles–Meudon region southwest of Paris. The fact that fossils of "huitres" (oysters) were found near Versailles—and about thirty meters below the surface—indicates the former presence of an ocean. Despite the separation of a valley of approximately ten kilometers in width, the strata for the two highest spots shown (Sataury and Meudon) are very similar, lending more support to the idea of a specific order of geologic layers.

WILLIAM MACLURE
1763–1840

CALLED the father of American geology, William Maclure was born in Scotland. At nineteen, he traveled to New York to enter upon a commercial career, eventually becoming a partner in an American firm in London. By 1797, he had made a fortune and retired to devote himself to the study of natural history, primarily mineralogy and geology. For the next twenty years, Maclure traveled widely in Europe and the United States. His journey from Maine to Georgia in 1808 resulted in the first geological map of the new country, published in the *Transactions of the American*

✷ Portrait of William Maclure. From Samuel George Morton's "A Memoir of William Maclure, Esq., Late President of the Academy of Natural Sciences of Philadelphia," in *American Journal of Science and Arts* 47 (1844): 1–17 [General Library Collection].

Philosophical Society in 1809. Back in the United States in 1816, accompanied by the French artist and naturalist Charles Alexandre Lesueur (1778–1846), whom he had hired as an assistant, Maclure set out again through New England and the Middle Atlantic states to make a thorough revision to his geological study, which he published in 1818 to widespread acclaim. (The general accuracy of Maclure's geological observations was corroborated in subsequent surveys.)

By then a resident of Philadelphia, Maclure became indelibly associated with the young Academy of Natural Sciences, financing its move to an expanded building and becoming its president, a position he held (1817–1840) until his death. His patronage was crucial to the development of American science before the creation of the Smithsonian Institution (1846). His European travels exposed him to the educational teachings of Johann Heinrich Pestalozzi (1746–1827), who championed practical education geared to the individual's unique intuition. When Maclure met the Welsh social reformer Robert Owen (1771–1858) in 1824, he became intrigued with the socialist's plan for a utopian community in [New] Harmony, Indiana, and agreed to invest heavily in it. In December 1825, Maclure and others recruited from the Academy of Natural Sciences traveled by boat to the new community. (Also aboard Owen's boat was John Chappelsmith; see his entry in the Meteorology section.) There, Maclure took charge of its educational program; established a journal and a printing press, which published notable works by Lesueur on ichthyology and Thomas Say's groundbreaking volumes, *American Conchology*; and continued his financial support even after the community fell apart as a result of incessant bickering.

He retired to Mexico in 1828, where he lived the rest of his life. Unmarried, Maclure left no descendants; his estate was divided among his scientific and educational interests.

✷ [*Overleaf*] "Map of the United States of America, Designed to Illustrate the Geological Memoir of Wm. Maclure, Esqr." Copperplate map, with added color, 31.4 × 42.7 cm. From Maclure's article "Observations on the Geology of the United States of North America, with Remarks on the Probable Effects That May Be Produced by the Decomposition of the Different Classes of Rocks on the Nature and Fertility of Soils: Applied to the Different States of the Union, Agreeably to the Accompanying Geological Map," which he read before the American Philosophical Society on May 16, 1817, and published in *Transactions of the American Philosophical Society, Held at Philadelphia, for Promoting Useful Knowledge* 1 (new ser., 1818): 1–91 [Rare Books Division].

First geological map of the United States, published by the important, Scottish-born American mapmaker John Melish. This is the revised, larger version of the map that Maclure originally published in the *Transactions* in 1809. Here, in broad strokes, he identifies six different geological classes: primitive rocks, transition, secondary, alluvial, old red sandstone, and salt/gypsum. (Note that the chain of the Appalachian Mountains is correctly labeled as containing the most primitive, or oldest, rock.) Maclure avoids speculating on the origins

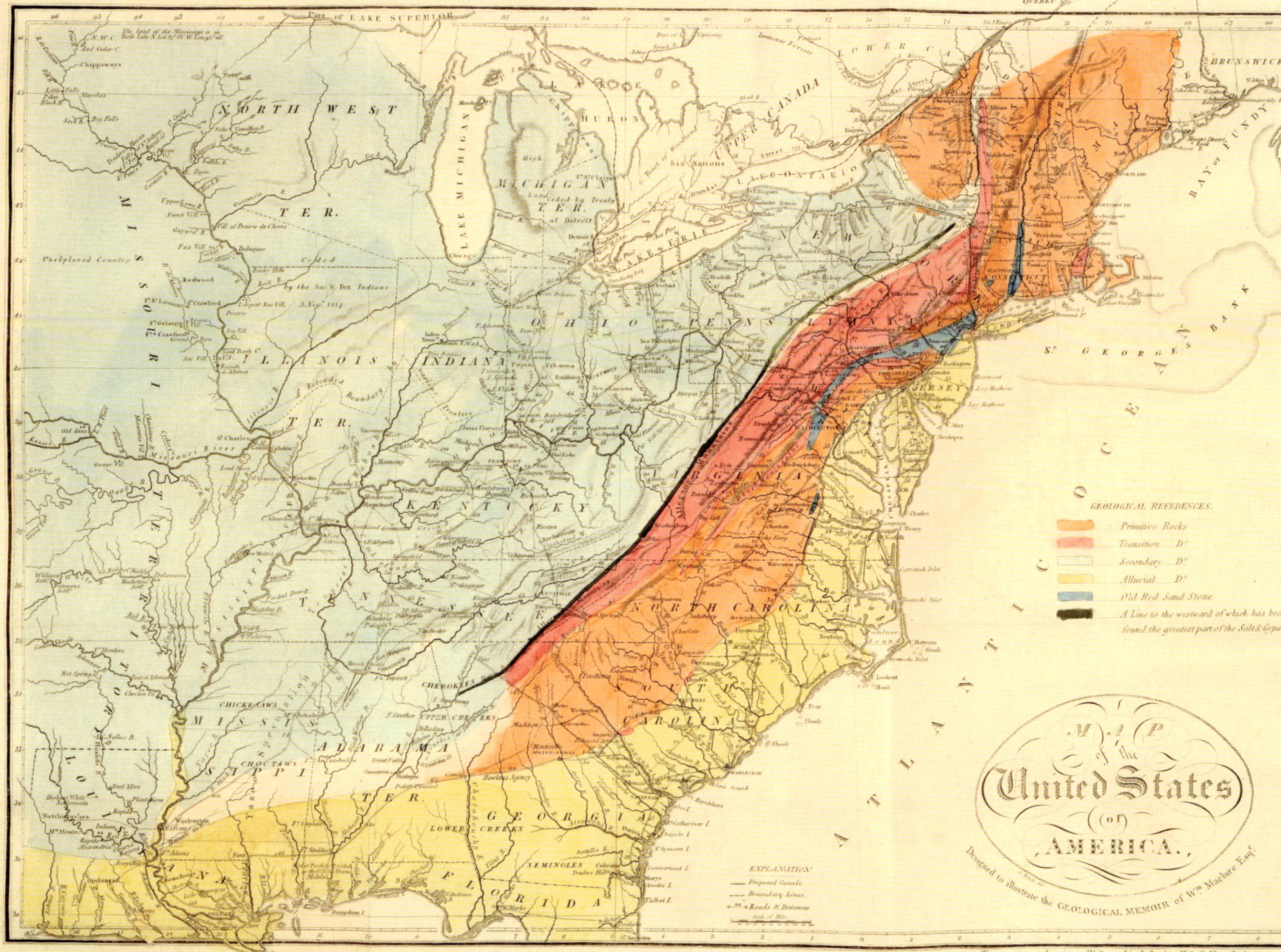

Entered as the Act directs, and Published by JOHN MELISH, Philadelphia.

Transactions American Philosophical Society Vol. I New Series.

or agents of geological change, which he believes is not productive, and instead directs his attention to making observations that will have practical uses:

> A knowledge of the nature and properties of rocks, and the results of their decomposition, enables us to judge of their hardness, easy or difficult decomposition, their component parts, mode of splitting, &c., by which we judge of their fitness for house buildings, roofing, road making, burning for lime, china or pottery, brick making, glass making, hearths for forges and furnaces, &c. [p. 5].

He hopes for the day when college students will study the properties and uses of such substances to the extent they now devote to the study of "mere words."

After the presentation of his geological findings, Maclure takes the opportunity to draw some political conclusions from the country's topography and to make some rather astute prognostications:

> Placed on an extensive coast, accessible at all points to the depredations of a superior fleet, he [the inhabitant of the Atlantic region] is easily persuaded by his rulers to keep up a fleet and an army to protect commerce, &c. tending doubtless to involve us in all the wars of Europe, at the enormous expense it must always cost a government such as this. Taxes follow in proportion. The inhabitants of the west pay their proportion of these taxes without the same feeling or interest. The breach widens by the natural gravitation of interest arising out of situation; and nothing can long keep them together but the utmost prudence and economy in the federal rulers, by avoiding war and every cause of expense [p. 89].

Maclure foresees a bright future for the residents of the Mississippi basin, where a naturally protected country with diverse climates and easy inland navigation provides a better environment for perpetuating a free and equal representative government. For the need (excuse) to maintain a fleet or standing army, he notes, has always produced the ruin of such governments.

> Bottomed on a free and equal representation of men, they [the western inhabitants] will most probably be governed by the majority; not like the greatest part of the Atlantic states, which are founded on a representation of property, and liable to be governed by the few or minority. Monopoly of property ensures monopoly of power, and the means of perpetuating it, as is proven by the experience of all other nations [p. 90].

Still, he indulges the hope that the United States will "long be governed by the positive majority, and remain a place of refuge to oppressed humanity" [ibid.].

✷ [*Overleaf*] "Plate II." Copperplate chart, with added color, plate size 20 × 26.5 cm. From Maclure's 1818 geological article.

The chart provides five cross sections of the United States, north to south (I to V), from the "great secondary basin of the Mississippi" River (left side) to the Atlantic seashore (right side). The colors identifying different strata correspond to those used on his map.

EDWARD HITCHCOCK
1793–1864

ORDAINED as a Congregational minister, Edward Hitchcock became a professor of chemistry and natural history, then a professor of natural theology and geology, at Amherst College in Amherst, Massachusetts. His course on geology became a requirement for graduation. From 1845 to 1854, he was president of the college (its third), overseeing a religious revival at the institution. During those years he was also leading geological surveys in Massachusetts and neighboring states. He was appointed state geologist in 1830, a post he held until 1833 and, again, from 1837 to 1841. His 1833 *Report on the Geology, Mineralogy, Botany, and Zoology of Massachusetts* was the first of such state-authorized reports and became a recognized standard. In 1840, he cofounded the Association of American Geologists, which would later reorganize as the American Association for the Advancement of Science (AAAS) and grow into the world's largest general scientific society. In both his geological and paleontological publications, he tried to reconcile his religious beliefs with his discoveries, at one point interpreting a single Hebrew character in Genesis to imply the passage of vast spans of time in the earth's history. The collection of fossil footmarks (dinosaur tracks) begun by Hitchcock with his finds along the Connecticut River Valley is now the largest

I
II
III
IV
Oxbow
Wellsboro
L. Champlain
White Hills
Kennebeck R
Camden
Ithica
Della
Catskill Mt
Hudson R
Green Mt
Springfield
Plymouth
Pittsburgh
Allegany Mt
York
Near Phil a
Egg Har
Abingdon
Greenville
Martinsville
Williesville
Roanocke R
Lunenburg
Harris
Smithfield
Norfolk
Land Haven B
C Henry
Warm Spring
Union
Catawba R
Pedee R
Smithville
C Fear
Miles
6000
1000

Geology

cm, accompanying Hitchcock's article "Remarks on the Geology and Mineralogy of a Section of Massachusetts on Connecticut River, with a Part of New-Hampshire and Vermont." From *American Journal of Science, More Especially of Mineralogy, Geology, and the Other Branches of Natural History; Including Also Architecture and the Ornamental as Well as Useful Arts* 1, no. 2 (1819): 105–116 [Historic Maps Collection].

Earliest detailed geological map of an American region. Included is a profile of the strata of rocks from Hoosac Mountain (in Massachusetts) to a point eleven miles east of the Connecticut River. In his article, Hitchcock notes some interesting anthropological (and other) discoveries made in the Deerfield area:

> The plain on which the village of Deerfield stands, with the adjoining meadows, is sunk 50 or 60 feet below the general alluvial tract, and was undoubtedly the bed of a pond, or small lake.... On digging below the surface, stones are found calcified by fire. These are probably the spots where Indian wigwams formerly stood. Many vestiges of the aboriginals are frequently found in Deerfield, such as beads, stone pots, mortars, pipes, axes, and the barbs of arrows and pikes.... In the meadows, logs, leaves, butternuts, and walnuts are found undecayed, 15 feet below the surface; and stumps of trees are observed at that depth, standing yet firmly where once they grew. In the same meadows, a few years since, several toads were dug up from 15 feet below the surface, and three feet in gravel. They soon recovered from a torpid state and hopped away [pp. 107–108].

❋ Portrait of Edward Hitchcock. From W. S. Tyler's *History of Amherst College during Its First Half Century, 1821–1871* (Springfield, Mass.: C. W. Bryan, 1873) [General Library Collection].

in the world and resides in the Beneski Museum of Natural History at Amherst College.

❋ [*Below & overleaf*] "A Geological Map of a Part of Massachusetts on Connecticut River, 1817." Engraved map, with added color, 37 × 18 cm on sheet 45 × 21

❋ [*Overleaf*] "Paleontological Chart." Lithograph chart, with added color, 29.7 × 35 cm. From Hitchcock's *Elementary Geography: A New Edition, Revised, Enlarged, and Adapted to the Present Advanced State of the Science, with an Introductory Notice by John Pye Smith*, 30th ed.

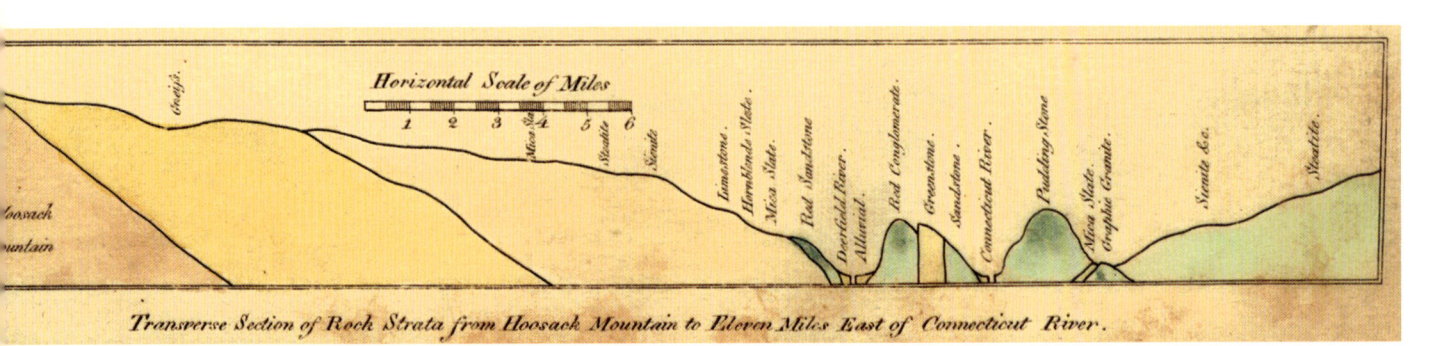

Transverse Section of Rock Strata from Hoosack Mountain to Eleven Miles East of Connecticut River.

A
Geological
MAP
of a part of Massachusetts on
Connecticut River
1817.
Primitive Rocks
Transit Argillite
Secondary
Alluvial
MARLBOROUGH
BRATTLEBOROUGH
CHESTERFIELD
West River
Ashuelot River
HALIFAX
GUILFORD
HINSDALE
VERNON
Vermont Line
New Hampshire Line
LEYDEN
BERNARDSTON
COLRAIN
Green River
NORTHFIELD
GILL
GREENFIELD
Unincorporated Tract
Millers River
SHELBURNE
Deerfield River
MONTAGUE
WENDELL
CONWAY
DEERFIELD
LEVERET
SUNDERLAND
Connecticut River
SHUTESBURY
WILLIAMSBURGH
WHATELEY
HATFIELD
PELHAM
AMHERST
NORTH HAMPTON
HADLEY
WEST HAMPTON
BELCHERTOWN
EASTHAMPTON
SOUTH HADLEY
SOUTHAMPTON
GRANBY

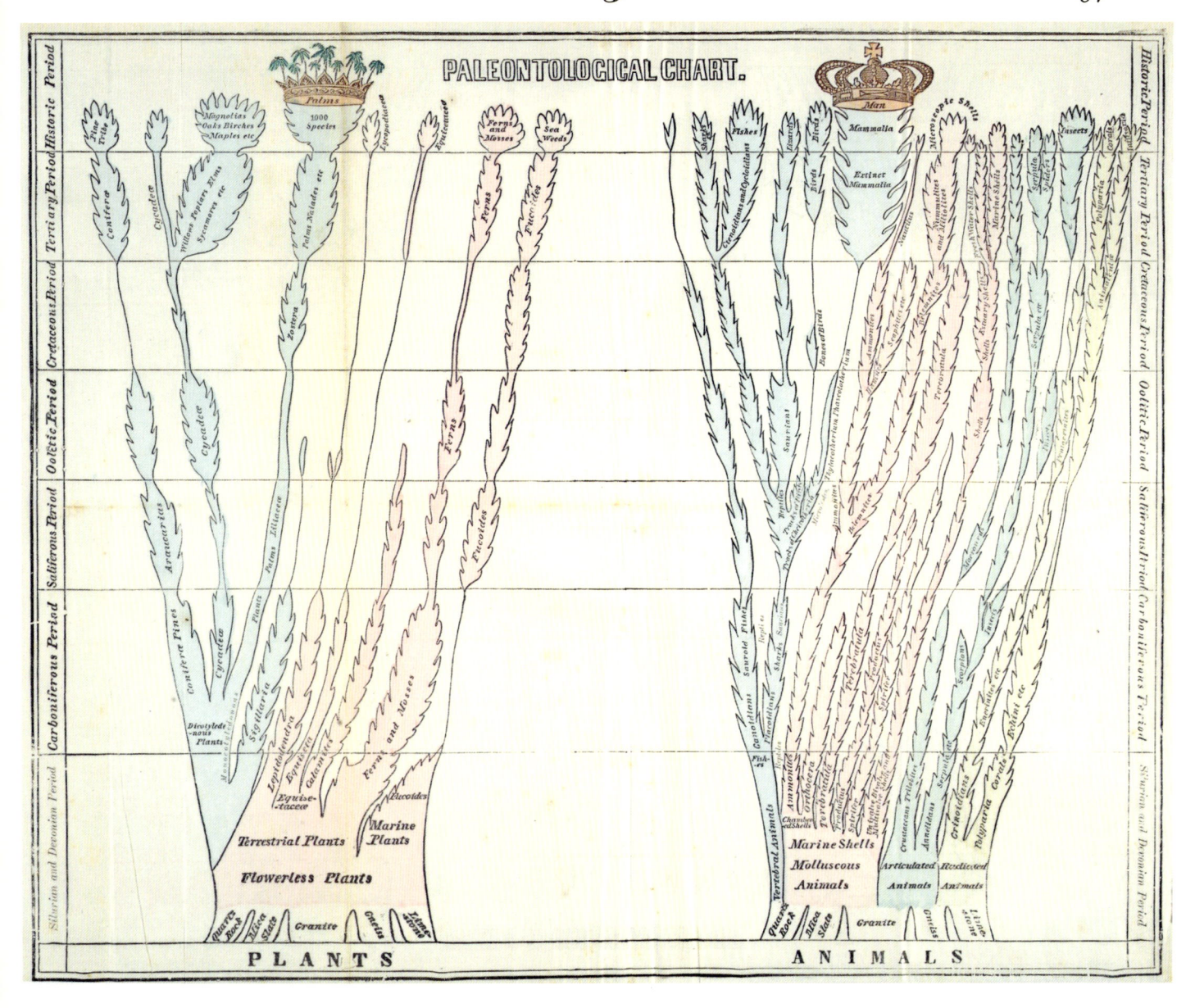

(New York: Ivison & Phinney, 1857) [Historic Maps Collection].

Based on Hitchcock's Amherst teaching, this was the first truly American textbook on the subject, not merely an Americanized version of a European work. It was extremely popular and went through thirty editions before the Civil War. First appearing in the 1840 edition, the exhibited chart is the earliest known to graphically link paleontological evidence of ancient plants and animals with geological eras using the concept of a tree with branches, which was Hitchcock's innovation. (Several years earlier, German geologist Heinrich Georg Bronn had published a similar chart, but in circular form, in his *Lethæa Geognostica*.) Whereas humans are shown to be the crowning achievement of animals, palm trees hold that position for plants; as Hitchcock explains, they have developed in great abundance, with more than one thousand species described.

As a fervent Christian, Hitchcock, of course, believed that species were introduced and extinguished by a Supreme Being at appropriate times in the earth's history, and he rejected the theory of evolution. "[T]he principles of science, rightly understood, should not contradict the statements of revelation, rightly interpreted"

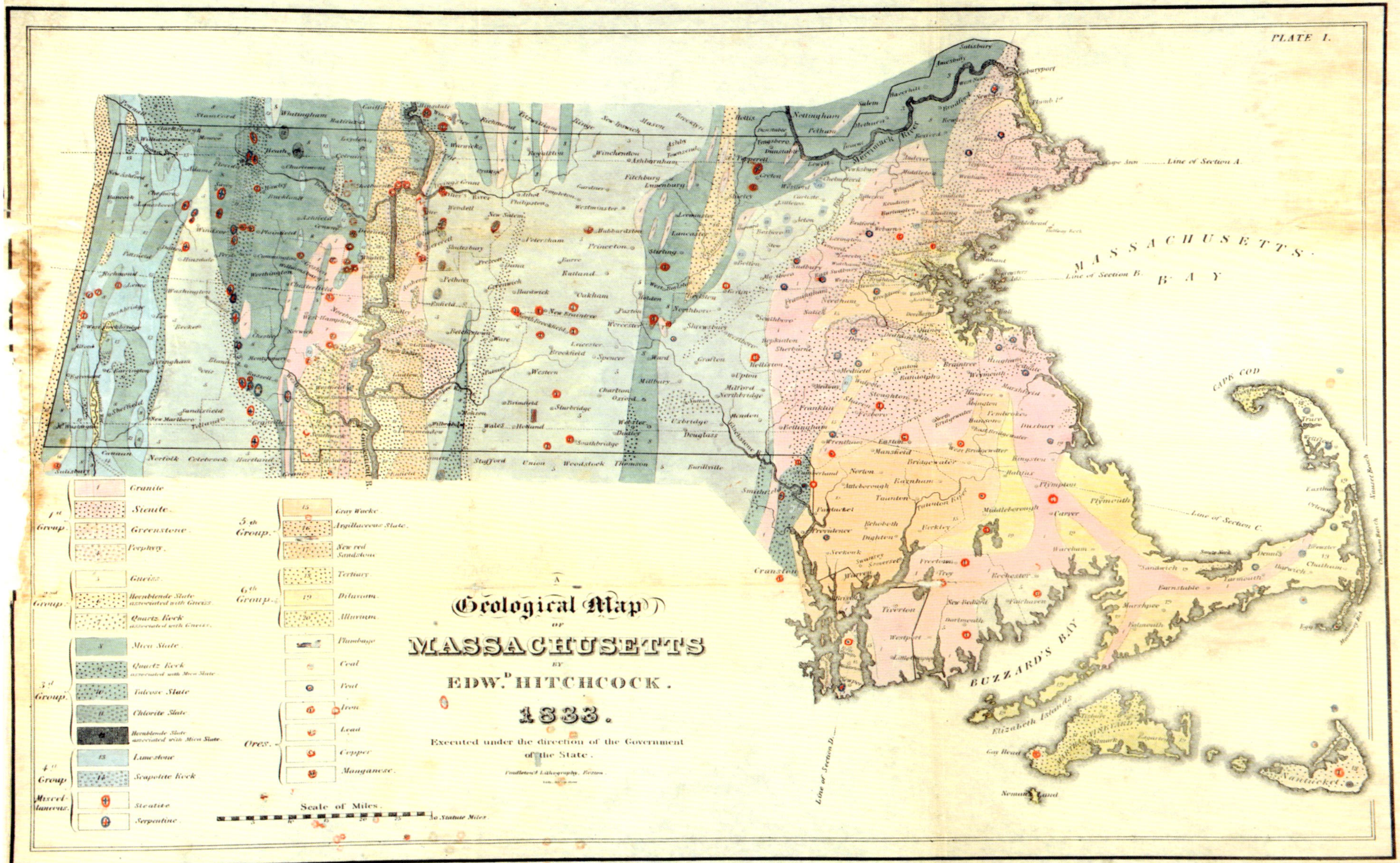
PLATE I.
A
Geological Map
of
MASSACHUSETTS
BY
EDWD. HITCHCOCK.
1833.
Executed under the direction of the Government of the State.
MASSACHUSETTS BAY
BUZZARD'S BAY
CAPE COD
Elizabeth Islands
Nantucket
Line of Section A.
Line of Section B.
Line of Section C.
Line of Section D.
Connecticut R.
1st Group.
Granite
Sienite
Greenstone
Porphyry
2nd Group.
Gneiss
Hornblende Slate associated with Gneiss
Quartz Rock associated with Gneiss
3d Group.
Mica Slate
Quartz Rock associated with Mica Slate
Talcose Slate
Chlorite Slate
Hornblende Slate associated with Mica Slate
4th Group.
Limestone
Scapolite Rock
Miscellaneous.
Steatite
Serpentine
5th Group.
Gray Wacke
Argillaceous Slate
New red Sandstone
6th Group.
Tertiary
Diluvium
Alluvium
Ores.
Plumbago
Coal
Peat
Iron
Lead
Copper
Manganese
Scale of Miles.
Statute Miles

Geology

(*Elementary Geology*, 1857 ed., p. 345). Hence, after Charles Darwin published his *On the Origin of Species* (1859), Hitchcock dropped the chart from his textbook, for a "tree of life" then became synonymous with an evolutionary tree.

✱ [*Opposite*] "A Geological Map of Massachusetts." Lithograph map, with added color, 44 × 70 cm. From the atlas volume accompanying Hitchcock's *Report on the Geology, Mineralogy, Botany, and Zoology of Massachusetts* (Amherst, Mass.: Press of J. S. and C. Adams, 1833) [Graphic Arts Collection].

First geological map of a U.S. state, greatly expanding the Massachusetts part of the map of the Connecticut River Valley that he had published in the *American Journal of Science and Arts* in 1823.

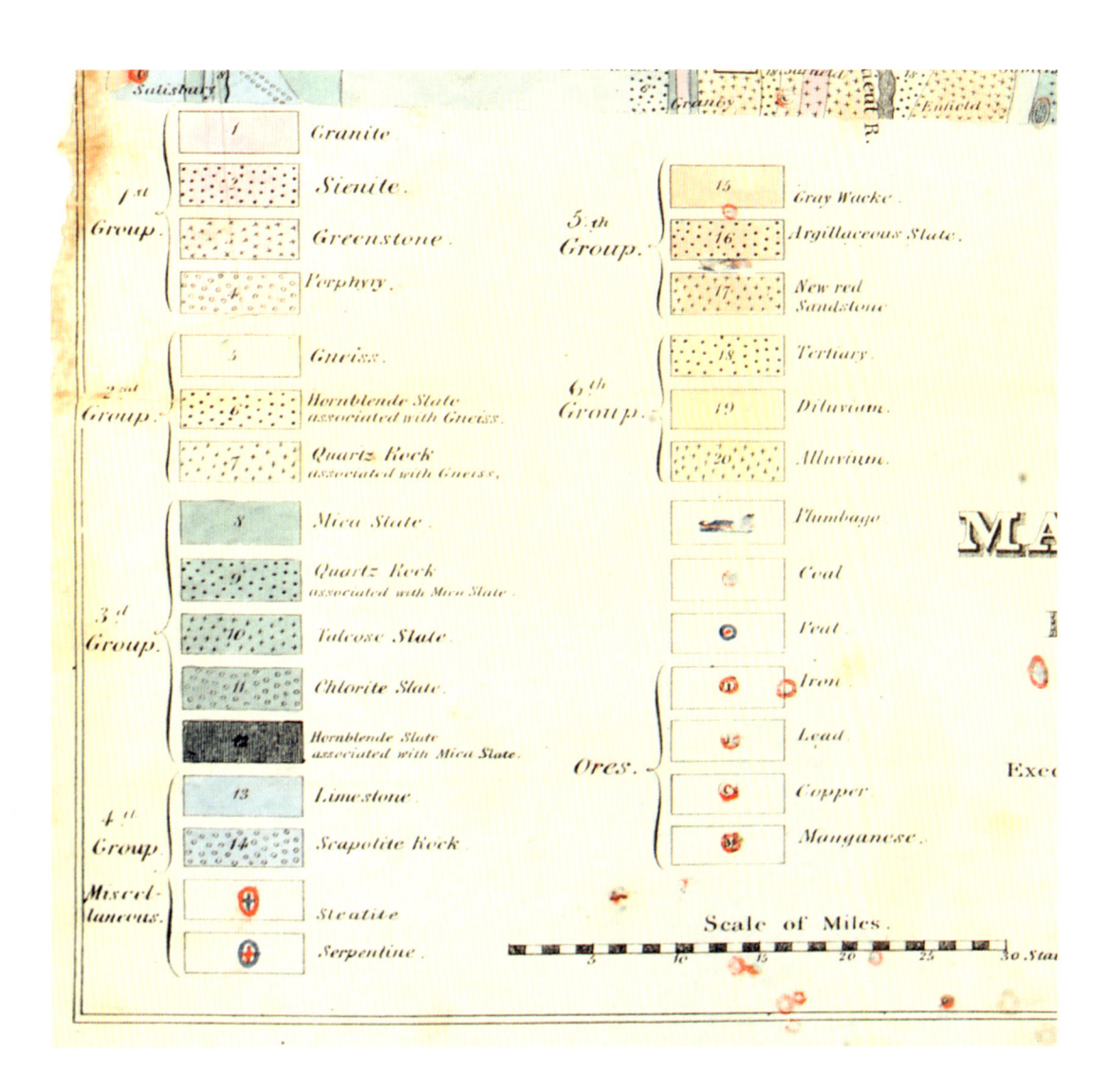

✱ Key to Edward Hitchcock's "A Geological Map of Massachusetts."

Explanation.

System of Drainage. — The coloured Lines indicate the Waterparting or the natural separation between Rivers flowing off in opposite directions. — Five Great natural Divisions of the United Kingdom are thus established, depending on the Drainage of the waters into the
  1. Central Basin or River System of the Irish Sea
  2. River System of the German Ocean or Eastern Coast of Great Britain
  3.   "   "   "   Western Coast of Ireland and that of Gt. Britain not included in the Central Basin
  4.   "   "   "   Northern Coasts
  5.   "   "   "   Southern Coasts

River Basins. — The subdivisions of the five Systems define the Basins of each River, draining an area of 500 English Square miles and upwards.

The name and area of each Basin in English Square miles is inscribed thus: **THAMES 6160.**

Basins drained through subterraneous Channels are coloured thus

The Main streams are distinguished from tributaries throughout their entire course by broader lines.

The Shading at the Mouths of Rivers exhibits their legal extent:

The small Figures along the River courses, Canal lines and Lakes, indicate the Height above the Level of the Sea in English feet.

Fishing Stations and the principal large Towns are inserted in light characters, thus: *Richmond*. LONDON.

Signs:
- Tideway
- Navigable extent
- Extent of Steam Navigation
- Subterraneous Channels
- Waterfalls and Cataracts
- Canals
- Leats and other artificial Channels supplying large Towns with water
- Artificial Channels draining Bogs, Fens &c.
- Railways completed in July 1849.

Character of Letters: RIVERS, Rivers
  LAKES with an area of 20 Engl. Square miles and upwards
  Lakes   "   "   from 20 to 5
  Lakes   below 5 Engl. Square miles

Abbreviations:

B. – Burn (in Northn. Ct. of England-Beck)	D. – Dale	Hd. – Head	W. – Water	**In Wales:**
	F. – Fall	L. – Lake or Lough	Wh. – White	A. – Afon (River)
Br. – Brook	Fo. – Force (Waterfall in Cumberland)	M. – Mere	Wl. – Waterfall	Ll. – Llyn (Pool or Lake)
C. – Cascade		R. – River		P. – Pistill (Waterfall)
Cr. – Creek	G. – Gill	T. – Tarn		Rh. – Rhayder (do.)

Hyetography. — The Figures within small Circles (30) denote the average yearly amount of Rain falling in various localities, in Inches. Places of observations are distinguished thus:

✶ Key to August Petermann's "… Hydrographical Map of the British Isles …" (1849).

HYDROGRAPHY

HYDROGRAPHY, generally defined, is the study of the depth and movement of bodies of water—streams, rivers, lakes, oceans—and of their coastal land areas, particularly in the context of navigation.

ATHANASIUS KIRCHER
1602–1680

OFTEN COMPARED to Leonardo da Vinci for the breadth and depth of his interests, Kircher was a German Jesuit scholar who spent most of his life in Rome. His numerous publications amounted to encyclopedic works on a wide range of topics, including magnetism, Egyptology (and hieroglyphics), geology, and music theory. He examined the blood of plague victims under a microscope, concluding the disease was caused by microorganisms; he constructed a magnetic clock; he designed a cat piano which would drive spikes into the tails of cats so they would yowl to specified pitches (though he is not known to have constructed it!). He was the first scientist to support himself from his writings. The *Encyclopædia Britannica* describes him as a "one-man intellectual clearinghouse for cultural and scientific information."

✻ [*Overleaf*] "Tabula geographico hydrographica motus oceani currentes…." Copperplate map, 28.1 × 53.7 cm, within larger border. From Kircher's *D'onderaardse weereld in haar goddelijk maaksel en wonderbare uitwerkselen aller dingen…*, 2 vols. in 1 (Amsterdam, 1682) [Rare Books Division]. Reference: Shirley, *Mapping of the World*, 436.

Landmark map of ocean currents, first published in Kircher's *Mundus subterraneus* (1665). Note, though, that there are no arrows to indicate direction. Kircher theorized that there was a worldwide underground network of canals and caverns through which water flowed (via tidal flux and reflux), connecting to counterparts on the surface, such as rivers and currents. He has drawn dotted lines where he believes tunnels link the Caspian

✻ Portrait of Athanasius Kircher. From his *Romani collegii Societatus* [!] *Jesu musaeum celeberrimum …* (Amsterdam: Ex Officina Janssonio-Waesbergiana, 1678) [Rare Books Division].

Sea, Black Sea, and Persian Gulf, and pass through the Sinai Peninsula, site of today's Suez Canal. The small, circled dots indicate whirlpools where water is sucked down into the subterranean system; the largest one, not shown, is at the North Pole.

EBERHARD WERNER HAPPEL
1647–1690

EBERHARD WERNER HAPPEL was a German journalist and author of formulaic historical fiction and popular treatises on natural science.

✻ [*Overleaf*] "Die Ebbe und Fluth auff einer flachen Landt-Karten fürgestelt" [Ulm: s.n., 1675]. Copper-

{ 101 }

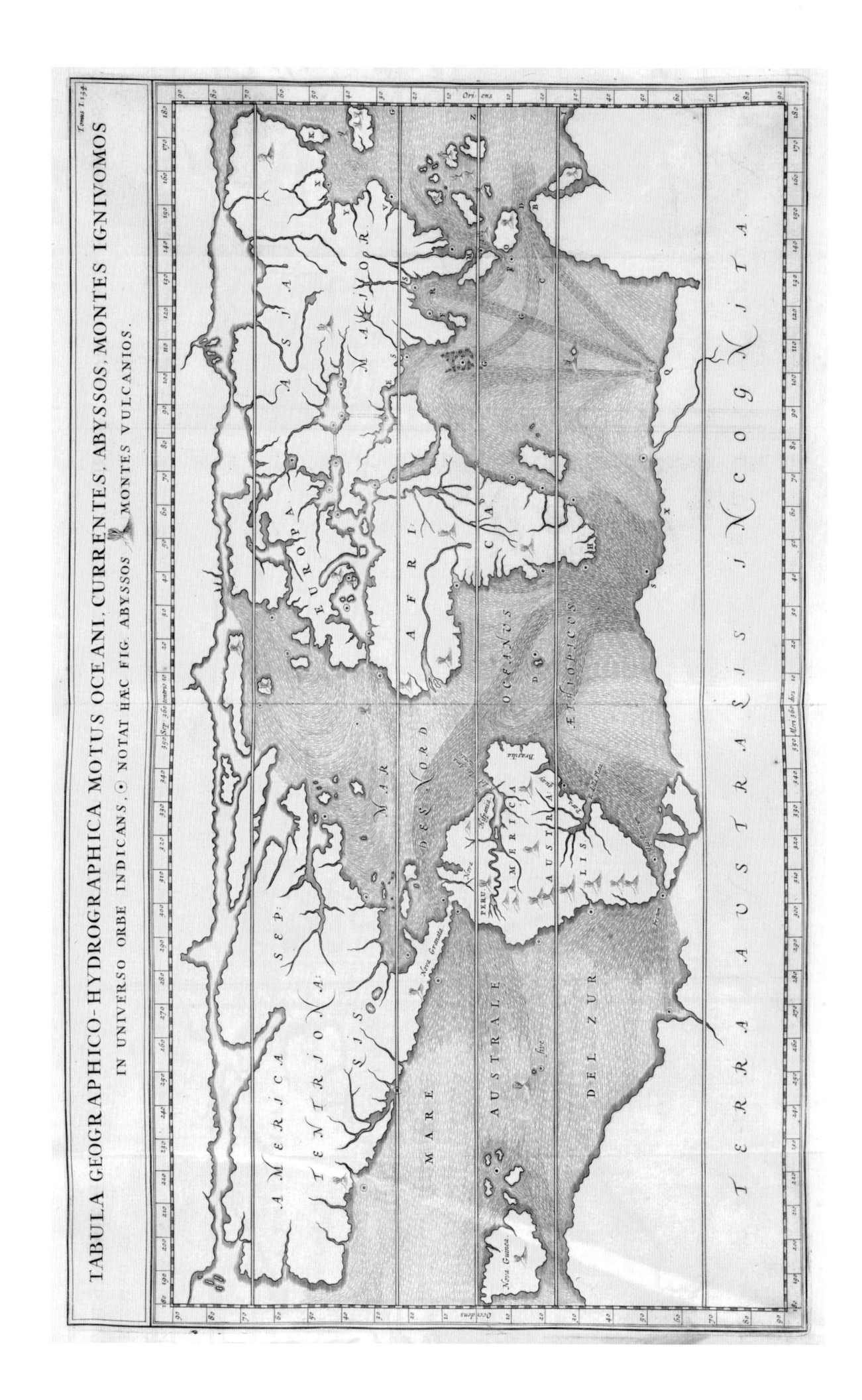

TABULA GEOGRAPHICO-HYDROGRAPHICA MOTUS OCEANI, CURRENTES, ABYSSOS, MONTES IGNIVOMOS IN UNIVERSO ORBE INDICANS. NOTAT HÆC FIG. ABYSSOS. MONTES VULCANIOS.

plate map, 20 × 28 cm [Historic Maps Collection]. Reference: Shirley, *Mapping of the World*, 468.

One of the earliest thematic maps, showing ebb and flow of the earth's waters—but, again, no directions. Obviously, this is a derivative of Kircher's 1665 map, but it is more defined and includes a man-made feature, the Great Wall of China. Both maps are very early attempts to rectify actual mariners' observations with semiscientific theory.

BENJAMIN FRANKLIN
1706–1790

ONE MIGHT have expected that a naturally curious, scientifically minded man like Benjamin Franklin would one day help to create an important map. That it is one of the earliest American thematic map productions only adds to our growing fascination with this colonial jack-of-all-trades.

As early as 1726, in a crossing of the Atlantic from London to Philadelphia, Franklin noted effects of an ocean current in his journal. In 1768, in his role as deputy postmaster of the British colonies in North America, Franklin began hearing complaints about the practical implications of this current: something was delaying the New York mail. Boston customs officials observed a two-weeks' difference in the arrival times of ships sailing east to west from England to New York versus England to Rhode Island. He consulted a cousin, Nantucket mariner Timothy Folger, about the problem. Folger was certain that the Gulf Stream was the culprit, for Rhode Island captains were aware of the current through their whaling activities, whereas those of the English packet boats were not. Franklin asked

Quantitative Thematic Maps

Published in England circa 1768, the map was mostly ignored by the stubborn English navigators. Though few copies of this English version seem to have survived (Library of Congress has one), Franklin also had the chart printed in France around 1785, and he published it again with his article "Sundry Maritime Observations" in the *Transactions of the American Philosophical Society* in 1786. However, it took a long time before the British followed Franklin's advice on how to avoid fighting this current.

✴ [*Below*] Section of an autograph letter by Franklin, dated 27 May 1762, to Sir John Pringle, who would become president of the Royal Society in 1772 and physician to King George III in 1774 [Andre De Coppet Collection, Manuscripts Division].

Franklin's first mention of the Gulf Stream. In his letter to Dr. Pringle, Franklin discusses the Admiral Bartholomew De Fonte myth of a Northwest Passage, which he believes has merit—and also touches upon the prevailing winds:

> The Trade Wind blowing over the Atlantic Ocean constantly from the East, between the Tropics, carries a Current to the American Coast, and raises the Water there above its natural Level. From thence it flows off thro' the Gulf of Mexico, and all along the North American Coast to & beyond the Banks of Newfoundland in a strong Current, called by Seamen *the Gulph Stream*.... [T]he Waters are mov'd away from the North American Coast towards the Coasts

✴ Portrait of Benjamin Franklin. From vol. 1 of Evert A. Duyckinck's *Portrait Gallery of Eminent Men and Women of Europe and America* (New York: Johnson & Miles, 1873) [General Library Collection].

Folger to add the location and dimensions of this current to an available chart so that he could communicate the information to the English sea captains.

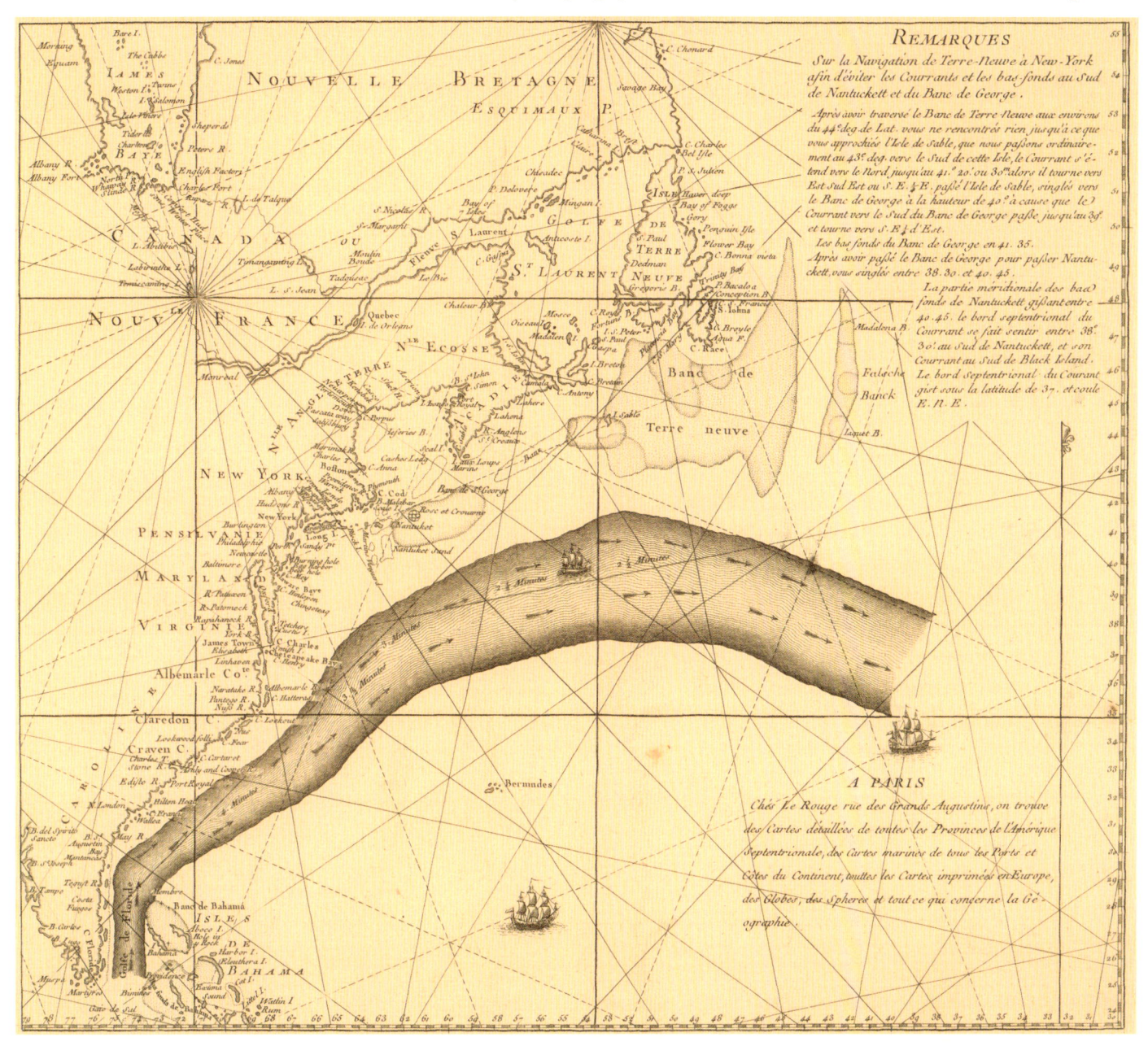

of Spain & Africa, whence they get again into the Power of the Trade Winds, & continue the Circulation [Franklin's underlining].

✷ [*Above*] "Remarques sur la navigation de terre-neuve à New-York afin d'eviter les courrants et les bas-fonds au sud de Nantuckett et du Banc de George" (Paris: Chés Le Rouge, rue des Grands Augustine…, [ca. 1785]). Copperplate map, 32 × 36 cm on sheet 46 × 61 cm [Historic Maps Collection].

First map of the Gulf Stream, which gave it its name. It is often referred to as the Franklin–Folger map because of Folger's major role.

AUGUST PETERMANN
1822–1878

Prussian-born cartographer August Petermann spent seven years (1847–1854) in London, where he founded his own business in 1850. He was also a fellow of the Royal Geographical Society. (For more on Petermann, see his entry in the Landmark Thematic Atlases section.)

✻ [*Opposite*] "To Her Most Excellent Majesty Queen Victoria This Hydrographical Map of the British Isles, Exhibiting the Geographical Distribution of the Inland Waters" (London: published for the author by Wm. S. Orr, 147, Strand, July 1849). Engraved map, with added color, 81 × 53 cm [Historic Maps Collection].

One of the most important products from Petermann's London years and probably the earliest and largest such map devoted to Great Britain's hydrography. Petermann first presented this map at the annual meeting of the British Association for the Advancement of Science, held at Swansea, Wales, in August 1848. It identifies 1,550 rivers, 440 lakes and ponds, and 40 waterfalls. The fall of the principal rivers and the elevation of the major canals are illustrated in the inset. Of the rivers that drain more than five hundred square miles, twenty are in England, ten in Scotland, and ten in Ireland. According to Petermann, the length of the rivers and the area of their basins are drawn from "careful Original calculations."

GEORG BAUERKELLER
fl. 1830–1870

Georg Bauerkeller was a relief cartographer and globe maker.

✻ [*Overleaf*] "Hydrogr. Karte von Europa" (Paris: Farbendruck und Prägung von Bauerkeller et Cie, ca. 1845). Embossed lithograph map, 47 × 59 cm [Historic Maps Collection].

This is an extremely rare and early map of European hydrography, employing an unusual printing process. (No copies of it are listed in the WorldCat database, which represents the holdings of more than ten thousand libraries worldwide; a title search retrieves no results through Google.) The orange dots identify the major towns and cities of the countries.

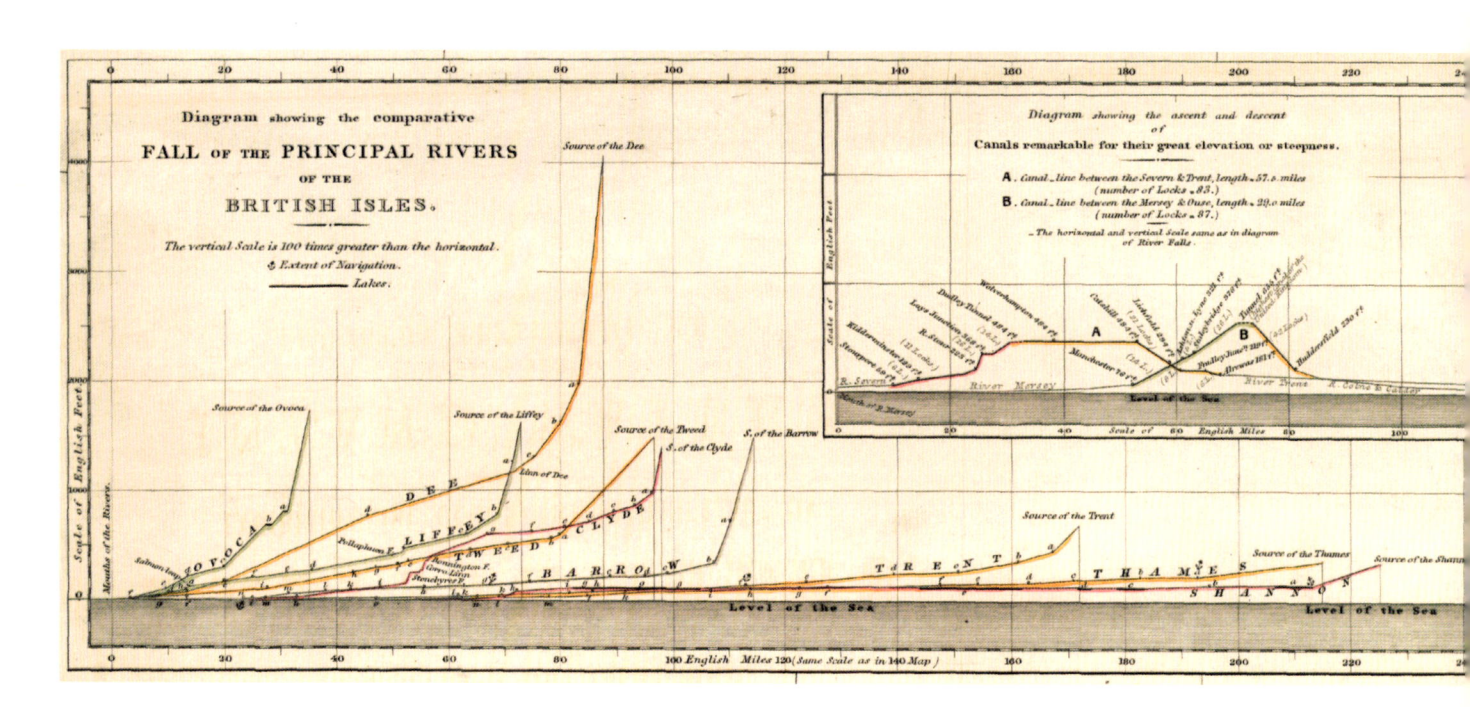

✻ Detail from Petermann's hydrographical map of the British Isles.

To Her Most Excellent Majesty
QUEEN VICTORIA
THIS HYDROGRAPHICAL MAP
OF THE
BRITISH ISLES,
EXHIBITING THE GEOGRAPHICAL DISTRIBUTION
OF THE
INLAND WATERS,
Constructed by
AUGUSTUS PETERMANN, F.R.G.S.,
Honorary Member of the Geographical Society of Berlin,
by Her Majesty's gracious permission most humbly dedicated
By the Author.

LONDON, July 1849, published for the Author by Wm. S. ORR & CO. 147. Strand.

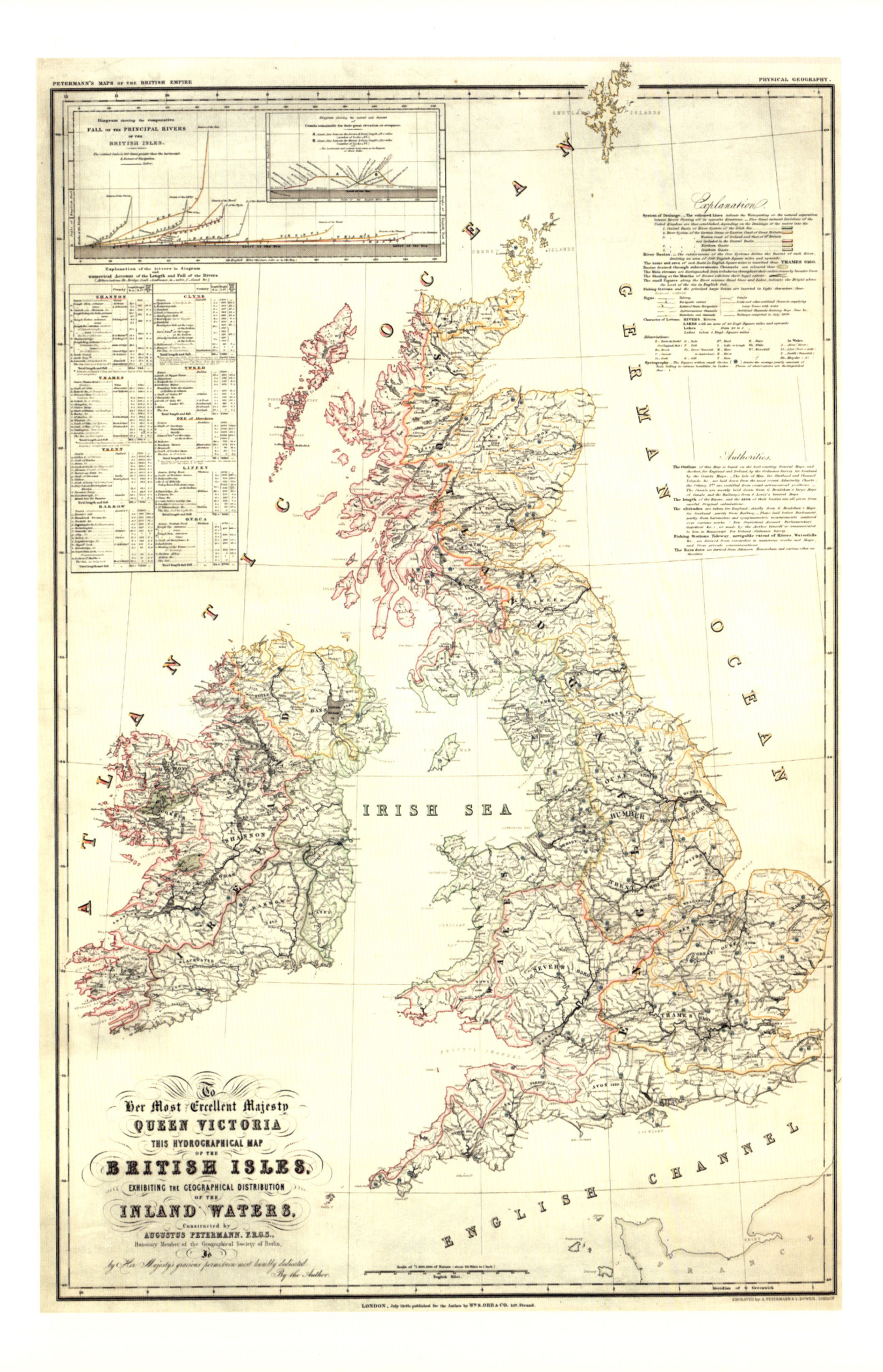

HYDROGR. KARTE VON EUR[OPA]

FARBENDRUCK UND PRÄGUNG VON BAUER

PA VON BAUERKELLER.

...ELLER & Cie PRIVILEGIRT IN PARIS.

✻ Key to Joakim Frederik Schouw's "Taf V. Verbreitungsbezirk und Vertheilungsweise der Gertreide-arten" (1823).

NATURAL HISTORY

NATURAL HISTORY has become a more inclusive subject in recent times, embracing many diverse, focused scientific disciplines. Modern natural history museums, for example, often include elements of anthropology, geology, paleontology, ecology, and astronomy besides botany and zoology. Historically, however, it usually has been associated with the observational study of plants and animals in their environments.

EBERHARD AUGUST WILHELM VON ZIMMERMANN
1743–1815

EBERHARD AUGUST WILHELM VON ZIMMERMANN taught college mathematics and natural history at the Collegium Carolinum in the former duchy of Brunswick in central Germany. One of his pupils was Carl Friedrich Gauss (1777–1855), who became one of history's most influential mathematicians. Zimmermann traveled throughout Europe to study economic conditions and natural resources. Today, he is considered one of the founders of animal geography.

✻ [*Overleaf*] "Tabula mundi geographico zoologica sistens quadrupedes hucusque notos sedibus suis adscirptos" (1783). Copperplate map, with added outline color, 47 × 66 cm [Historic Maps Collection]. Probably issued in Zimmermann's *Geographische Geschichte des Menschen, und der allgemein verbreiteten vierfüssigen Thiere* ... (Leipzig: In der Weygandschen Buchhandlung, 1778–1783).

First map of animal geography. Originally published under a different title in Zimmermann's *Specimen zoologiae geographicae, Quadrupedum domicilia et migrationes sistens* (Leiden, 1777), this world map of 390° reflects some updated geography, including English Captain James Cook's discovery of the Sandwich Islands (Hawaii). Note, however, that only the most basic place names are provided. It is the addition and geographical placement of the Latin names of quadrupeds that distinguishes the map from anything previously published. *Castor* (beaver), for example, appears throughout northern North America; *leo* (lion) in Africa; and *kanguro* (kangaroo) in northeastern Australia, where Cook's men first sighted one. Though very rudimentary in style and accuracy, the map marks an auspicious moment in the history of thematic mapping.

✻ [*Above*] Title page of Zimmermann's *A Political Survey of the Present State of Europe: In Sixteen Tables; Illustrated with Observation on the Wealth and Commerce, the Government,*

{ III }

Map: Western Hemisphere

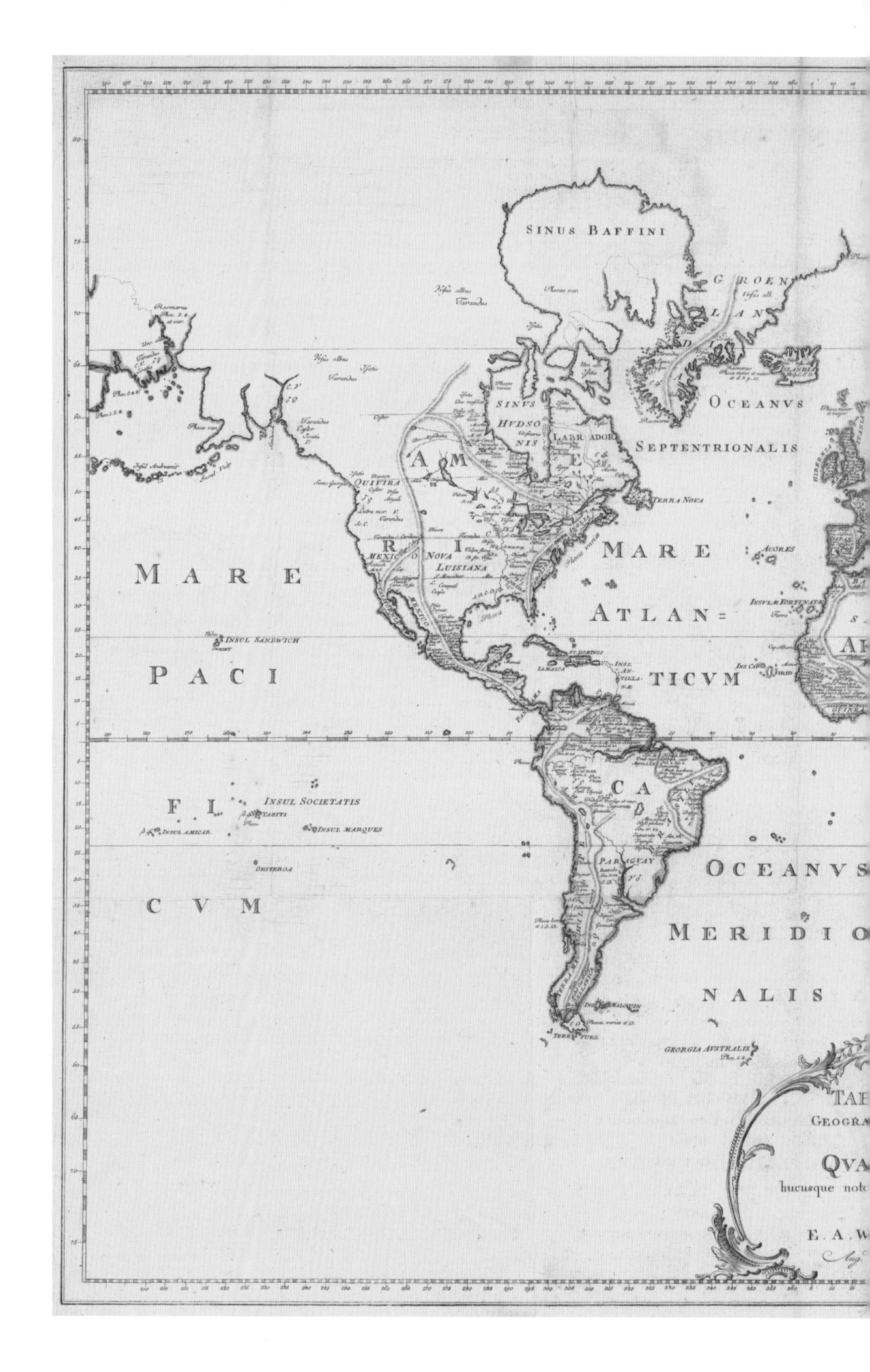

SINUS BAFFINI

G. ROENLAN D

OCEANVS SEPTENTRIONALIS

SINUS HUDSONIS

LABRADOR

TERRA NOVA

A M E R I C A

QUIVIRA

MEXICO NOVA LUISIANA

MARE ATLAN=TICVM

ACORES

INSVLÆ FORTVNATÆ

MARE PACIFICVM

INSUL SANDWICH

ST DOMINGO
IAMAICA
INSÆ ANTILLÆ

INSUL SOCIETATIS
TAHITI
INSUL AMICAB.
INSUL MARQUES

OHITEROA

PARAGUAY

OCEANVS MERIDIONALIS

I. MALOUIN
TERRA FUEG.

GEORGIA AVSTRALIS

TAB. GEOGRA... QVA... hucusque noto...

E. A. W...

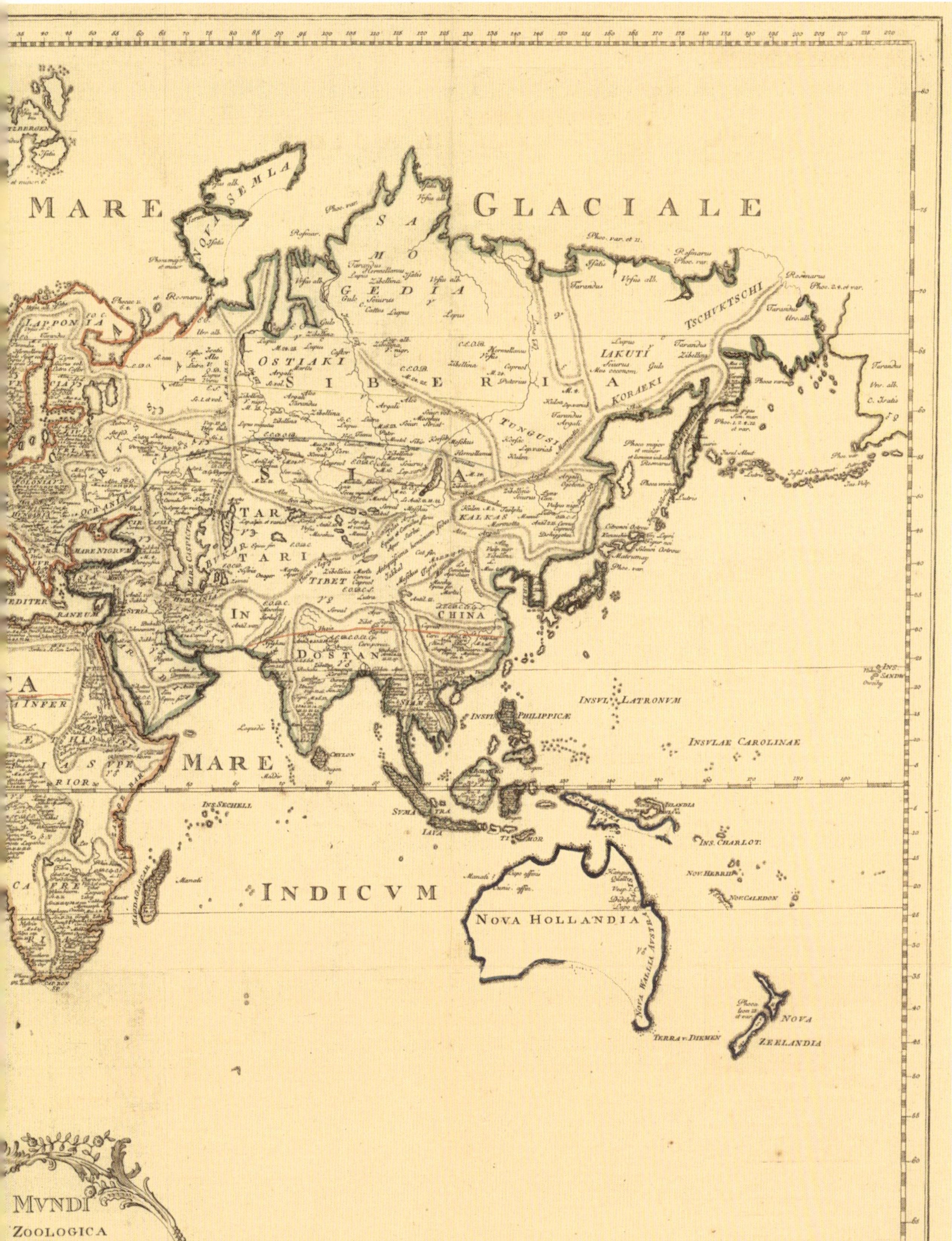

Finances, Military State, and Religion of the Several Countries (Dublin: L. White, 1788) [Rare Books Division]. This particular copy belonged to John Witherspoon, president (1768–1794) of the College of New Jersey (now Princeton University) and bears his ownership inscription. The first edition of the book was printed in London in 1787.

Around the time that English political economist William Playfair began charting data, Zimmermann published this statistical work containing tabular data, thus heralding a new science:

> It is about forty years ago that that branch of political knowledge, which has for its object the actual and relative power of the several modern states, the power arising from their natural advantages, the industry and civilization of their inhabitants, and the wisdom of their governments, has been formed, chiefly by German writers, into a separate science. It used formerly to be improperly connected with geography; and it was but superficially treated amidst the topographical and descriptive details of the larger geographical works.... [T]his science, distinguished by the new-coined name of *Statistics*, is become a favourite study in Germany" [pp. i–ii; Zimmermann's emphasis].

According to the *Oxford English Dictionary*, this is one of the earliest appearances of the word "statistics" in the English language, continuing its original association with political science. For each of his statistical tables, Zimmermann cites the sources of information (many German) that served as his authorities, including dictionaries, geographies, manuals, histories, periodicals, and even travel writings. Zimmermann was eager to showcase German efforts, but he was also an admirer of English government and society and wanted them to embrace this science. A strong motive behind its publication, he states, was his desire to provide young English travelers with a useful, non-bulky reference book to accompany them on their *grand tour* through Europe.

✻ Portrait of Joakim Frederik Schouw. Frontispiece to his *Die Erde, die Planzen und der Mensch: Populäre Naturschilderungen* (Leipzig: Carl B. Lorck, 1851).

JOAKIM FREDERIK SCHOUW
1789–1852

THE SON OF a Danish wine merchant, Joakim Frederik Schouw became a lawyer before building a career as a pioneering botanist in the field of phytogeography. The turning point came in 1812, when he accompanied Christen Smith, a Norwegian botanist, on a botanical trip in the mountains, where he began to note how vegetation was organized into altitudinal zones. In Copenhagen, he devoured botanical literature, particularly that of Alexander von Humboldt and Göran Wahlenberg. He earned a Ph.D. in 1816, writing on the origin and evolution of plant species. A three-year travel grant took him through the Alps and southern Europe; on his return he visited Humboldt in Paris. In 1820, he began teaching botany at Copenhagen University. From 1831, he edited the weekly Danish periodical *Dansk Ugeskrift* (1831–1846) where many of his popular science lectures appeared, increasing his reputation. He became curator of the botanical gardens of Copenhagen in 1841. Schouw was also one of the main leaders of the political movement that lead to the first democratic constitution of Denmark in 1849. During the later part of his life, he was active in promoting Scandinavism, the idea of a unified Scandinavian region, and advocated the division of the southern Jutland region of Schleswig between Denmark and Germany.

✳ [*Below*] "Tafel III." Foldout table from the text volume of Schouw's *Grundzüge einer allgemeinen Pflanzengeographie* (Berlin: Gedruckt und verlegt bei G. Reimer, 1823) [Historic Maps Collection]. First German edition, translated by Schouw from the Danish version that he published in the previous year.

Schouw's *Grundzüge einer allgemeinen Pflanzengeographie*

Tafel III.

zu Seite 212.

	Polar-Grenze			Obere Grenze			Aequatorial-Grenze	Vortheilhafteste Verhältnisse	
	Paris [1]	London [2]	Ofen [3]	Zürich [4]	Geneve [5]	Sicilien [6]	Cairo [7]	Rom [8]	Palermo [9]
Januar	+ 2° 99	+ 1° 92	− 2° 69	− 3° 17	1° 16	+ 4° 78	+14° 37	+ 7° 18	+10° 78
Februar	4° 01	3° 27	+ 0° 65	+ 0° 94	2° 87	4° 78	13° 17	8° 18	10° 78
März	6° 14	5° 95	3° 61	4° 51	5° 86	6° 11	18° 20	10° 71	12° 11
April	10° 46	7° 80	9° 63	7° 58	9° 74	8° 51	25° 60	13° 71	14° 51
Mai	13° 60	11° 95	18° 37	15° 30	13° 75	11° 71	25° 80	18° 11	17° 71
Juni	16° 64	15° 16	20° 19	16° 35	16° 06	14° 48	28° 66	21° 58	20° 48
Juli	17° 98	16° 66	21° 82	18° 17	17° 72	16° 38	29° 86	23° 18	22° 38
August	17° 56	16° 46	22° 01	18° 43	17° 70	17° 18	29° 86	22° 88	23° 18
September	15° 10	13° 54	16° 77	14° 14	14° 85	15° 57	25° 84	20° 07	21° 57
October	10° 04	9° 09	11° 01	9° 60	10° 01	13° 77	22° 04	16° 77	19° 77
November	6° 18	4° 99	4° 69	3° 58	5° 50	9° 57	16° 84	12° 07	15° 57
December	2° 77	2° 57	− 0° 50	− 1° 21	2° 22	6° 38	16° 07	8° 48	12° 38
Winter	+ 3° 26	+ 2° 58	− 0° 85	− 1° 15	+ 2° 08	+ 5° 31	+14° 53	+ 7° 95	+11° 31
Frühling	+10° 07	+ 8° 57	+10° 55	+ 9° 13	+ 9° 78	+ 8° 78	+23° 20	+14° 18	+14° 78
Sommer	+17° 39	+16° 09	+21° 34	+17° 82	+17° 16	+16° 02	+29° 46	+22° 55	+22° 02
Herbst	+10° 44	+ 9° 21	+10° 82	+ 9° 10	+10° 12	+12° 97	+21° 57	+16° 30	+18° 97
Jahr	+10° 29	+ 9° 12	+10° 46	+ 8° 73	+ 9° 79	+10° 77	+22° 19	+15° 24	+16° 77

1) Ohngefähr bei der Polargrenze. Nach 5 Jahren (1816 — 1820) annales de Chimie et de Physique; media der täglichen Extreme, aber wie die folgenden, auf wahre media zurückgeführt.

2) Beinahe 3 Grade nördlich von der Polargrenze. Nach Howards Observationen der täglichen Extreme in 7 Jahren (1815 — 21) zu Tottenham. Thomson annals of Philosophy.

3) Ein bis anderthalb Grad südlicher als die Polargrenze. Nach Observationen der täglichen Extreme in 6 Jahren. Wahlenbergs Flora Carpat.

4) Ohngefähr die obere Grenze. Observationen der täglichen Extreme in 6 Jahren. Wahlenbergs Tentamen p. LXVII.

5) Etwas unter der oberen Grenze. Observationen der täglichen Extreme in 7 Jahren (1815 — 1821). Bibliothéque universelle.

6) Die Temperatur bei 3000 Fuß nach der von Palermo (cfr. Note 9), das in der 3ten Hauptabtheilung angenommene Gesetz der Abnahme vorausgesetzt, berechnet.

7) Nach Humboldts lignes isothermes Tab. III. ad p. 602. Die von ihm angegebenen media sind aus Novets Beobachtungen der täglichen Extreme gezogen. Doch sind diese Beobachtungen mangelhaft (cfr. Description de l'Egypte).

8) Nach Contis und Calendrellis Observationen in 7 J. (1811 — 1817). Die Observationen sind um 7 U. v. M. 2 und 9 U. n. M. angestellt.

9) Nach Marabittis Beobachtungen in 5 Jahren (1813 — 1817) der täglichen maxima und minima. Cfr. Scinà Topografia di Palermo. Note 177.

Quantitative Thematic Maps

[Fundamental features of a general plant geography] is the first vegetation atlas, consisting of twelve pairs of eastern and western hemisphere maps on facing pages, showing the global distribution of various classes of plants, with a companion volume in which he discusses his and others' related plant research. Annual temperature ranges of geographic regions is a critical factor in his botanical analysis. In this table, Schouw charts the monthly, seasonal, and annual average temperatures across a variety of mostly European cities, and provides his sources for the information at the bottom (Humboldt, of course, is one). Accordingly, temperatures in Rome and the Sicilian city of Palermo seem particularly advantageous for a range of plant growth.

✻ [*Opposite*] "Taf V. Verbreitungsbezirk und Vertheilungsweise der Gertreide-arten." Copperplate map, with added color, diameter of 33.8 cm. From the atlas volume of Schouw's *Grundzüge einer allgemeinen Pflanzengeographie* (1823) [Historic Maps Collection]. This atlas volume was added for the German edition.

Only the eastern hemisphere part of the map is shown. Broad strokes of color illustrate the distribution and range of five basic grain types (in order from the top): barley and oats, rye, wheat, rice, corn.

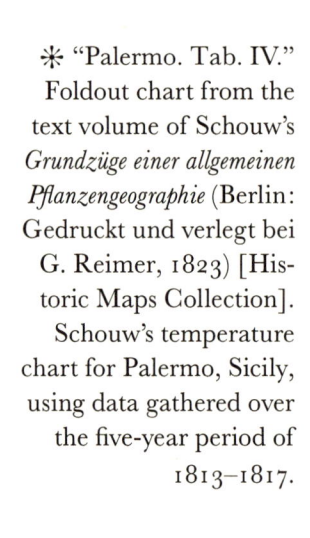

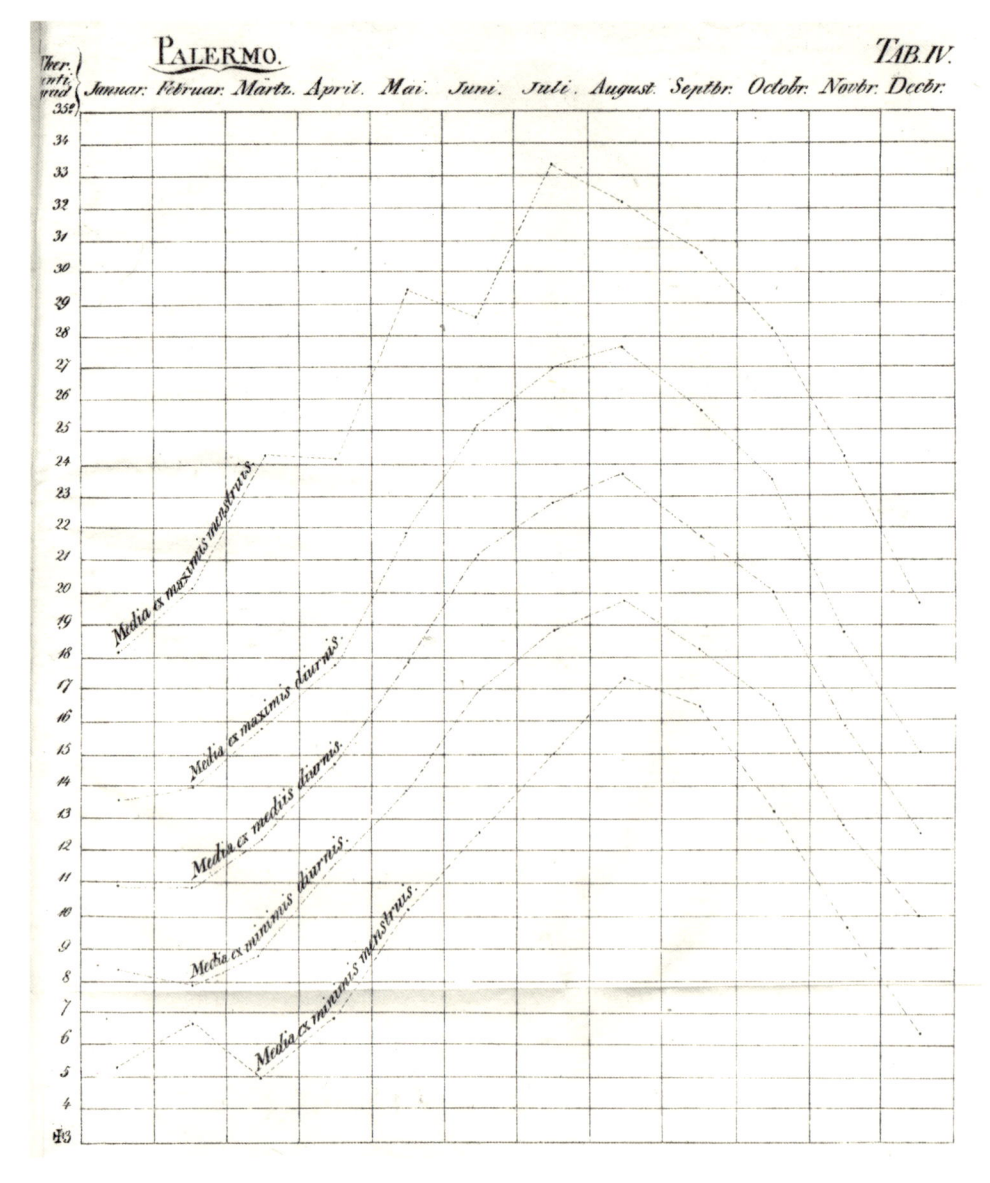

✻ "Palermo. Tab. IV." Foldout chart from the text volume of Schouw's *Grundzüge einer allgemeinen Pflanzengeographie* (Berlin: Gedruckt und verlegt bei G. Reimer, 1823) [Historic Maps Collection]. Schouw's temperature chart for Palermo, Sicily, using data gathered over the five-year period of 1813–1817.

V.
Vertheilungsweise der
arten.

- Gerste u. Hafer.
- Roggen.
- Weitzen.
- Reis.
- Mais.

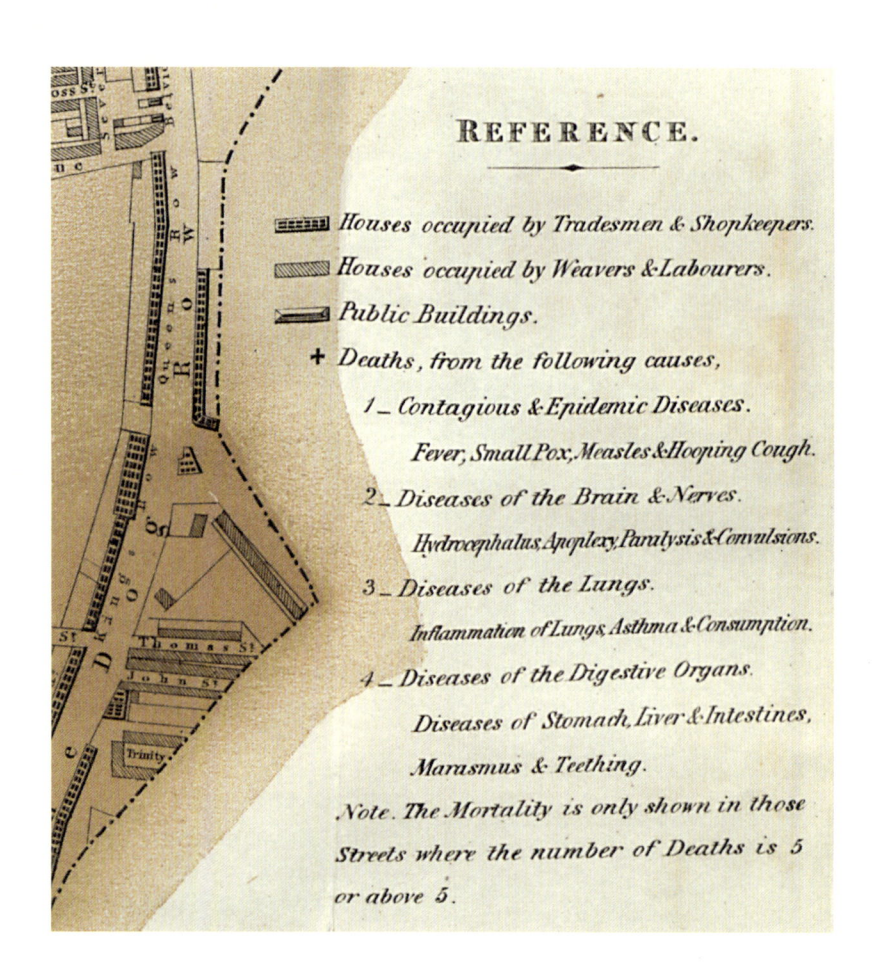

✳ Key to Edwin Chadwick's " Map of Bethal Green Parish ... " (1842).

MEDICINE

EARLY "medical" maps lacked precise data, but their creators' impulses were definitely Hippocratic. Topographies of disease started to appear regularly in the 1830s and 1840s, as epidemics lent themselves well to cartographic expression. Cholera, the first truly global disease, was a major focus of these early maps. Ultimately, they played a decisive role in identifying the source of the scourge.

GIOVANNI MARIA LANCISI
1654–1720

GIOVANNI MARIA LANCISI was an Italian physician and anatomist, trained at the Pontificia Università Gregoriana and Università di Roma in Rome. He was physician to Popes Innocent XI, Clement XI, and Innocent XII.

✻ [*Overleaf*] Untitled copperplate map ("page 154"), 18.2 × 37.2 cm. From Lancisi's *De noxiis paludum effluviis, eorumque remediis: Libri duo* [On the noxious effluvia of marshes and their remedies] (Rome: Typis Jo. Mariae Salvioni…, 1717) [Rare Books Division].

In this important work, Lancisi argues that mosquito-infested swamps are the breeding ground for malaria and recommends draining them to prevent it. He believes that trees have important ecological value, and he deplores the destruction of forests. His map of the area between the gulfs of Astura and Terracina, south-southeast from Rome (shown in the upper left), identifies twenty-six forested quarters ("quarti delle selve") and four ruined lands ("terre dirute"). The directions of the major winds are also given. The Roman statesman and orator Cicero had owned a villa in the area.

VALENTINE SEAMAN
1770–1817

SON OF A SUCCESSFUL New York City merchant, Valentine Seaman resisted the pressure to join his father in business and, instead, followed his heart into

✻ Portrait of Giovanni Maria Lancisi. Frontispiece to his *De motu cordis et aneurysmatibus opus postumum …* (Neapoli: Felix-Carolus Musca, 1738).

medicine. He began his medical studies under the care of Dr. Nicholas Romayne (born "Romeyn"), a dynamic New York medical figure who is considered today one of the founders of Columbia University's College of Physicians and Surgeons—then furthered his training at the city's almshouse. In 1791, Seaman went to the University of Pennsylvania in Philadelphia to study under Benjamin Rush, Adam Kuhn, and others; he graduated with his M.D. the following year. He made his home in New York on Beekman Street, opposite the Old Brick Church, where he and his wife had ten children.

pag. 154

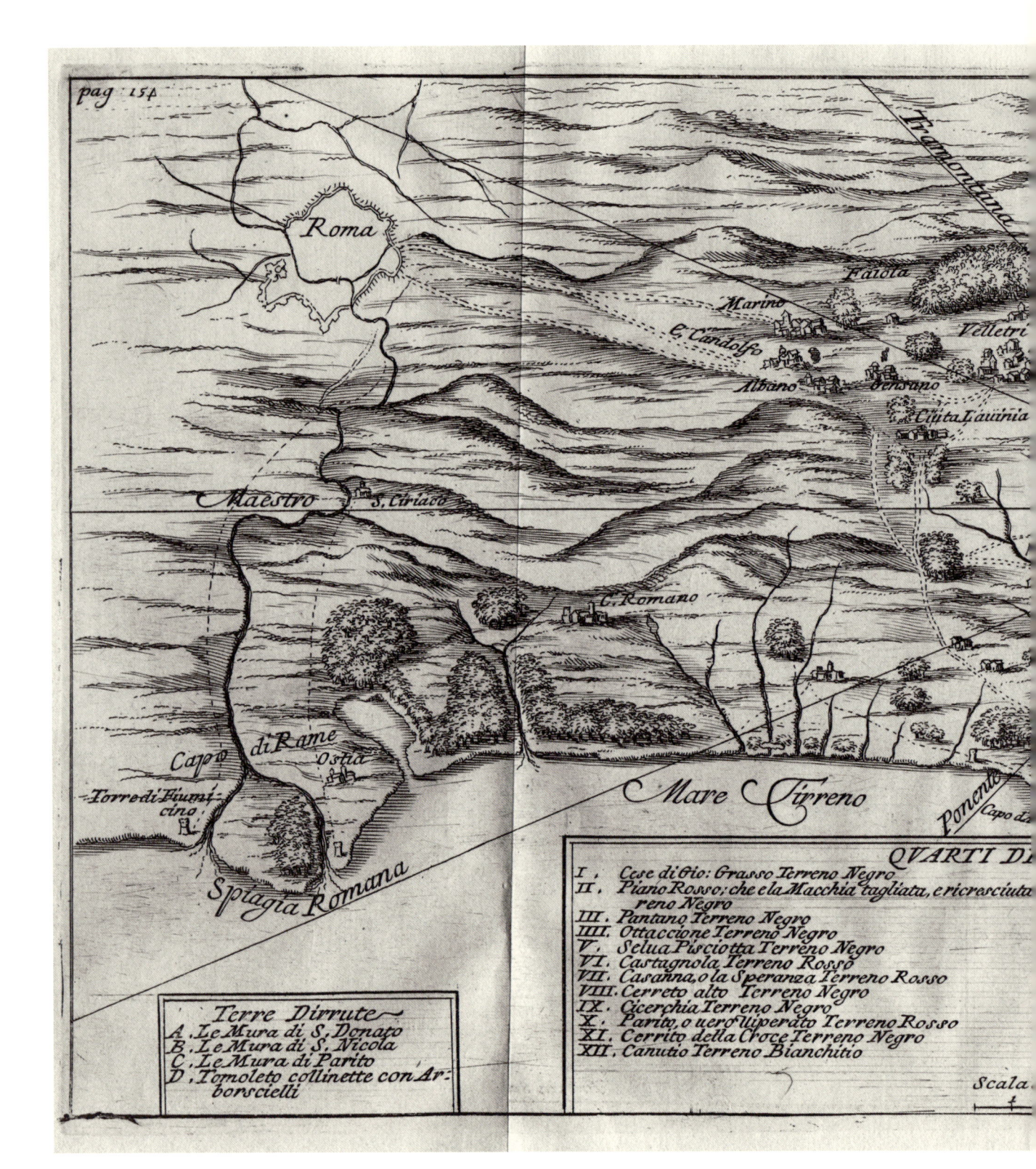

Tramontana

Roma

Faiola
Marino
C. Candolfo
Velletri
Albano
Gensano
Ciuta Lauinia

Maestro   S. Ciriaco

C. Romano

Capo di Rame
Ostia
Torre di Fiumicino

Mare Tirreno   Ponente
Capo d.

Spiagia Romana

QVARTI DI

I. Cese di Gio: Grasso Terreno Negro
II. Piano Rosso: che e la Macchia tagliata, e ricresciuta
    reno Negro
III. Pantano Terreno Negro
IIII. Ottaccione Terreno Negro
V. Selua Pisciotta Terreno Negro
VI. Castagnola Terreno Rosso
VII. Casanna, o la Speranza Terreno Rosso
VIII. Cerreto alto Terreno Negro
IX. Cicerchia Terreno Negro
X. Parito, o uero Uiperato Terreno Rosso
XI. Cerrito della Croce Terreno Negro
XII. Canutio Terreno Bianchitio

Terre Dirrute
A. Le Mura di S. Donato
B. Le Mura di S. Nicola
C. Le Mura di Parito
D. Tomoleto collinette con Arborscielli

Scala

SELVE

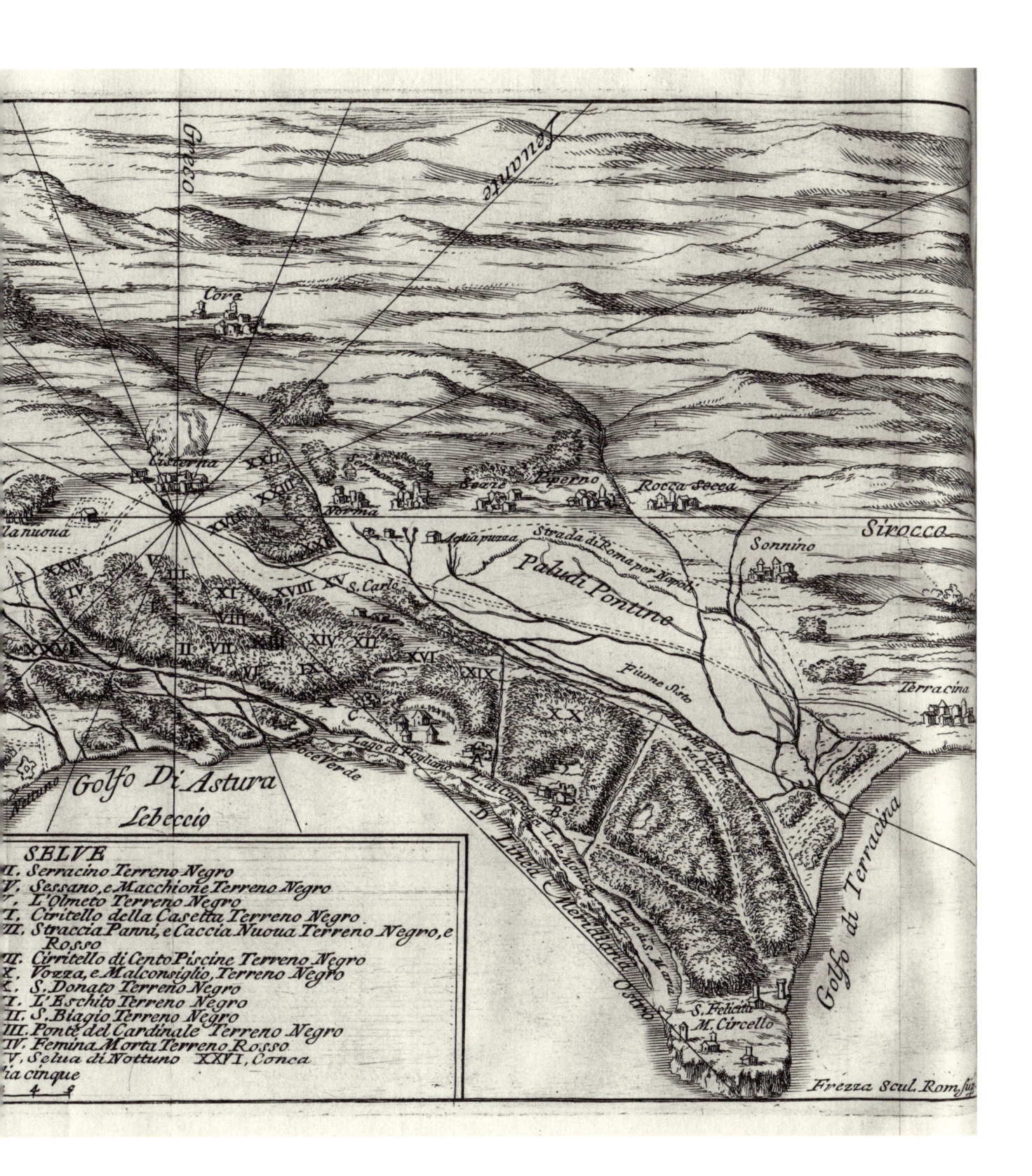

- II. Serracino Terreno Negro
- V. Sessano, e Macchione Terreno Negro
- ?. L'Olmeto Terreno Negro
- ?. Ciritello della Casetta Terreno Negro
- VII. Straccia Panni, e Caccia Nuoua Terreno Negro, e Rosso
- ?II. Ciritello di Cento Piscine Terreno Negro
- ?X. Vozza, e Malconsiglio, Terreno Negro
- X. S. Donato Terreno Negro
- ?I. L'Eschito Terreno Negro
- ?II. S. Biagio Terreno Negro
- ?III. Ponte del Cardinale Terreno Negro
- ?V. Femina Morta Terreno Rosso
- V. Selua di Nottuno   XXVI. Conca

Frezza Scul. Rom. fig.

✱ Portrait of Valentine Seaman. Photograph of oil painting by Lewis T. Ives [courtesy of Larry McCurdy].

After he lost his first child to smallpox in 1795, Seaman obtained serum from English doctor Edward Jenner, who had made great inroads against the disease by inoculating subjects with fluid taken from cowpox lesions. Seaman used it successfully first on his son and then others, and thus he is credited with introducing the practice to New York. He was also instrumental in improving the art of midwifery by offering formal classes to women and writing *The Midwives Monitor* (1800), the first instruction manual on midwifery published in the United States. Seaman belonged to the Society of Friends, for which slavery was anathema, and he became an active member of the New York Manumission Society, which sought the liberation and well-being of slaves. When he died of tuberculosis at the age of forty-seven, Seaman left behind a progressive public health legacy.

✱ [*Above & facing*] Plate I and Plate II from Seaman's "An Inquiry into the Cause of the Prevalence of the Yellow Fever in New-York," dated March 10, 1797. *Medical Repository*, 1 (1800, 2nd edition): 303–323 [Rare Books Collection].

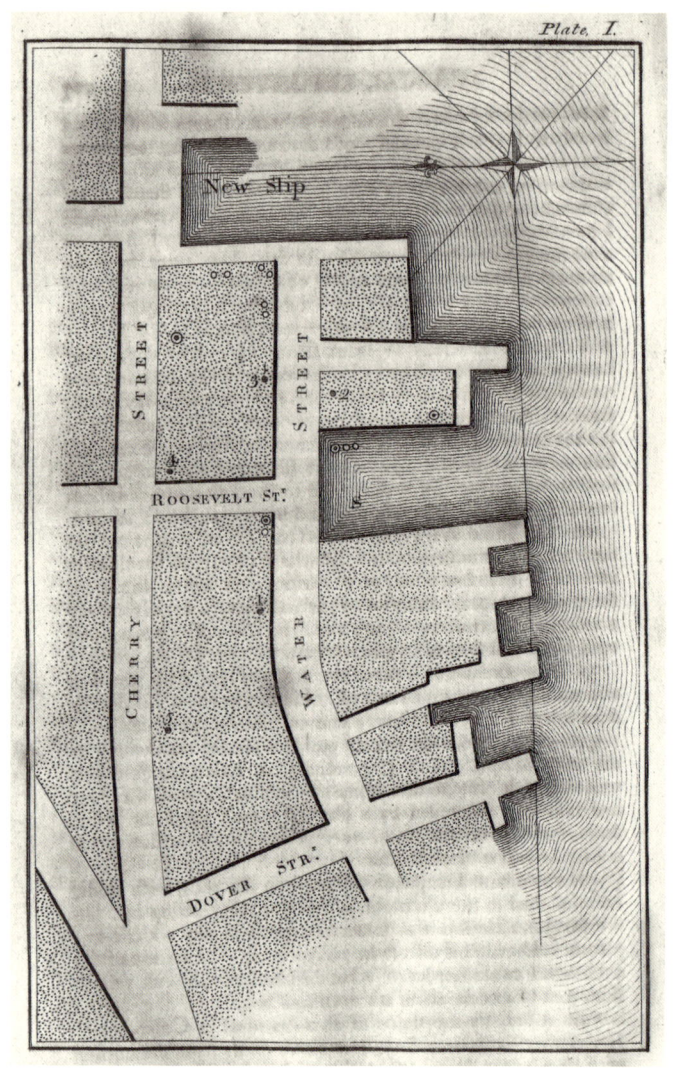

Describing recent fatal cases of yellow fever and plotting the addresses of the victims on these plates, Seaman concludes his review with several observations about the disease. His main point, emphasized in italics, is "*that no Yellow Fever can spread, but by the influence of putrid effluvia*" [p. 322]. In the case of the first plate, a sewer drain empties at the end of Roosevelt Street; in the second, the slips on each side of the end of Pine Street are filled with "rubbish and filth of every description." Both areas are low-lying and so often contain stagnant, putrid water. Eliminating "these pools of putrefaction" would help safeguard residents against the disease. Cartographically, Seaman notes that he lacks the symbols to adequately locate all the other cases, for the result would be "objectionable" [p. 309]—that is, probably too dense to be intelligible. The mapmaker's technique could not match the physician's thematic need.

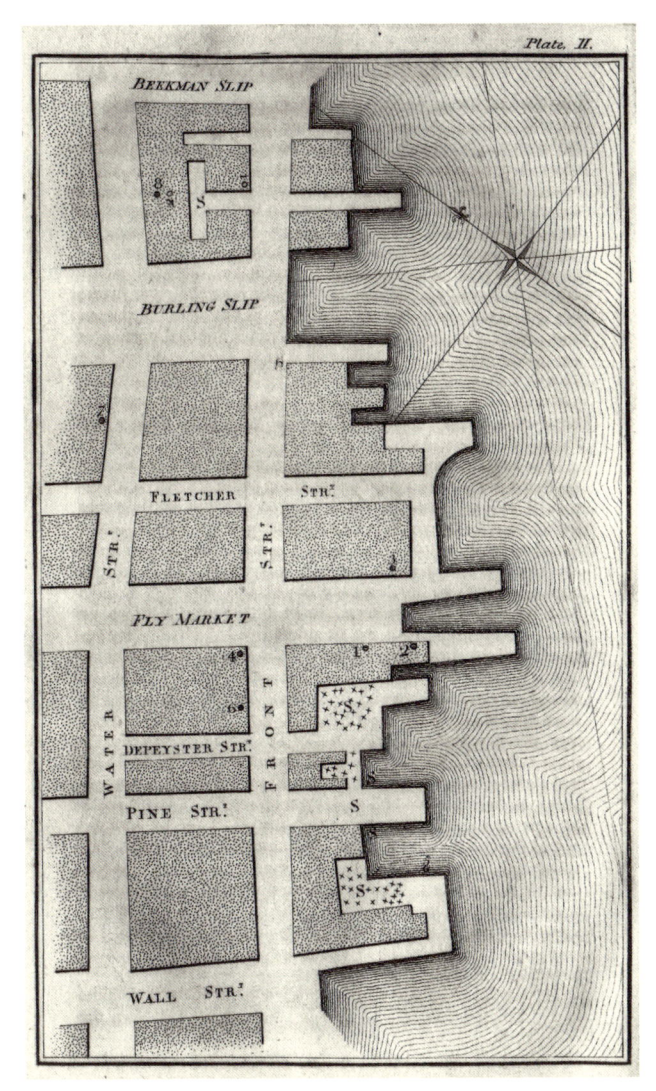

AMARIAH BRIGHAM
1798–1849

AN AMERICAN PHYSICIAN and asylum superintendent, Amariah Brigham was one of the founders of the Association of Medical Superintendents of American Institutions for the Insane (1844), which became the American Psychiatric Association, and he was the first editor of the *American Journal of Insanity* (now known as the *American Journal of Psychiatry*). In

✱ Portrait of Amariah Brigham. Engraved by H. B. Hall from a daguerreotype. From "Images from the History of Medicine," National Library of Medicine, Bethesda, Md.

1835, he published *Observations on the Influence of Religion upon the Health and Physical Welfare of Mankind*, in which he argued that the misuse of religion, particularly the emotional pitch aroused by evangelists in their protracted meetings, was harmful to the nervous system. Brigham was influential in advocating for the institutionalization of the mentally ill (rescuing them from jails and poor houses), implementing active treatment plans, and educating the public about its responsibility for such dependent people. His moral therapy included individual attention in a familylike setting that offered educational, occupational, recreational, and religious programs.

✱ [*Overleaf*] "Chart Showing the Progress of the Spasmodic Cholera." Engraved map, with outline color, 24 × 43 cm. Frontispiece to Brigham's *A Treatise on Epidemic Cholera: Including an Historical Account of Its Origin and Progress, to the Present Period* (Hartford, Conn.: Huntington, 1832) [Historic Maps Collection].

CHART
Shewing the Progress
of the
SPASMODIC CHOLERA
Longitude from Washington
Longitude West 82 from Greenwich
Longitude 75 East from 90 Greenwich
ATLANTIC OCEAN
INDIAN OCEAN
AFRICA
ASIA
EUROPE
CHINESE EMPIRE
MONGOLIA
ARABIA
PERSIA
INDOSTAN
BARBARY
GUINEA
ABYSSINIA
MEDITERRANEAN
Tropic of Cancer
Equator
Arctic Circle
LOWER CANADA
UPPER CANADA
NORTH WEST TERRIT.
NEW YORK
PENNSYLVANIA
VIRGINIA
KENTUCKY
TENNESSEE
NORTH CAROLINA
SOUTH CAROLINA
GEORGIA
ALABAMA
MISSISSIPPI
FLORIDA
OHIO
INDIANA
ILLINOIS
MICHIGAN
LAKE SUPERIOR
LAKE MICHIGAN
LAKE HURON
LAKE ERIE
ONTARIO
BAHAMA ISLANDS
FRANCE
SPAIN
ITALY
GERMANY
DENMARK
SWEDEN
FINLAND
LAPLAND
BLACK SEA
CASPIAN SEA
BALTIC SEA
EAST INDIA ISLANDS
BORNEO
SUMATRA
CHINA SEA
Philipine Isles
COREA
MEKRAN
CABUL
Nepaul
Bay of Bengal
Calcutta
Madras
Bombay
Ceylon
Archangel
Petersburg
Moscow
Orenburg
Astracan
Constantinople
Vienna
Paris
London
Pekin
Nankin
Canton
Java
Batavia
MADAGASCAR

One of the first world charts of a disease. The map traces the spread of cholera from two main sources, India (1817) and China (1820), across Asia and the Middle East via trade routes, to France and England in 1832—and thence to North America. More of a compendium, drawing on numerous reports and other publications, than a product of personal experience, Brigham's study functions on several levels by providing the historical context of the disease, describing the medical community's current understanding of its operation, and summarizing the latest, best advice for preventing it. According to Brigham's literature research, positive spirits (no fear); ventilation; avoidance of chills (dress warmly); exercise; cleanliness; a diet of well-cooked meats, fresh vegetables, and fruit; and sobriety—all habits commonly associated with good health—are anticholeric.

EDWIN CHADWICK
1800–1890

EDWIN CHADWICK is remembered as a British social reformer whose most lasting legacy is in the improvement of sanitary conditions and public health. Ironically, as secretary to social theorist Jeremy Bentham, Chadwick earlier had authored the Royal Commission's report behind the British Poor Law Amendment Act (1834), which created public workhouses where working conditions were notably vile. Their purpose was to get the lazy, shiftless poor to perform socially profitable work; however, he soon learned that sickness prevented many of the poor from working, not their lack of desire or bad work habits. Logically, he argued that it would be less expensive to promote and create a healthier environment for workers. Hence, his motivation was not primarily humanitarian but, rather, more economic. In his research, Chadwick was one of the first to correlate class/income and population density with the incidence of disease. From 1848 to 1849, he was commissioner of the Metropolitan Commission of Sewers in London and, from 1848 to 1854, commissioner of the General Board of Health. He tried unsuccessfully to get house drains hooked up to public sewers; more epidemics followed. He retired in 1854 but continued to volunteer his time on sanitation mat-

✱ Portrait of Edwin Chadwick. From Maurice Marston's *Sir Edwin Chadwick, 1800–1890* (London: Parsons, [1925]) [General Library Collection].

ters. In recognition of his public service, Chadwick was knighted in 1889.

✱ [*Overleaf*] "Sanitary Map of the Town of Leeds." Lithograph map, 17.3 × 37.8 cm. "Map of Bethal Green Parish...." Lithograph map, 31.5 × 40.5 cm. Both from Chadwick's "Report on the Sanitary Conditions of the Labouring Population of Great Britain," published in the Poor Law Commissioners' *Report to Her Majesty's Principal Secretary of State for the Home Department, from the Poor Law Commissioners, on an Inquiry into the Sanitary Condition of the Labouring Population of Great Britain, with Appendices* (London: W. Clowes and Sons, 1842) [Historic Maps Collection]. Chadwick's 457-page report constitutes the entire Poor Law Commissioners' report.

In the Leeds map, Chadwick identifies two groups of dwellings: houses of the working class and "shops, workhouses, and houses of tradespeople." Dots (blue for cholera and orange for other contagious diseases)

SANITARY MAP of the Town of LEEDS.

Reference to the Wards

I	North Ward	V	Kirkgate Ward
II	North East	VI	Mill Hill
III	East	VII	West
IV	South	VIII	North West

WARDS.	Population.	Population on each Acre.	No. of Streets	Good Streets	Bad Streets	Births to Population	Deaths to Population
Nos. I & II	28,775	207		64	109	1 in 22	1 in 25
III, IV & V	27,039	118		60	100	1 in 26	1 in 30
VI, VII & VIII	30,306	84		120	130	1 in 23	1 in 36

Reference to the Public Buildings

1. St Peter's Church
2. St John's do.
3. Trinity do.
4. St Paul's do.
5. St James's do.
6. St George's do.
7. Christ Church
8. St Mark's do.
9. St Mary's Church
10. Dispensary
11. General Infirmary
12. House of Recovery
13. National School
14. Workhouse
15. Mixed Cloth Hall
16. White Cloth Hall
17. Public Baths

Note
Houses of the Working Classes do.
Shops, Warehouses and Houses of Tradespeople
Houses of the first Class
Whether Vested, Cotton Mills, or Flax Mills.
The Blue spots designate localities in which Cholera prevailed.
The Red do. do. do. the House of recovery from 1834 to 1839.
The less shaded Districts are marked in Buff Brown

Engraved & printed in colours by Stephen. By H. Beaufort Street
For her Majesty's Stationary Office.

Scale of Yards — ¼ a Mile

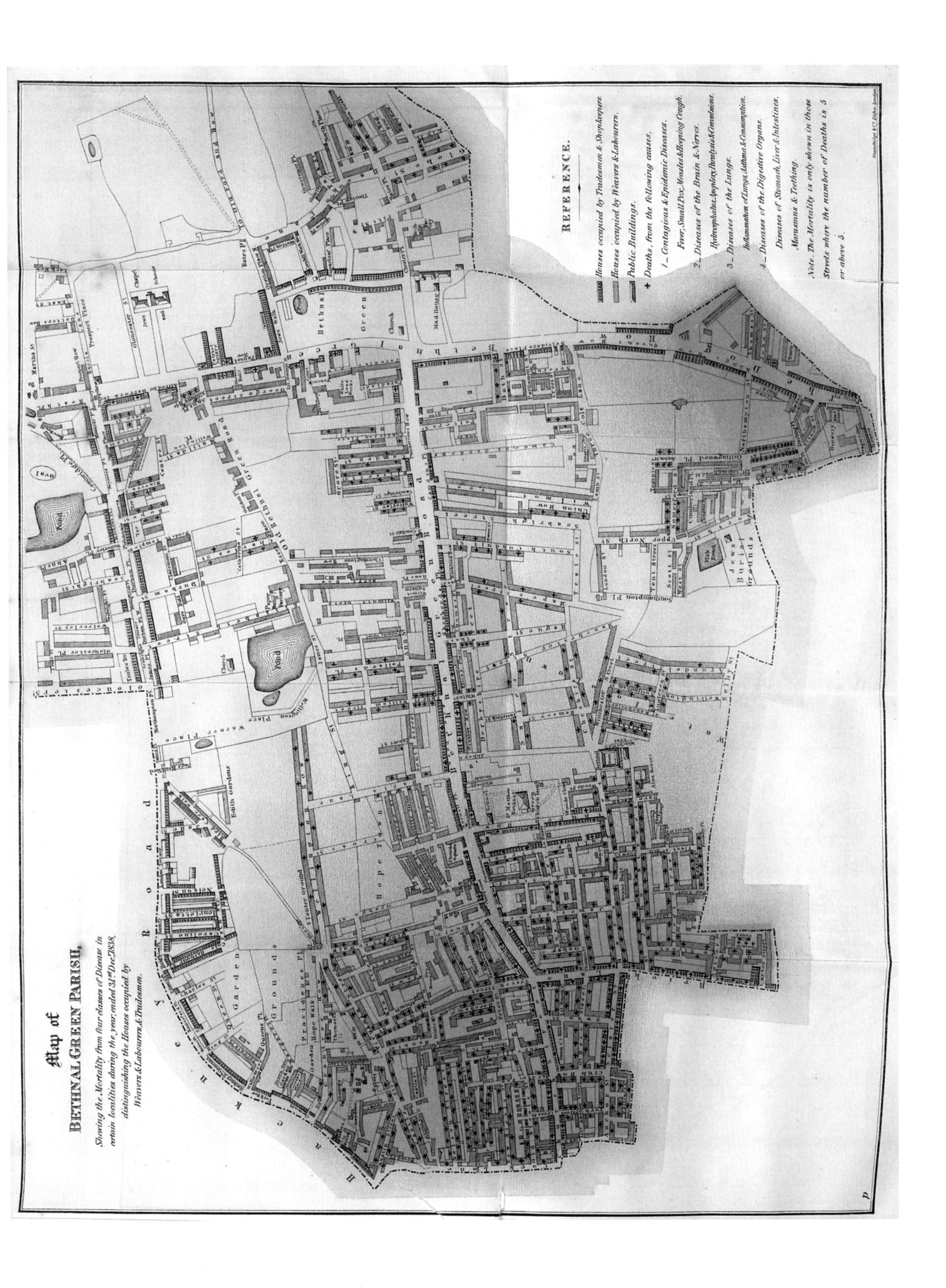

Map of BETHNAL GREEN PARISH,

Showing the Mortality from four classes of Disease in certain localities during the year, ended 31st Dec. 1838, distinguishing the Houses occupied by Weavers & Labourers, & Tradesmen.

REFERENCE.

▓ Houses occupied by Tradesmen & Shopkeepers.
▥ Houses occupied by Weavers & Labourers.
▬ Public Buildings.
✚ Deaths, from the following causes.

1 — Contagious & Epidemic Diseases.
    Fever, Small Pox, Measles & Hooping Cough.
2 — Diseases of the Brain & Nerves.
    Hydrocephalus, Apoplexy, Paralysis & Convulsions.
3 — Diseases of the Lungs.
    Inflammation of Lungs, Asthma & Consumption.
4 — Diseases of the Digestive Organs.
    Diseases of Stomach, Liver & Intestines,
    Marasmus & Teething.

Note. The Mortality is only shown in those Streets where the number of Deaths is 5 or above 5.

proliferate in the working-class areas. Note that these are not contiguous regions but are sprinkled around the map.

The Bethal Green map shows deaths (+) in the parish for 1838, caused by four classes of disease—contagious/epidemic diseases, diseases of the brain and nerves, diseases of the lungs, diseases of the digestive organs. What is interesting about this landmark map is that Chadwick distinguishes between the houses occupied by weavers/laborers and tradesmen/shopkeepers; in other words, he relates classes of housing to disease. From the map, it is clear that many more deaths occurred in the crowded, poor homes of the laborers, a conclusion that led Chadwick to closely examine housing conditions.

In fact, Chadwick found that prison conditions often were healthier (in terms of general cleanliness, ventilation, and water) than those he found among the working populations living in cellars in Liverpool, Manchester, and Leeds. Much of his report is devoted to recommending better layouts in the construction of cottages and living quarters for the working class. Overall, he concludes that

> ... the public loss from the premature deaths of the heads of families is greater than can be represented by an enumeration of the pecuniary burdens consequent upon their sickness or death.... The primary and most important measures [for improving health], and at the same time the most practicable, and within the recognized province of public administration, are drainage, the removal of all refuse of habitations, streets, and roads, and the improvement of the supplies of water [pp. 369–370].

THOMAS SHAPTER
1809–1902

A GRADUATE of Edinburgh University, Thomas Shapter spent most of his medical career in Exeter, England, where he arrived in 1832, the year of a great cholera epidemic. His subsequent, detailed study of that disease, with its important map, made his reputation. The British Parliament's Cholera Prevention Act of 1832, following upon the creation of local boards of health, enabled communities like Exeter to benefit

✸ Portrait of Thomas Shapter in the Royal Devon and Exeter Hospital, by an unknown painter. From the Wellcome Gallery (London).

from better collection of data relating to that disease. By the time Shapter began his book about that year's outbreak, however, many of those health reports had been lost, thus requiring him to make an exhaustive effort to unearth every relevant document and to interview survivors. He explains in the preface to *The History of the Cholera in Exeter in 1832* (1849) that the map

> which forms the frontispiece, has been constructed with great care and attention to particulars, and at the expense of much labour; for I have not only consulted the official returns, the registers of deaths, and the registers of burials, but personally and diligently sought information from those engaged in the burials themselves ... [p. ix].

Shapter's volume was embellished with thirty woodcuts of Exeter scenes by his artist friend John Gendall. A curious subject of one of the book's chapters is the efficacy of flannel belts, worn around the waist, in protecting people against the disease. According to Shapter, the Exeter Board of Health resolved in the fall of 1831 to

Medicine 129

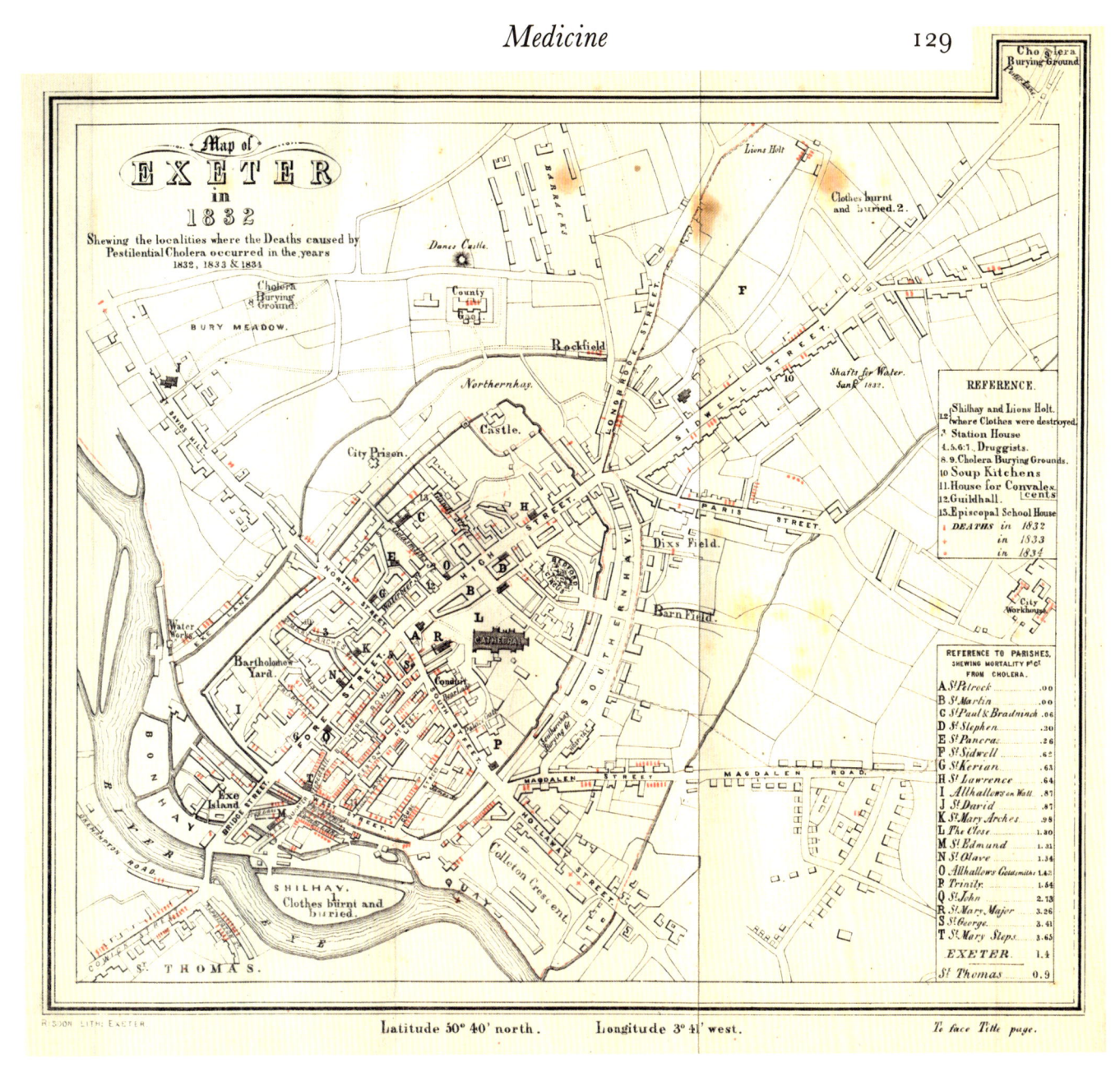

give such articles of clothing to poor people, and 7,440 were distributed. Shapter thought the idea was useless and a waste of money, but he recorded the incident anyway in his role as historian of the Exeter epidemic.

The visual power of Shapter's map may have influenced John Snow (see the John Snow entry in this Medicine section) to include a map in the second edition (1854) of his famous study of cholera in London, for the first edition (1849) had contained only tabular data.

✻ [Above] "Map of Exeter in 1832 Shewing the Localities Where the Deaths Caused by Pestilential Cholera Occurred in the Years 1832, 1833 & 1834." Lithograph map, 16.6 × 19.5 cm. Frontispiece to Shapter's *The History of the Cholera in Exeter in 1832* (London: John Churchill…; Exeter: Adam Holden…, 1849) [Historic Maps Collection].

Using red bars (1832), red diamonds (1833), and red dots (1834), Shapter locates the individual cholera deaths of those years. Numbered in the top map key are sites identified with the city's response to the epidemic, such as places where contaminated clothes were burned and buried, convalescent homes, druggists, burying grounds (see far upper right corner of the map, for example), and soup kitchens. In the other legend box, the parishes of Exeter are listed by the percentage of their populations affected by the disease, and each is assigned an alphabetic letter on the map. For Shapter, the evidence in the map was irrefutable: cholera was rampant in low-lying areas of dense habitation, near the river, where drainage was poor and waste and refuse accumulated—in others words, the disease was miasmatic.

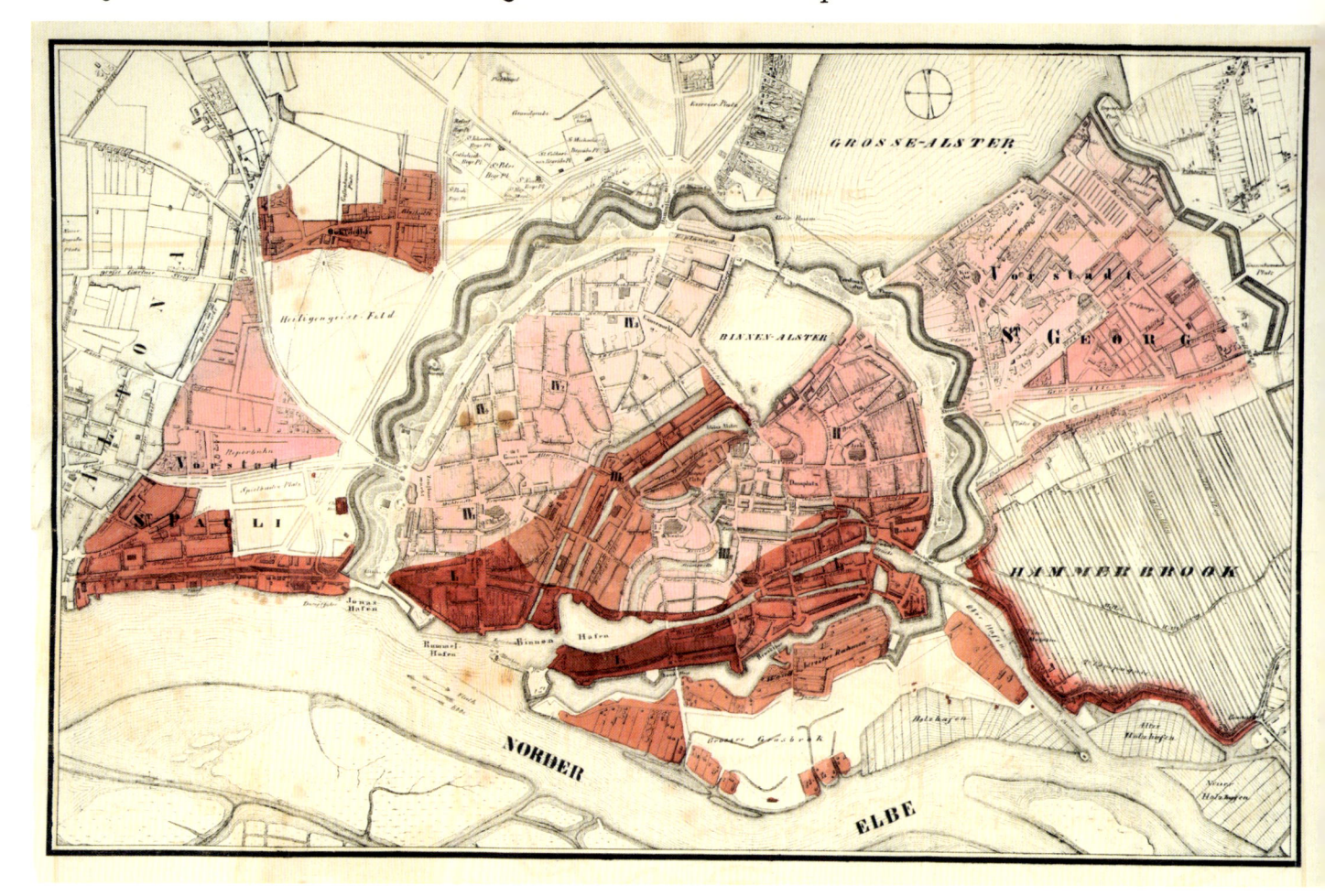

✳ [*Above*] "Zu Rothenburg's Cholera-Epidemie des Jahres 1832 in Hamburg." Lithograph map, with added color, 27.7 × 43.6 cm. From J. N. C. Rothenburg's *Die Cholera-Epidemie des Jahres 1832 in Hamburg: Ein Vortrag, gehalten im der wissenschaftlichen Versammlung des ärztlichen Vereins, am 17 November 1835* (Hamburg: Perthes & Besser, 1836) [Historic Maps Collection].

Another mapping of cholera in 1832, on a coarser scale, was made in Hamburg, Germany, by Dr. Rothenburg, using hand-colored gradations of red—via the chloropleth method—to show the relative, aggregate incidence of the disease. It was reprinted in an 1850 British parliamentary report on cholera, emphasizing the international appeal of this cartography.

✳ [*Opposite*] "Cholera Consultation / The Central Board of Health" ([London:] S. Knights, Feby. 27th. 1832). Lithograph print by George Cruikshank, with added color, 20 × 32.5 cm [Graphic Arts Collection].

In the midst of the 1832 cholera epidemic, British caricaturist and book illustrator Cruikshank pulls no punches in lampooning fat, self-serving doctors charged with the care of public health:

> "While Drs. defer & deny—
> The country bleeds & patients die."

JOHN SNOW
1813–1858

THE OLDEST of nine children born to a poor York coal yard worker, John Snow became a pioneer in the use of anesthesia, and he is recognized today as one of the founders of epidemiology. Family connections earned him an apprenticeship with a surgeon/physician at age fourteen. Subsequently, he worked at various locations as a medical and apothecary assistant and then went to the Hunterian School of Medicine in London; in 1837, he worked at Westminster Hospital and later set up his own private practice in the Soho area of London. In 1844, he graduated from the University of London and was admitted to the Royal College of Physicians in 1850.

In the 1840s, Snow progressed from practicing general medicine to publishing his medical research and becoming a specialist in anesthesia, which had first been demonstrated in London in 1846. His clinical textbook on the subject, *On the Inhalation of the Vapour of Ether in Surgical Operations* (1847), secured his reputation as a leading practitioner of the science. Later, he administered chloroform to Queen Victoria when she gave birth to her last two children, Leopold (1853) and Beatrice (1857).

During this period cholera returned to England (1849 and 1854) and was particularly virulent in the Soho area where Snow lived. He began to concentrate his attention and research on the disease and its causes, developing a theory that ran counter to the prevailing view that miasmatic, foul airs carried the disease from urban refuse. Snow believed the disease was waterborne and spread from individual to individual. The Thames River was the city's primary source of drinking water and also its principal sewer. In a large-scale South London study, Snow showed that water supplied by the Southwark and Vauxhall Company, compared with

✻ Portrait of John Snow in 1857. Frontispiece to his *Snow on Cholera, Being a Reprint of Two Papers by John Snow, M.D. ...* (New York: The Commonwealth Fund, 1936) [Rare Books Division].

that from the Lambeth Company or other sources, was associated with ten times more cholera deaths. Southwark and Vauxhall drew from sources Snow believed were polluted by the city's waste; Lambeth used sources farther from the city.

But it was Snow's other, focused study on the Broad Street neighborhood of Soho that made him famous. Here, he began with a thesis, collected data, and used a map to confirm his argument. Snow personally investigated hundreds of cholera deaths (of all classes), seeking the sources of the household water used by the decedents; he mapped more than five hundred cases. The results conclusively led him to a water pump on Broad Street. The handle to the pump was removed, and the intensity of the cholera outbreak declined. The "cholera poison," Snow believed, was cell-like, reproduced quickly, and was invisible to the eye. However, not everyone who had drawn water from that source became infected. Also, miasmatic theorists believed that Snow's evidence did not necessarily undermine their position, for some kind of localized outbreak would be expected from a noxious miasma.

The debate over the cause of cholera continued well after Snow's death from the effects of a stroke in 1854. Coincidentally, in the same year, the Italian anatomist Filippo Pacini isolated the microscopic culprit of the disease, the bacillus *Vibrio cholera*, but his work was ignored until 1885, when the renowned German physician Robert Koch, studying cholera in Egypt, made a similar discovery.

✻ [*Opposite*] "Map 1." Printed map, 37.9 × 40.4 cm. From Snow's *Snow on Cholera ...* (1936). The map originally accompanied the second edition of Snow's *Of the Mode of Communication of Cholera* (London: John Churchill, 1854).

Snow's decisive, iconic map, showing how cholera deaths clustered around the Broad Street water pump. Using a commercial map of the Soho District, Snow stacked his black line symbols that represented individual deaths inward from the street address. This visual innovation combined an accurate location with a measure of intensity. (In another version of the map, Snow drew a dotted line of equidistance, by foot travel, between the Broad Street pump and other local pumps. Plotted cholera deaths diminished or ceased entirely at every point where residences were nearer other pumps: another visual confirmation of his argument.) Snow argued for a stringent regime of cleanliness: in the water supply, in the household (separating washing areas from cooking, etc.), and in personal hygiene.

HENRY WENTWORTH ACLAND
1815–1900

ENGLISH physician and educator Henry W. Wentworth Acland took the cholera debate in another direction in his comprehensive study (1856) of the disease in Oxford, England. Its examination of cholera outbreaks there from 1830 to 1854—the most exhaustive of its day, using charted data and maps—concluded that altitude was more closely related to mortality from cholera than any other known factor (such as class, age, occupation, or sex). Accurate and rigorous in his mapping, Acland failed, however, to observe that people living at higher elevations usually obtained their water from aquifers or streams far removed from polluted rivers. But he was a strong advocate for improving sanitation and drainage in towns and homes as the best method for fighting the disease.

Educated at Harrow and Oxford, Acland became a physician in the Radcliffe Infirmary there and, later, was appointed to the Regius Professor of Medicine post at Oxford University. He had a large role in its school of medicine and in promoting the study of natural science. Interested in public health issues, Acland served on a royal sanitation commission and published pamphlets, as well as his landmark study, on related matters. He was a lifelong friend of the Victorian art critic John Ruskin.

✽ Portrait of Henry W. Acland. From vol. 2 of Henry Barraud's *The Medical Profession in All Countries Containing Photographic Portraits from Life* (London: J. & A. Churchill, 1874).

✽ [*Opposite*] "Map of Oxford." Lithograph map, 45 × 62 cm. From Acland's *Memoir on the Cholera at Oxford, in the Year 1854, with Considerations Suggested by the Epidemic* (London: John Churchill ... and J. H. and J. Parker...; Oxford: J. H. and J. Parker, 1856) [Historic Maps Collection].

Covering three epidemics of cholera, Acland's map relates altitude to occurrences of the disease. Black contour lines mark altitude in five-foot intervals, from the lowlands near the rivers to the town's highest point, the summit of Carfax. Brown dots indicate spots previously described by investigators as unhealthy. Visually, it is clear that cholera affected many more people living in the low spots than in the higher areas of town, despite designations of "unhealthy." The conclusion Acland drew was that cholera was more of a miasmatic disease that festered and settled in low-lying airs. (From today's skeptical vantage point, Acland's altitude scale—five feet, ten feet, fifteen feet, etc.—seems so small as to be irrelevant to any study.)

✽ [*Overleaf*] "Diagram Shewing the Daily Number of New Cases of Cholera, Choleraic Diarrhœa, and Diarrhœa Reported in Oxford, During the Epidemic of 1854, Together with the Daily Maximum of Temperature of the Air, the Amount of Rain, Degree of Moisture in the Air, the Mean Height of the Barometer, the Force and Direction of the Wind at 10 a.m. and 2 p.m., and the Amount of Cloud." Lithograph chart, 60.2 × 42.8 cm. From Acland's *Memoir on the Cholera at Oxford ...* (1856) [Historic Maps Collection].

In discussing the tables of climatic data in his text, Acland noted the

> ... extraordinary nature of 1854. Except in the solitary condition of mean temperature, every thing is abnormal. Excessive in atmospheric pressure, and daily variations of temperature, deficient in rain and wind, abnormal in the direction of the wind, excessive in the display of electrical phenomena—as if to complete a meteorological paradox, this same year, remarkable for the abundance of its harvest, was not less remarkable for pestilence and its consequent mortality [p. 63].

Acland's general observations provided more supporting "evidence" for miasmatic theorists, for he suggested that meteorological factors at lower altitudes could promote choleraic airs. However, in his accompanying chart, none of the data elements exhibit, in my view, any unusual activity relative to the choleraic incidents displayed in red over the epidemic period of September–October 1854.

FLORENCE NIGHTINGALE
1820–1910

INTERNATIONALLY celebrated for her pioneering nursing work in the Crimean War, Florence Nightingale is also recognized for combining statistics with sanitary reform, which she was able to dramatize with her innovative polar area diagrams. Born in Florence, Italy (her namesake), of an upper-class English family, she rejected, at an early age, the traditional expectations

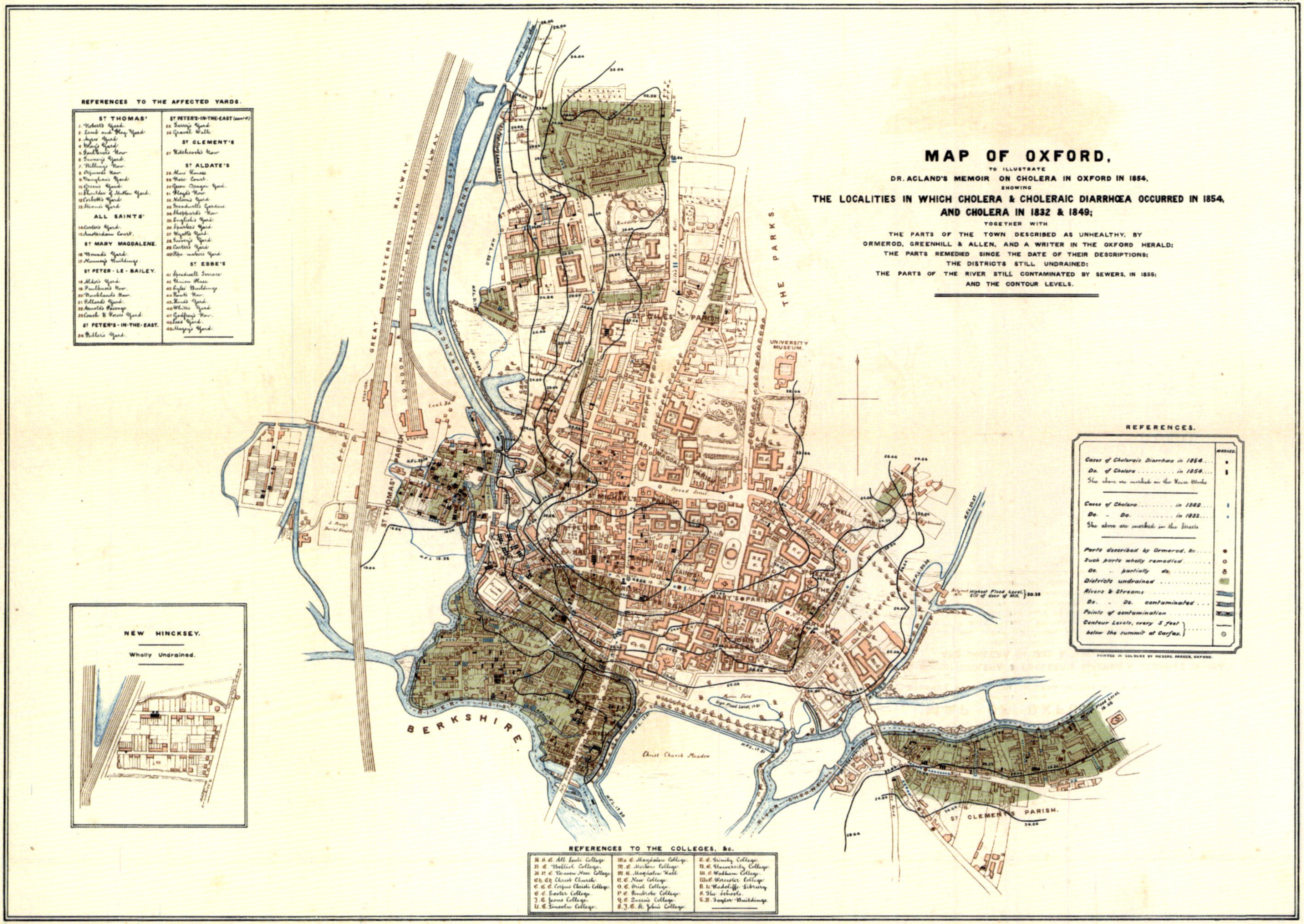

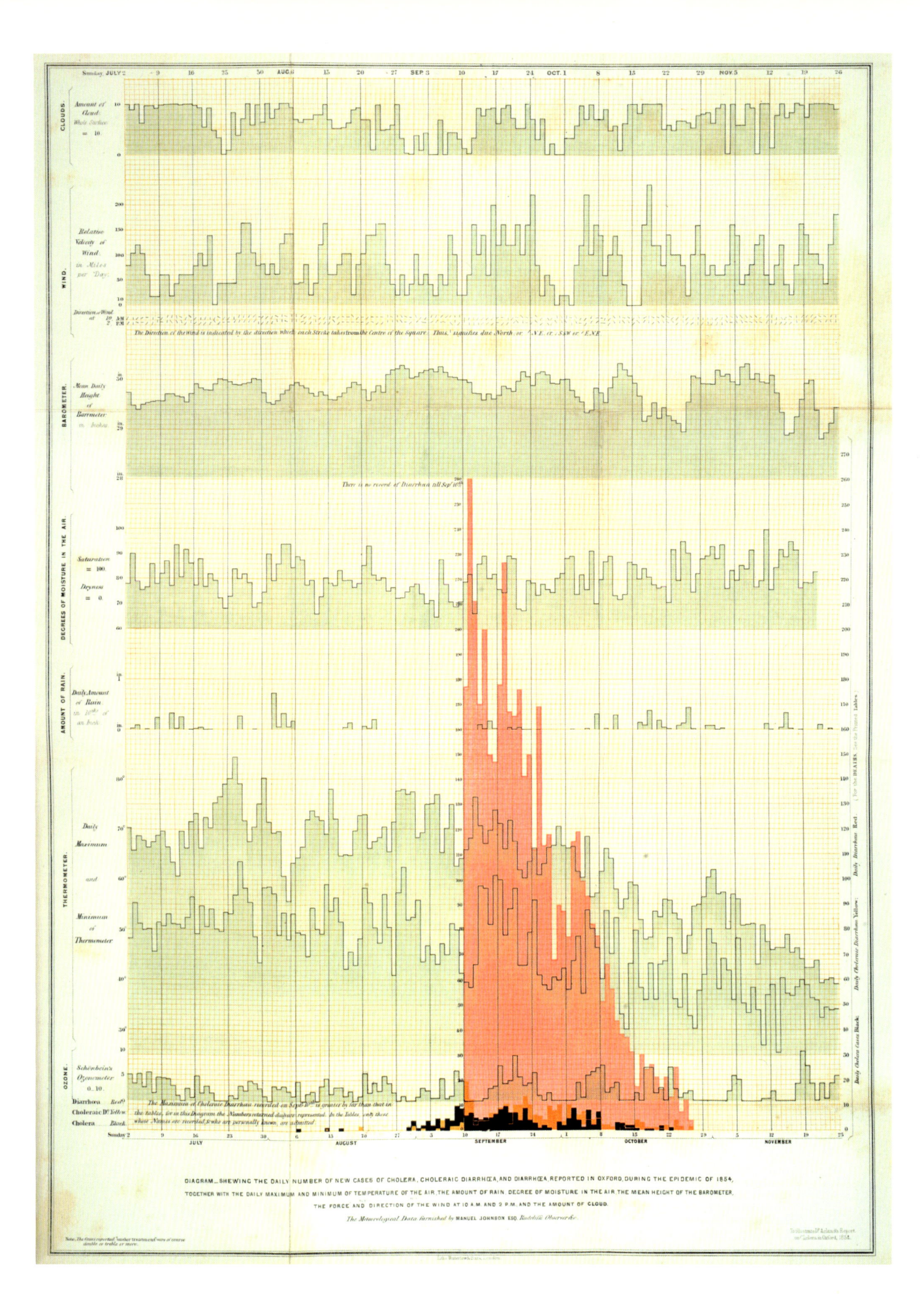

DIAGRAM – SHEWING THE DAILY NUMBER OF NEW CASES OF CHOLERA, CHOLERAIC DIARRHŒA, AND DIARRHŒA REPORTED IN OXFORD, DURING THE EPIDEMIC OF 1854, TOGETHER WITH THE DAILY MAXIMUM AND MINIMUM OF TEMPERATURE OF THE AIR, THE AMOUNT OF RAIN, DEGREE OF MOISTURE IN THE AIR, THE MEAN HEIGHT OF THE BAROMETER, THE FORCE AND DIRECTION OF THE WIND AT 10 A.M. AND 2 P.M. AND THE AMOUNT OF CLOUD.

The Meteorological Data furnished by MANUEL JOHNSON ESQ. *Radcliffe Observer &c.*

✳ Portrait of Florence Nightingale. Undated *carte de visite* [Laurence Hutton Photograph Albums, Manuscripts Division].

of her sex and status, choosing instead a life of service to the sick. Against her mother's strong wishes, she entered nursing school in 1844 and was superintendent of the Institute for the Care of Sick Gentlewomen (London) when the Crimean War broke out in March 1854. Sent by the secretary of war to the Ottoman Empire (now Turkey), across the Black Sea from the British Army's main camp at Balaklava (Sevastopol, Ukraine), Nightingale arrived in November with a staff of volunteer nurses she had trained herself. She earned the epithet "Lady with the Lamp" from her nighttime ministerings to the wounded at the Selimiye Barracks in Scutari, a district of modern Istanbul. Nightingale and her nurses improved conditions where limited supplies of medicine, poor hygiene, and lack of quality food had been leading to illnesses that were ten times more fatal to the men than battle wounds.

The Nightingale Fund for training nurses was created in 1855 to recognize Nightingale's war work. From fund donations, in 1860, she established what is now called the Florence Nightingale School of Nursing and Midwifery in London. Her *Notes on Nursing* (1859) is considered a classic introduction to the profession of nursing, and she also wrote on improving sanitation and administration in civilian and military hospitals. Under her father's tutorship, Nightingale had excelled in mathematics as a youngster; in midlife she was adept at using statistics to promote her nursing agenda and was the first female elected to the Royal Statistical Society (1858). In 1907, she was also the first woman to receive the Order of Merit.

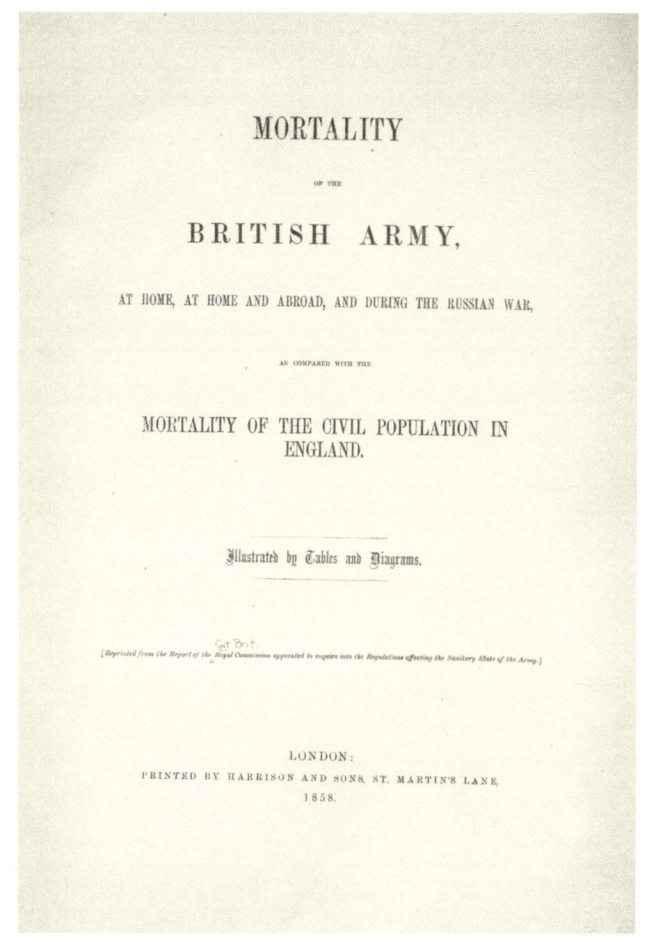

Intermittently bedridden and suffering from depression for much of her later life, Nightingale continued to be productive—in social reform, hospital planning, and nursing education. Beyond numerous monuments, museums, and memorials, Nightingale's legacy survives in the women's movement and global health awareness.

✳ [*Above*] Title page from *Mortality of the British Army: At Home, at Home* [*sic*] *and Abroad, and during the Russian War, as Compared with the Mortality of the Civil Population in England* (London: Printed by Harrison and Sons,

138   *Quantitative Thematic Maps*

1858) [Historic Maps Collection]. One of two thousand copies. Reprinted from the report of the royal commission appointed to inquire into the regulations affecting the sanitary state of the army. Nightingale arranged for the printing of this version of her appendix to the government's report—the same content but with better layout.

Diagrams are of great utility for illustrating certain questions of vital statistics by conveying ideas on the subject through the eye, which cannot be so readily grasped when contained in figures [p. 1].

✳ [*Below*] "(K) Diagrams Representing the Relative Mortality from Zymotic Diseases (blue [appears greenish]), from Wounds &c. (red), and from All Other Causes (black), in the Hospitals of the Army in the East, for Each Month from April 1854 to March 1856." From *Mortality of the British Army …* (1858) [Historic Maps Collection].

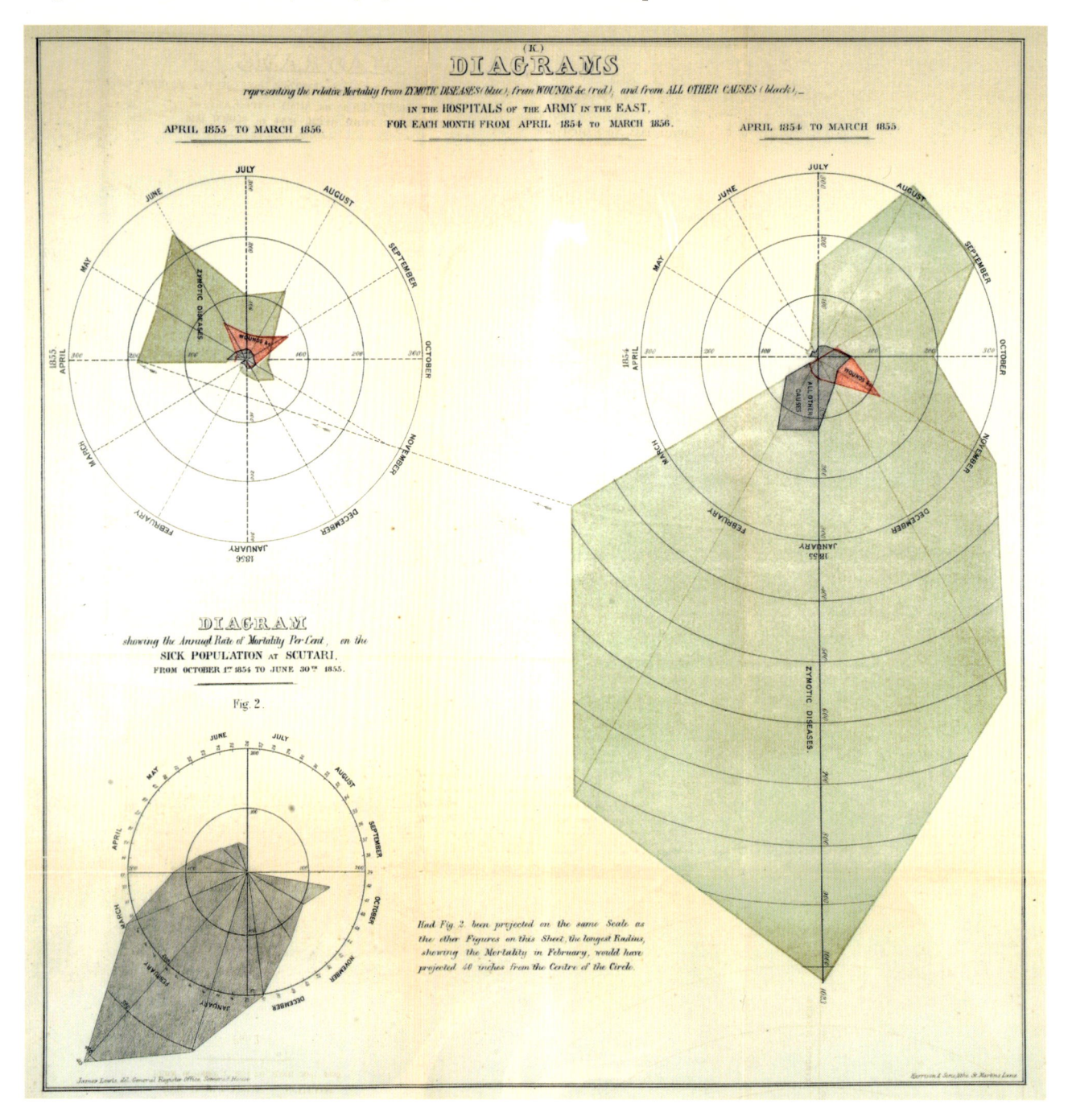

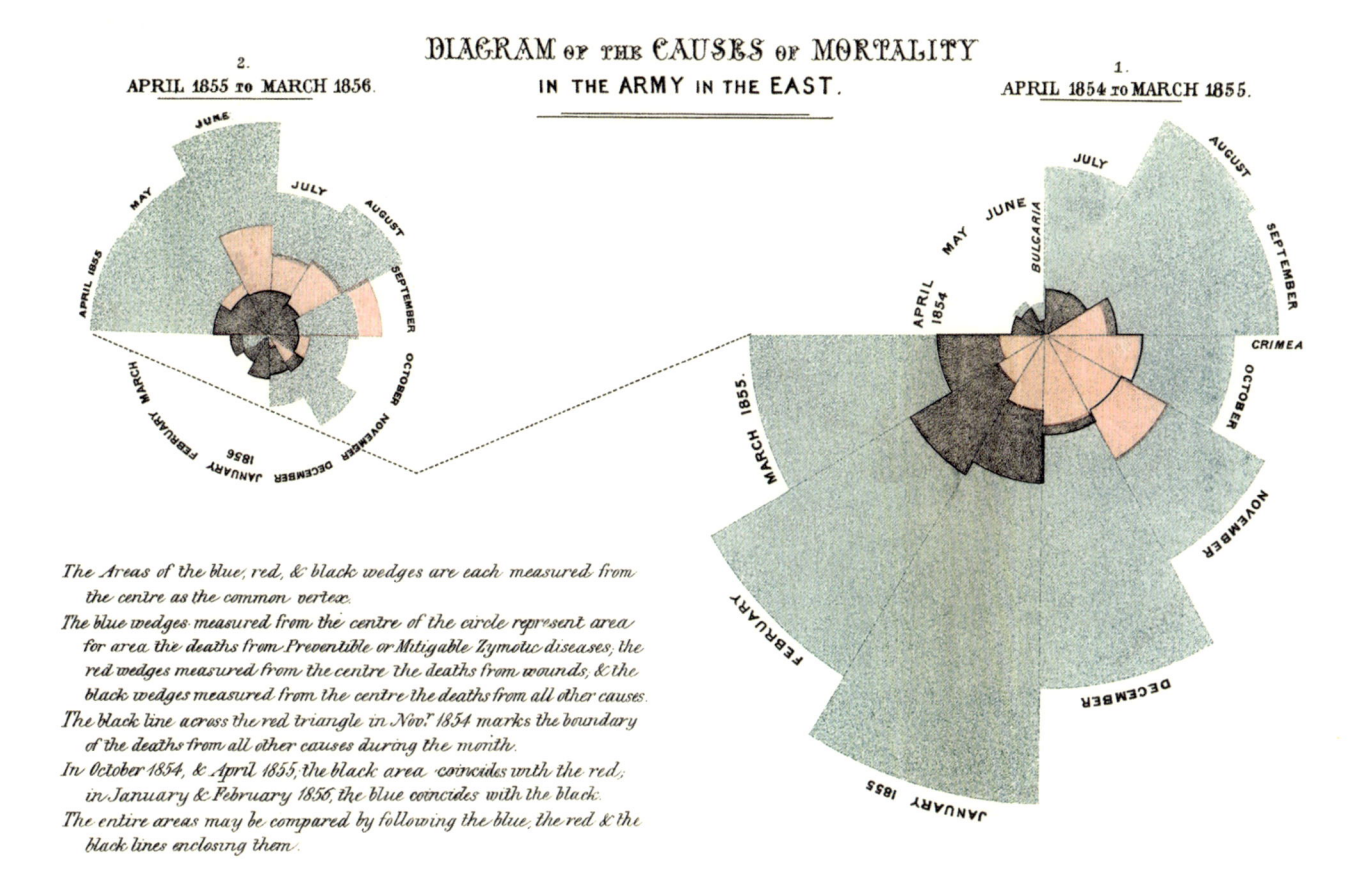

Medicine

DIAGRAM OF THE CAUSES OF MORTALITY IN THE ARMY IN THE EAST.

2. APRIL 1855 TO MARCH 1856.

1. APRIL 1854 TO MARCH 1855.

The Areas of the blue, red, & black wedges are each measured from the centre as the common vertex.

The blue wedges measured from the centre of the circle represent area for area the deaths from Preventible or Mitigable Zymotic diseases, the red wedges measured from the centre the deaths from wounds, & the black wedges measured from the centre the deaths from all other causes.

The black line across the red triangle in Novr 1854 marks the boundary of the deaths from all other causes during the month.

In October 1854, & April 1855, the black area coincides with the red; in January & February 1856, the blue coincides with the black.

The entire areas may be compared by following the blue, the red & the black lines enclosing them.

Often referred to as "bat wings," these diagrams dramatically summarize Nightingale's argument:

> The immense preponderance of zymotic diseases has been already referred to, and a glance at Diagram K will show that these diseases were the cause of the whole catastrophe. The total mortality from wounds at Alma, Inkermann, and during the five months in the trenches, exclusive of the killed in action, is all comprised in the small pink cone in the centre. The small black patch adjacent comprehends the total mortality from diseases not zymotic. The irregular blue surface, like the tail of a portentous comet, shows the zymotic diseases, the pests and scourges of camps and armies now, as they were of cities and towns in the middle ages, before the dawn of sanitary knowledge [p. 5].

However, it is the length of the radial line that is proportional to the death rate, not the area, and yet the text suggests it is the shaded areas that are proportional. Nightingale recognized this error, and in her subsequent publication replaced the "bat wings" with wedges, sometimes called "coxcombs" (see above).

✻ [*Above*] "Diagram of the Causes of Mortality in the Army in the East" [*Wikipedia*]. From *Notes on Matters Affecting the Health, Efficiency, and Hospital Administration of the British Army*, a confidential report to the government that Nightingale printed privately in 1858.

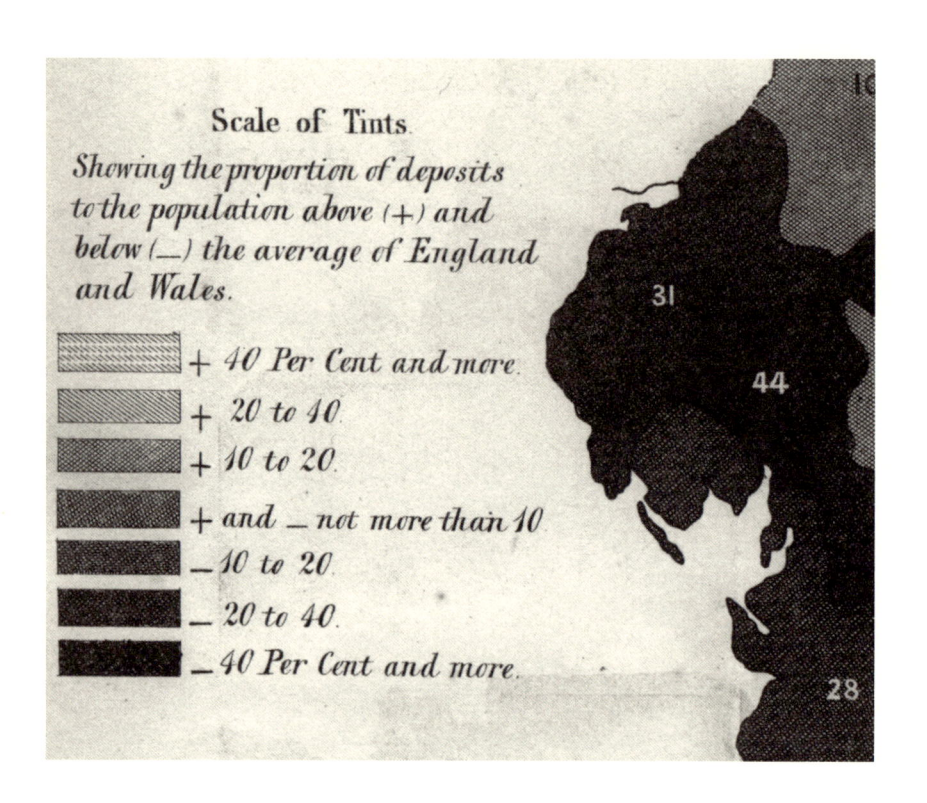

✻ Key to Joseph Fletcher's "Deposits in the Savings Banks in England & Wales in Proportion to the Population" (1849).

SOCIOLOGY & ECONOMICS

("Moral Statistics")

PROBABLY the most intuitive areas for thematic map use are the social and economic environments, where subjects like trade, population, crime, and poverty come readily to mind. And these are also the areas where governmental bodies and institutional organizations historically focused their initial statistical efforts. But who first was responsible (where and how) for making this kind of information available visually in charts and maps?

WILLIAM PLAYFAIR
1759–1823

AN OPPORTUNIST, a scoundrel, a genius—William Playfair tried and failed at many things in his life but left a permanent mark on statistical graphics, pioneering the way that we have visualized data ever since. A chart of his own life would show a line spiraling downward across the axis of years, asterisked with explanatory text:

* Educated by older brother John after the death of his Scottish clergyman father when he was thirteen (John would become a distinguished geologist and mathematician).
* Served an apprenticeship with James Watt, of steam engine fame.
* Failed with a silversmith and plate-making business he had set up with a partner.
* Tried to develop a rolling mill in France with Louis XVI's approval.
* Lived in France at the time of the French Revolution and assisted in the storming and capture of the Bastille.
* Partnered with Joel Barlow (American lawyer and poet) in the Scioto Land Company, which attempted to establish French settlers along the Ohio River but subsequently collapsed amid embezzlement charges.
* Failed with a London bank he had co-partnered.
* Edited short-lived publications (a daily paper and a weekly).
* Was convicted of swindling.
* Edited the first critical edition of Adam Smith's *Wealth of Nations*.
* Attempted extortion.

Playfair never realized the "grand scheme." But in his lifetime he wrote more than a hundred pamphlets and books. In 1786, he produced *The Commercial and Political Atlas*, the first publication to contain statistical charts (but no maps), including the first bar graph and line graphs. (These latter were probably inspired by Joseph Priestley's chronological diagrams, which Playfair had seen.) In 1801, Playfair published *The Statistical Breviary*, which included the first pie chart, using different size slices to represent the extent of their corresponding geographical regions. None of these graphic innovations was recognized as a major achievement by his countrymen. Abroad, however, he had important supporters. Presented with a copy of Playfair's *Atlas*, French King Louis XVI thought the charts were very clear and readily understandable. German naturalist-geographer Alexander von Humboldt acknowledged his debt to Playfair in his *Political Essay on the Kingdom of New Spain* (1811) in which he graphed, in a similar manner, the silver and gold mining operations of Mexico.

Playfair died in poverty. His obituaries made no mention of his graphical inventions, concentrating, instead, on his unpopular political and economic writings. One of his sons emigrated to Canada, became prominent and successful, and founded the town of Playfairville in Ontario. Two centuries after Playfair's death, the pie chart, bar graph, and line graph remain fundamentally the same—and they are universally ubiquitous.

✻ [*Overleaf*] Title page of *The Commercial and Political Atlas: Representing, by Means of Stained Copper-plate Charts, the Progress of the Commerce, Revenues, Expenditure and Debts of England during the Whole of the Eighteenth Century*, 3rd ed. (London: T. Burton for J. Wallis, etc., 1801) [Rare Books Division]. The first edition had appeared in 1786; the second in 1787.

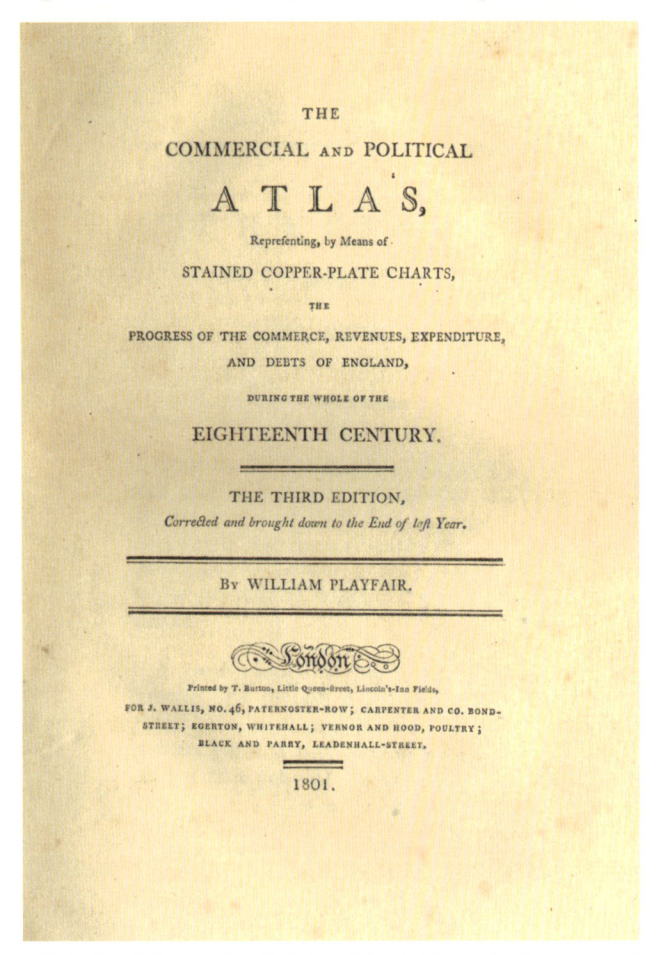

> As knowledge increases amongst mankind, and transactions multiply, it becomes more and more desirable to *abbreviate* and *facilitate* the modes of conveying information from one person to another, and from one individual to the many [p. vii].

This is not a quote from a current smartphone advertisement; rather, it is how Playfair begins the third edition of his landmark work, which he felt necessary to update because of the great change "operating in Europe"—certainly a reference to the French Revolution and its aftereffects. To him, the reasons for new and improved graphic representations were clear (as they continue to be today): they enabled him to give form and shape to abstract ideas.

That I have succeeded in proposing and putting into practice a new and useful mode of stating accounts, has been generally acknowledged, that it remains only for me to request that those who do not, at the first sight, understand the manner of inspecting the Charts, will read with attention the few lines of directions facing the first Chart, after which they will find all the difficulty entirely vanish, and as much information may be *obtained in five minutes as would require whole days to imprint on the memory, in a lasting manner, by a table of figures* [p. xii; his emphasis].

✲ [*Opposite*] "A Map of France with the Proposed Divisions." Copperplate map, with added color, 35.1 × 31.9 cm. From Playfair's *Thoughts on the Present State of French Politics and the Necessity and Policy of Diminishing France, for Her Internal Peace, and to Secure the Tranquillity of Europe* (London: Printed for John Stockdale, 1793) [Rare Books Division].

Grown disenchanted with the revolutionaries, Playfair became a resolute Royalist. His attitude on the French Revolutionary Wars is made abundantly clear with these words printed under his name on the title page: "The French Democrats will be like other Madmen, they have begun by insulting and attacking all their Neighbours, and will finish their Career in a strait Waistcoat." His thematic map proposes a solution to the current danger of France's revolutionary fever: break the country up and offer pieces of its territory to neighboring states "as an indemnity for expenses occasioned by France"; then reconstitute its diminished state under the House of Bourbon.

✲ [*Opposite*] "Exports & Imports to and from All North America." Copperplate chart, with added color, 8 × 15.4 cm. Plate 5 from Playfair's *The Commercial and Political Atlas* (1801) [Rare Books Division].

This chart dramatically exhibits the effect of the American Revolution on trade between England and its former colonies: brought to a standstill during the war, it quickly recovered and expanded. In his accompanying notes, Playfair argues that his country's idea of keeping America "in a state of dependence was rapacious, impolitic, and unjust" [p. 22], for England's trade advantage is now greater than ever.

A MAP of FRANCE with the proposed Divisions.

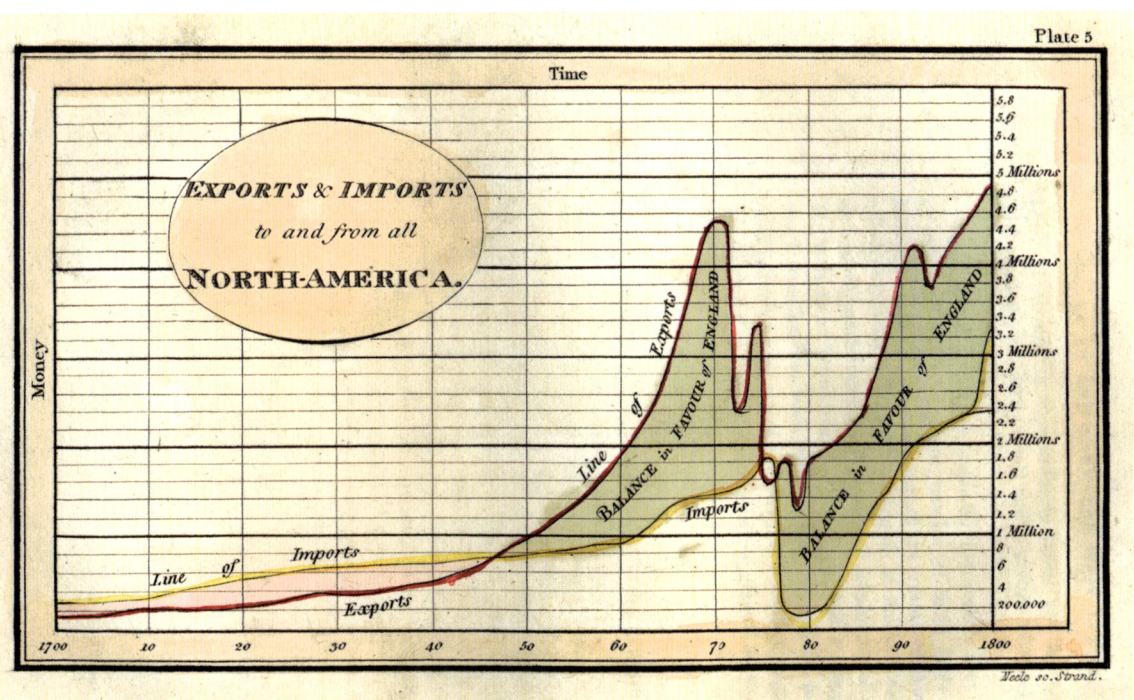

Plate 5

EXPORTS & IMPORTS to and from all NORTH-AMERICA.

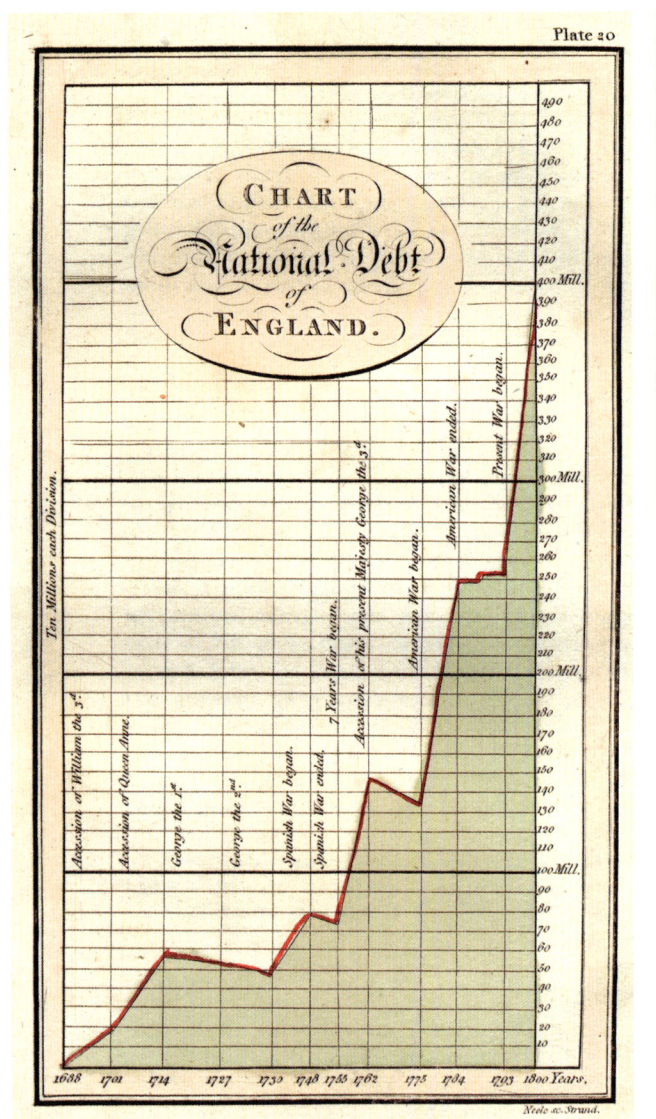

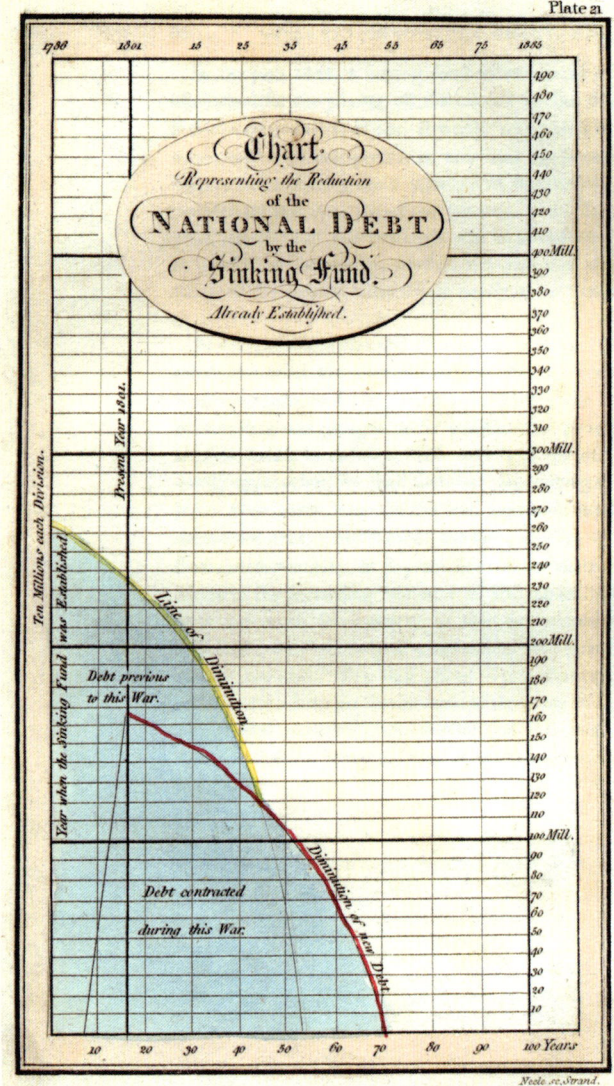

✳︎ [Above] "Chart of the National Debt of England." Copperplate chart, with added color, 15.3 × 8.4 cm. Plate 20 from Playfair's *The Commercial and Political Atlas* (1801) [Rare Books Division].

Similarly, in this chart, inferences are clear: wars increase national debt. Playfair is not content with drawing obvious conclusions, however. His observations are as keenly relevant today as they were when he published them over two hundred years ago:

> The effect, which is before us in the chart, is the natural one of perpetual loans; for though it might have been managed a little better, or a little worse, as long as it continued upon this plan, it must have increased, unless as much money had been levied in time of peace, as would pay off the debt contracted in the previous war; but if this were done, it would be the same with annuities, because it would be raising taxes to pay off, at a certain time, the capital of the debt. That, however, has not been done, except, during this last war, content with getting possession of the money, we have left to future generations the trouble of repaying it [p. 85].

And he concludes with the prediction that heavy taxation will result in the "general penury of the middle and lower classes" [p. 86]. (Compare to Francis Amasa Walker's U.S. public debt chart of 1870 in the Landmark Atlases section.)

Sociology & Economics

✳ [*Opposite*] "Chart Representing the Reduction of the National Debt by the Sinking Fund, Already Established." Copperplate chart, with added color, 15.3 × 8.4 cm. Plate 21 from Playfair's *The Commercial and Political Atlas* (1801) [Rare Books Division].

Playfair's companion chart to the previous one, with the same dimensions, allowing the viewer to make an exact comparison. Governments and corporate bodies establish sinking funds, primarily from surpluses, to retire debt. Great Britain first used them in the eighteenth century, but its war with France in the 1790s greatly limited their viability—and this projection of Playfair proved more wishful than useful.

✳ [*Below*] "Chart Shewing the Value of the Quarter of Wheat in Shillings & in Days Wages of a Good Mechanic [*i.e.*, smith, mason, carpenter] from 1565 to 1821." Copperplate chart, with added color, 13.5 × 28.7 cm. From Playfair's *A Letter on Our Agricultural Distresses, Their Causes and Remedies: Accompanied with Tables and Copper-plate Charts, Shewing and Comparing the Prices of Wheat, Bread, and Labour, from 1565 to 1821. Addressed to the Lords and Commons* (London: Printed for William Sams, 1821) [Rare Books Division].

This is one of Playfair's final works, an interesting example of his smaller publications addressing national economic issues.

I have adopted, for the sake of illustration, the method I invented nearly forty years ago, of representing, by charts and diagrams, the progress and proportional amounts of prices; that method having met with much approbation on the Continent, and Baron Humboldt [Alexander von Humboldt] having declared it to be the best mode of impressing on the mind proportional quantities.—The unqualified approbation of that great philosopher and traveler is deemed a sufficient reason for adopting that mode of illustration on this important subject [p. iv].

His graph argues his point, which he presents "[f]or the sake of putting an end to mistaken theories, and to shew that the wages of labour never bore so favourable a proportion to the price of wheat as they do at this time" [pp. 51–52]. Wages equivalent to seventy-three days of work were required in Queen Elizabeth's time to buy the same amount of wheat as that purchased with less than fourteen days during the reign of George IV.

✳ [*Overleaf*] "Linear Chronology, Exhibiting the Revenues, Expenditure, Debt, Price of Stocks & Bread, from 1770 to 1824." Copperplate chart, with added color, 12 × 39.4 cm. From *Chronology of Public Events and Remarkable Occurrences within the Last Fifty Years; or from 1774 to 1824* (London: G. and W. B. Whittaker, 1824) [Rare Books Division].

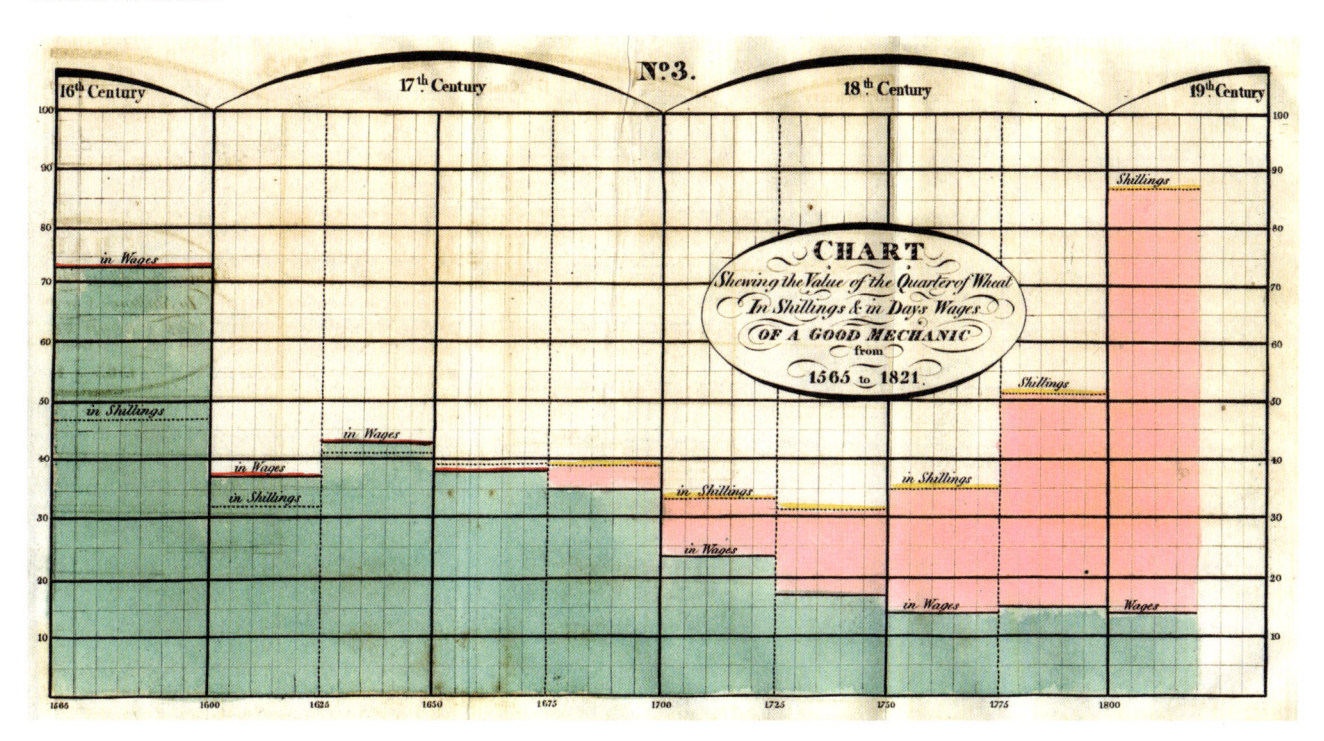

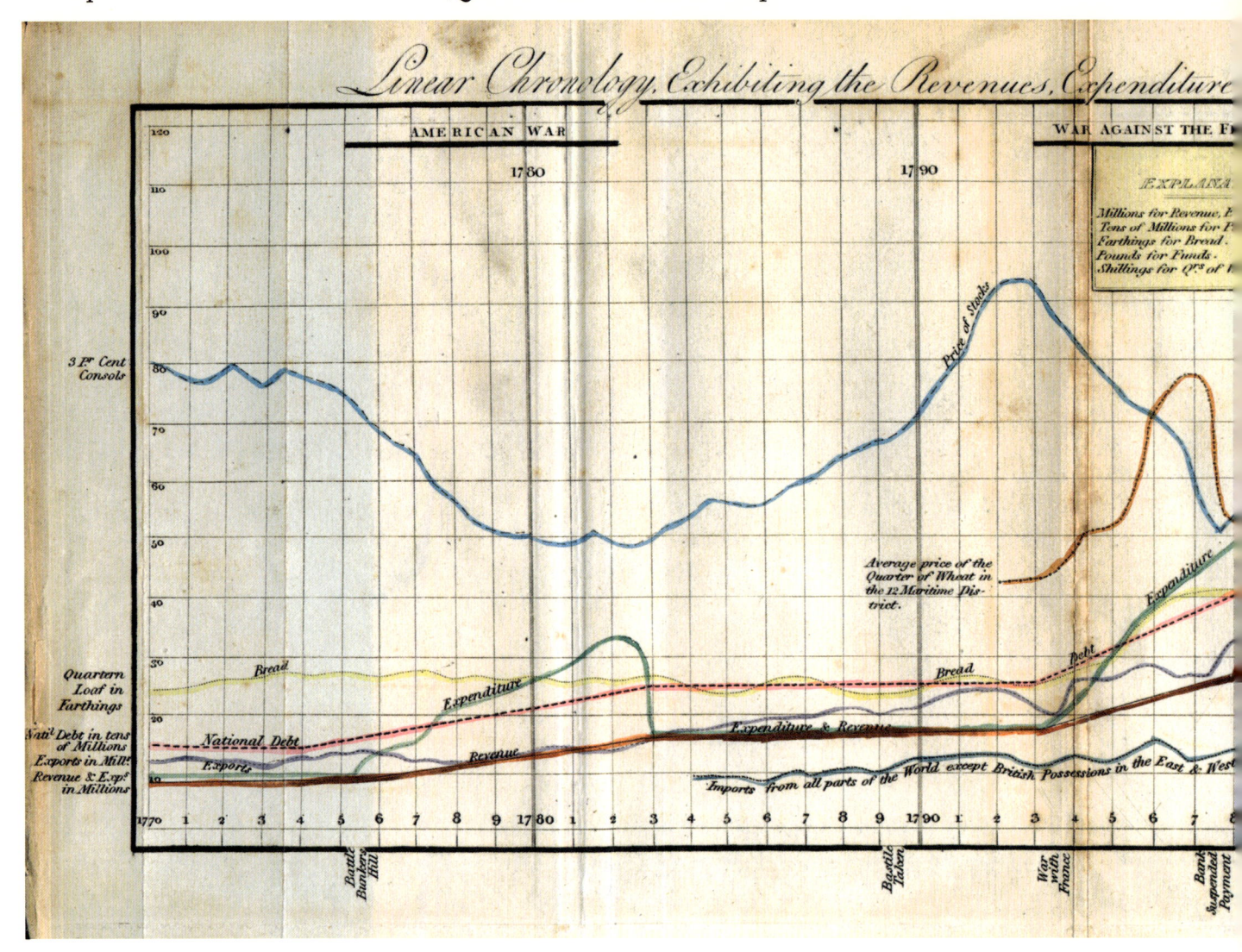

This volume was intended to be a perpetual publication, adding a year on at the end while removing one from the beginning, so that it would continually present a record of the last fifty years. Here, Playfair's popular time line has been extrapolated beyond his death (1823) for another year.

CHARLES DUPIN
1784–1873

THE MIDDLE SON of a French lawyer and legislator, Charles Dupin made his mark in mathematics, economics, and education. In 1803 he graduated from the École Polytechnique (Paris) as a naval engineer; among early assignments, he restored France's damaged arsenal on the island of Corfu (1808–1811) and exhaustively toured English commercial and military dockyards and installations to report (in six volumes) on their technical advances. He made numerous contributions in the field of geometry, including the "Dupin cyclide," the "Dupin indicatrix," and "Dupin's theorem." From 1819 to 1854, he was professor of mechanics at the Paris Conservatoire des Arts et Métiers, where his free public lectures on mathematics and mechanics were very popular. King Louis XVIII made him a baron in 1824. In later life, Dupin was active in politics, becoming a member of the senate in 1852. He was a strong advocate for the construction of schools, roads, and canals, and favored the use of steam power. Among his many writings on economic topics, none had a more powerful impact than his detailed study of French commercial activity (2 vols., 1827). Its associated chloropleth map on public education, a key to prosperity, provided a new vista for viewing sociological data.

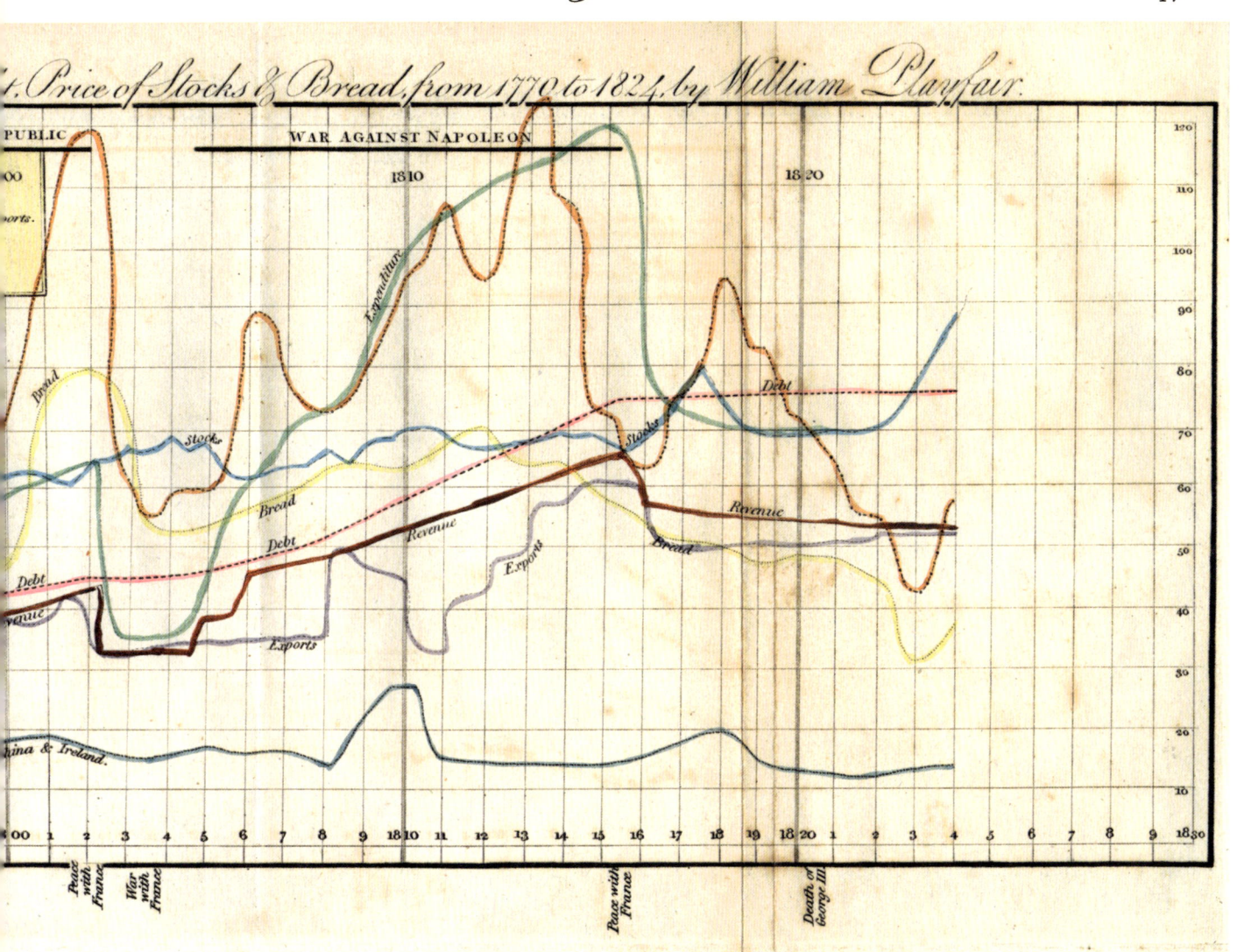

✻ [*Overleaf*] Title page of vol. 1 of Dupin's *Forces productives et commerciales de la France* (Paris: Bachelier, 1827) [General Library Collection].

The first work with a thematic map on "moral statistics."(Unfortunately, many copies lack the important map.) Princeton's copy is inscribed by Dupin on the half title page.

✻ [*Overleaf*] Autograph letter by Dupin to George Richardson Porter, director of the statistical office of the British Board of Trade, dated 7 September [or October?] 1836, Dover [England] [Wild Autograph Collection, Manuscripts Division].

Dupin had recently attended the August meeting of

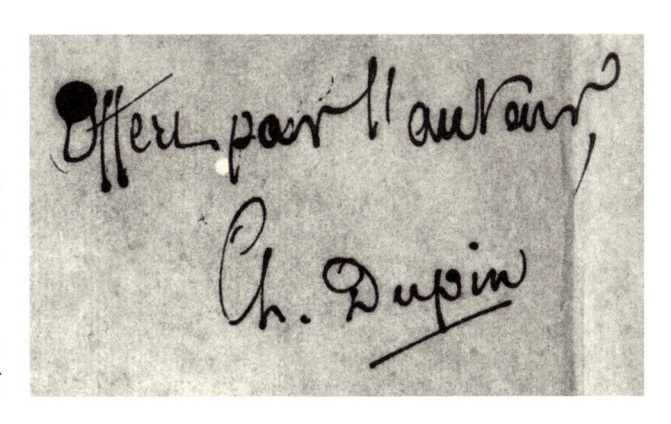

148 · Quantitative Thematic Maps

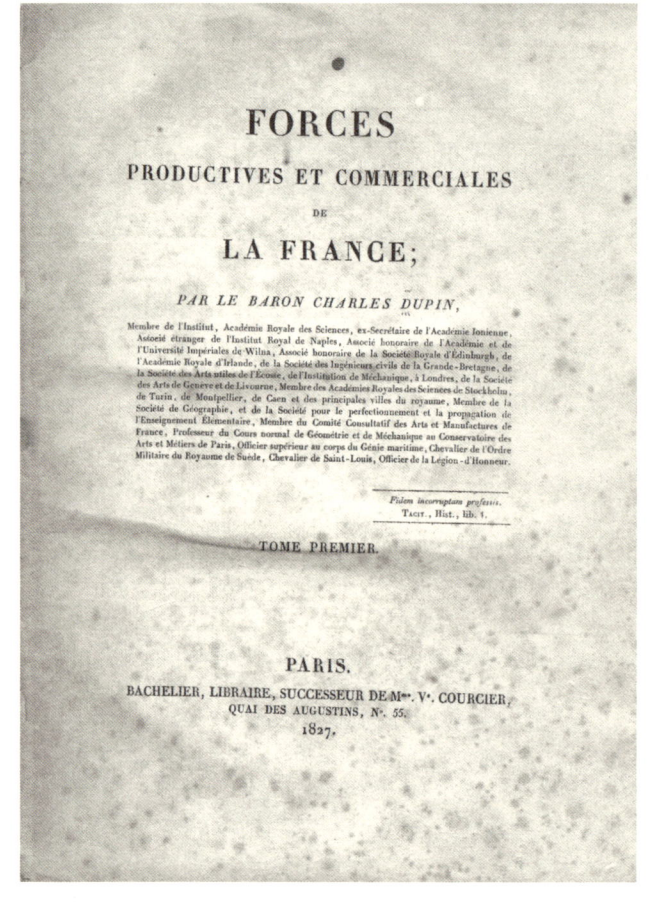

the Statistical Section of the British Association for the Advancement of Science in Bristol, England, presenting a paper on the relationship of the price of grain to population growth in France. He found that price had no influence on the number of births or deaths. Two days later,

> The Baron Dupin exhibited a map of England, illustrating the proportion of crime to the density of

---

✱ [*Above*] Caricature of Baron Charles Dupin by Honoré Daumier, published in *Le Charivari* (Paris) on 18 June 1849, from his series on French legislators [Graphic Arts Collection].

population, from which it appeared that the ratio of crime generally increased proportionally with that of density, especially in offences against property [*Proceedings of the Statistical Society of London*, 1, no. 8. (1836–37): 190].

In this letter to Porter, Dupin admits to not having had the time to arrange with "Mr. Ch Knight" for the printing of his comparative map on population and criminality—this task he leaves to Porter. (Charles Knight was the publisher of the Society's journal and a number of other important publications. Apparently, the map was never published, for no copy is known.) In addition, Dupin reminds Porter that he was promised statistical data "for this year" on Britain's finance, army, and navy.

Trying to understand the social transformations that were underway in early Victorian society motivated statisticians and public reformers in England to form several statistical societies in the 1830s. These developments were influenced by their European counterparts like Frenchman Dupin and, even more directly, by the Belgian Adolphe Quetelet. (See his entry in this Sociology and Economics section.) Dupin's letter illustrates the cross-fertilization of this period.

ESSAI
SUR LA
STATISTIQUE MORALE
DE
LA FRANCE,
PRÉCÉDÉ D'UN RAPPORT A L'ACADÉMIE DES SCIENCES,
PAR MM. LACROIX, SILVESTRE ET GIRARD;
PAR A. M. GUERRY,
AVOCAT A LA COUR ROYALE.

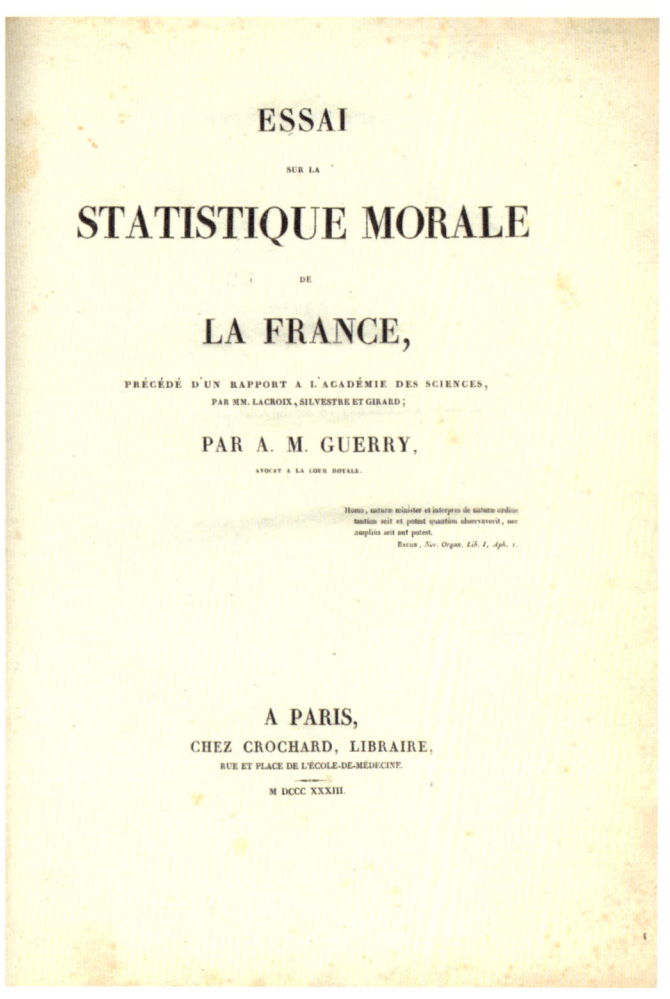

Homo, naturæ minister et interpres de naturæ ordine
tantum scit et potest quantum observaverit, nec
amplius scit aut potest.
Bacon, Nov. Organ. Lib. I, Aph. 1.

A PARIS,
CHEZ CROCHARD, LIBRAIRE,
RUE ET PLACE DE L'ÉCOLE-DE-MÉDECINE.
M DCCC XXXIII.

ANDRÉ-MICHEL GUERRY
1802–1866

An only child, A.-M. Guerry broke from the usual family pattern of blue-collar work and became a lawyer. Around 1825, he was admitted to the bar in Paris as a royal advocate (prosecutor). Soon afterwards he began working in the Ministry of Justice on crime statistics drawn from the *Compte générale de l'administration de la justice*. Commissioned by the Ministry in 1825, this was a massive project to compile criminal justice data for the whole nation, the first centralized system of its kind, a forerunner of modern national crime databases. These statistics became Guerry's life's work, for he realized their importance in developing public policy. He abandoned law to devote himself exclusively to analyzing and interpreting this data and gathering additional data on his own. He was appointed the Ministry's director of criminal statistics after the Revolution of 1830.

Guerry's publications based on his statistical research gained widespread attention. His first was a collaborative effort (1829) with the Italian geographer and ethnographer Adriano Balbi (1782–1848), a large broadside containing three thematic maps of France: crimes against persons, crimes against property, and literacy. The relationship between crime and education was a particular interest for him. His magnum opus was a comparative study of England and France using "moral statistics": *Statistique morale de l'Angleterre comparée avec la statistique morale de la France, d'après les comptes de l'administration de la justice criminelle en Angleterre et en France, etc.* (Paris, 1864). It was awarded the French Academy of Sciences' grand prize in statistics.

❋ Title page of Guerry's *Essai sur la statistique morale de la France, précédé d'un rapport à l'Académie des sciences, par MM. Lacroix, Silvestre et Girard* (Paris: Crochard, 1833) [Historic Maps Collection]. Note that Guerry quotes Sir Francis Bacon's famous aphorism here.

First use of the term "moral statistics": what today would fall under the umbrella of sociology. In his introduction, Guerry makes reference to the authoritative words of Alexander von Humboldt and William Playfair to help justify his reasons for employing new graphical techniques to display his data—but that perhaps is not necessary, he believes, for the results are striking and speak for themselves. He does not subscribe to any theory; rather, he identifies his information sources so that others may be assured of his exactitude and sincerity.

The basic conclusion that Guerry draws, convincingly—after the presentation of all of his statistics and maps—is that

> … la plupart des faits de l'ordre moral, considérés dans les masses, et non dans les individus, sont déterminés par des causes régulières, dont les variations sont renfermées dans d'étroites limites, et qu'ils peuvent être soumis, comme ceux de l'ordre matériel, à l'observation directe et numérique [p. 69]. [On a population basis, most facts related to the "moral sphere" have recurring causes whose exceptions are narrowly confined, and that can be analyzed, as they are in the physical world, by statistical observation.]

Here is a strong and early advocacy of the "science" in social sciences. The volume was awarded the 1833 Prix Montyon for statistics and remains a foundational study of criminology and sociology.

✳ [*Overleaf*] "Crimes contre les personnes." Lithograph map with data table, 25.6 × 20 cm. Plate I from Guerry's *Essai sur la statistique morale de la France* ... (1833) [Historic Maps Collection].

A chloropleth map, a form pioneered by Charles Dupin (see his entry in this Sociology and Economics section) which uses gradations of shading to show changes in levels of data. Here, from dark brown to white, the shades of the eighty-six administrative departments of France reflect six to seven different levels of crime against persons (as opposed to crimes against property, the subject of another map). Moreover, the departments are numbered in order of crime rate, from highest to least. The exact crime numbers for the specific departments are provided in the table at the bottom. Visually, one easily can see that the southern regions of France, and those directly bordering Germany, have the most crime. Corsica has the highest rate of all: 1 out of every 2,199 people has been accused of committing a crime against someone else. In the accompanying text, Guerry provides a table showing how the rate of this kind of crime has grown for each of five regions (south, east, north, west, central) over the years from 1825 to 1830. The average rate for France as a whole for the six-year period was 1 crime per 17,085 inhabitants.

✳ [*Overleaf*] "Donations aux pauvres." Lithograph map with data table, 25.6 × 20 cm. Plate V from Guerry's *Essai sur la statistique morale de la France*... (1833) [Historic Maps Collection].

A similar chloropleth map utilizing data taken from the government's *Bulletin des lois*, showing the frequency of donations/bequests to the poor per number of residents. (This is independent of the value of each gift.) An interesting detail that strikes one immediately, in comparison with the previous map, is that Corsica has the fewest number of such gifts but the highest crime rate (learned from the other map). Guerry notes that donations are higher in regions where Catholic clergy are more widespread. These kinds of "relationships"—if, indeed, there is one—are amplified in a thematic map.

✳ [*Overleaf*] "Suicides." Lithograph map with data table, 25.6 × 20 cm. Plate VI from Guerry's *Essai sur la statistique morale de la France* ... (1833) [Historic Maps Collection].

Another chloropleth map based on the unpublished data on suicides in Paris that Guerry collected over many years as well as official records published in the *Compte générale de la justice criminelle* for the years 1827 to 1830. (Reported suicides, Guerry argues, are fewer than those known.) The map confirms what one might expect: the highest suicide rate is in Paris (Seine department); in fact, the rate increases as one approaches the capital. However, what is remarkable about this phenomenon, according to Guerry, is that it does not seem specifically related to population density, level of education, distribution of clergy, or level of crime in the surrounding districts—only their proximity to Paris. If men like Voltaire and Montesquieu cannot agree on the cause of suicide, Guerry says that he will not presume to know the reason—yet. Clearly, he concludes, more study is needed.

✳ [*Overleaf*] "Résultats divers." Plate VII from Guerry's *Essai sur la statistique morale de la France* ... (1833) [Historic Maps Collection].

A tabular rendition of various different views of Guerry's moral statistics: crimes against persons and property by sex and then by month, type of murder victim following adultery (for example, "outraged husband" or "wife's lover"), literacy by region, and suicides by age and method (gun or hanging). Except for the literacy graph, there are no geographical aspects to the data, hence no possibility for thematic map versions.

GEORGE POULETT SCROPE
1797–1876

GEORGE POULETT SCROPE is best known as a geologist who specialized in, and made notable contributions to, the study of volcanoes. He explored volcanic regions in Italy and France and, in fact, was present at the 1822 eruption of Mt. Vesuvius. His work *Considerations on Volcanos* (1825), later amplified and retitled *Volcanos* (1862), was a classic textbook on the subject, promoting a theory of the earth born out of fire

CRIMES CONTRE LES PERSONNES.

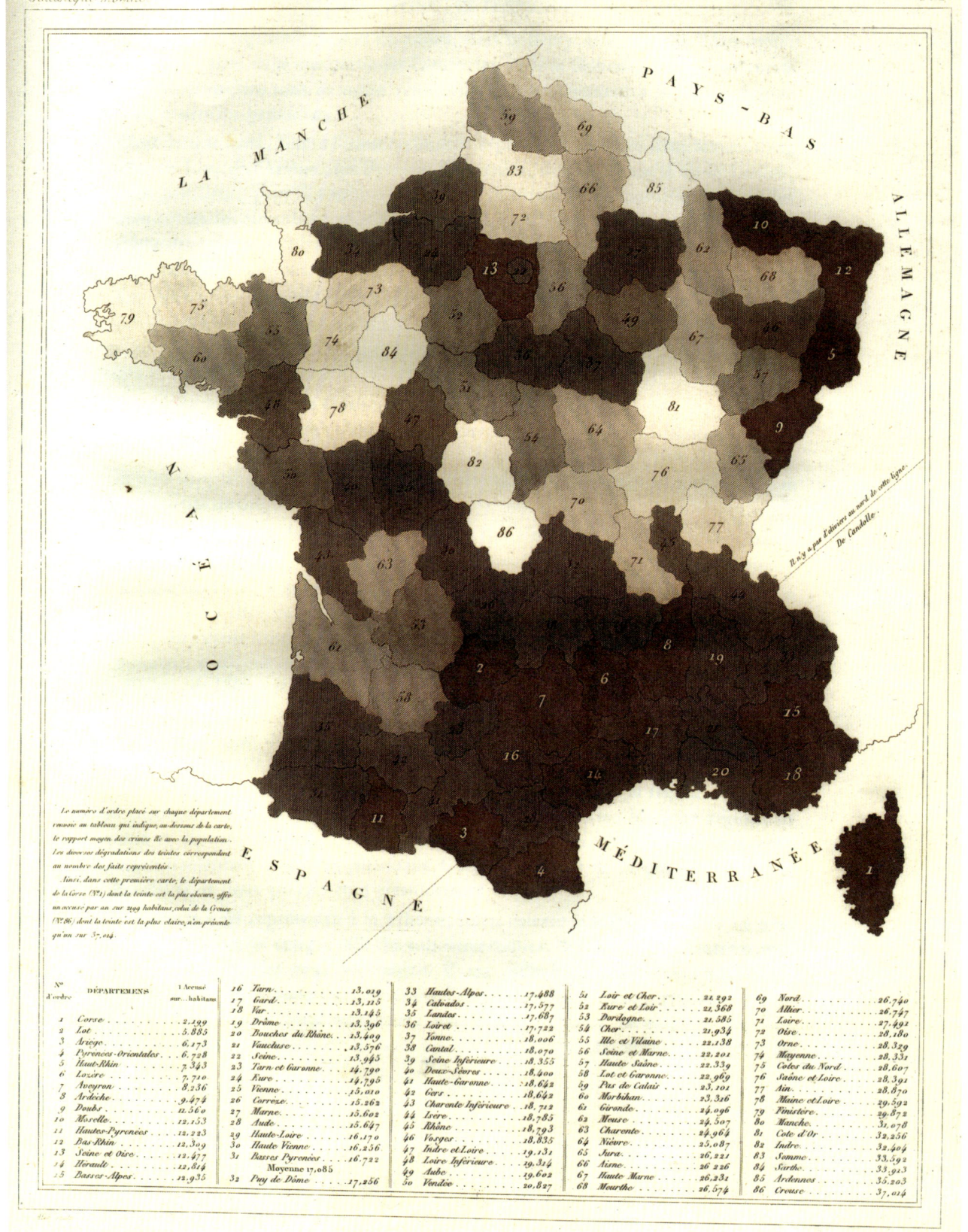

Statistique morale.   Pl. I.

Il n'y a pas d'accusés au nord de cette ligne.
De Candolle.

Le numero d'ordre placé sur chaque département renvoie au tableau qui indique, au-dessous de la carte, le rapport moyen des crimes là avec la population. Les diverses dégradations des teintes correspondent au nombre des faits représentés.

Ainsi, dans cette première carte, le département de la Corse (N°1) dont la teinte est la plus obscure, offre un accusé par an sur 2199 habitans, celui de la Creuse (N°86) dont la teinte est la plus claire, n'en présente qu'un sur 37,014.

N° d'ordre	DÉPARTEMENS	1 Accusé sur habitans										
1	Corse	2,199	16	Tarn	13,029	33	Hautes-Alpes	17,488	51	Loir et Cher	21,292	69	Nord	26,740
2	Lot	5,885	17	Gard	13,115	34	Calvados	17,577	52	Eure et Loir	21,368	70	Allier	26,747
3	Ariège	6,173	18	Var	13,145	35	Landes	17,687	53	Dordogne	21,585	71	Loire	27,492
4	Pyrénées-Orientales	6,728	19	Drôme	13,396	36	Loiret	17,722	54	Cher	21,934	72	Oise	28,180
5	Haut-Rhin	7,343	20	Bouches du Rhône	13,409	37	Yonne	17,722	55	Ille et Vilaine	22,138	73	Orne	28,329
6	Lozère	7,710	21	Vaucluse	13,576	38	Cantal	18,006	56	Seine et Marne	22,201	74	Mayenne	28,331
7	Aveyron	8,236	22	Seine	13,945	39	Seine Inférieure	18,070	57	Haute Saône	22,339	75	Côtes du Nord	28,607
8	Ardèche	9,474	23	Tarn et Garonne	14,790	40	Deux-Sèvres	18,355	58	Lot et Garonne	22,969	76	Saône et Loire	28,391
9	Doubs	11,560	24	Eure	14,795	41	Haute-Garonne	18,400	59	Pas de Calais	23,101	77	Ain	28,870
10	Moselle	12,153	25	Vienne	15,010	42	Gers	18,642	60	Morbihan	23,316	78	Maine et Loire	29,592
11	Hautes-Pyrénées	12,223	26	Corrèze	15,262	43	Charente Inférieure	18,712	61	Gironde	24,096	79	Finistère	29,872
12	Bas-Rhin	12,309	27	Marne	15,602	44	Isère	18,785	62	Meuse	24,507	80	Manche	31,078
13	Seine et Oise	12,477	28	Aude	15,647	45	Rhône	18,793	63	Charente	24,964	81	Côte d'Or	32,256
14	Hérault	12,814	29	Haute-Loire	16,170	46	Vosges	18,835	64	Nièvre	25,087	82	Indre	32,404
15	Basses-Alpes	12,935	30	Haute Vienne	16,256	47	Indre et Loire	19,131	65	Jura	26,221	83	Somme	33,592
			31	Basses Pyrénées	16,722	48	Loire Inférieure	19,314	66	Aisne	26,226	84	Sarthe	33,913
				Moyenne	17,085	49	Aube	19,602	67	Haute Marne	26,231	85	Ardennes	35,203
			32	Puy de Dôme	17,256	50	Vendée	20,827	68	Meurthe	26,574	86	Creuse	37,014

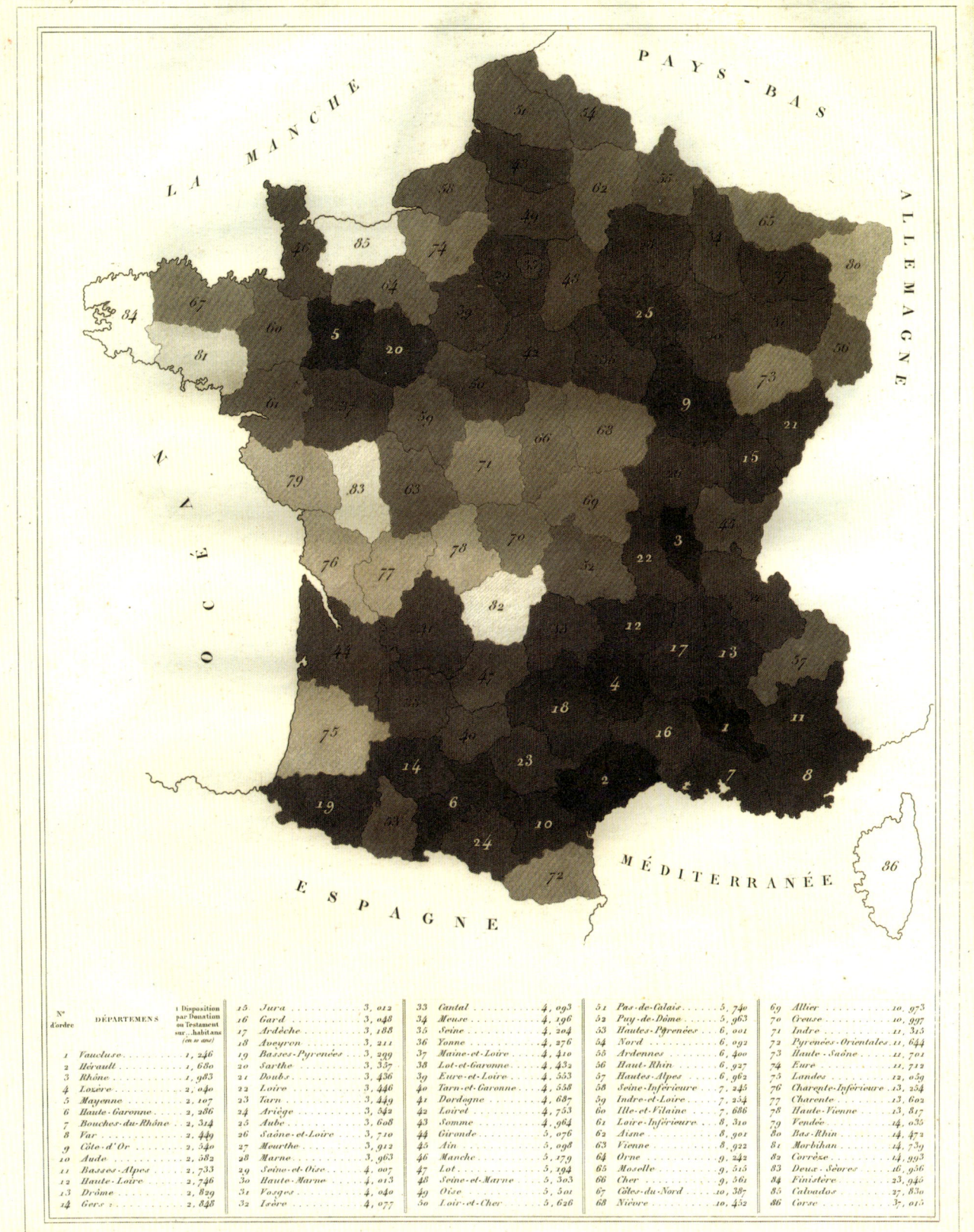

Statistique morale. DONATIONS AUX PAUVRES. Pl. V.

Nº d'ordre	DÉPARTEMENS	1 Disposition par Donation ou Testament sur ..habitans (en 10 ans)
1	Vaucluse	1,246
2	Hérault	1,680
3	Rhône	1,983
4	Lozère	2,040
5	Mayenne	2,107
6	Haute-Garonne	2,286
7	Bouches-du-Rhône	2,314
8	Var	2,449
9	Côte-d'Or	2,540
10	Aude	2,582
11	Basses-Alpes	2,733
12	Haute-Loire	2,746
13	Drôme	2,829
14	Gers	2,848
15	Jura	3,012
16	Gard	3,048
17	Ardèche	3,188
18	Aveyron	3,211
19	Basses-Pyrénées	3,299
20	Sarthe	3,337
21	Doubs	3,436
22	Loire	3,446
23	Tarn	3,449
24	Ariège	3,542
25	Aube	3,608
26	Saône-et-Loire	3,710
27	Meurthe	3,912
28	Marne	3,963
29	Seine-et-Oise	4,007
30	Haute-Marne	4,013
31	Vosges	4,040
32	Isère	4,077
33	Cantal	4,093
34	Meuse	4,196
35	Seine	4,204
36	Yonne	4,276
37	Maine-et-Loire	4,410
38	Lot-et-Garonne	4,432
39	Eure-et-Loire	4,553
40	Tarn-et-Garonne	4,558
41	Dordogne	4,687
42	Loiret	4,753
43	Somme	4,964
44	Gironde	5,076
45	Ain	5,098
46	Manche	5,179
47	Lot	5,194
48	Seine-et-Marne	5,303
49	Oise	5,501
50	Loir-et-Cher	5,626
51	Pas-de-Calais	5,740
52	Puy-de-Dôme	5,963
53	Hautes-Pyrénées	6,001
54	Nord	6,092
55	Ardennes	6,400
56	Haut-Rhin	6,927
57	Hautes-Alpes	6,962
58	Seine-Inférieure	7,245
59	Indre-et-Loire	7,254
60	Ille-et-Vilaine	7,686
61	Loire-Inférieure	8,310
62	Aisne	8,901
63	Vienne	8,922
64	Orne	9,242
65	Moselle	9,515
66	Cher	9,561
67	Côtes-du-Nord	10,387
68	Nièvre	10,452
69	Allier	10,973
70	Creuse	10,997
71	Indre	11,315
72	Pyrénées-Orientales	11,644
73	Haute-Saône	11,701
74	Eure	11,712
75	Landes	12,059
76	Charente-Inférieure	13,254
77	Charente	13,602
78	Haute-Vienne	13,817
79	Vendée	14,035
80	Bas-Rhin	14,472
81	Morbihan	14,739
82	Corrèze	14,993
83	Deux-Sèvres	16,956
84	Finistère	23,946
85	Calvados	27,830
86	Corse	37,015

SUICIDES.

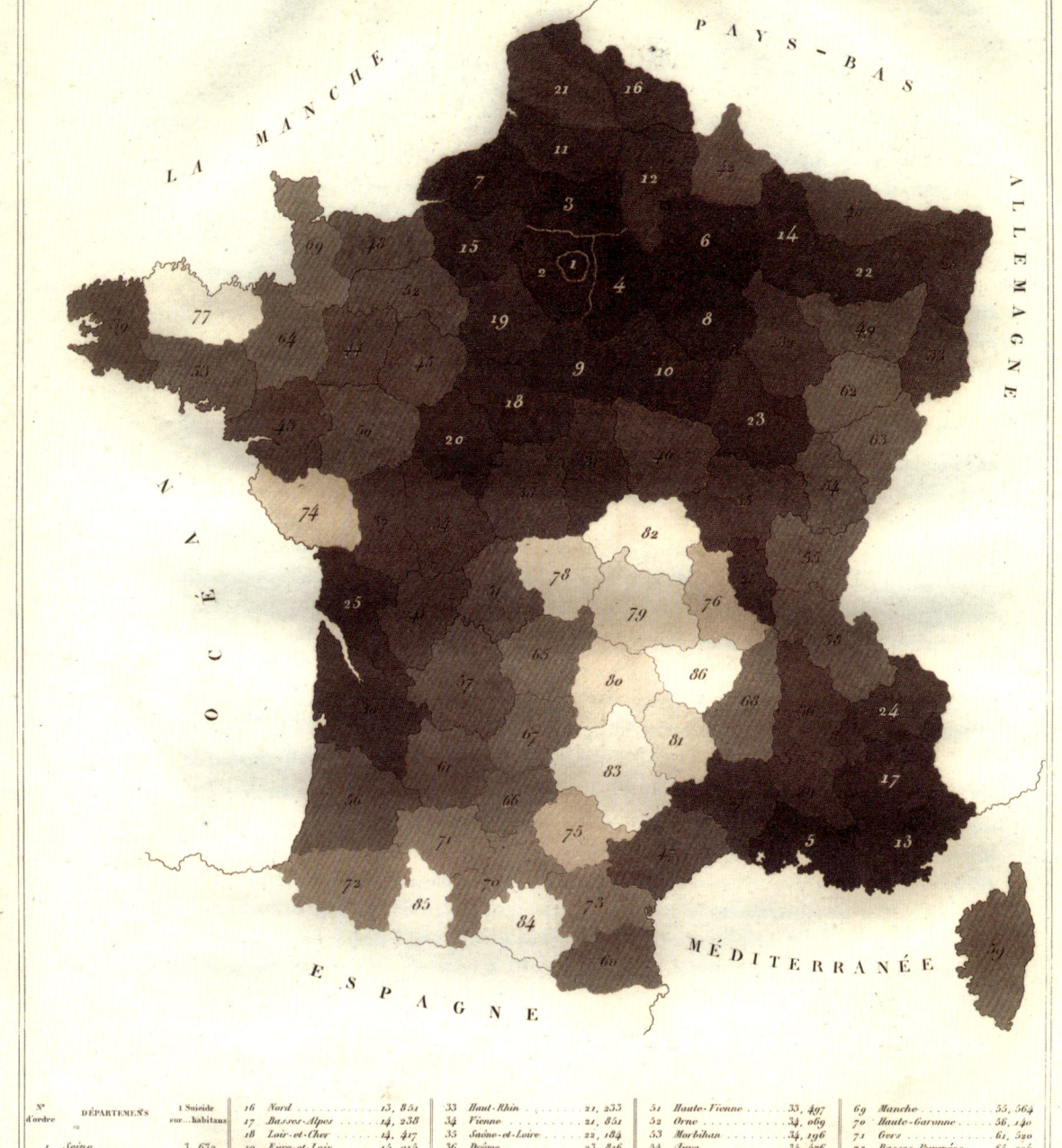

Statistique morale.   Pl. VI

N° d'ordre	DÉPARTEMENS	1 Suicide sur... habitans
1	Seine	3,632
2	Seine-et-Oise	5,460
3	Oise	5,994
4	Seine-et-Marne	7,315
5	Bouches-du-Rhône	8,107
6	Marne	8,334
7	Seine-Inférieure	9,523
8	Aube	10,989
9	Loiret	11,815
10	Yonne	12,789
11	Somme	12,836
12	Aisne	12,883
13	Var	13,380
14	Meuse	13,465
15	Eure	13,493
16	Nord	13,851
17	Basses-Alpes	14,238
18	Loir-et-Cher	14,417
19	Eure-et-Loir	15,015
20	Indre-et-Loire	15,272
21	Pas-de-Calais	15,400
22	Meurthe	15,652
23	Côte-d'Or	16,128
24	Hautes-Alpes	16,171
25	Charente-Inférieure	16,798
26	Rhône	17,063
27	Gard	18,292
	Moyenne	18,520
28	Bas-Rhin	18,625
29	Vaucluse	19,024
30	Gironde	19,220
31	Cher	19,497
32	Haute-Marne	19,586
33	Haut-Rhin	21,233
34	Vienne	21,851
35	Saône-et-Loire	22,184
36	Drôme	23,816
37	Deux-Sèvres	24,533
38	Indre	25,014
39	Finistère	25,143
40	Moselle	25,572
41	Charente	25,720
42	Ardennes	26,198
43	Loire-Inférieure	27,289
44	Mayenne	28,331
45	Sarthe	29,280
46	Nièvre	29,381
47	Hérault	30,869
48	Calvados	31,807
49	Vosges	33,029
50	Maine-et-Loire	33,358
51	Haute-Vienne	33,497
52	Orne	34,069
53	Morbihan	34,196
54	Jura	34,476
55	Ain	35,039
56	Landes	35,375
57	Dordogne	36,024
58	Isère	36,275
59	Corse	37,016
60	Pyrénées-Orientales	37,843
61	Lot-et-Garonne	38,501
62	Haute-Saône	39,714
63	Doubs	40,690
64	Ille-et-Vilaine	45,180
65	Corrèze	47,480
66	Tarn-et-Garonne	48,317
67	Lot	48,785
68	Ardèche	52,547
69	Manche	55,564
70	Haute-Garonne	56,140
71	Gers	61,520
72	Basses-Pyrénées	65,995
73	Aude	66,496
74	Vendée	67,963
75	Tarn	68,980
76	Loire	71,564
77	Côtes-du-Nord	75,056
78	Creuse	77,825
79	Puy-de-Dôme	78,148
80	Cantal	87,338
81	Lozère	111,022
82	Allier	114,121
83	Aveyron	116,671
84	Ariège	123,525
85	Hautes-Pyrénées	148,039
86	Haute-Loire	163,242

RÉSULTATS DIVERS.

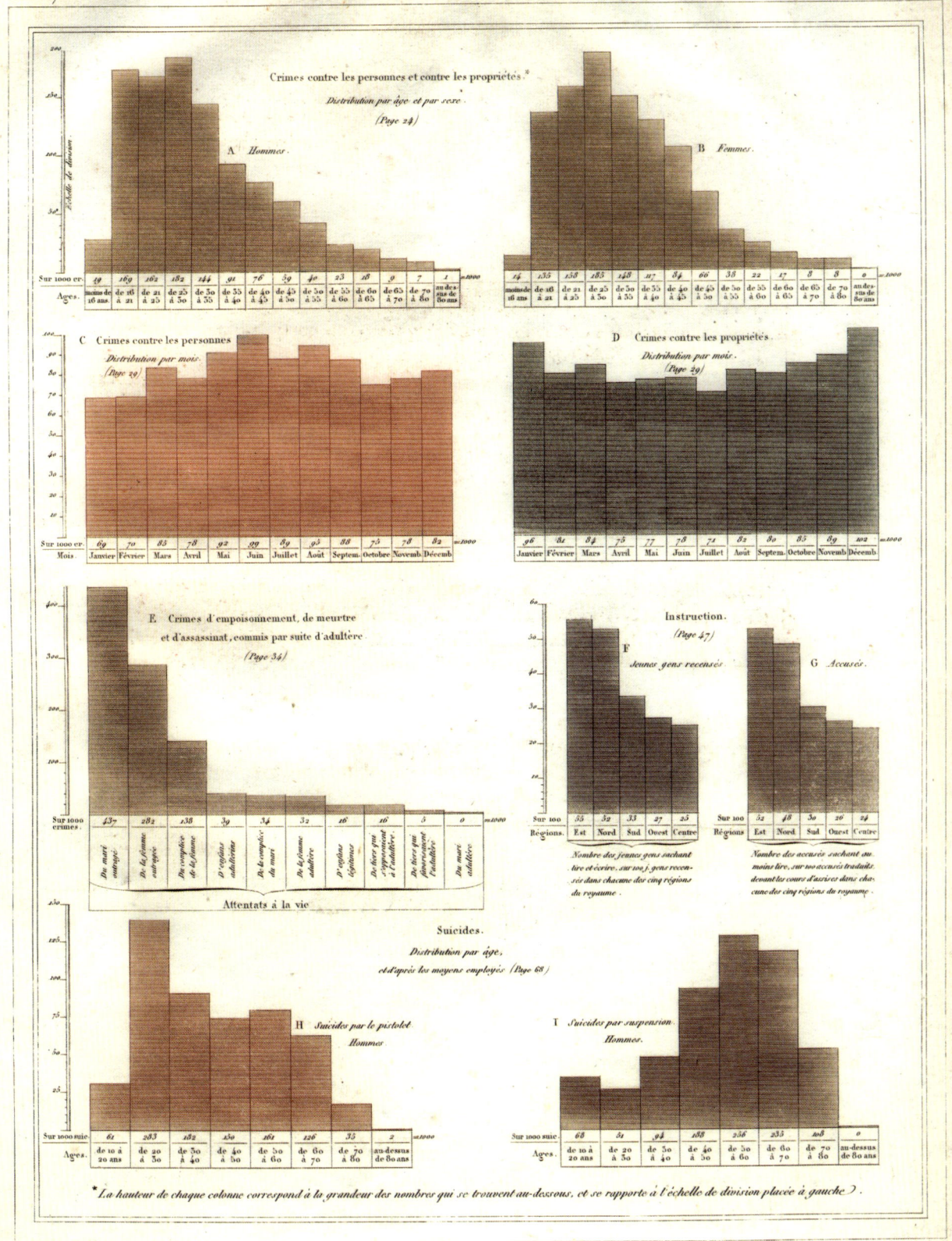

✷ Portrait of George Poulett Scrope. From vol. 2 of Sir Archibald Geikie's *Life of Sir Roderick I. Murchison...* (London: J. Murray, 1875) [General Library Collection].

(volcanism) rather than water (neptunism, the crystallization of minerals from the oceans). Scrope believed that present volcanic processes provided windows into the past. In 1867, he was awarded the prestigious Wollaston Medal by the Geological Society of London (see also the William Smith entry in the Geology section).

Born George Julius Poulett Thomson, Scrope changed his surname after marrying heiress Emma Phipps Scrope in 1821. For more than thirty years, he held a seat in the British House of Commons, where his major interests were political economy and welfare economics. He authored several dozen papers and pamphlets, but his most important theoretical work was *Principles of Political Economy, Deduced from the Natural Laws of Social Welfare, and Applied to the Present State of Britain* (1833). Considering himself a man of the people, he dedicated the book to his constituents: "Mutual regard, reciprocal confidence, and a general agreement on political principles, now form the bond of union between a parliamentary trustee and those who appoint him" [p. v]. Though much of what he writes has a relevant, contemporary air, the work has received more attention—at least from cartographic quarters—for its innovative world map.

✷ [*Opposite*] "Map Exhibiting the Comparative Extent of the Fully-Peopled, the Under-Peopled, and the Yet Un-Peopled Parts of the Earth." Lithograph map, 7.4 × 11.5 cm. Frontispiece to Scrope's *Principles of Political Economy* ... (London: Longman, Rees, Orme, Brown, Green & Longman, 1833) [Historic Maps Collection].

First world map to show population density. Scrope divides the land area into regions "averaging more than 200 inhabitants to the square mile" (black), "from ten to 200" (gray), and "less than ten inhabitants & rarely so much as one" (blank). Where he acquired his data is not given, and the map is not mentioned in the book.

ADOLPHE QUETELET
1796–1874

BELGIAN MATHEMATICIAN Adolphe Quetelet was among the first to apply probability and statistics to social phenomena in order to better understand the underlying causal factors. He was extremely influential in the development of European social science. His research interests also included astronomy and meteorology, and he succeeded in raising public and private funds for the building of an observatory in Brussels, which he then directed for the rest of his life.

In the early 1830s, Quetelet had an important role in forming the Statistical Section of the British Association for the Advancement of Science and the Statistical Society of London (now the Royal Statistical Society); he was the first foreign member of the American Statistical Association, founded in 1839. In 1853, he organized the first international statistics conference, held in Brussels. From 1834 onward, Quetelet served as secretary to Belgium's Royal Academy of Sciences.

One of Quetelet's best-known contributions, still used internationally today, is the concept of a body mass index, also called the Quetelet Index (QI). This is a simple mathematical tool that classifies a person's weight in comparison to an ideal weight for that person's height. The formula is QI = weight (in kilograms)

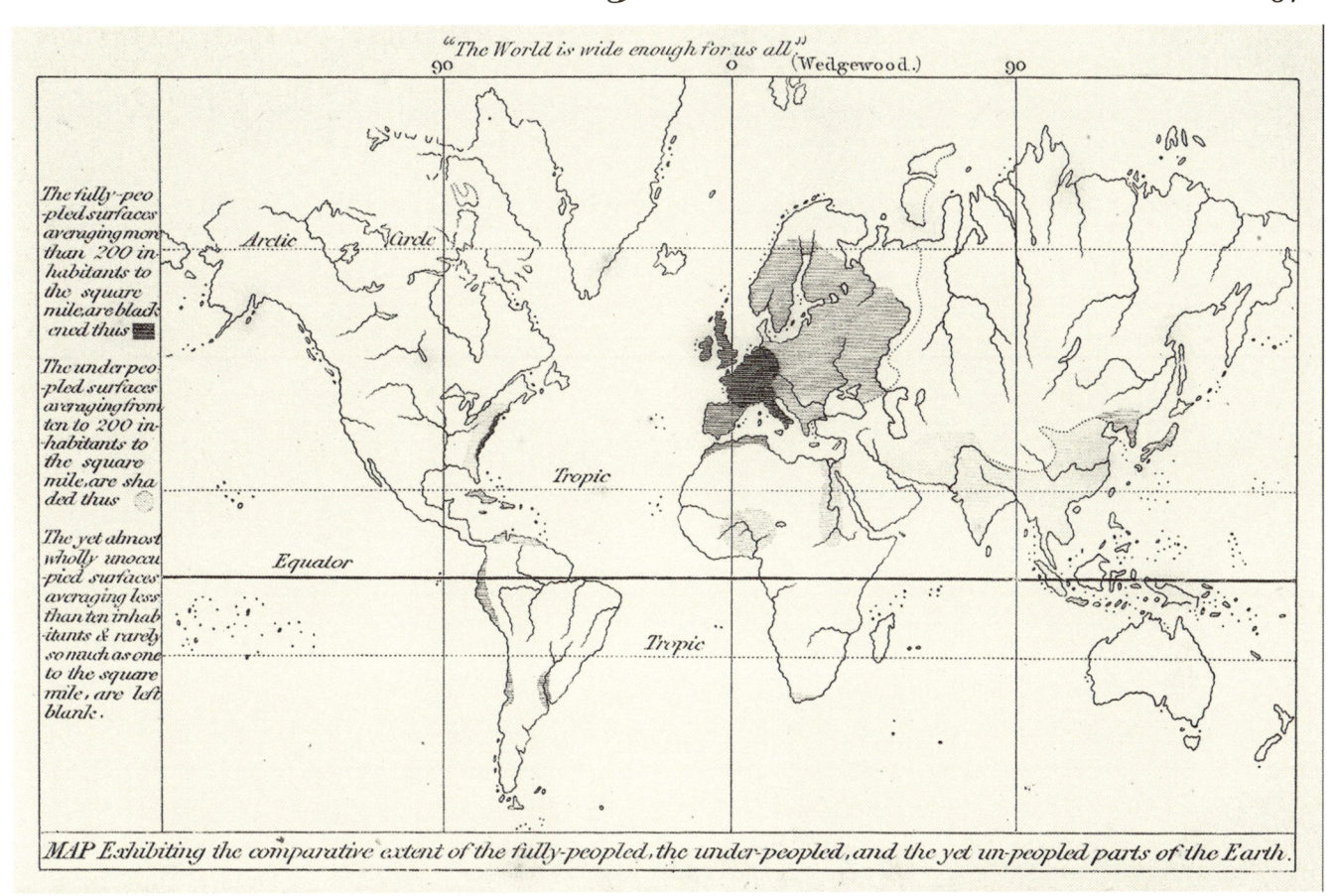

MAP Exhibiting the comparative extent of the fully-peopled, the under-peopled, and the yet un-peopled parts of the Earth.

"The World is wide enough for us all" (Wedgewood.)

The fully-peopled surfaces averaging more than 200 inhabitants to the square mile, are blackened thus ■

The under peopled surfaces averaging from ten to 200 inhabitants to the square mile, are shaded thus

The yet almost wholly unoccupied surfaces averaging less than ten inhabitants & rarely so much as one to the square mile, are left blank.

/ height (in meters)^2. Anyone with a QI that is greater than 30 is considered to be officially obese. The formula has had a significant role in fostering public health debates.

But it is Quetelet's concept of the average man (*l'homme moyen*) that has had the most profound effect on modern social research. As he wrote in his groundbreaking two-volume work, *Sur l'homme et le développement de ses facultés; ou, Essai de physique sociale* (1835),

> L'homme que je considère ici est, dans la société, l'analogue du centre de gravité dans les corps; il est la moyenne autour de laquelle oscillent les elements sociaux: ce sera, si l'on veut, un être fictif pour qui toutes les choses se passeront conformément aux resultants moyens obtenus pour la société [1836 ed., vol. 1, pp. 21–22]. [The man that I have in mind here is to society what the center of gravity is to the body, the middle around which orbit social phenomena; a fictional being, if you wish, for whom everything that happens conforms to the average outcomes achieved by society.]

✲ Portrait of Adolphe Quetelet. From *Annuaire de l'Académie royale des sciences, des lettres et des beaux arts de Belgique* 41 (1875): 108 [General Library Collection].

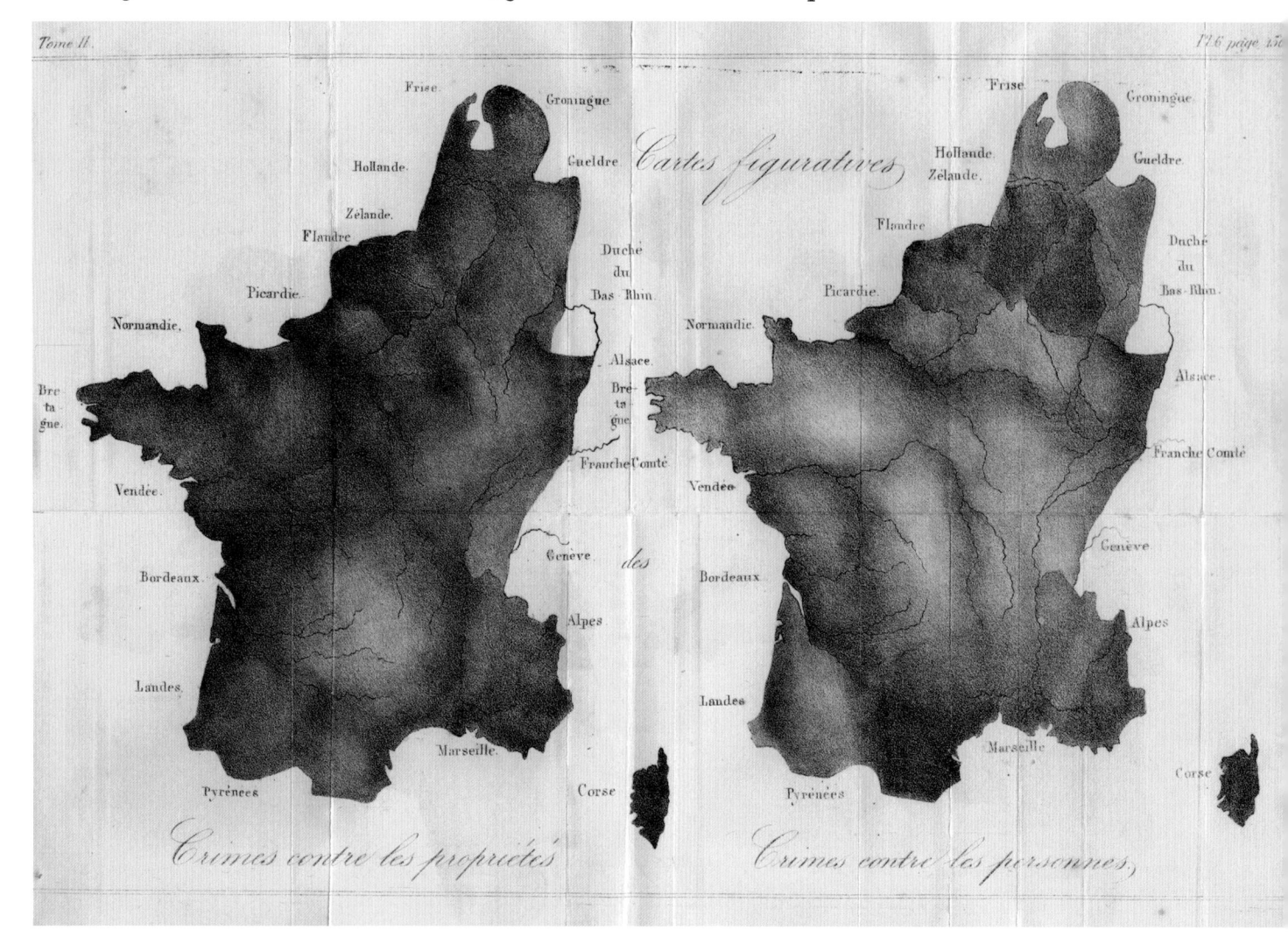

In his world of "social physics" (his coined phrase), Quetelet found the "average man" in the mean values of variables that followed a normal, or Gaussian, distribution (i.e., a bell curve). Much of his research focused on collecting data on those variables.

In his later work, Quetelet ventured to suggest that the average man was an ideal type toward which nature strove. The English naturalist Charles Darwin was aware of Quetelet's research in probability theory, but he went in an opposite direction: Darwin saw variations from the mean as evolution's raw materials for natural selection, whereas Quetelet saw such variations as accidents from the species' prototype.

Among those influenced by Quetelet's work were nursing pioneer Florence Nightingale (see her entry in the Medicine section), who met the statistician in 1860, and Sir Francis Galton (see his entry in the Meteorology section), who, building on Quetelet's bell-curve research, developed what he would call "eugenics."

✻ [*Above*] "Cartes figurative: Crimes contre les propriétés / Crimes contre les personnes." Two lithograph maps within one border, 21.5 × 33 cm. From Quetelet's *Sur l'homme et le développement de ses facultés; ou, Essai de physique sociale*, 2 vols. in 1 (Brussels: Louis Hauman, 1836) [Historic Maps Collection].

Landmark chloropleth maps on crime in France, showing a smoother, seamless distribution in their graphic presentation than those exhibited in similar maps by fellow countryman A.-M. Guerry (see his entry in this Sociology and Economics section). These were originally published in 1831.

ADOLPHE D'ANGEVILLE
1796–1856

SON OF A LANDOWNER in the Jura region of France bordering Switzerland, Adolphe d'Angeville spent his youth as a naval officer. His sister Henriette in 1838 became the second woman to climb Mont Blanc. From 1834 to 1848, d'Angeville held a seat in the Chamber of Deputies, the lower house of the French parliament. He synthesized data collected in Paris before and during that period into his great statistical work, *Essai sur la statistique de la population française, considerée sous quelques-uns de ses rapports physiques et moraux* (1836). This is now considered to be the first sweeping application of thematic cartography to national industrial and population data. However, during the French Revolution of 1848, d'Angeville returned to his family estate and met a jeering crowd that threw rocks at him and called him a *malthusien* (after Thomas Robert Malthus, the influential English demographer), which was then a great insult. Clearly, his work was not understood or appreciated in his time.

✳ [*Opposite*] Title page of d'Angeville's *Essai sur la statistique de la population française, considerée sous quelques-uns de ses rapports physiques et moraux* (Bourg: Impr. de F. Dufour, 1836 [i.e., 1837, appendix dated "juin 1837"]) [Historic Maps Collection].

Presentation copy to Monsieur Fazy-Pasteur with inscription by the author.

✳ [*Overleaf*] "Statistique de la population française. 1re. Carte." Lithograph map, 24.1 × 19.1 cm. From d'Angeville's *Essai sur la statistique de la population française …* (1836) [Historic Maps Collection].

One of the earliest chloropleth maps of population density. Using data from 1831, d'Angeville calculated density values for square myriamètres (kilometers) and then graphically displayed the results on his map by using darker shades/denser patterns for denser regions. Five different levels of density are shown; regions with close density values share the same shading. Crediting the example of fellow statistician Charles Dupin (see his entry in this Sociology and Economics section), d'Angeville praises the effect of this graphic representation of data:

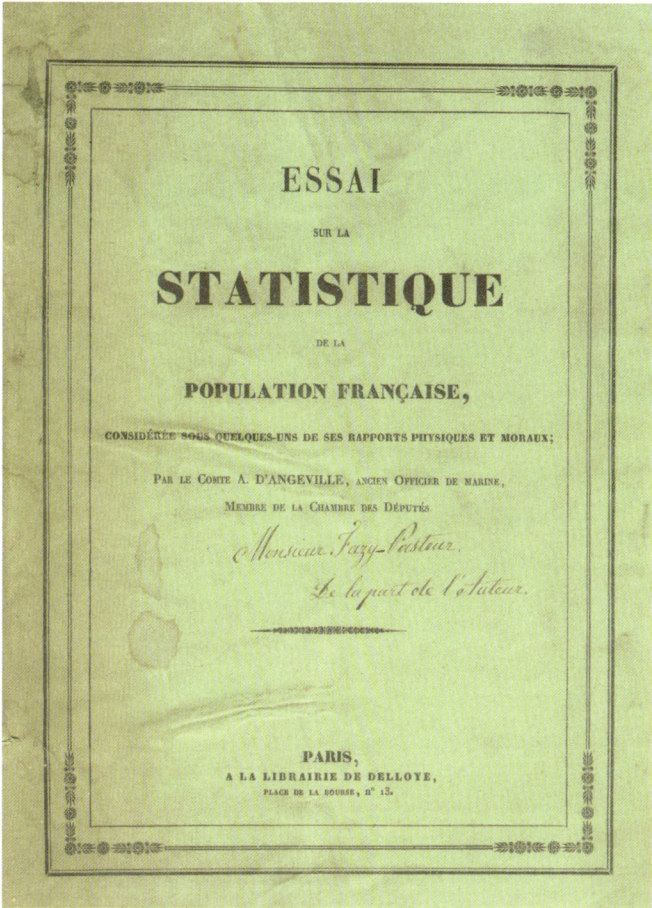

> Le moyen de parler aux yeux, que nous avons employé dans la 4me. Partie [the map section], … c'est que nous avons éprouvé souvent combien les moyens graphiques suppléent à l'aridité des énumerations; on arrive ainsi sans aucune fatigue d'esprit [p. 15]. [Speaking to the eyes with graphic methods avoids the aridity of numbers that fatigues the spirit.]

D'Angeville applies the same chloropleth technique in fifteen succeeding maps dealing with other sociological aspects of the French population, such as life expectancy, completion of primary education, level of crime, and illegitimate birth rate. An unusual statistic that he maps is the number of doors and windows found in homes per one hundred residents (from tax records)—presumably the greater number of openings in a house leads to more light and a healthier interior environment, and reflects higher incomes. The average in France at the time was 112 per 100 residents.

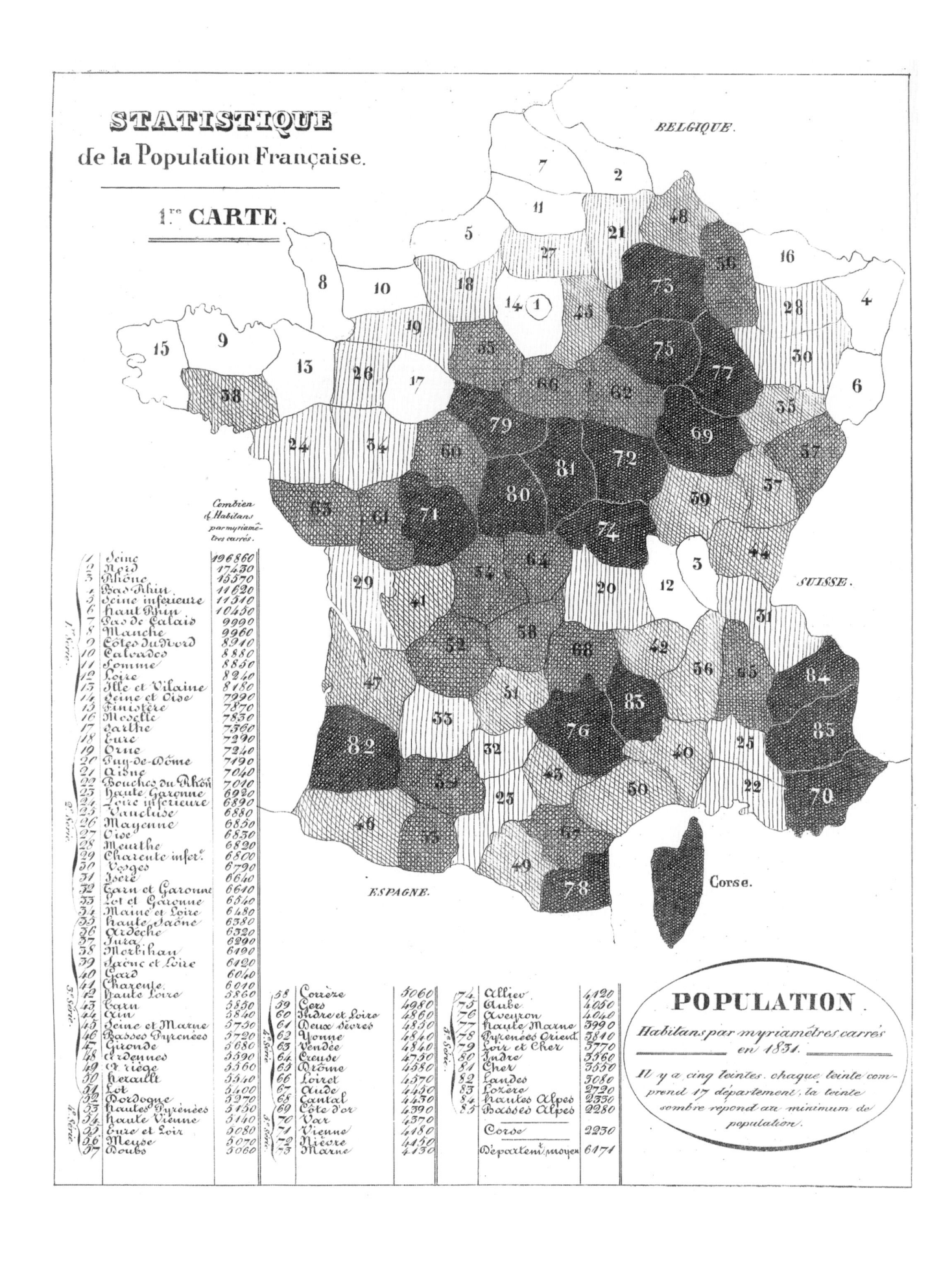

STATISTIQUE de la Population Française.

1re CARTE.

POPULATION.
Habitans par myriamètres carrés en 1831.

Il y a cinq teintes, chaque teinte comprend 17 départements, la teinte sombre répond au minimum de population.

Combien d'Habitans par myriamètres carrés.

1	Seine	196860
2	Nord	17430
3	Rhône	15570
4	Bas-Rhin	11620
5	Seine inférieure	11510
6	Haut Rhin	10450
7	Pas de Calais	9990
8	Manche	9960
9	Côtes du Nord	8910
10	Calvados	8880
11	Somme	8850
12	Loire	8240
13	Ille et Vilaine	8180
14	Seine et Oise	7990
15	Finistère	7870
16	Moselle	7830
17	Sarthe	7360
18	Eure	7290
19	Orne	7240
20	Puy-de-Dôme	7190
21	Aisne	7040
22	Bouches du Rhône	7010
23	Haute Garonne	6920
24	Loire inférieure	6890
25	Vaucluse	6880
26	Mayenne	6850
27	Oise	6830
28	Meurthe	6820
29	Charente inférê	6800
30	Vosges	6790
31	Isère	6640
32	Tarn et Garonne	6640
33	Lot et Garonne	6540
34	Maine et Loire	6480
35	Haute Saône	6380
36	Ardèche	6320
37	Jura	6290
38	Morbihan	6190
39	Saône et Loire	6130
40	Gard	6040
41	Charente	6010
42	Haute Loire	5860
43	Tarn	5850
44	Ain	5840
45	Seine et Marne	5730
46	Basses Pyrénées	5720
47	Gironde	5680
48	Ardennes	5590
49	Ariège	5560
50	Hérault	5340
51	Lot	5400
52	Dordogne	5270
53	Hautes Pyrénées	5150
54	Haute Vienne	5140
55	Eure et Loir	5080
56	Meuse	5070
57	Doubs	5060
58	Corrèze	5060
59	Gers	4980
60	Indre et Loire	4860
61	Deux Sèvres	4850
62	Yonne	4840
63	Vendée	4840
64	Creuse	4750
65	Drôme	4580
66	Loiret	4570
67	Aude	4450
68	Cantal	4430
69	Côte d'Or	4390
70	Var	4370
71	Vienne	4180
72	Nièvre	4150
73	Marne	4130
74	Allier	4120
75	Aube	4050
76	Aveyron	4040
77	Haute Marne	3990
78	Pyrénées Oriente	3810
79	Loir et Cher	3770
80	Indre	3560
81	Cher	3550
82	Landes	3080
83	Lozère	2720
84	Hautes Alpes	2330
85	Basses Alpes	2280
	Corse	2230
	Départent moyen	6171

JOSEPH FLETCHER
1813–1852

EDUCATED as a barrister, Joseph Fletcher used his skills as a statistician to improve the health and well-being of his British compatriots. He was given several government appointments, including secretary of the children's employment commission and inspector of state schools (1844), and his resulting statistical reports led to useful legislation in those areas. He was honorary secretary of the Statistical Society of London and editor of the *Statistical Journal*, and he published several treatises on education, which was one of his major interests.

Fletcher's *Summary of the Moral Statistics of England and Wales* (London: privately printed, 1849?) compiles the tables and maps from his contributions to the *Journal of the Statistical Society* in 1847, 1848, and 1849. In his first paper about the subject, which he read before the Statistical Section of the British Association in June 1847, Fletcher saw an important role for the fledging science of statistics in an open society:

> I wish to submit to the Section a few facts illustrative of the moral and intellectual condition of the English people. These facts form a very imperfect body of evidence; but gentlemen who are acquainted with the true nature of Statistics, or of science in general, will not therefore reject it, if it be the result of continuous and conscientious labour, applied to remove the frontier of doubt and ignorance which surrounds us but one step further back. Those who have expected our science to spring into existence ready armed like another Minerva, and complain that Statistics can know nothing because they do not know everything in the field of investigation which they propose to themselves, ask of us what they ask the labourers in no other department of inquiry.... It might rather be rejoined, that the more neglected are Statistics, the greater the reproach upon the age and the country in which their consequent imperfection is witnessed [*Journal of the Statistical Society of London* 10, no. 3 (September 1847): 193].

For his data, Fletcher drew from the latest census; income tax returns; reports of the registrar-general of births, deaths, and marriages; Home Office tables of criminal offenders; the latest reports of the Poor Law Commissioners; and a summary of savings banks published by the barrister who was appointed to certify their rules.

Reminiscent of A.-M. Guerry's work (1833) on the "moral statistics" of France (see his entry in this Sociology and Economics section), Fletcher provides twelve maps on similar subjects, such as ignorance, crime, poverty, and illegitimate births. Generally, he observes that

> the figures here adduced bear conclusive evidence to the fact of the immediate alliance of all the moral evils of which we can yet obtain statistical cognizance with *ignorance*; and that this ignorance is the denser and more wide spread wherever there is the least active intervention of persons blessed with means, education, and a missionary spirit ... [p. 29; Fletcher's emphasis].
>
> The conclusion is therefore irresistible that *education* is not only essential to the security of modern society, but that such education should be solid, useful, and above all, Christian ... [p. 131; Fletcher's emphasis].

Many of Fletcher's views would still find resonance today, more than 150 years later.

✻ [*Overleaf*] "Dispersion of the Population in England and Wales 1841." Lithograph map, 23.9 × 19.2 cm. Plate I from Fletcher's *Summary of the Moral Statistics of England and Wales* (1849) [Historic Maps Collection].

Probably the earliest population density map of England. In seven shades, the map shows the proportion of inhabitants per one hundred acres that are below (lighter) or above (darker) the average of all of England and Wales. The forty-four counties are ranked (least dense to most), and their rank numbers are indicated on the map. As one would expect, the metropolitan/industrial areas of London, Liverpool, and Birmingham appear darkest.

✻ [*Overleaf*] "Improvident Marriages in England & Wales (Those of Males under 21, Being So Designated.) 1844." Lithograph map, 23.9 × 18.9 cm. Plate IX from Fletcher's *Summary of the Moral Statistics of England and Wales* (1849) [Historic Maps Collection].

In all of his maps, Fletcher associates darker tints

Moral Statistics of England and Wales, by Mr. Fletcher.

DISPERSION of the POPULATION IN ENGLAND & WALES
1841

Scale of Tints.
Shewing the proportion of inhabitants to 100 acres, below (−) and above (+) the average of all England & Wales

− 50 Per Cent & more
− 30 to 50
− 10 to 30
− and + less than 10
+ 10 to 30
+ 30 to 70
+ 170 & more

Standidge & Co. Litho. Old Jewry.

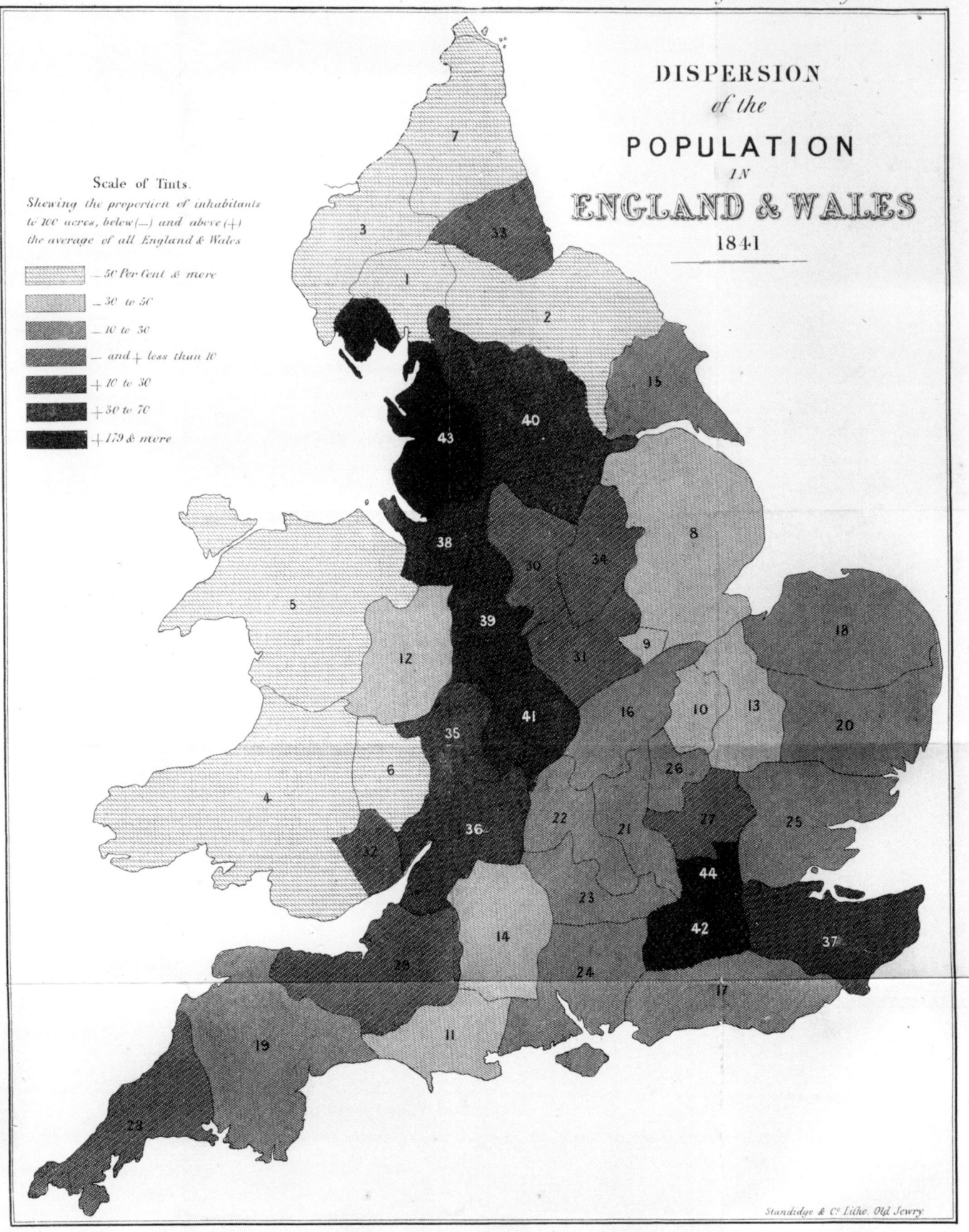

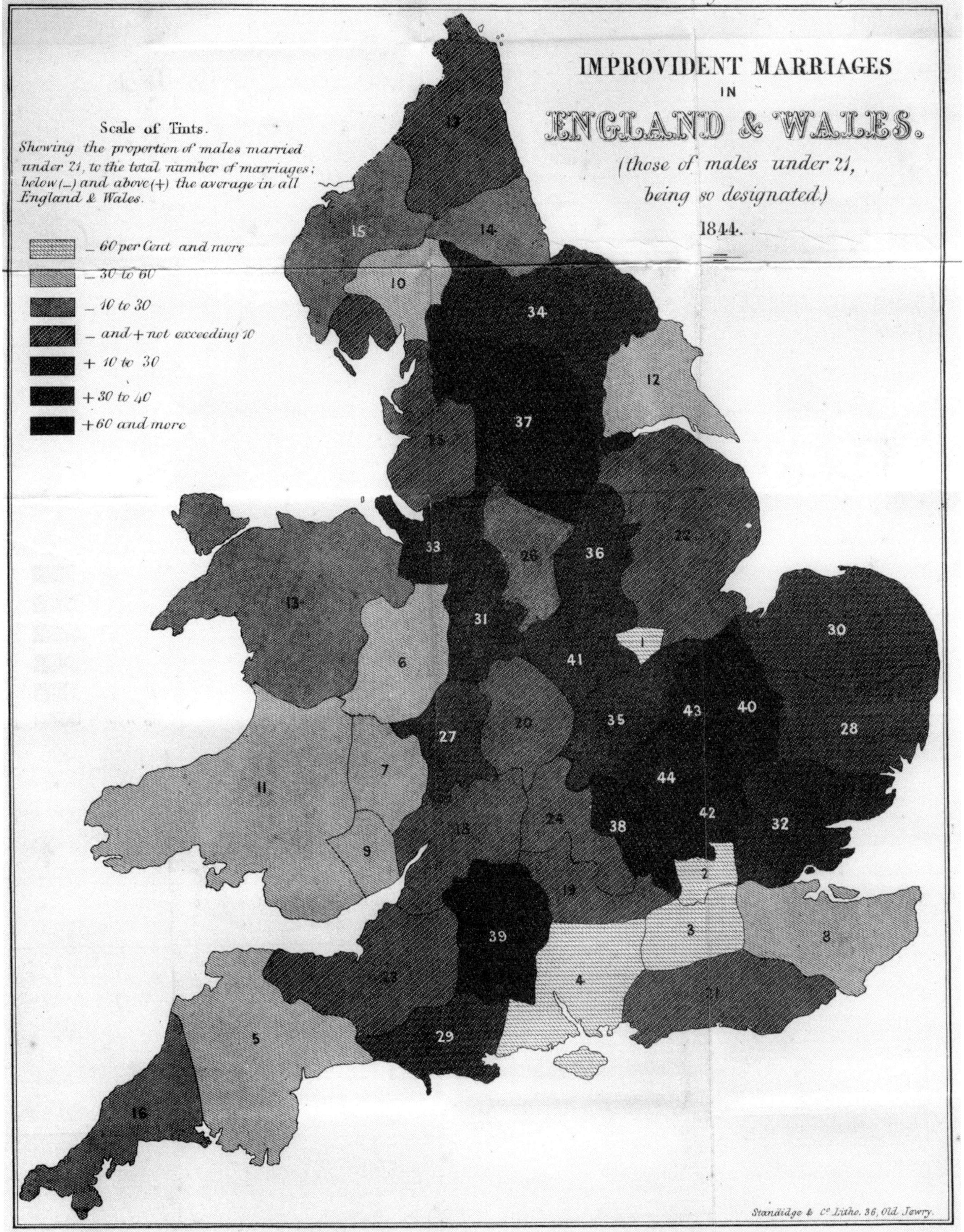

Pl. IX.　　　　　　　　　　　　　　　　　　　　　Moral Statistics of England and Wales by Mr. Fletcher.

IMPROVIDENT MARRIAGES
IN
ENGLAND & WALES.
(those of males under 21, being so designated.)
1844.

Scale of Tints.
Showing the proportion of males married under 21, to the total number of marriages; below (−) and above (+) the average in all England & Wales.

- − 60 per Cent and more
- − 30 to 60
- − 10 to 30
- − and + not exceeding 10
- + 10 to 30
- + 30 to 60
- + 60 and more

Standidge & Co. Litho. 36, Old Jewry.

DEPOSITS IN THE SAVINGS BANKS IN ENGLAND & WALES in proportion to the POPULATION.

Moral Statistics of England and Wales, by Mr. Fletcher

Scale of Tints

Showing the proportion of deposits to the population above (+) and below (−) the average of England and Wales.

- + 40 Per Cent and more.
- + 20 to 40.
- + 10 to 20.
- + and − not more than 10
- − 10 to 20.
- − 20 to 40.
- − 40 Per Cent and more.

Standidge & C° Litho. Old Jewry.

with the "unfavourable end of the scale, whether of influence or results." In this map, the counties are ranked from those having the lowest percentage of underage marriages to those having the highest, when compared with the average in all of England and Wales. Rutland (1), Middlesex (2), and Surrey (3) counties lead with the smallest proportions; Herts (42), Huntingdon (43), and Bedford (44) have the greatest. In attempting to explain these results in his text, Fletcher acknowledges that illegitimate births and underage marriages tend to run counter to each other; however, he believes that pauperism and ignorance are major influences in channeling youthful "incontinence."

✳ [*Opposite*] "Deposits in the Savings Banks in England & Wales in Proportion to the Population." Lithograph map, 24 × 18.9 cm. Plate XII from Fletcher's *Summary of the Moral Statistics of England and Wales* (1849) [Historic Maps Collection].

Essentially a map of prosperity, showing Wales to be near the bottom in terms of "persons of independent means" who maintain savings accounts. As that is essential, in Fletcher's view, for the development and support of education, one would expect—and Fletcher's statistics support—that these poorer counties rank near the top on his map of ignorance. He admits, though, that nothing is the result of one cause, and that the field of statistics is only beginning to identify the predominant moral influences.

CHARLES JOSEPH MINARD
1781–1870

FRENCHMAN Charles Joseph Minard made most of his pioneering contributions to thematic mapping after a long career as a civil engineer. He worked on a number of canal and bridge projects in Europe, served as superintendent of the École Nationale des Ponts et Chaussées (National School of Bridges and Roads) from 1830 to 1836, and was inspector general of bridges when he retired in 1851. His most famous work, published in 1869, is "Carte figurative des pertes successives en hommes de l'Armée Française dans la campagne de Russie 1812–1813." This flow map charts the disastrous campaign of Napoleon's army in Russia, showing the movements of the troops and the huge losses of men against a scale of declining temperatures.

Prior to that chart, Minard had published a number of large lithographic maps that utilized innovative graphic designs to emphasize thematic concerns. In fact, American geographer and educator Arthur H. Robinson identified fifty-one separate thematic maps that Minard published from 1845 to 1869; most are very rare and exist only in the holdings of national institutions like the Bibliothèque Nationale de France and the archives of his government employer. Subjects covered include tonnage of cargo handled by large European ports (1856), tonnage of merchandise carried on the waterways and railroads of France (1859), coal distribution in England (1866), and European railroad passenger movements for 1862 (1865).

> When the complete story of the development of thematic cartography during the nineteenth century is finally added to the annals of the history of cartography, the name of Charles Joseph Minard (1781–1870) will again take on some of the lustre it had during the latter part of his lifetime.… Minard was a pioneer in many respects, both in terms of his cartographic symbolism and in the handling of the data with which he worked [Robinson, *Imago Mundi* 21 (1967): 95].

Minard belonged to no major professional societies and published his maps privately—how and where they were distributed remains a mystery—yet his importance is clearly and widely recognized today.

✳ [*Overleaf*] Minard's "Carte figurative des pertes successives en hommes de l'Armée Française dans la campagne de Russie 1812–1813" [map showing the successive losses in men of the French Army in the Russian campaign of 1812–1813]. Lithograph map, 30 × 62 cm [*Wikipedia*].

HENRY MAYHEW
1812–1887

ONE OF SEVENTEEN children, Henry Mayhew spent his early years on the sea. Back home by 1829, he tried his hand at freelancing as a journalist, writing a play, and managing a theater house. Deep in debt by 1835, he had to flee creditors and spent more than ten years in Paris, where he met and became friends with other English writers like William Makepeace Thackeray and Douglas William Jerrold.

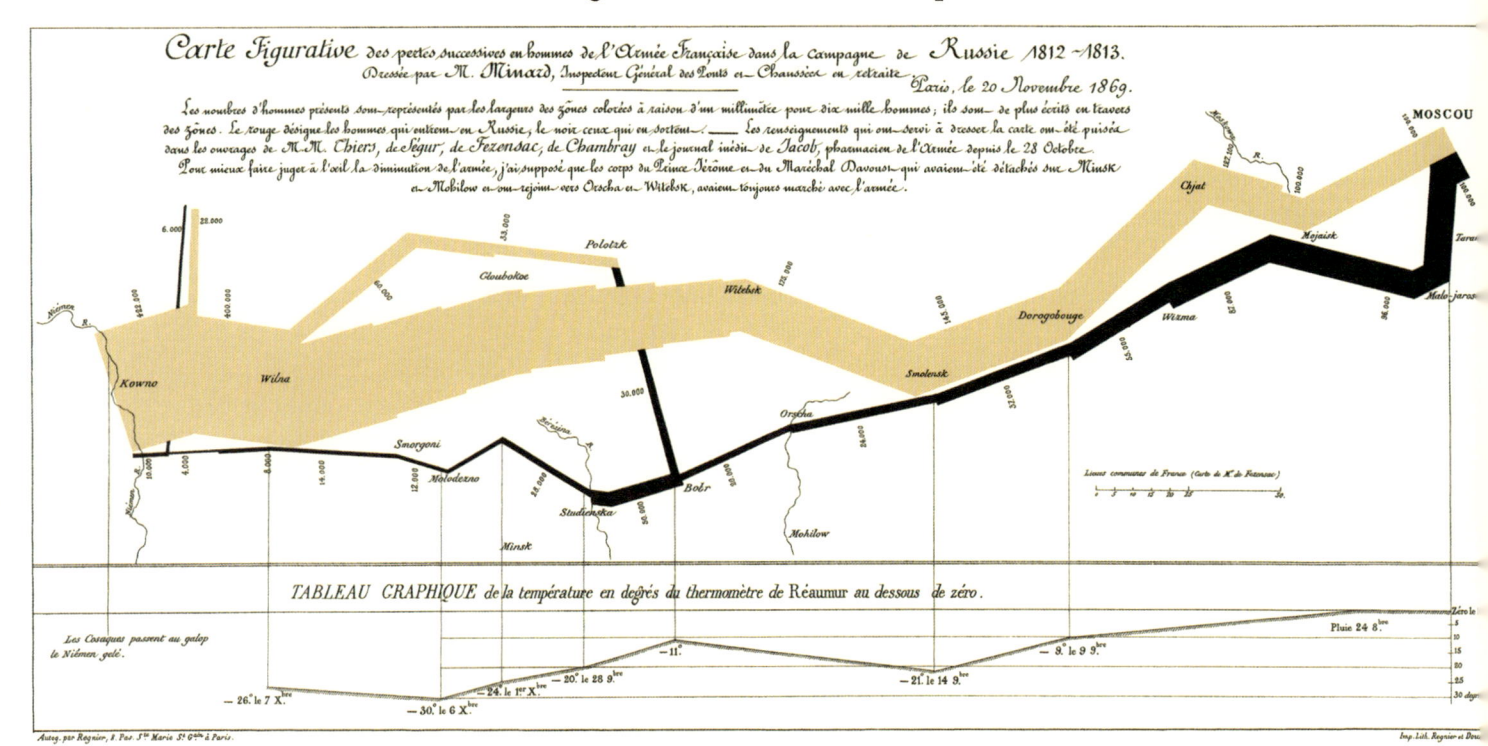

In 1841, Mayhew cofounded *Punch*, a weekly magazine of humor and satire that became extremely popular (it closed in 1992). Mayhew used some of the same talented illustrators for his groundbreaking, influential *London Labour and the London Poor*. Comprised of articles he had written for the *Morning Chronicle*, the work initially appeared in three volumes in 1851; an expanded version in four volumes was published in 1861–1862. The work's statistics-driven maps, combined with compelling graphics, provided unprecedented access into the lives of the Victorian poor. The appendix to volume 4 contains tabular data and fifteen associated maps "illustrating the criminal statistics of each of the counties of England and Wales in 1851." Map subjects include the density of the population, intensity of criminality, intensity of ignorance, number of illegitimate children, number of early marriages (under age twenty-one), committals for rape, committals for bigamy, and criminality of females. Among the general population, ignorance was determined from marriage registers by

✻ Portrait of Henry Mayhew. From vol. 1 (1861) of his *London Labour and the London Poor: A Cyclopædia of the Condition and Earnings of Those That Will Work, Those That Cannot Work, and Those That Will Not Work*, 4 vols. (London: Griffin, Bohn, and Company, 1861–1862) [Graphic Arts Collection].

tabulating the number of males and females who signed their names with marks.

Mayhew's research was used by politicians and other writers advocating social reform. It is believed that novelist Charles Dickens was heavily influenced by Mayhew's descriptions of London underclass life.

✳ [*Below*] "The Crippled Street Bird-Seller." From vol. 2 (1861) of Mayhew's *London Labour and the London Poor* ... [Graphic Arts Collection].

What was unique about Mayhew's work was the breadth and depth of his firsthand accounts:

> It surely may be considered curious as being the first attempt to publish the history of a people, from the lips of the people themselves—giving a literal description of their labour, their earnings, their trials, and their sufferings, in their own "unvarnished" language; and to pourtray the condition of their homes and their families by personal observation of the places, and direct communion with the individuals. ... Within the last two years some thousands of the humbler classes of society must have been seen and visited with the especial view of noticing their condition and learning their histories ... [vol. 1, p. iii].

The index to each volume reads like a vaudevillian "who's who" of London street life and employment options of the poor: ballast-getters, beetle-destroyers, bone grubbers, chalker on flag-stones, cigar-end finders,

MAP No. IX.   485

MAP

SHOWING THE NUMBER OF

PERSONS COMMITTED FOR KEEPING DISORDERLY HOUSES

IN EVERY 10,000,000 OF THE POPULATION,

IN THE SEVERAL COUNTIES OF

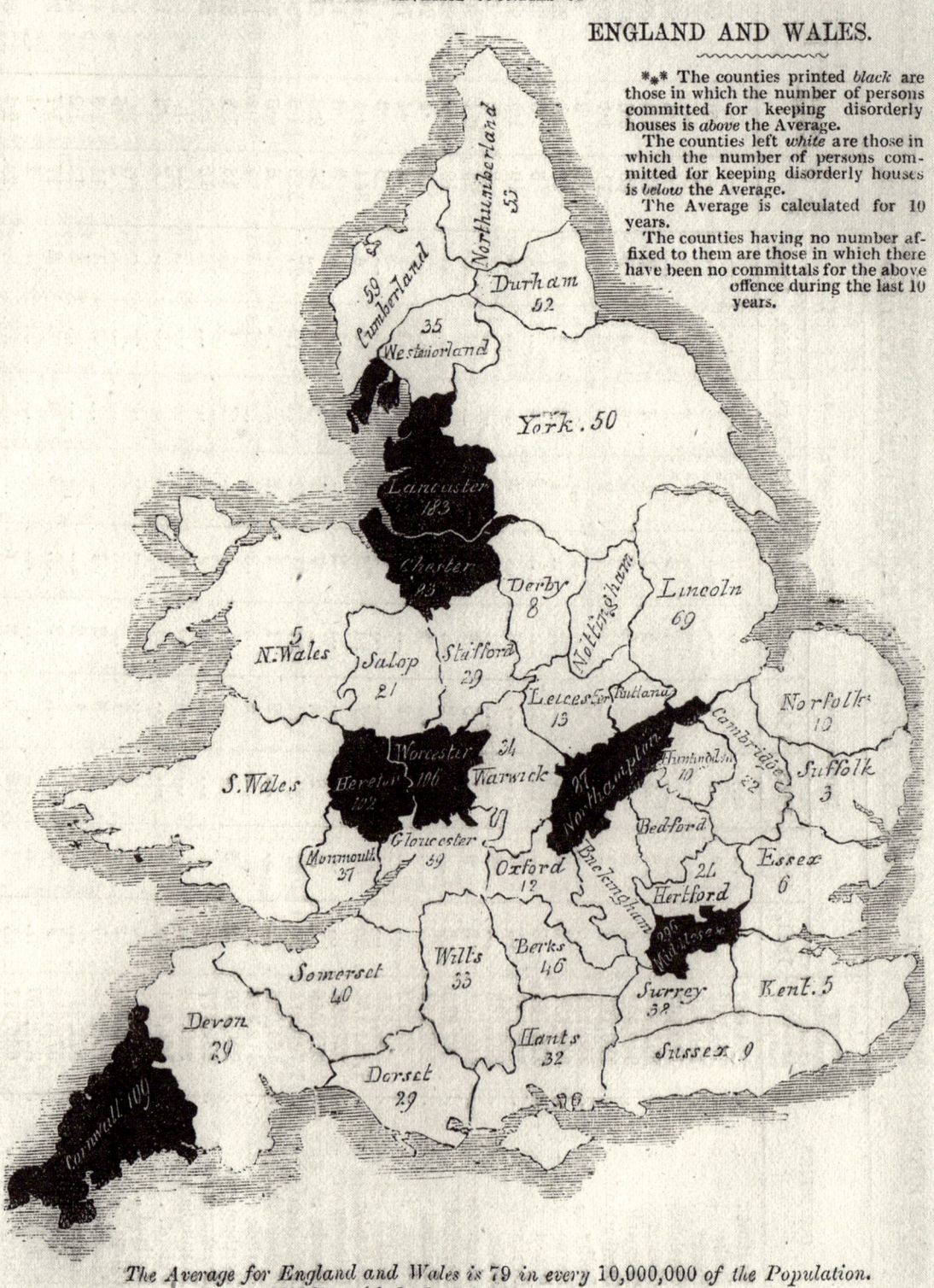

ENGLAND AND WALES.

*** The counties printed *black* are those in which the number of persons committed for keeping disorderly houses is *above* the Average.

The counties left *white* are those in which the number of persons committed for keeping disorderly houses is *below* the Average.

The Average is calculated for 10 years.

The counties having no number affixed to them are those in which there have been no committals for the above offence during the last 10 years.

The Average for England and Wales is 79 in every 10,000,000 of the Population.
" *Middlesex (the highest) is 296*   "   "

Sociology & Economics

dog-collar seller, dustmen, glee-singers, penny mouse-trap maker, punchmen, rag gatherers, stilt vaulters, street poets and authors, water-cress girl. According to Mayhew, "there are about 40,000 people engaged in selling articles in the streets of London" [vol. 2, p. 97].

✳ [*Below*] "A View in Rosemary-Lane." From vol. 2 (1861) of Mayhew's *London Labour and the London Poor* … [Graphic Arts Collection].

> One side of the lane is covered with old boots and shoes; old clothes, both men's, women's, and children's; new lace for edgings, and a variety of cheap prints and muslins.… Some of the wares are spread on the ground on wrappers, or pieces of matting or carpet.… And amidst all this motley display the buyers and sellers smoke, and shout, and doze, and bargain, and wrangle, and eat and drink tea and coffee, and sometimes beer [vol. 2, p. 40].

✳ [*Opposite*] "Map Showing the Number of Persons Committed for Keeping Disorderly Houses [brothels] in Every 10,000,000 of the Population, in the Several Counties of England and Wales." Lithograph map, 19.3 × 12 cm. From vol. 4 (1862) of Mayhew's *London Labour and the London Poor* … [Graphic Arts Collection].

This map clearly shows/confirms that brothels (with implications for associated prostitution) are more prevalent in the country's industrial areas and cities, including major ports.

EXPLANATION

1. Egyptians
2. Moors & Arabs
3. Libyan or Berber or Tuaryk Race
4. Tibbo
5. Garamantes or Fezzaners
6. Ababdeh & Bisharein
7. Barabra or Nubians
8. Nouba of Kordofan
9. Shangalla
10. Amharas and other Abyssins
11. Hazorta Race
12. Galla Race
13. Nouba or Negroes of Borgho
14. Begharmi
15. Bornowy
16. Hausa Race Eastern Sudan
17. Race of Western Sudan
18. Fulah or Felatah Race
19. Mandingo Race
20. Jaloff Race
21. Felups & other Negroes near Sierra Leone
22. Susus & Buloms
23. Kroo Race and other Tribes
24. Race of Ashanti & Fanti
25. Widah or Dahomeh Race
26. Binin Race
27. Great South African Family of Nations
28. Kongo Race
29. Mosambique Nations
30. Kafirs
31. Hottentots or Quaiquai Race

Qualitative Thematic Maps

✶

QUALITATIVE thematic maps are not dependent on numbers (data). For example, I can map the hospitals in Manhattan without counting them. I may only be interested in their locations to see where health care gaps exist. Then I could layer the map with population data to determine how many people are served, theoretically, by each one—and then compare that ratio with ones for the other boroughs of New York City.

✶ Key to James Cowles Prichard's "Ethnographical Map of Africa, from the Earliest Times, Illustrative of Dr. Prichard's Natural History of Man and His Researches into the Physical History of Man" (1851).

✱ Portrait of Abraham Ortelius, 1527–1598. From his *Theatrvm orbis terrarvm* ... (Antwerp: imp. C. Plantinus, 1579) [Rare Books Division].

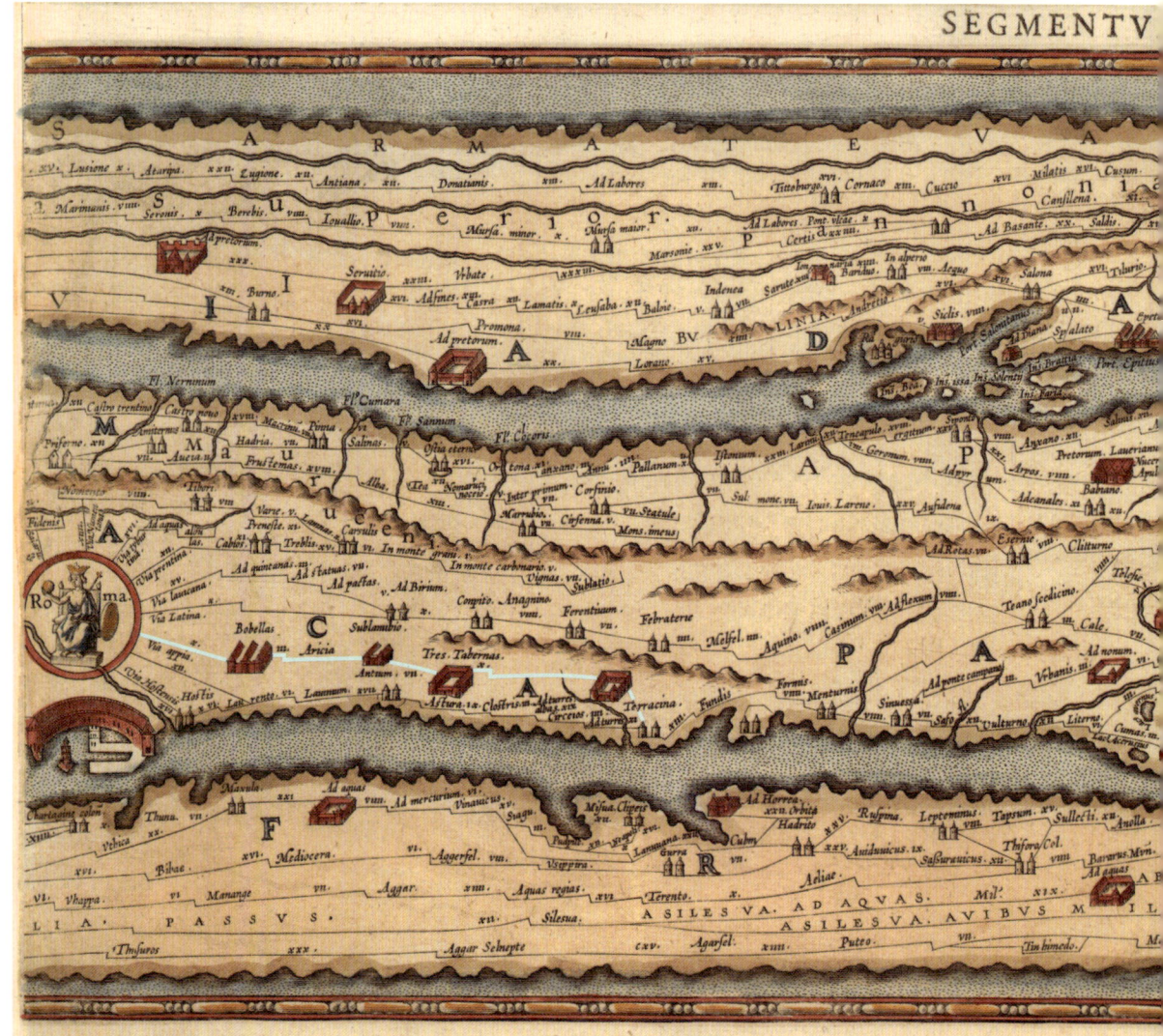

COMMUNICATION & TRANSPORTATION

ROADS

FLEMISH CARTOGRAPHER Abraham Ortelius created the first modern atlas of uniform map sheets, *Theatre Orbis Terrarum* [Theater of the world], in 1570. Below his portrait, the Latin text says: Ortelius gave mortals the world to gaze at; Galle [Philippe Galle, the engraver] gave the world Ortelius to admire.

✽ [*Below*] Segment IV of Ortelius's "Tabula itineraria ex illustri Peutingerorum Bibliotheca quae Augustae Vindel. Est." Copperplate map in eight segments on four sheets, with added color, each segment 19 × 52 cm, on sheets 41 × 53 cm. From Petrus Bertius's *Theatrum geographiæ veteris, duobus tomis distinctum* (Amsterdam: Ex officina Iudoci Hondij, 1619) [Historic Maps Collection]. Ortelius supervised the engraving of these sheets in 1598 but died before seeing them in print. Dutch cartographer Bertius added offprints of them to his atlas.

Commonly referred to as the Peutinger Table, this is the oldest road map in the world. More accurately, it is a sixteenth-century printed copy of a thirteenth-century manuscript version of a fourth- or early-fifth-

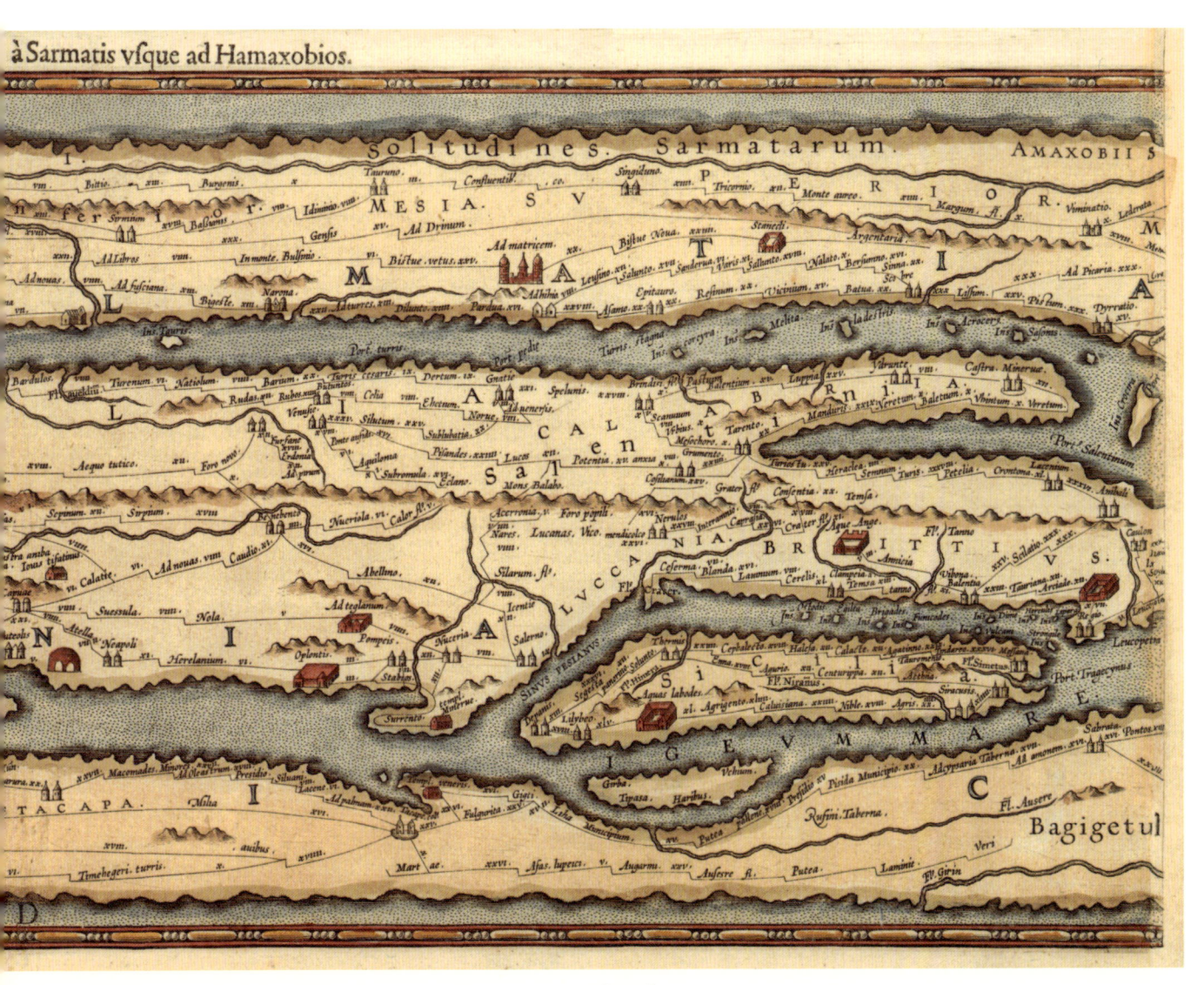

{173}

century map, which most scholars believe was a descendant of a Roman chart that was engraved in marble and featured in the Porticus Vipsaniae monument in ancient Rome. It is also probably the first printed facsimile of a classical map. (The source manuscript is now housed in the Österreichische Nationalbibliothek in Vienna, Austria.) The subject is the Roman *cursus publicus*, or network of roads originally created for the use of couriers of the emperors. It is definitely a thematic map showing various itineraries. Actually, it is rather sophisticated in its AAA TripTik–approach, using a right-angle hook to show a day's travel and symbols for spas where one could expect to find water, food, and lodging. See, for example, the stretch from Rome to the coast along the historic Appian Way (Via Appia), highlighted in light blue.

POST

✻ Portrait of Nicolas Sanson, 1600–1667. From Hans Harms's *Künstler des Kartenbildes: Biographien und Porträts*. Oldenburg (Oldb): E. Völker [1962] [courtesy of Ernst Völker]. A tutor in geography to two French kings (Louis XIII and Louis XIV), Nicolas Sanson became *géographe ordinaire du roi* in 1630. Thereafter, most of his maps bore that honorable appellation. The Sanson family—*le père*'s map business was continued by two of his sons and a grandson into the eighteenth century—became synonymous with the golden age of French cartography.

✻ [*Opposite*] "Carte géographicque des postes qui trauersent la France" (Paris: Par Melchior Tauernier…, 1632). Copperplate map, with added outline color, 41 × 52 cm [Historic Maps Collection].

First postal road map—also the first important map issued by Sanson. The map shows all of the routes used by the royal posts of the time, identifying the stops along the way; it was reprinted many times during the seventeenth century. Curiously, the cartouche for the dedication has been left blank. The French postal system dates back to 1477, when King Louis XI set up a Royal Postal Service that employed mounted couriers. The timing of this map is relevant, for private mail delivery had just been legalized several years earlier (1627), so both services were operating over the same major routes. In 1672, France made postal service a government-only function.

✻ [*Overleaf*] John Senex, 1678–1740. "A New Map of France: Shewing the Roads & Post Stages Thro-out That Kingdom, as Also the Errors of Sanson's Map Compard with ye Survey Made by Order of ye Late French King" ([London: J. Senex], 1719). Copperplate map, with added color, 50 × 56 cm [Historic Maps Collection].

English cartographer Senex compares his postal map to Sanson's (see previous entry), over which he has superimposed a "corrected" version. The outline of Sanson's map can be seen along the Atlantic and Mediterranean coasts. "[Y]e Survey Made by Order of ye Late French King" was a plan, approved by King Louis XIV (1638–1715) in 1679, for a much more accurate map of France based on the latest scientific techniques. This

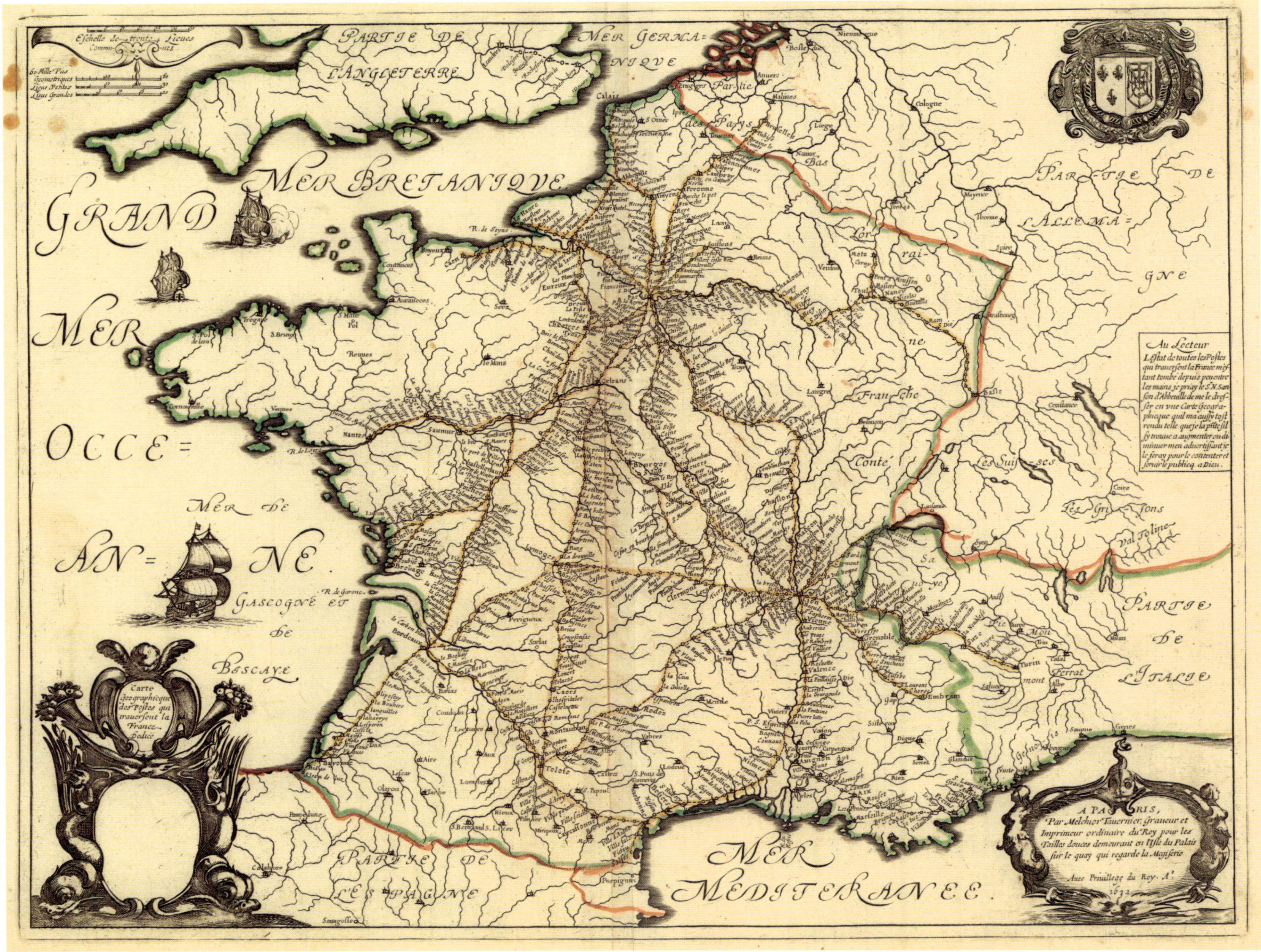
Carte Geographique des Postes qui traversent la France. Dedié
A PARIS, Par Melchior Tavernier, graveur et Imprimeur ordinaire du Roy pour les Tailles douces demeurant en l'Isle du Palais sur le quay qui regarde la Megisserie
Avec Privillege du Roy. A°. 1632
Au Lecteur
L'Estat de toutes les Postes qui traversent la France m'estant tombé depuis peu entre les mains, je priay le S.N. Sanson d'Abbeville de me le dresser en une Carte Geographique qu'il m'a aussy tost rendu telle que je la presente. S'il s'y trouve a augmenter ou diminuer, m'en advertissant, je le feray pour le contenter et servir le public. a Dieu.
Eschelle de trente Lieues Communes
MER BRETANIQUE
GRAND MER OCCE= AN= NE
MER DE GASCOGNE ET DE BISCAYE
MER GERMANIQUE
MER MEDITERANEE
PARTIE DE L'ANGLETERRE
PARTIE DE L'ALLEMAGNE
PARTIE DE L'ITALIE
PARTIE DE L'ESPAGNE

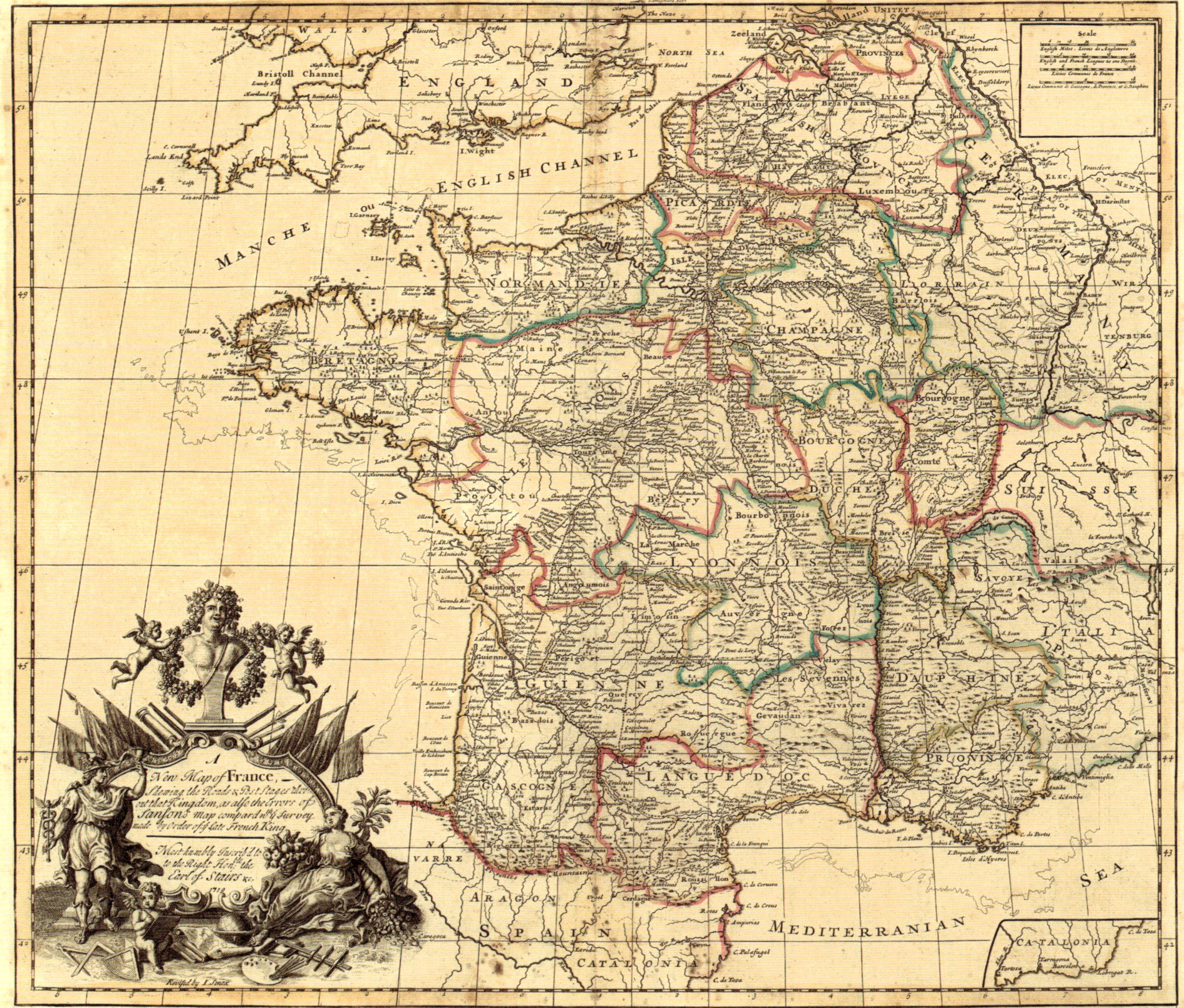
A
New Map of France,
Shewing the Roads & Post Stages thro-
out that Kingdom, as also the Errors of
Sansons map compard wth ye Survey
made by Order of ye late French King
Most humbly Inscrib'd to
to the Right Honble the
Earl of Stairs &c.
1719
Revised by I. Senex
Scale
ENGLAND
WALES
Bristoll Channel
ENGLISH CHANNEL
MANCHE
NORTH SEA
PICARDIE
NORMANDIE
BRETAGNE
Maine
Anjou
Poitou
Saintonge
Angoumois
Limosin
CHAMPAGNE
LORRAIN
BOURGOGNE
Comté
LYONNOIS
Bourbonnois
Auvergne
Forez
Les Sevennes
Gevaudan
Vivarez
DAUPHINE
PROVINCE
LANGUE D'OC
GUIENNE
Quercy
Perigort
GASCOGNE
Bazadois
Estarac
Rouergue
SAVOYE
Valais
SUISSE
ITALIA
PIEMONT
GERMANY
Luxembourg
PROVINCES
Zeeland
Brabant
Lyege
ARAGON
SPAIN
CATALONIA
NAVARRE
MEDITERRANIAN SEA
I. Wight
Lands End
Scilly I.
C. de Creus
C. Palafugel
Roses
Ampurias
Isles d'Hyeres

was begun by Jean Picard (1620–1682) and continued by Giovanni Domenico Cassini (1625–1712); preliminary work, based on triangulation, revised the outlines of the country and appeared in the 1693 map "Carte de France corrigée par ordre du roy sur les observations de Mss. de l'Academie des Sciences." That is the source that Senex used for this "new" postal map. The postal routes have greatly expanded in the interim years—see Normandy, for example.

TELEGRAPH

✳ [*Overleaf*] "The Electric and International Telegraph Company's Map of the Telegraph Lines of Europe, 1856" (London: published under the authority of the Electric Telegraph Company, by Day & Son, lithrs...., August 1, 1856). Lithograph map, mounted on linen, 68 × 97 cm, on sheet 76 × 112 cm [Historic Maps Collection].

Sending messages with electrical signals developed quickly in the 1830s and became practical and commercial in the 1840s. Founded in Great Britain in 1846, the Electric Telegraph Company was the world's first public telegraph company. It merged with the International Telegraph Company, an English-Dutch venture begun in 1852, in 1855. This is the first map of the consolidated company, showing the extent of the burgeoning communications system. Current and future telegraph lines are shown in full and dotted red lines; all of the English and Continental stations, between which messages can be sent, are indicated with red circles and listed on the map's margins. According to the note at the top right, messages to and from the Continent had to be addressed "via Amsterdam."

✳ [*Below*] Henry Howe, 1816–1893. "Map of the Submarine Telegraph between America & Europe, with the Various Communications on the Two Continents." Printed map, with added color, 17.2 × 45.6 cm. Frontispiece to his *Adventures and Achievements of Americans: A Series of Narratives Illustrating Their Heroism, Self-Reliance, Genius and Enterprise*, illus. by F. O. C. Darley and others (New York: Geo. F. Tuttle; Cincinnati: H. Howe, 1858) [Graphic Arts Collection].

Beginning his story with Nathan Hale, martyr of the American Revolution, Howe builds up to, and concludes with, a chapter on "The Atlantic Telegraph." "It is a happy circumstance that a volume like this can be closed by an account of the rise, progress, and completion of the great work which is properly regarded as the crowning triumph of scientific discovery and

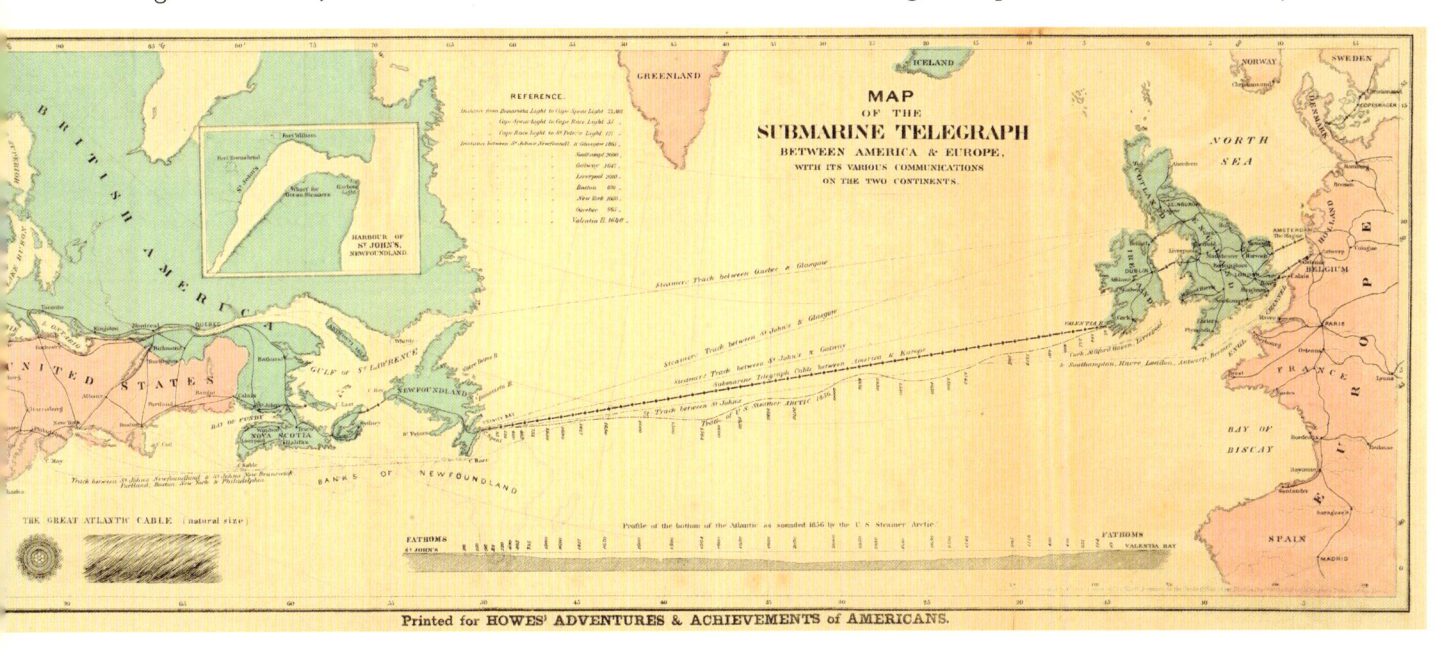

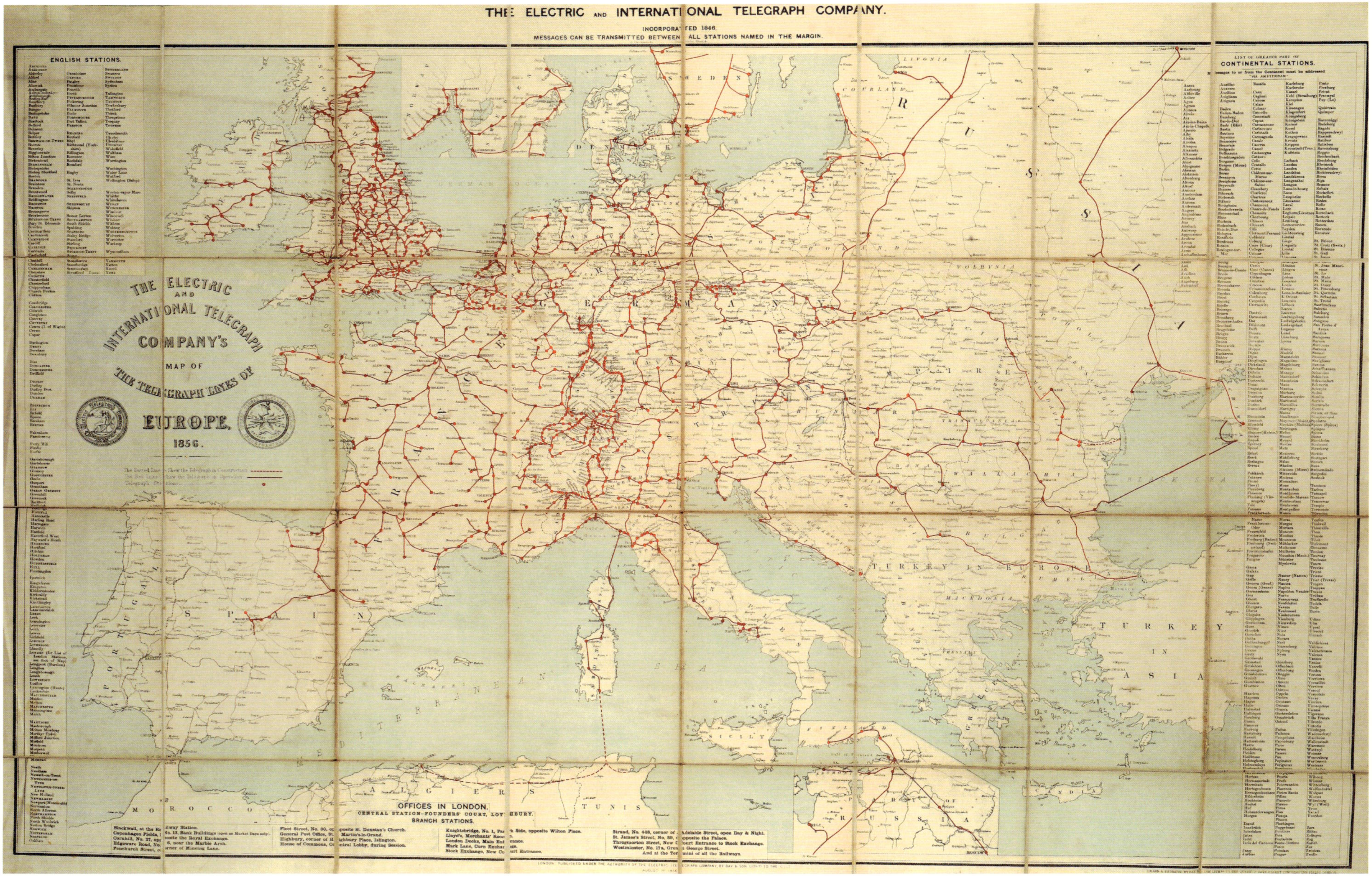
THE ELECTRIC AND INTERNATIONAL TELEGRAPH COMPANY.
INCORPORATED 1846.
MESSAGES CAN BE TRANSMITTED BETWEEN ALL STATIONS NAMED IN THE MARGIN.
ENGLISH STATIONS.
CONTINENTAL STATIONS.
THE ELECTRIC AND INTERNATIONAL TELEGRAPH COMPANY'S MAP OF THE TELEGRAPH LINES OF EUROPE.
1856.
OFFICES IN LONDON.
CENTRAL STATION–FOUNDERS' COURT, LOTHBURY.
BRANCH STATIONS.
RUSSIA
GERMANY
FRANCE
SPAIN
PORTUGAL
TURKEY IN EUROPE
TURKEY IN ASIA
MACEDONIA
WALLACHIA
SWEDEN
DENMARK
LIVONIA
COURLAND
VOLHYNIA
ALGIERS
TUNIS
MOROCCO
MEDITERRANEAN SEA
BLACK SEA

mechanical ingenuity" [p. 653]. The first transatlantic telegraph cable was laid in the late summer of 1858, linking Newfoundland to Valentia Island, off Ireland's southwest coast. Hence, Howe's work was extraordinarily current.

HIGHWAY AND BUS

✳ [*Overleaf*] John C. Mulford. "National Highways Map of the United States Showing One Hundred Fifty Thousand Miles of National Highways Proposed by the National Highways Association" (Washington, D.C.: National Highways Association, 1918). Lithograph map, 76 × 125 cm, on sheet 102 × 157 cm [Historic Maps Collection].

Organized by millionaire Charles Henry Davis in 1911, the National Highways Association—its slogan, "Good Roads Everywhere"—proposed a nationwide system of highways for the federal government to construct and maintain. The timing was not good, as World War I would consume the government's attention and funds. The interstate highway system that we know today did not develop until the 1950s, under President Dwight D. Eisenhower's administration.

✳ [*Overleaves*] Greyhound Lines. "A Good-Natured Map of the United States: Setting Forth the Services of the Greyhound Lines and a Few Principal Connecting Bus Lines" (N.p.: Greyhound Lines, [1937?]). Lithograph map, 47 × 72 cm [Historic Maps Collection].

Probably the first version of a popular pictorial map depicting the routes of the fast-growing Greyhound Bus Lines. The first Greyhound bus began operation in Hibbing, Minnesota, in 1914 (see the illustration at the top center of the map). The Golden Gate Bridge had just opened (1937). The "good nature" of the map condones social and racial stereotypes that proliferate in the map's pictorials—Native American Indians snake dancing, African-Americans picking cotton—all captioned with "down home" lingo. At the time of the map, black passengers faced segregated buses and facilities in the South.

AVIATION

✳ [*Overleaves*] Rand McNally and Company. "Aviation Map of United States: Featuring Landing Fields." Printed map on sheet 69 × 117 cm. From rear pocket of *The Complete Camp Site Guide and Latest Highway Map of U.S.A., Together with Official Directory of Aeroplane Landing Fields* (Waterloo, Iowa: United States Touring Information Bureau, 1923) [Historic Maps Collection].

After World War I, many American fighter pilots became barnstormers, venturing into small communities across the nation to entertain crowds with their aerial antics and to offer rides for hire. At the same time, the United States Postal Service began experimenting with air mail service. Commercial aviation began on a very small scale during the mid-to-late 1910s in Florida. This map, therefore, provides a snapshot of this very early, first stage of American aviation, before the creation of the great airlines like Pan American Airways (1927), which would radically change everything about flying.

RADIO

✳ [*Overleaves*] George F. Cram Company. "Cram's Detailed Radio Map of the United States & Canada" (Indianapolis: George F. Cram Co., [1926]). Printed map, 47 × 73 cm, on sheet 69 × 86 cm [Historic Maps Collection].

Pre-network era map. Revised to December 5, 1926, the map includes listings of radio stations by place and by call letters. Generally, the first letter is K for stations west of the Mississippi and W for those east of it, but there are a number of exceptions. Symbols are used to

PREPAREDNESS

WE ARE ALL FOR IT. SOME FOR WAR
THERE CAN BE NO REAL PREPAREDNESS
NATIONAL HIGHWAYS AN[D] ... *Farm* MUST BE JOINED

GOOD ROADS
FOUR FOLD SYSTEM OF HIGHWAYS — NATIONAL HIGHWAYS

NATIONAL HIGHWAYS MAP OF THE UNITED STATES
SHOWING
ONE HUNDRED FIFTY THOUSAND MILES OF
NATIONAL HIGHWAYS
PROPOSED BY THE
NATIONAL HIGHWAYS ASSOCIATION
WASHINGTON, D.C.

PUBLISHED UNDER DIRECTION OF THE
NATIONAL HIGHWAYS ASSOCIATION
GENERAL COLEMAN DU PONT, CHAIRMAN BOARD OF NATIONAL COUNCILLORS
CHARLES HENRY DAVIS, C.E., PRESIDENT
FREDERIC REMSEN HUTTON, M.E., Sc.D., GENERAL SECRETARY
AND ISSUED UNDER JOINT AUSPICES OF THE
NATIONAL HIGHWAYS ASSOCIATION
AND ITS
TRUSTEES, COUNCILS, DIRECTORS, BOARDS AND COMMITTEES, AND ITS
HIGHWAY DEPARTMENTS AND DIVISIONS

"OUR QUESTION OF QUESTIONS — ARM OR DISARM?"
REAR ADMIRAL W. W. KIMBALL, U.S.N. RETIRED

NATIONAL HIGHWAYS vs. PANAMA CANAL
FREE SEAS — ATLANTIC TO PACIFIC — GULF TO LAKES — FREE ROADS

"ROAD BUILDERS"

DEDICATION
To the only power capable of teaching us, the people, what we should do about armament — the only power competent to make us do it:
THE NEWSPAPER PRESS

"A military people are a peaceful people, free from the danger of preventable war, from the danger of being conquered, and from all danger of being infected with militarism."

"NATIONAL HIGHWAYS
Will do more than any other one thing for real development and defense of our country."

"GOOD ROADS EVERYWHERE"

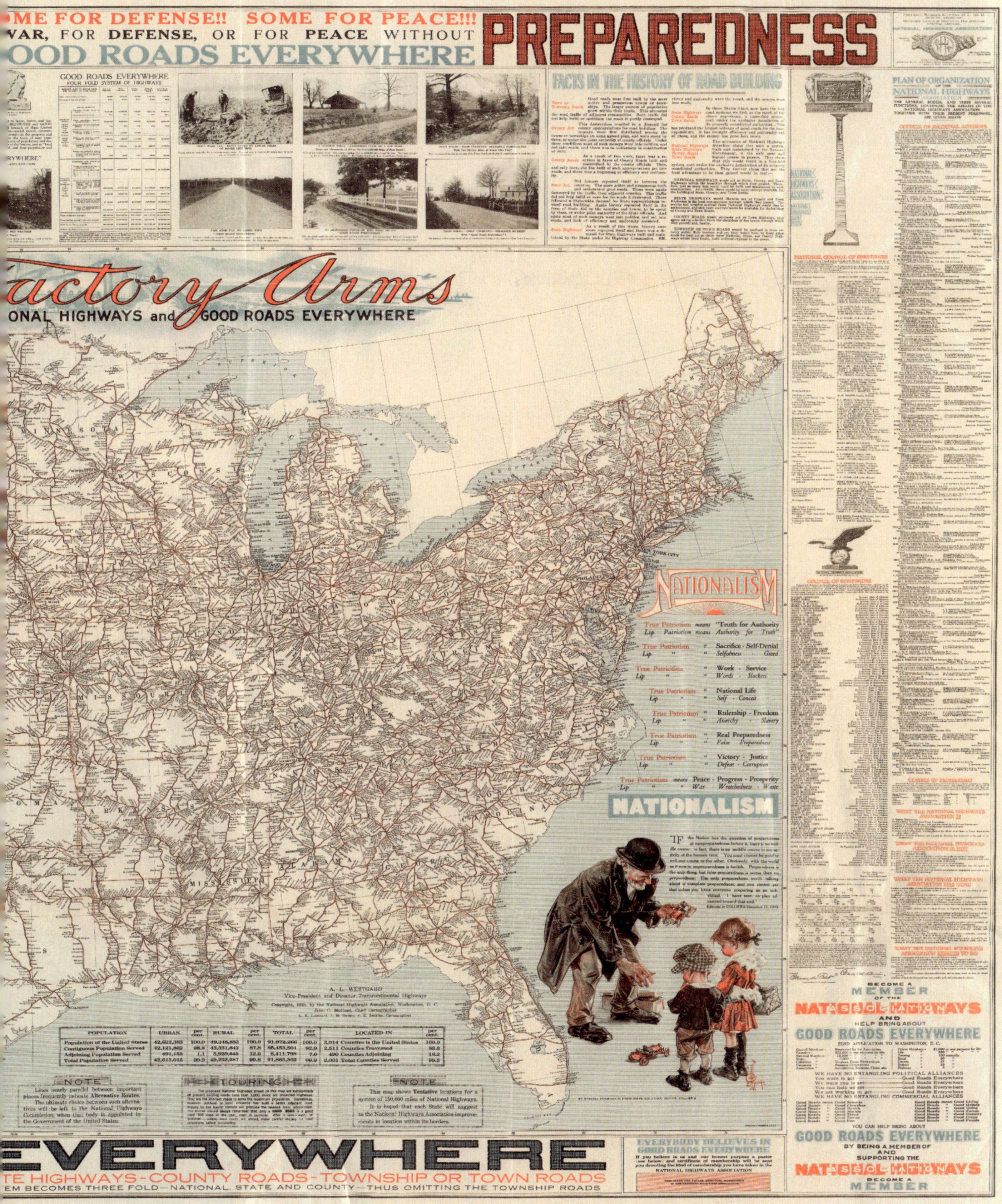
ME FOR DEFENSE!! SOME FOR PEACE!!!
VAR, FOR DEFENSE, OR FOR PEACE WITHOUT
OOD ROADS EVERYWHERE
PREPAREDNESS
GOOD ROADS EVERYWHERE
FOUR FOLD SYSTEM OF HIGHWAYS
FACTS IN THE HISTORY OF ROAD BUILDING
PLAN OF ORGANIZATION
OF THE
NATIONAL HIGHWAYS
ASSOCIATION
THE GENERAL BODIES, AND THEIR SEVERAL FUNCTIONS, GOVERNING THE AFFAIRS OF THE NATIONAL HIGHWAYS ASSOCIATION TOGETHER WITH THEIR PRESENT PERSONNEL, ARE GIVEN BELOW
actory Arms
ONAL HIGHWAYS and GOOD ROADS EVERYWHERE
NEW YORK CITY
NATIONALISM
True Patriotism means "Truth for Authority
Lip Patriotism means Authority for Truth"
True Patriotism " Sacrifice - Self-Denial
Lip " " Selfishness - Greed
True Patriotism " Work - Service
Lip " " Words - Slackers
True Patriotism " National Life
Lip " " Self - Conceit
True Patriotism " Rulership - Freedom
Lip " " Anarchy - Slavery
True Patriotism " Real Preparedness
Lip " " False Preparedness
True Patriotism " Victory - Justice
Lip " " Defeat - Corruption
True Patriotism means Peace - Progress - Prosperity
Lip " " War - Wretchedness - Waste
NATIONALISM
"IF the Nation has the question of preparedness or nonpreparedness before it, there is no middle course; in fact, there is no middle course in any activity of the human race. You must choose for good or evil, one course or the other. Obviously, with the world as it now is, unpreparedness is foolish. Preparedness is the only thing, but false preparedness is worse than no preparedness. The only preparedness worth talking about is complete preparedness, and you cannot get that unless you have everyone
A. L. WESTGARD
Vice-President and Director Transcontinental Highways
Total Population Served | 42,613,015 | 99.9 | 49,252,287 | 99.8 | 91,865,302 | 99.9 | 3,001 Total Counties Served | 99.5
NOTE
Lines nearly parallel between important places frequently indicate Alternative Routes.
The ultimate choice between such alternatives will be left to the National Highways Commission, when that body is appointed by the Government of the United States.
TOURING
NOTE
This map shows Tentative locations for a system of 150,000 miles of National Highways.
It is hoped that each State will suggest to the National Highways Association improvements in location within its borders.
EVERYWHERE
TE HIGHWAYS - COUNTY ROADS - TOWNSHIP OR TOWN ROADS
EM BECOMES THREE FOLD—NATIONAL, STATE AND COUNTY—THUS OMITTING THE TOWNSHIP ROADS
EVERYBODY BELIEVES IN GOOD ROADS EVERYWHERE
BECOME A
MEMBER
OF THE
NATIONAL HIGHWAYS ASSOCIATION
AND
HELP BRING ABOUT
GOOD ROADS EVERYWHERE
SEND APPLICATION TO WASHINGTON, D. C.
WE HAVE NO ENTANGLING POLITICAL ALLIANCES
You want to get ——— Good Roads Everywhere
We want you to get ——— Good Roads Everywhere
You can help us get ——— Good Roads Everywhere
We are working to get ——— Good Roads Everywhere
WE HAVE NO ENTANGLING COMMERCIAL ALLIANCES
YOU CAN HELP BRING ABOUT
GOOD ROADS EVERYWHERE
BY BEING A MEMBER OF
AND
SUPPORTING THE
NATIONAL HIGHWAYS ASSOCIATION
BECOME A
MEMBER

A good-nature
settin
THE GR
and a few
VANCOUVER
BELLINGHAM
SEATTLE
TACOMA
SPOKANE
PORTLAND
TILLAMOOK
PENDLETON
LEWISTON
EUGENE
BEND
BOISE
GLACIER NAT. PARK
POCATELLO
OGDEN
RENO
WINNEMUCCA
ELKO
SALT LAKE CITY
EUREKA
REDDING
CHICO
SACRAMENTO
SAN FRANCISCO
MONTEREY
FRESNO
BAKERSFIELD
LOS ANGELES
SAN DIEGO
LAS VEGAS
NEEDLES
KINGMAN
PHOENIX
TUCSON
EL PASO
RAWLINS
LARAMIE
CHEYENNE
DENVER
SANTA FE
ALBUQUERQUE
AMARILLO
ROSWELL
SAN ANTONIO
LAREDO
MONTERREY
PACIFIC
OCEAN
GULF OF CALIFORNIA
LOWER CALIFORNIA
MEXICO
RIO GRANDE
Explanation
GREYHOUND BUS ROUTES
PRINCIPAL CONNECTING LINES
STATE BOUNDARIES

e United States
ND LINES
DOMINION of CANADA
LAKE SUPERIOR
LAKE MICHIGAN
LAKE HURON
GEORGIAN BAY
LAKE ONTARIO
LAKE ERIE
QUEBEC
MONTREAL
OTTAWA
TORONTO
SAULT STE. MARIE
PORT ARTHUR
DULUTH
SUPERIOR
MINNEAPOLIS
ST. PAUL
EAU CLAIRE
OSHKOSH
LA CROSSE
MILWAUKEE
MUSKEGON
GRAND RAPIDS
BATTLE CREEK
DETROIT
FLINT
CHICAGO
SOUTH BEND
TOLEDO
CLEVELAND
BUFFALO
ERIE
SYRACUSE
ALBANY
PLATTSBURG
PORTLAND
PORTSMOUTH
BOSTON
CONCORD
SPRINGFIELD
PROVIDENCE
HARTFORD
NEW HAVEN
NEW YORK
PT. PLEASANT
PHILADELPHIA
ATLANTIC CITY
BALTIMORE
WASHINGTON
QUANTICO
PITTSBURGH
AKRON
CANTON
COLUMBUS
DAYTON
CINCINNATI
INDIANAPOLIS
FT. WAYNE
TERRE HAUTE
SPRINGFIELD
BLOOMINGTON
ST. LOUIS
KANSAS CITY
ST. JOSEPH
DES MOINES
DUBUQUE
CEDAR RAPIDS
DAVENPORT
BURLINGTON
ROCKFORD
MANKATO
ROCHESTER
EVANSVILLE
LOUISVILLE
LEXINGTON
CHARLESTON
HUNTINGTON
ROANOKE
LYNCHBURG
RICHMOND
NORFOLK
NEWPORT NEWS
VIRGINIA BEACH
BRISTOL
KNOXVILLE
NASHVILLE
GLASGOW
CAIRO
PADUCAH
MEMPHIS
JACKSON
LITTLE ROCK
HOT SPRINGS
TEXARKANA
SHREVEPORT
JOPLIN
CHATTANOOGA
ASHEVILLE
WINSTON-SALEM
GREENSBORO
CHARLOTTE
ROCKINGHAM
GREENVILLE
COLUMBIA
FLORENCE
CHARLESTON
FORT SUMTER
AUGUSTA
ATLANTA
MACON
SAVANNAH
BIRMINGHAM
MONTGOMERY
MERIDIAN
JACKSON
GREENWOOD
NATCHEZ
MOBILE
PENSACOLA
TALLAHASSEE
DOTHAN
JACKSONVILLE
ST. AUGUSTINE
LAKE CITY
OCALA
DAYTONA BEACH
ORLANDO
TAMPA
ST. PETERSBURG
PALM BEACH
MIAMI
FT. MYERS
KEY WEST
NEW ORLEANS
BATON ROUGE
ALEXANDRIA
HOUSTON
GALVESTON
BEAUMONT
PORT ARTHUR
"I WANNA GO HOME"
"HI, STRANGER"
"I CAN'T WALK ANOTHER MILE"
GULF OF MEXICO
ATLANTIC OCEAN
The GREYHOUND LINES

SAN FRANCISCO AND VICINITY

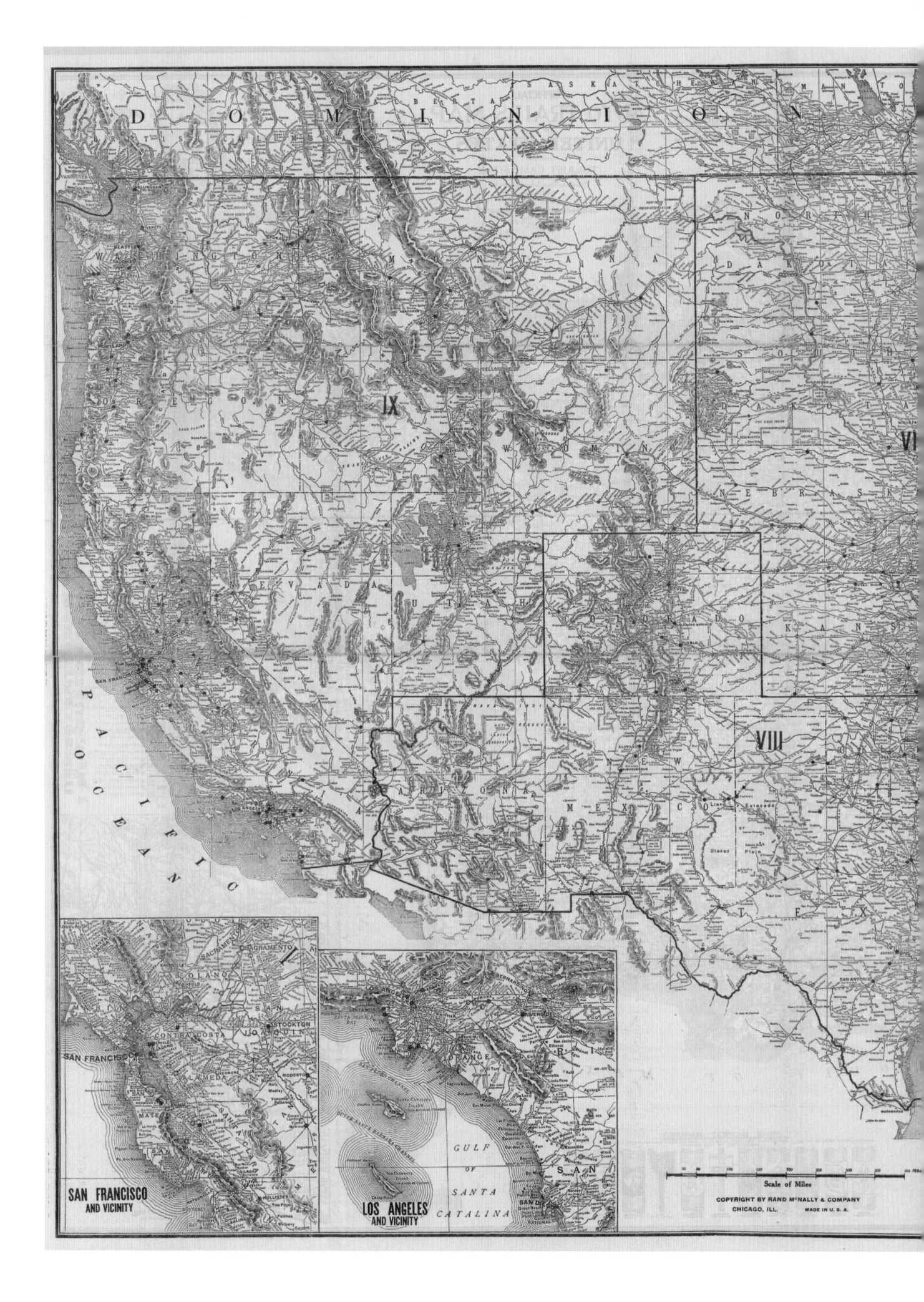

LOS ANGELES AND VICINITY

Scale of Miles

COPYRIGHT BY RAND McNALLY & COMPANY
CHICAGO, ILL.   MADE IN U.S.A.

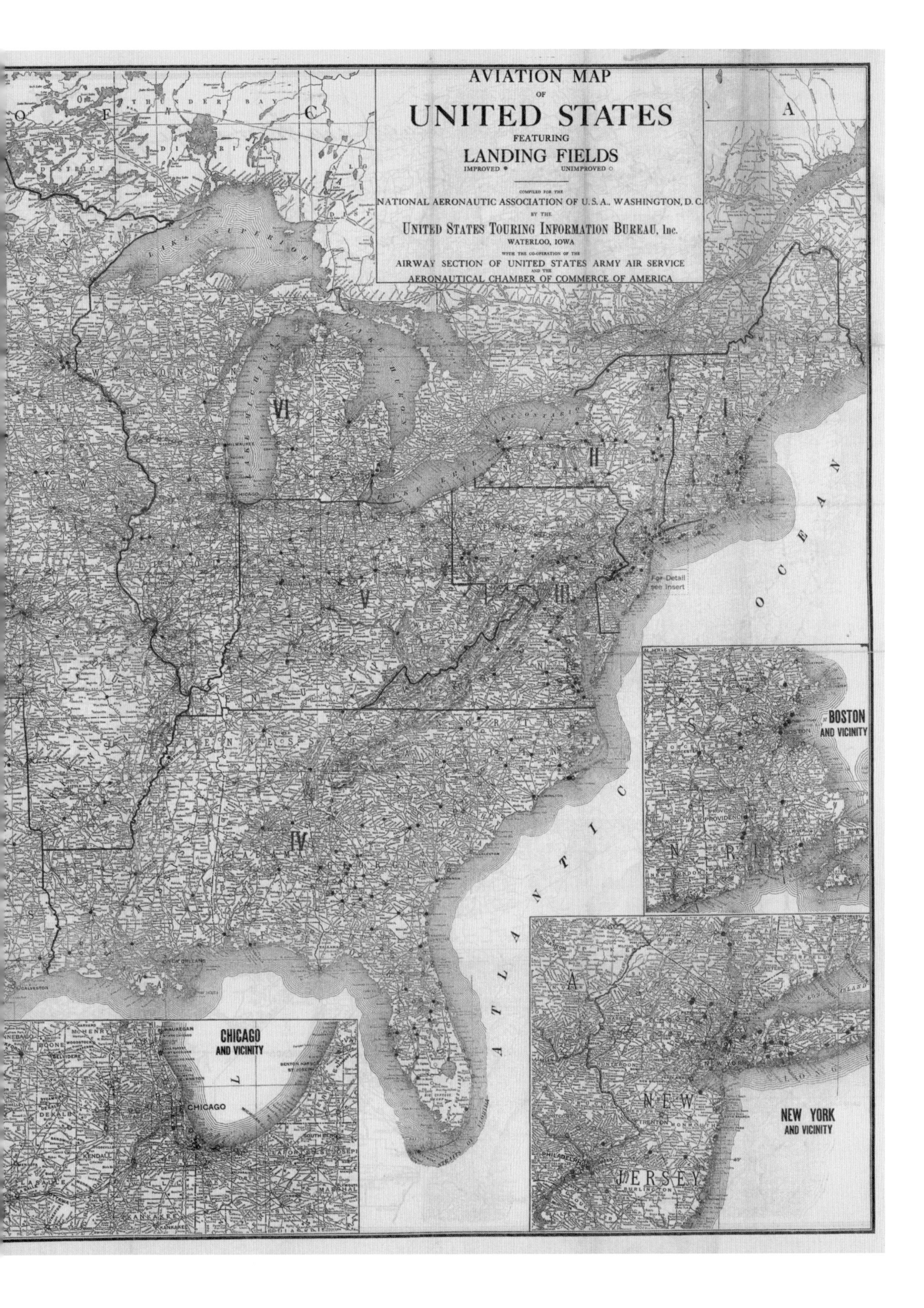

AVIATION MAP
OF
UNITED STATES
FEATURING
LANDING FIELDS
IMPROVED ●   UNIMPROVED ○

COMPILED FOR THE
NATIONAL AERONAUTIC ASSOCIATION OF U.S.A., WASHINGTON, D.C.
BY THE
UNITED STATES TOURING INFORMATION BUREAU, Inc.
WATERLOO, IOWA
WITH THE CO-OPERATION OF THE
AIRWAY SECTION OF UNITED STATES ARMY AIR SERVICE
AND THE
AERONAUTICAL CHAMBER OF COMMERCE OF AMERICA

BOSTON AND VICINITY

CHICAGO AND VICINITY

NEW YORK AND VICINITY

186   *Radio*

indicate the power (in watts) of each station, from fifty or less to more than a thousand. The first radio network broadcast, by NBC (National Broadcasting Company), took place on November 15, 1926—too late for the network to be indicated on the map.

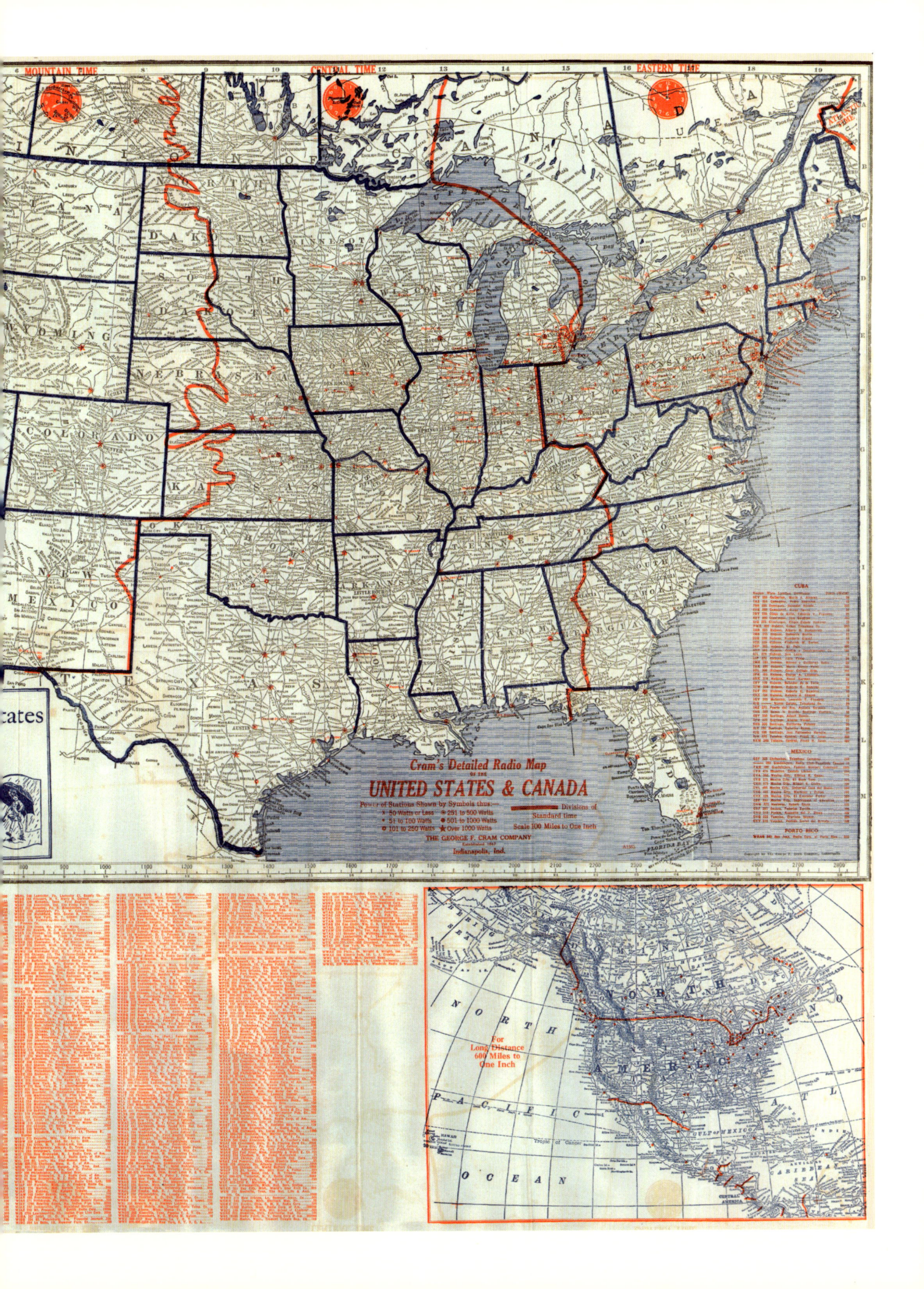

Cram's Detailed Radio Map of the
UNITED STATES & CANADA

ETHNOGRAPHICAL MAP OF AFRICA, IN THE EARLIEST TIMES,

ILLUSTRATIVE OF

DR PRICHARD'S Natural History of Man.

AND HIS RESEARCHES INTO THE PHYSICAL HISTORY OF MANKIND

EXPLANATION
1. Egyptians
2. Moors & Arabs
3. Libyan or Berber or Tuaryk Race
4. Tibbo
5. Garamantes or Fezzaners
6. Ababdeh & Bishareen
7. Barabra or Nubians
8. Nouba of Kordofan
9. Shangalla
10. Amharas and other Abyssins
11. Hazarta Race
12. Galla Race
13. Nouba or Negroes of Borgho
14. Begharmi
15. Bornowy
16. Hausa Race Eastern Sudan
17. Race of Western Sudan
18. Fulah or Felatah Race
19. Mandingo Race
20. Jaloff Race
21. Felups & other Negroes near Sierra Leone
22. Susus & Bulloms
23. Krou Race and other Tribes
24. Race of Ashanti & Fanti
25. Widah or Dahomeh Race
26. Binin Race
27. Great South African Family of Nations
28. Kongo Race
29. Mozambique Nations
30. Kafirs
31. Hottentots or Quaquai Race

ETHNOGRAPHY

TRAINED AS A physician, Englishman James Cowles Prichard is considered a precursor of Charles Darwin and a founder of racial studies. He was one of the first ethnologists to believe that all races originated from the same species in Africa. In medicine, he specialized in nervous system disorders—what we call psychiatry—and was the first to define senile dementia.

✻ [*Opposite*] "Ethnographical Map of Africa, from the Earliest Times, Illustrative of Dr. Prichard's Natural History of Man and His Researches into the Physical History of Man." Engraved map, with added color, 58.3 × 48 cm. From Pritchard's *Six Ethnographical Maps ...*, 2nd ed. (London, New York: H. Baillière, 1851) [Historic Maps Collection].

Prichard's set of ethnographical maps, originally published in 1843, was the first of its kind. In his cover note, he recognizes that "it is impossible to represent in one map the positions of nations in periods of time very distant from each other. These positions vary through the effect of migrations and conquests" [p. 1]. Hence, some anachronism results. In respect to his Africa map, Pritchard admits that much of the representation of the interior is conjectural; divisions of regions and countries is based on authorities. The color key identifies thirty-one different races.

✻ [*Overleaf*] Gustaf Kombst. "Ethnographic Map of Europe." Engraved map, with added color, 46.9 × 56.8 cm. From Alexander Keith Johnston's *The National Atlas of Historical, Commercial, and Political Geography: Constructed from the Most Recent and Authentic Sources ... Accompanied by Maps and Illustrations of the Physical Geography of the Globe by Heinrich Berghaus, and an Ethnographic Map of Europe by Gustaf Kombst* (Edinburgh: J. Johnstone; W. & A. K. Johnston..., 1846) [Rare Books Division]. The first edition of the atlas appeared in 1843, the same year as Pritchard's publication. The volume's five maps of physical geography (four by Berghaus and this one by Kombst) are thought to constitute the beginning of

✻ Portrait of James Cowles Prichard, 1786–1848. From D. J. Cunningham's "Anniversary Address," *Journal of the Royal Anthropological Institute of Great Britain and Ireland* 38 (January–June 1908): 10–35 [General Library Collection].

Johnston's landmark thematic atlas of 1848 (see his section in the Landmark Thematic Atlases section).

Kombst accompanies his map with four lengthy pages of descriptive notes. Though they are dated March 1844 in this edition, the map first appeared as a separate publication in 1841. He begins by talking generally about the utility of such mapping:

> An Ethnographic Map would be of great use in History and Statistics, but of still greater use in the Natural History of Man.... Circumstances have so

{189}

ETHNOGRAPHIC MAP
OF
EUROPE
BY
Dr GUSTAF KOMBST
ARCTIC OCEAN
SCANDINAVIA
ATLANTIC OCEAN
MEDITERRANEAN SEA
AFRICA
TURKEY
IN ASIA
BLACK SEA
Reference to the Colours.

Ethnography

far favoured the projector of this Map, as to enable him to see the three great varieties of the so called Caucasian species in Europe, viz., the Celtic, Teutonic, and Sclavonian, in several countries inhabited by them. He has devoted to the subject of the physical differences of these varieties, their origin, connection, &c., undiminished attention for a great number of years. Yet, as *this is the first Ethnographic Map ever published*, based upon the principle of the natural physical difference of the different varieties of the Caucasian species inhabiting Europe, he is fully aware, that it must in many respects still remain deficient.... But a beginning must be made, and in this matter, as in many others, it requires the co-operation of a great number of minds, and a long series of observations by each, to arrive at complete scientific correctness, at which stage such studies may turn out to be highly useful in many more points than can at present be anticipated [p. 53; my italics].

Clearly, he is an advocate of the Baconian approach to the acquisition of knowledge. Among possible benefits of such ethnographic study, according to Kombst, is information on the intellectual and moral character of nations, their languages, and forms of government. One interesting conclusion he has drawn so far is that nations are so differently constituted that no one form of government can be applicable, at the same time, to all of them. (Something for U.S. foreign policymakers to ponder?)

The map's coloring is purposeful. For the three main Caucasian species, Kombst uses blue for Celtic, yellow for Teutonic, and red for Sclavonion. To indicate a crossing of these varieties, he has mixed the colors in such a manner that the dominant color in the mixture indicates the dominant national element—more blue, more Celtic, for example.

✻ Key to Gustaf Kombst's ethnographic map.

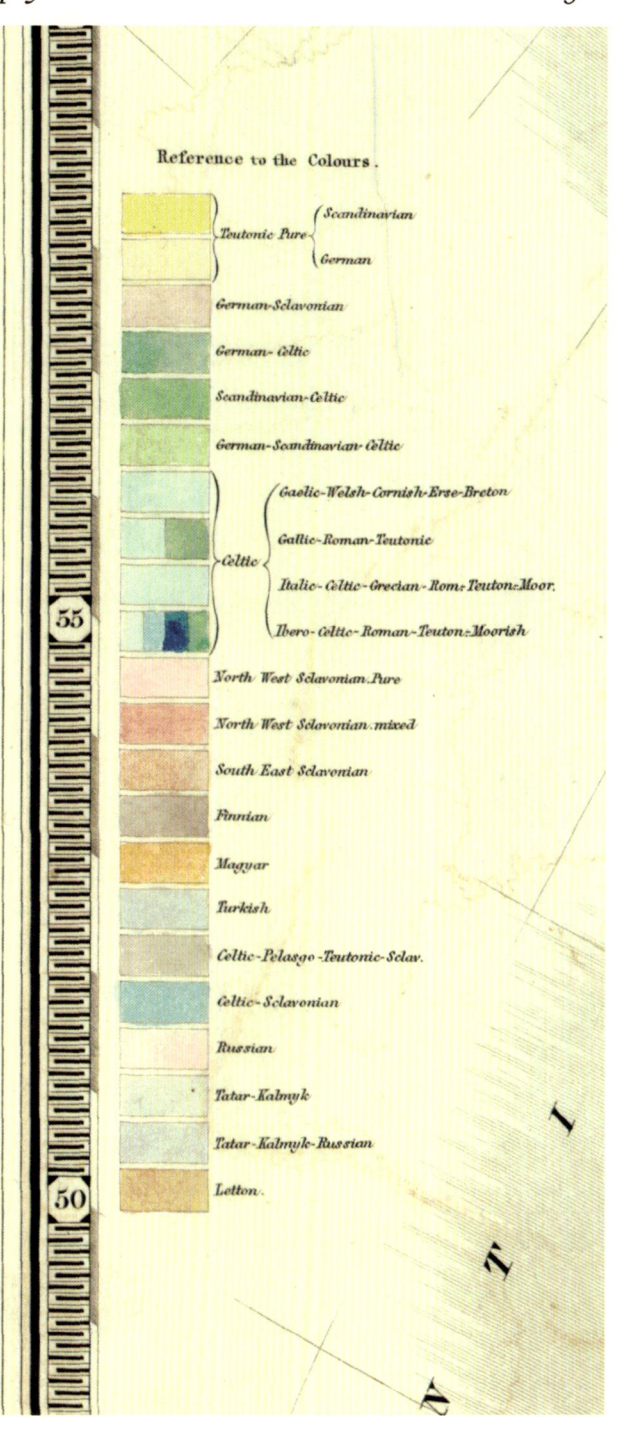

EUROPA
MARE GERMANICUM
MARE MEDITERRANEUM
PONTUS EUXINUS
Opera Godofr. Hensilii delineata
Excusa prostat in Officina Homanniana

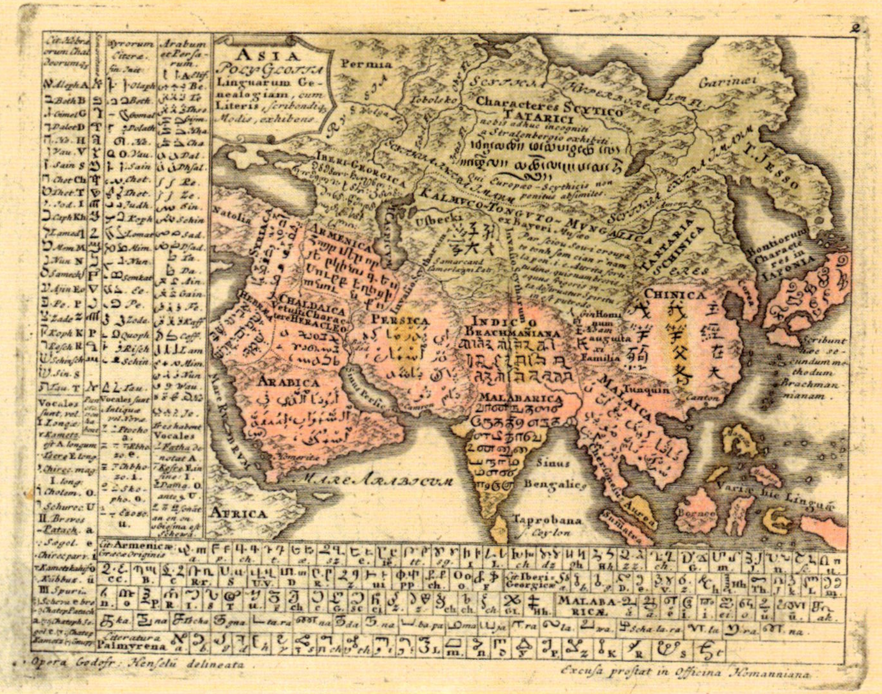
ASIA Polyglotta Linguarum Genealogiam, cum Literis scribendique Modis, exhibens
ARABICA
PERSICA
CHINICA
MARE ARABICUM
AFRICA
Opera Godofr. Hensilii delineata
Excusa prostat in Officina Homanniana

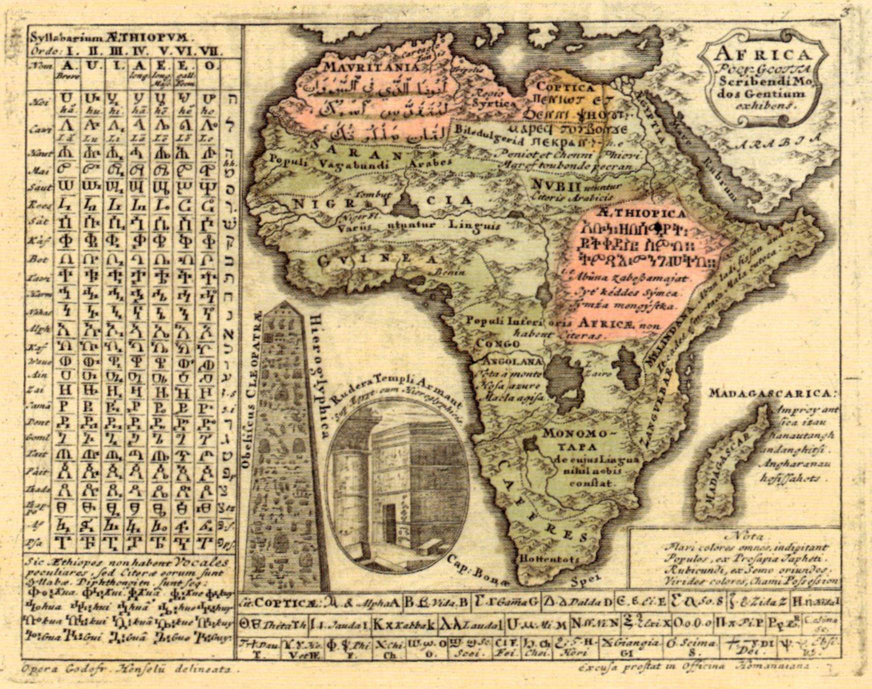
Syllabarium ÆTHIOPUM
AFRICA Polyglotta Scribendi Modos Gentium exhibens
MAURITANIA
COPTICA
ÆTHIOPICA
NIGRITIA
GUINEA
CONGO
ANGOLANA
MONOMOTAPA
CAFFRES
MADAGASCARICA
Hieroglyphica
Obeliscus CLEOPATRÆ
Cap. Bonæ Spei
Opera Godofr. Hensilii delineata
Excusa prostat in Officina Homanniana

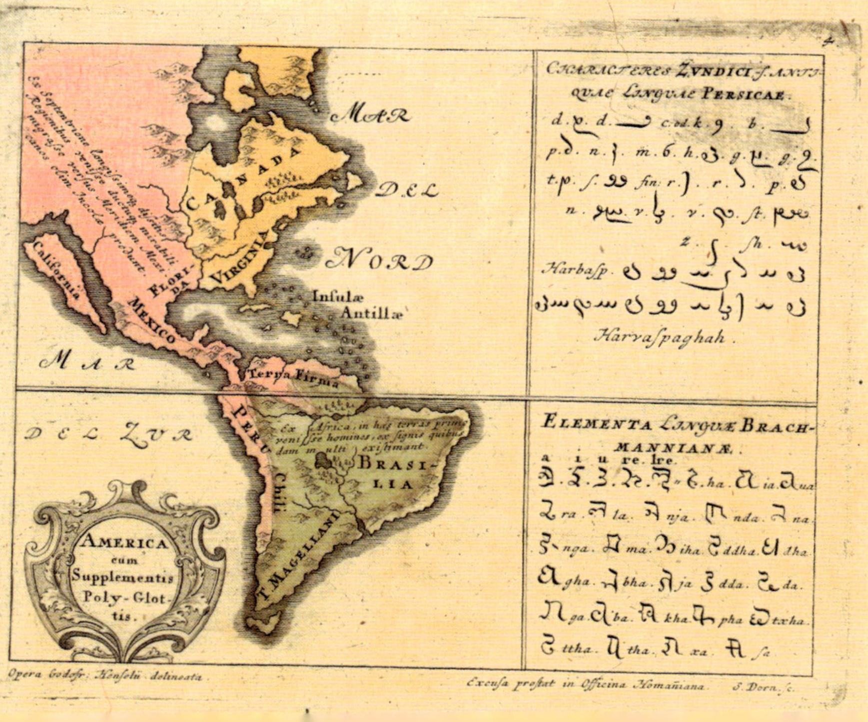
MAR DEL NORD
CANADA
VIRGINIA
FLORIDA
MEXICO
California
Insulæ Antillæ
Terra Firma
PERU
BRASILIA
Chili
T. MAGELLANICA
MAR DEL ZUR
AMERICA cum Supplementis Poly-Glottis
CHARACTERES ZUNDICI ANTIQUÆ LINGUÆ PERSICÆ
ELEMENTA LINGUÆ BRACHMANNIANÆ
Opera Godofr. Hensilii delineata
Excusa prostat in Officina Homanniana
S. Dorn

LINGUISTICS

✻ [*Opposite*] Gottfried Hensel, b. 1689? "Europa poly glotta: Linguarum genealogiam exhibens, una cum literis, scribendiq[ue] modis, omnium gentium" ([Nuremberg]: Excusa prostat in Officina Homanniana, [1741]). Four copperplate maps, with added color, each 16 × 21 cm, on one sheet 51 × 57 cm [Historic Maps Collection]. From his *Synopsis vniversae philologiae* ... (Nuremberg: Homann, 1741).

THE EARLIEST linguistic maps of the four continents. Where he can, German philologist Hensel translates the first few words of the Lord's Prayer ("Our Father, who art in Heaven, hallowed be thy name") into local languages. Elsewhere, as in America and Africa, he notes human migrations. In Brazil, for example, evidence suggests, he says, that the first humans there came from Africa. In the box at the bottom right of Africa, he states that the map colors mark areas settled by descendants of the three sons of Noah: Japhet ("rubicundi," here pink), Shem ("oriundos," here yellow-orange), and Ham ("virides," here olive green). Along the sides and at the bottom of the four maps are alphabet tables that cover most known written languages.

Here, California continues its mythical status as an island.

{ 193 }

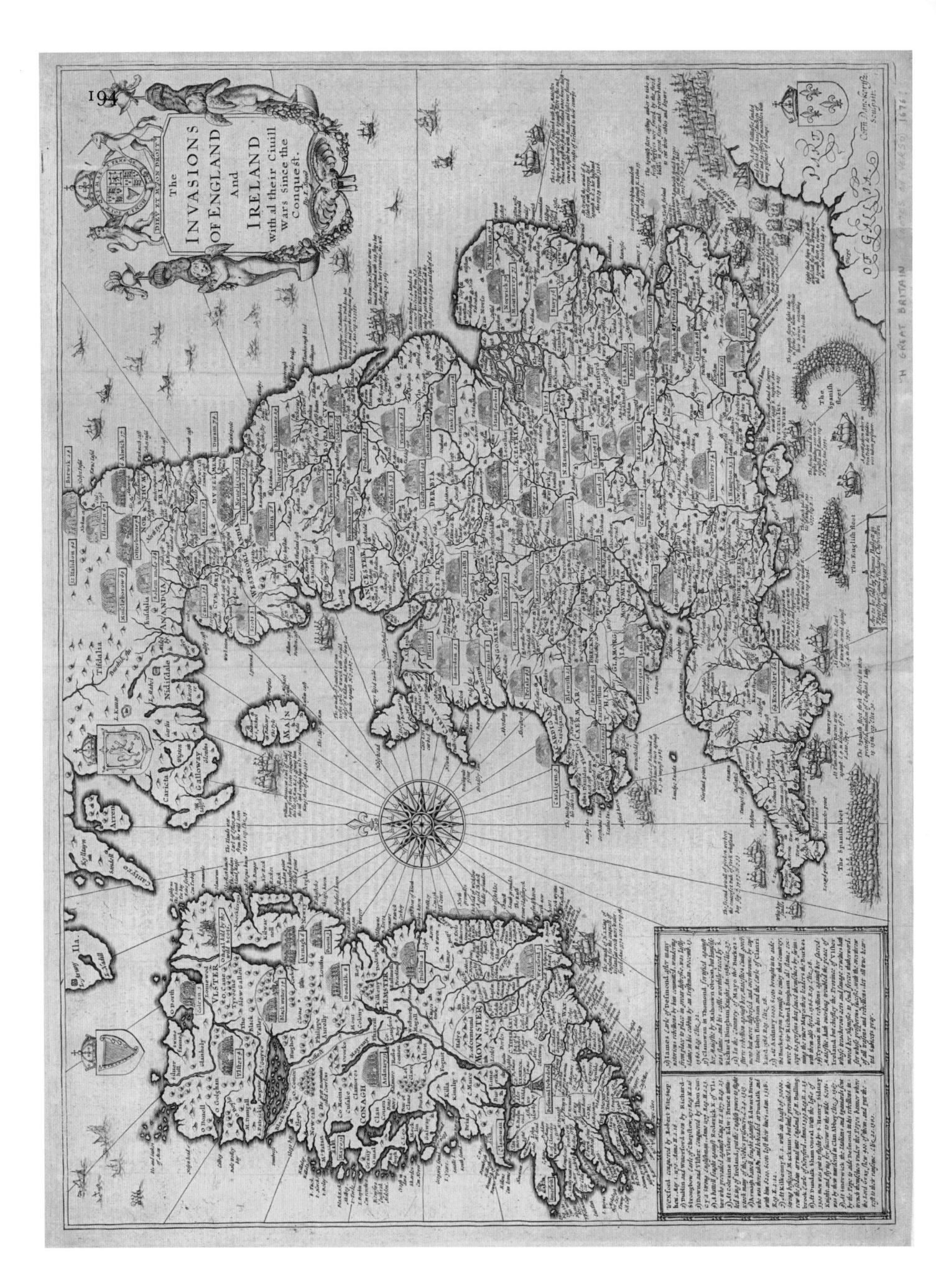

The INVASIONS Of ENGLAND And IRELAND with al their Ciuill wars Since the Conquest.

MILITARY HISTORY

JOHN SPEED came into mapmaking late in life, having worked in his father's tailoring business until he was about fifty. An interest in history brought him in contact with Sir Fulke Greville, who offered financial support, and Queen Elizabeth I, who allowed him working space in the Custom House. His 1611/1612 atlas, *The Theatre of the Empire of Great Britaine*, was the first comprehensive English atlas, and it contained the first set of English county maps, most with town plans; these probably constitute his most significant contributions to English cartography.

✳ [*Opposite*] "The Invasions of England and Ireland: With Al Their Ciuill Wars since the Conquest." Copperplate map, 38 x 51 cm [Historic Maps Collection]. From Speed's *A Prospect of the Most Famous Parts of the World* (London: Printed for Thomas Basset … and Richard Chiswel…, 1676). Published as a complement to Speed's earlier work, *A Prospect* was the first world atlas published by an Englishman; the first edition appeared in 1627.

This map covers the period from the Norman Invasion of 1066 through the Spanish Armada of 1588, but its focus is on battles fought among Britons. The sites of the battles are marked with small banners containing a place name and number. (Several pages of text in the atlas, keyed to the numbers, identify the combatants and summarize the action.) Most of the battles feature miniature groups of pikemen facing each other, forming a canopy with their tall weapons; several show cavalry engagements. The ships of the Spanish Armada take center stage at the bottom. In Ireland, there are two, more descriptive, scenes: "Oneal kild by the wild Scots" (1567) and "Desmond beheded" (1468). In all, more than eighty-five military encounters are noted on the map.

✳ Portrait of John Speed (1552?–1629) by Solomon Savery [Graphic Arts Collection].

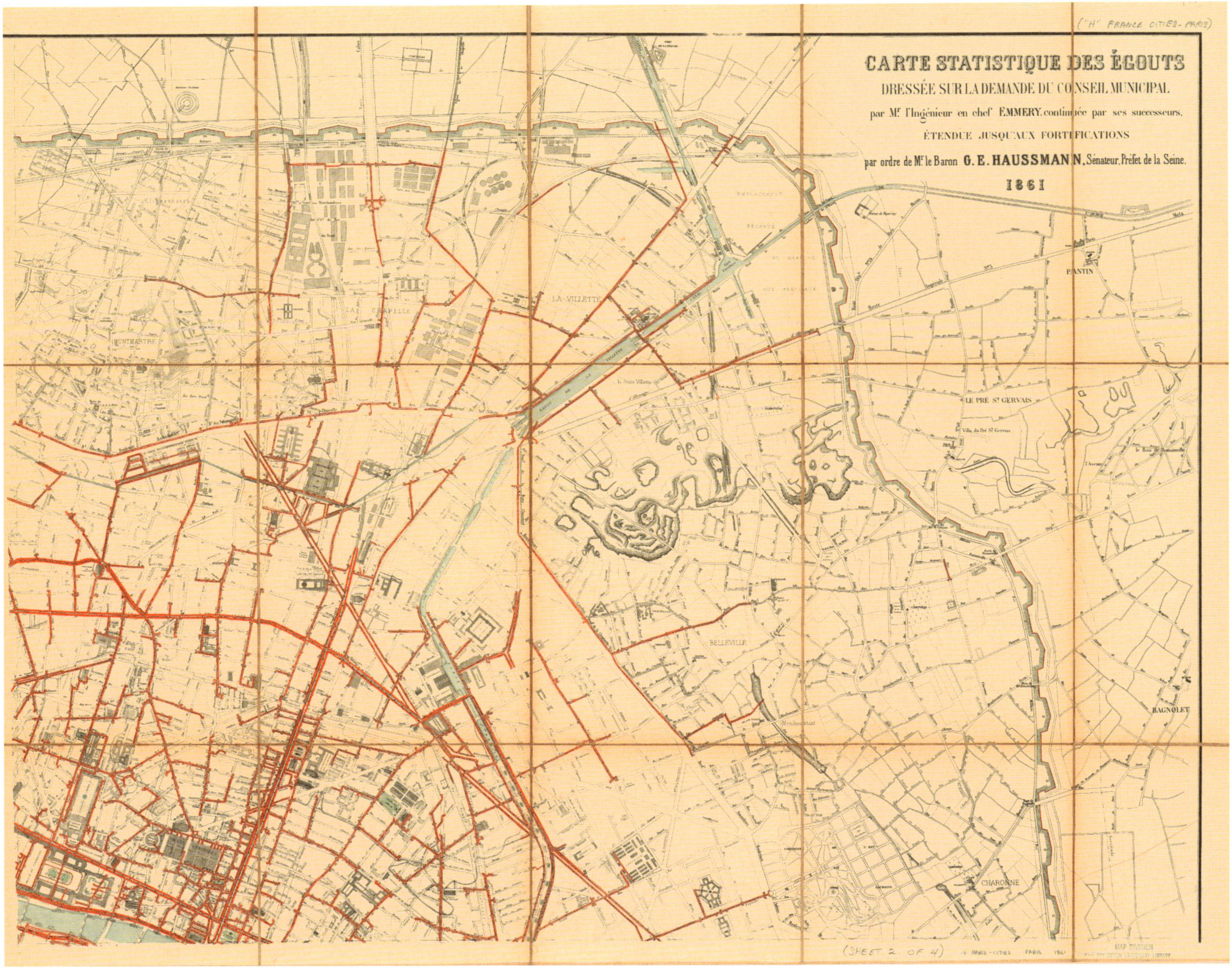

CARTE STATISTIQUE DES ÉGOUTS
DRESSÉE SUR LA DEMANDE DU CONSEIL MUNICIPAL
par Mr l'Ingénieur en chef EMMERY, continuée par ses successeurs.
ÉTENDUE JUSQU'AUX FORTIFICATIONS
par ordre de Mr le Baron G. E. HAUSSMANN, Sénateur, Préfet de la Seine.
1861
("H" FRANCE CITIES - PARIS)
PANTIN
LA VILLETTE
LA CHAPELLE
MONTMARTRE
LE PRÉ St GERVAIS
BELLEVILLE
BAGNOLET
CHARONNE
(SHEET 2 OF 4)
MAP DIVISION

URBAN PLANNING

Appointed préfet de la Seine (head of the city's administration) by Napoleon III in 1853, Baron Georges Eugène Haussmann is associated with the rebuilding and modernizing of Paris. Among his many changes/improvements to the city's landscape were wide boulevards radiating from the Arc de Triomphe, expansive gardens, new bridges, a new water supply, and a huge new sewer system. His transformations affected more than 50 percent of the city's area. Historically, he has either been hated as the man who destroyed medieval Paris or loved as the one who created the modern metropolis we know today.

✻ [*Opposite*] Segment "Nord-Est, 1861" of Haussmann's "Carte statistique des égouts, dressée sur la demande du conseil municipal par M. l'ingénieur en chef Emmery, continuée par ses successeurs, étendue jusqu'aux fortifications, par ordre de Mr. le Baron G. E. Haussmann … 1861." Lithograph map in four segments, with added color, each segment dissected in fifteen pieces, mounted on cloth, 150 × 190 cm (Paris: imp. lith de V. Janson, [1861]) [Historic Maps Collection].

Certainly not the first sewer map of Paris, but the largest (roughly 5 feet × 6 feet) and most detailed of its time, indicative of the scope and scale of Haussmann's massive undertaking. Under his watch, the sewer system was quintupled, and tunnel sizes were greatly enlarged and standardized. Note the outer, numbered sections of the fortifications, which mark the boundaries of the city proper. (Compare with H. N. Maire's administrative maps of Paris in his Landmark Thematic Atlases section.)

✻ [*Right*] Detail from the Haussmann sewer map. Princeton's copy is signed in manuscript by "L'Inspecteur général, Directeur du Service Municipal des travaux Publics. Paris, le 23 Juin 1862. Michal."

✻ Portrait of Baron Georges Eugène Haussmann (1809–1881) in 1853. From vol. 2 of his *Mémoires du baron Haussmann …* (Paris: Victor-Havard, 1890–1893) [General Library Collection].

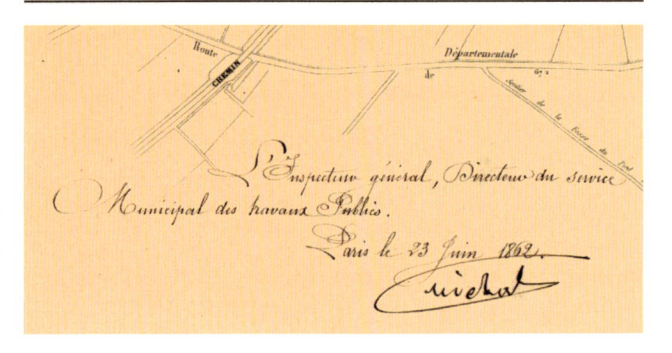

{ 197 }

LEOBELGICUS
ANGLIÆ PARS.
Norwich
Colchester
London
Douer
HOLLANDIA
ZELANDIA
BRABANTIA
ARTESIA
Amsterdam
Antwerpen
Breda
De Zuyder Zee
NOVUS XVII. INFERIORIS GERMANIÆ PROVINCIARUM.
Scala Milliar Germanica

Theme Maps (Fanta "Z")

✽

THESE MAPS are not layered with data in the thematic map sense; rather, they use fictional geography and/or shape to illustrate or symbolize themes.

✽ Famiano Strada, 1572–1649. "Novus XVII. inferioris Germaniæ provinciarum" (1653). Copperplate map, with added color, 18 × 13 cm [Historic Maps Collection]. From his *De bello Belgico*, novissima ed. (Rome: Apud Hermannum Scheus, 1653).

One of a number of versions of a map of the Low Countries in the form of a heraldic lion. The idea began in 1583 during the Dutch War of Independence (or Eighty Years' War, 1568–1648), when the "seventeen provinces"—the current Netherlands, Belgium, Luxembourg, northern France, and a small part of western Germany—revolted against Spain. The symbol of the lion derives from the coats of arms of several of the provinces.

THE PILGRIMS PROGRESS

Or Christians journey from the City of Destruction in this evil **WORLD** *to the* **CELESTIAL CITY** *in the* **WORLD** *that is to Come.*

Published July 1 1813 by J. Pitts No. 14 Great St. Andrew Street Seven Dials.

LITERATURE

✳ [*Opposite*] "The Pilgrims Progress, or, Christians Journey from the City of Destruction in This Evil World to the Celestial City in the World That Is to Come" ([London]: Published ... by J. Pitts, no. 14 Great St. Andrew Street Seven Dials, July 1, 1813). Copperplate map, with added color, 34 × 45 cm, on sheet 41 × 51 cm [Historic Maps Collection].

This anonymous map visually interprets English preacher John Bunyan's religious allegory *The Pilgrim's Progress from This World to That Which Is to Come: Delivered Under the Similitude of a Dream, Wherein Is Discovered the Manner of His Setting Out, His Dangerous Journey, and Safe Arrival at the Desired Country* (1678). (The book was probably written during his imprisonments for preaching without a license.) The protagonist, named Christian, faces temptations and digressions that could prevent him from reaching his goal, God's celestial city. The symbolic nature of the work lends itself to graphic illustration: the Slough of Despond, the Valley of the Shadow of Death, Vanity Fair—such "obstacles" have become iconic in Western literature. The universal resonance of Bunyan's work—it has been translated into more than two hundred languages—accounts for its never having been out of print.

✳ [*Right*] Lewis Carroll, 1832–1898. "Ocean Chart." Printed map, 13 × 8.2 cm. From Carroll's *The Hunting of the Snark: An Agony in Eight Fits* (London: Macmillan, 1876) [Rare Books Division]. With nine illustrations by Henry Holiday. Lewis Carroll, of course, is the pseudonym of Charles Lutwidge Dodgson, author of *Alice's Adventures in Wonderland* (1865).

Imagination at its most sublime and amusing: a blank map bearing only the accoutrements of orientation and an inscrutable scale.

> He had bought a large map representing the sea,
> Without the least vestige of land:
> And the crew were much pleased when they found it to be
> A map they could all understand.
>
> 'What's the good of Mercator's North Poles and Equators,
> Tropics, Zones, and Meridian Lines?'
> So the Bellman would cry: and the crew would reply,
> 'They are merely conventional signs!'
> 'Other maps are such shapes, with their islands and capes!
> But we've got our brave Captain to thank'
> (So the crew would protest) 'that he's bought us the best—
> A perfect and absolute blank!'

[pp. 15–16, from "Fit II. The Bellman's Speech"].

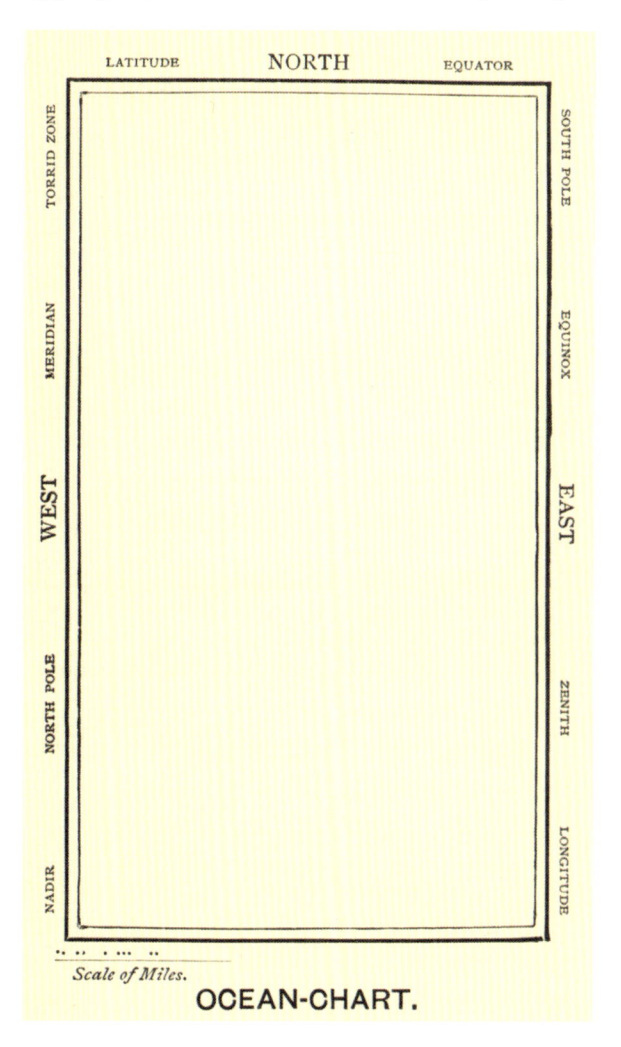

{ 201 }

Theme Maps (Fanta "Z")

FARANDOUL EN OCÉANIE

Jeté par la tempête, à l'âge de quatre mois, dans une des îles de l'archipel Pomotou, notre héros passe son enfance au sein d'une honnête tribu de singes. Un jour, poussé par un irrésistible instinct de voyageur, il quitte sa famille adoptive, ses frères et ses amis, pour se lancer dans l'inconnu.

Il est recueilli par le trois-mâts la Belle-Léocadie. Le lieutenant Mandibul apparaît pour la première fois dans sa vie. Ici commencent les grandes aventures. Démêlés avec les pirates du terrible Bora-Bora, sanglier à mitraille et gigantesque soupe à la tortue. Les écumeurs des îles de la Sonde sont vaincus! Apparition de la suave figure de Mysora, la perle de la Malaisie. L'amour au fond de la mer, chastes rendez-vous en scaphandre, Affreux malheurs!!!

Que dire du farouche Valentin Cronkuff, directeur de l'aquarium de Melbourne? Grâce à un concours d'évènements inouïs, il possède dans son aquarium la pauvre Mysora, toujours revêtue de son scaphandre et la séquestre rigoureusement. Mais des vengeurs surviennent. L'Océanie est agitée par de terribles évènements. Apparition d'armées quadrumanes.

Les singes sont aptes à la civilisation, Bimanes et quadrumanes vont former une belle nation mixte lorsque... un colonel quadrumane se laisse corrompre par la perfide Albion.

FARANDOUL EN AMÉRIQUE

Grandes chasses, pièges à serpents à sonnettes. Fortune immense! Farandoul et ses marins se dirigent vers le pays des Mormons. Ici complications nouvelles, 17 épouses!!! Des Apaches surviennent. Le poteau de la guerre, la danse du scalp. Farandoul peintre sur sauvages. Par malheur, son cœur a parlé encore une fois pour une jeune Apache répondant au nom poétique de la Lune-qui-se-lève. Aventures d'ours et de radeaux. Poursuite acharnée de Bison-Rouge, guerrier apache.

Autres aventures de Farandoul aux États-Unis. Gigantesque duel. Farandoul vogue vers l'Amérique du Sud. Les mines de diamants de la Patagonie. Rencontre extraordinaire du célèbre Philéas Fogg et de Passepartout, opérant avec monde, en plus de 80 jour Les Patagons arrivent. l Les États désunis du Nicar cavalerie sous-marine, l chloroforme, etc., la guerr à 8,000 mètres!!

FARAN

La mystérieuse Afrique

FRENCHMAN Albert Robida is the father of science fiction illustration. Though he trained to be a notary, he supported himself as an illustrator and caricaturist. He cofounded his own magazine, *Le Caricature*, in 1880, and authored a trilogy of futuristic novels: *Le vingtième siècle* (1883), *La guerre au vingtième siècle* (1887), and *Le vingtième siècle: La vie électrique* (1890). In these, he has often been compared to his contemporary countryman Jules Verne, whose own futuristic works such as

✻ Portrait of Albert Robida (1848–1926) by A. Brauer. From vol. 1 of *Figures contemporaines tirées de l'Album Mariani* (Paris: Ernest Flammarion, 1894) [General Library Collection].

[Illustration caption block:]

FARANDOUL EN ASIE

Salut, berceau du monde! L'Inde a-t-elle des secrets pour Farandoul? Non, plus de mystères. Salut! éléphants, rajahs et bayadères! Le rajah de Kafir a des intentions cruelles... mais n'anticipons pas. Farandoul sillonne l'Asie dans tous les sens; les éléphants aussi ont des vices; l'ivrognerie en est un. Et les amazones du roi de Siam! Farandoul explore la Chine, pays des mandarins; le Japon, la perle de l'extrême Orient. La encore que de dangers pour Farandoul! Daïmios et guerriers à trois sabres s'ouvrent le ven... vec fureur.

FARANDOUL EN EUROPE ET ETC.

Connaissons-nous bien notre vieille Europe? Farandoul y poursuit le cours de ses aventures et de ses découvertes, et couronne sa carrière par une petite excursion au pôle Nord!!

C'est tout un atlas qu'il faudrait pour indiquer clairement les routes suivies par Farandoul dans les cinq ou six parties du monde et même plus loin, mais nous espérons que l'intelligence de nos lecteurs suppléera aux nombreuses lacunes laissées dans notre carte, malgré toutes nos recherches et les indications de l'illustre voyageur lui-même, notre bienveillant ami.

SCEAUX, IMP. CHARAIRE ET FILS.

(in English) *Journey to the Center of the Earth* (1864) and *Twenty Thousand Leagues under the Sea* (1869) pioneered the genre. However, Robida's characters were not mad scientists, and his prescient imagination was more attuned to everyday life; his inventions, as a result, had social implications and consequences. For example, he envisaged wars fought with missiles and poison gas, flat-screen televisions that provided twenty-four-hour views of remote events, and urban settings that included flying cars and electric trains.

✴ [*Above*] "Carte des voyages très extraordinaires de Saturnin Farandoul: Pour servir a l'intelligence du texte." Lithograph map, with added color, 21.5 × 65 cm. From Robida's *Voyages très extraordinaires de Saturnin Farandoul: Dans les 5 ou 6 parties du monde et dans tous les pays connus et même inconnus de M. Jules Verne* (Paris: Librairie illustrée, [1879]) [Historic Maps Collection]. The 808-page book includes 453 drawings and 50 full-page color illustrations.

World map from Robida's first novel. Farandoul's adventures were serialized weekly, collected and published in five parts or books, and finally gathered into one large volume; the map first appeared in the first book. As one might expect from the title, Robida's work is a spoof on Jules Verne's "extraordinary voyages" series—in fact, the second part is titled "Le tour du monde en plus de

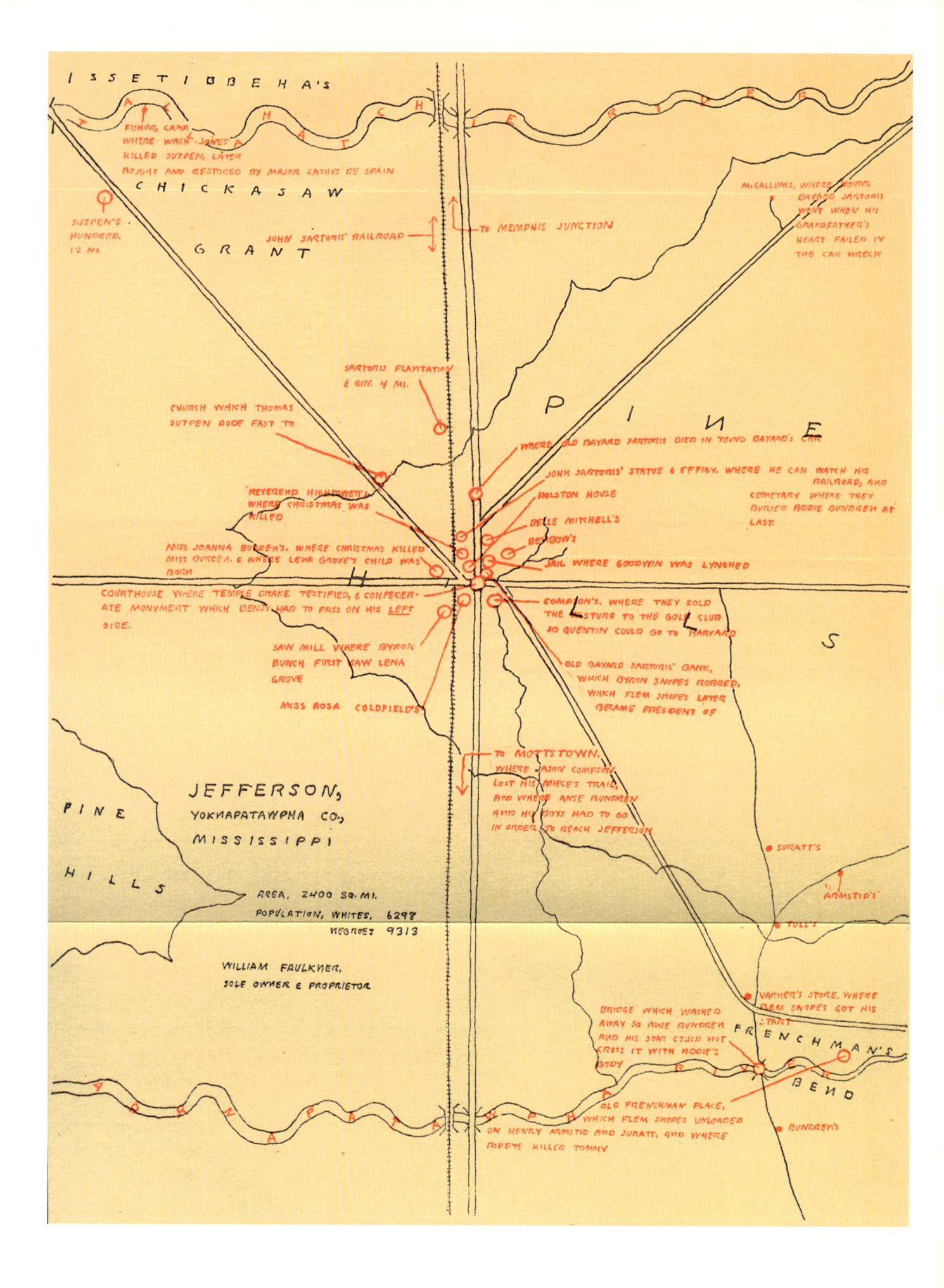

Jefferson, Yoknapatawpha Co., Mississippi

Area, 2400 sq. mi.
Population, Whites, 6298
Negroes 9313

William Faulkner, Sole Owner & Proprietor

Labeled locations:

- ISSETIBBEHA'S (TALLAHATCHIE RIVER)
- Fishing camp, where Wash Jones killed Sutpen, later bought and restored by Major Cassius de Spain
- CHICKASAW GRANT
- Sutpen's Hundred, 12 mi.
- John Sartoris' Railroad
- To Memphis Junction
- McCallum's, where young Bayard Sartoris went when his grandfather's heart failed in the car wreck
- PINE
- Sartoris Plantation & Gin, 4 mi.
- Church which Thomas Sutpen rode fast to
- Where old Bayard Sartoris died in young Bayard's car
- John Sartoris' statue & effigy, where he can watch his railroad, and cemetery where they buried Addie Bundren at last
- 'Reverend Hightower's' where Christmas was killed
- Holston House
- Belle Mitchell's
- Benbow's
- Miss Joanna Burden's, where Christmas killed Miss Burden, & where Lena Grove's child was born
- Jail where Goodwin was lynched
- Courthouse where Temple Drake testified, & Confederate Monument which Benjy had to pass on his LEFT side.
- Compson's, where they sold the pasture to the golf club so Quentin could go to Harvard
- HILLS
- Saw mill where Byron Bunch first saw Lena Grove
- Old Bayard Sartoris' Bank, which Byron Snopes robbed, which Flem Snopes later became president of
- Miss Rosa Coldfield's
- To Mottstown, where Jason Compson lost his niece's trail, and where Anse Bundren and his boys had to go in order to reach Jefferson
- PINE HILLS
- Suratt's
- Armstid's
- Tull's
- Varner's store, where Flem Snopes got his start
- Bridge which washed away so Anse Bundren and his sons could not cross it with Addie's body
- FRENCHMAN'S BEND
- Old Frenchman Place, which Flem Snopes unloaded on Henry Armstid and Suratt, and where Popeye killed Tommy
- Bundren's
- YOKNAPATAWPHA RIVER

80 jours," a clear reference to Verne's *Around the World in 80 Days* (1872). The map gives the reader a robust sense of the rollicking, continental range of Farandoul's world tour—and the exotic, formidable peoples and creatures he encounters—from his survival at the age of four months and seven days from a shipwreck on a remote Pacific island to his return years later as a grown man.

✻ [*Opposite*] William Faulkner, 1897–1962. "Jefferson, Yoknapatawpha Co., Mississippi." Printed map, 27 × 24.4 cm. From Faulkner's *Absalom, Absalom!* (New York: Random House, 1936) [Rare Books Division].

Probably the most famous map in American literature, bearing the statement "William Faulkner, Sole Owner & Proprietor"—in case there were any doubt of its authenticity. It is based on Oxford, Lafayette County, Mississippi, where Faulkner lived for most of his life, and locates much of Faulkner's fiction. Leading up to this novel were the remarkable achievements of *The Sound and the Fury* (1929), *As I Lay Dying* (1930), *Sanctuary* (1931), and *Light in August* (1932)—all have incidents in Yoknapatawpha, and so the map is not as much a revelation to readers as it is a confirmation of what they have learned from the previous fiction. Faulkner received the Nobel Prize for Literature in 1949.

✻ Dust jacket of Faulkner's *Absalom, Absalom!* (New York: Random House, 1936) [Rare Books Division].

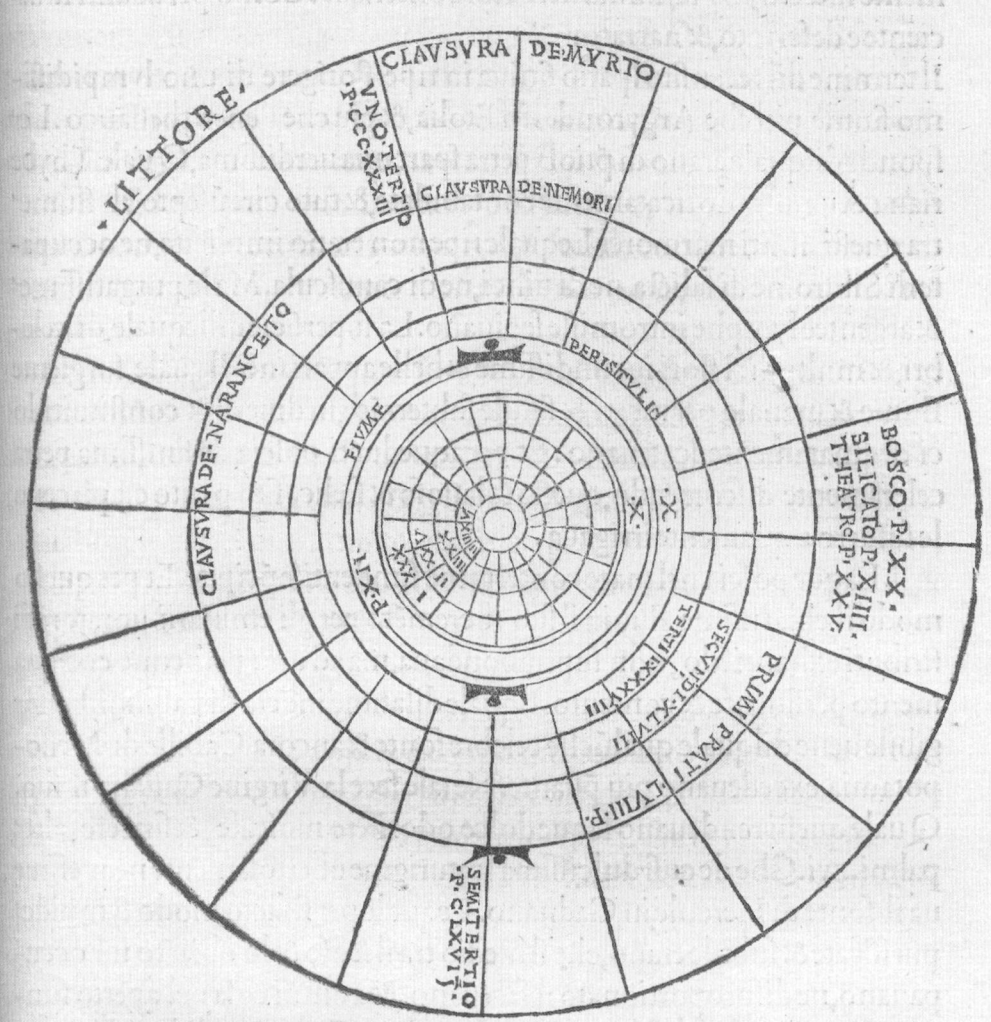

Per piu euidente dimonstratione, Il circuito di questa delitiosa & amœnissima insula di circumensuratione constaua di tre milliarii. La figura dillaquale di uno milliario il suo diametro præstaua. Ilquale in diuisione tripartito, uno tertio.333.passi continua uno pede, & dui palmi, & alquãto piu dal extremo labro dille litorale ripe fina al claustro naranceo. La mensura di uno semitertio, passi.166.& palmi.10.occupaua. Daquesto termine icominciauano gli prati uerso il centro tendenti, altro tanto semitertio. Distributo dúque acconciamente uno integro tertio, rimane uno semitertio a dispensare fina al meditulo, passi.166.& palmi.10. Dal peristylio antedicto, era conceduto alquanto di spatio rimasto per la contractione degli prati sopradicti, ad euitare l'ãgustia dille quadrature. Gliquali non haueuano il suo termine fina al cõpimto dil tertio, et questo solertemteaduene p proportionare alquãto il qdrato ultimo p le linee al pũcto di ducte. Ilquale spatio tra il flume & il peristylio intercalato, tuto gratiosa-

LOVE & MARRIAGE

THIS GENRE boasts a robust tradition dating from the beginning of printing. Though amusing and humorous, the maps are not "innocent," for they make contemporary cartographic commentary on their respective country's mores.

✱ [*Opposite*] Francesco Colonna, d. 1527. Untitled woodcut map ["Isola di Cithera"], 13.5 cm in diameter. From Colonna's *Hypnerotomachia Poliphili* (Venice: Aldus Manutius, Romanus, Dec. 1499) [Kane Collection, Rare Books Division].

"All human things are but a dream" states the preamble. This anonymous book (called in English "Polipho's Strife of Love in a Dream") is a fine example of early printing, the most lavishly illustrated incunable from Venice. Its romantic allegory, in which classical mythology figures prominently, was translated into French and English in the 1500s and remained popular well into the seventeenth century. From an acrostic formed from the elaborate first letter of each chapter, the work has been attributed to Colonna, a Dominican priest and monk who lived in Venice and preached at St. Mark's Cathedral.

In this part of his dream, Polipho and his love, Polia, take a barge, piloted by Cupid, to the island of Cythera, illustrated here in a woodcut map. The pie-shaped island is shown divided into equal slices, which are circled by alternating rows of groves, fields, colonnades, and hedges. Twenty paths from the shore (*littore*) converge at the center, where the fountain of Venus is concealed, we are told, by a sacred trellis structure. All of the design reflects Renaissance principles of perspective, and the text provides exacting measurements of its geometry. For example, the island's circumference is given as "tre milliarii" and its diameter as "uno milliario," a ratio that approximates the mathematical constant of *pi*.

Curiously, but appropriately in our mapping context, the work's elegant woodcut illustrations recently have been attributed to Italian editor and cartographer Benedetto Bordone (1460–1531) of *Isolario* fame.

✱ Portrait of Madeleine de Scudéry, 1607–1701. From vol. 2 of C. A. Sainte-Beuve's *Portraits of the Seventeenth Century, Historic and Literary*, trans. Katharine P. Wormeley (New York: G. P. Putnam's Sons, 1904) [General Library Collection].

A FRENCH AUTHOR of lengthy, conversational novels, Scudéry, commonly known as Mademoiselle de Scudéry, was a well-educated intellectual who started her own salon, Société du samedi (Saturday Society). She is considered to be the first "bluestocking" woman of France, predating her more famous English counterparts (Elizabeth Montagu et al.) by more than a century.

✱ [*Overleaf*] Untitled copperplate map ["Carte de tendre"], 20 × 29.5 cm. From vol. 1 of Scudéry's *Clélie:*

{ 207 }

fol. 399.
LA MER DANGEREVSE
Terres Inconnues
Reconnoissance F.
Tendre sur R.
Estime F.
Tendre sur E.
Constante amitie
Bonte
Obeissance
Tendresse
Tendre sur In.
Respect
Exactitude
LAC D'INDIFERENCE
MER D'INIMITIE
Sensibilite
Grands Services
Empressement
Inclination Fleuve
Probite
Grand Cœur
Assiduite
Sincerite
Oubli
Meschancete
Petits Soins
Billet doux
Legerete
Medisance
Soumission
Billet galant
Tiedeur
Perfidie
Complaisance
Iolis Vers
Inesgalite
Indiscretion
Grand esprit
Negligence
Orgueil
Nouvelle amitie
2 4 6 8 10
Lieues d'amitie

Histoire romaine dediée à Mademoiselle de Longueville (Paris: A. Courbé, 1654–1661) [Rare Books Division].

It is probably not surprising that Scudéry's map on love was originally conceived as a social game and only later incorporated into her romance *Clélie*. As geographer, Scudéry provides three different routes (or stages) for a woman to follow to the city of "Tendre" from her starting point, the city of New Friendship ("Nouvelle amitié"), given at the bottom of the map: along three different rivers, named Recognition, Esteem, and Inclination. (I'm not convinced that Scudéry's ideas, as expressed in the novel, are precisely depicted on the map, but one gets the general idea.) Departing on Inclination River, the main conveyance, she can pass by such towns as Fresh Eyes, Love Letter, Big Heart, and Generosity; on the other side of the river, the towns include Complacence, Little Care, Attendance, and Obeisance—alternating, it seems, between simple passions and social virtues. Constant Friendship (on the left) and Goodness (on the right) complete the other routes she might take. Beyond Tendre a woman should not venture, according to Scudéry, for a Dangerous Sea and Unknown Territory await. Similarly, deviating from New Friendship (left or right) will only bring a woman past places such as Indiscretion, Perfidy, and Wickedness, ending at the Sea of Enmity or the Lake of Indifference. Notice that "marriage" is not present in the map; its absence reinforces Scudéry's view that women should be emancipated from matrimony, as her heroine becomes in the novel—indeed, as her own name ("Mademoiselle") suggests.

The map was so popular, and widely debated, that Scudéry is often credited with originating this allegorical map genre.

FRENCH AUTHOR Eustache Le Noble produced a large number of pamphlets, stories, fables, histories, and translations of an entertaining but, mostly, mercenary nature during an adventurous life of travel and dissipation. He was imprisoned in La Conciergerie (Queen Marie Antoinette's prison) for forging documents, and penned many of his works there. One of his better-known publications in English is titled, ironically (ruefully?), *The Art of Prudent Behaviour, in a Father's Advice to His Son, Arriv'd to the Years of Manhood.*

✻ Portrait of Eustache Le Noble, 1643–1711. From his *Contes et fables, ou L'esprit du sage* (Paris: Chez Michel Brunet, 1697) [Kenneth McKenzie Fable Collection, Rare Books Division]. The caption under his portrait amusingly opines: "bark low" to keep your reputation.

✻ [*Overleaf*] "Carta dell'isola del maritaggio." Copperplate map, 22.5 × 34 cm. From Le Noble's *Carta topografica dell'isola del maritaggio di Monsieur Le Noble; per la prima volta tradotta dal francese in italiano* (Cosmopoli: s.n., 1765) [Rare Books Division]. This book was the

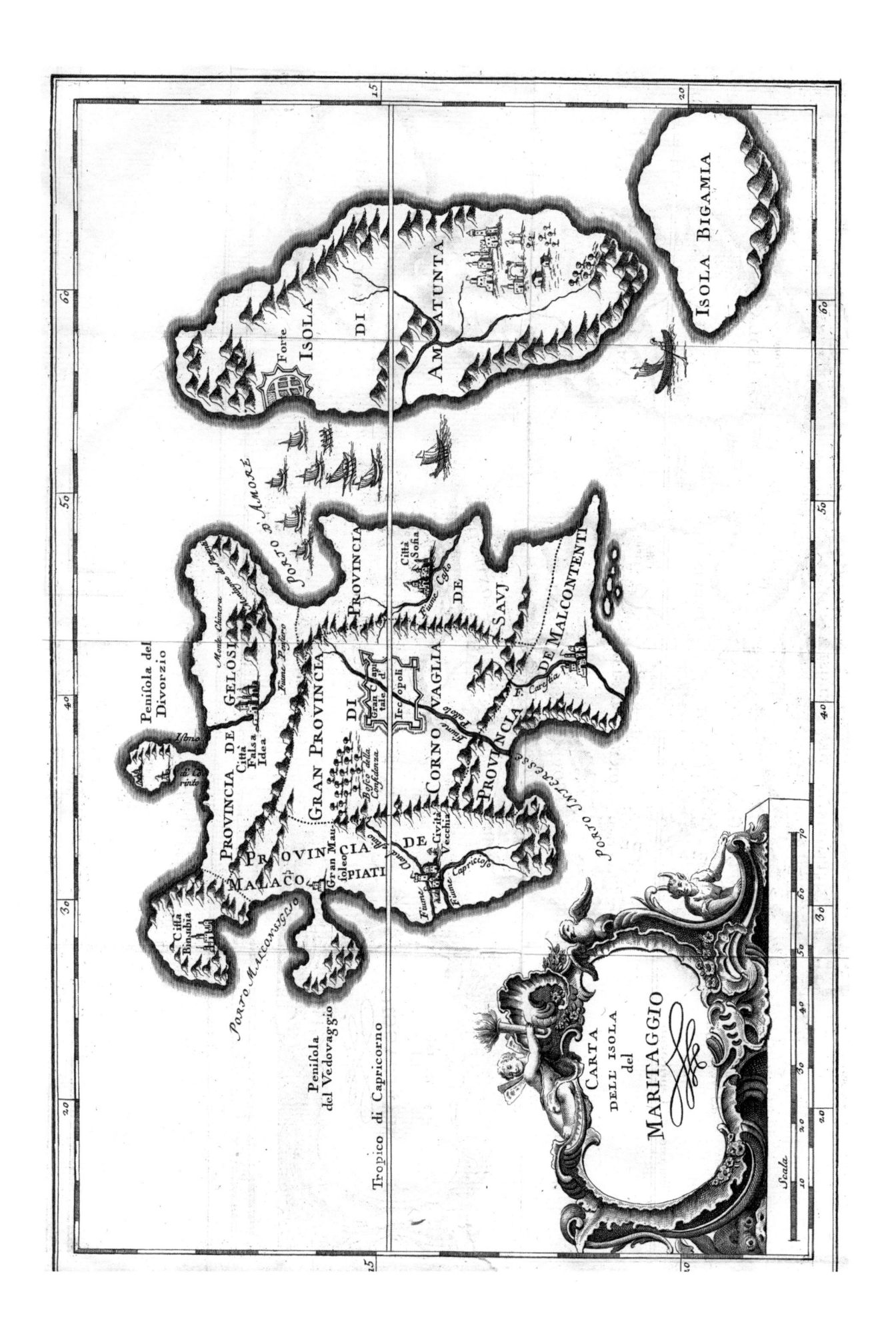

CARTA DELL' ISOLA del MARITAGGIO

Love & Marriage

first Italian printing of Le Noble's *Carte de l'isle de mariage* (Amsterdam, 1705).

The book's text offers instructions on how to reach this matrimonial island and describes the living options on it. The map's latitude and longitude scale place the island in the general area of Madagascar—far enough away from Europe to be exotic, but still "real." The island's central province is named *Cornovaglia*, or Great Province of Cuckolds (see the horned figure in the cartouche), and its heart is a great fortress whose largest ramparts point to the Port of Love as if prepared for perpetual attacks from that direction. The River of Covenant (symbolizing marriage vows?) runs through it as a constant, but fluid presence. To the north is the land of Jealousy with its peninsula of Divorce and Mountains of In-laws; to the south live the Discontented; to the west, the *Malacopiati*, or Incompatibles, with a peninsula for the Widowed. The Chaste River flows through the province of the Wise in the east, which shelters the Port of Love. Across an active, navigable channel lies a large Lovers Island, which neighbors Bigamy Island.

The imagery here is much more pessimistic than Scudéry's, presenting a sobering, if not negative, view of conjugal life, obviously colored by Le Noble's amatory experiences. "What are the advantages for a man," seems Le Noble's question, "who becomes a watchman constantly on the lookout for his usurper?" (Perhaps this is the reason Scudéry's map ignores matrimony altogether.)

MATTHAEUS SEUTTER was a talented German mapmaker of the early eighteenth century, who had apprenticed as an engraver in the print shop of esteemed countryman Johann Baptist Homann. Many of his maps were based on, or copied from, other cartographers, including Homann. (For more on Homann, see the following Utopia section.)

✶ [*Overleaf*] "Representation symbolique et ingenieuse projettée en siege et en bombardement comme il faut empecher prudemment les attaques de l'amour" ([Augsburg: M. Seutter, ca. 1730]). Copperplate map, with added color, 40 × 56 cm [Historic Maps Collection]. Title, captions, and key in both French and German. Reference: Hill, *Cartographical Curiosities*, 65.

✶ Portrait of Matthaeus Seutter, 1678–1756. From Hans Harms's *Künstler des Kartenbildes: Biographien und Porträts* (Oldenburg (Oldb): E. Völker, [1962]) [courtesy of Ernst Völker].

The concept of the fortified heart is taken to the extreme in this richly engraved and embellished map. The large cartouche shows Venus in her chariot being pulled by flying birds through clouds. Depicted below, as it were, a sophisticated battle scene (with ninety-five keyed features) unfolds, where forces are attacking and defending the fortress of Manhood that sits in a frozen, passionless sea. The side of Love, representing the fairer sex, employs four sets of artillery batteries (on the left) to bombard the walls with appeals to vanity, offering delightful surprises, charms, and joys, and plying with tenderness, wishful thinking, and "un certain je ne sais quoi." Over the walls, naval ships lob such feminine wiles and virtues as beauty, pleasant conversation, gentleness, and "regards languissant" (languishing looks).

Methode pour défendre et conserver son coeur contre les attaques de l'amour.

Representation Symbolique et ingenieuse projettée en Siege et en Bombardement,

comme il faut empecher prudemment les attaques de **L'AMOUR**.

Symbolische Sinnreiche in einer Belagerung u. Bombardirung entworffene Vorstellung wie man den anfällen und Versuchungen der **LIEBE** Klug und tapffer zu begegnen, zur Belustigung u. Sittlicher Belehrung verfertiget von MATTH. SEUTTER S.C. Maj. Geogr. in Augsp.

Die Methode sein Hertz wider die Angriffe der Liebe zu bewahren.

Love's forces are camped for the duration (at the lower left), commanded by their general, Cupid.

As the key states, there are also methods for defending and conserving one's heart against this unrelenting onslaught: memory, prudence, industry, experience (see the lettered outposts along the fortress walls). Ultimately, however, it is a war of attrition. As the trail winding through the fortress and along the coastline proves, the love-struck victim surrenders, retreating to his friends for advice, deliberation, and information, before moving onward to the garden of pleasure and his first encounter with his beloved. (Seutter's ornate and symmetrical "Jardin de plaisir" reflects the precisely structured love bower of Colonna.) From there, via a subterranean passage, he arrives at the Palace of Love—note the change from fortress to palace—which resides in a sea of peace. Entering is easy, according to the note, but leaving is impossible without losing one's liberty. Another definition of a prison?

JOHANN GOTTLOB IMMANUEL BREITKOPF was a German music publisher and typographer who revolutionized the printing of music with moveable type.

✻ Portrait of Johann Gottlob Immanuel Breitkopf, 1719–1794. From Hans Wahl's *Goethe und seine welt; unter mitwirkung von Ernst Beutler herausgegeben von Hans Wahl und Anton Kippenberg* (Leipzig: Insel-verlag, 1932) [General Library Collection].

✻ [*Opposite*] "Das Reich der Liebe: Zweyter Landchartensatz-Versuch" (Leipzig: Aus Breitkopfs Buchdr., 1777). Printed map, with added color, 18 × 23 cm [Historic Maps Collection]. From Breitkopf's *Beschreibung des Reichs der Liebe, mit beygefügter Landcharte: Ein zweyter Versuch im Satz und Druck geographischer Charten, durch die Buchdruckerkunst* (Leipzig: Aus der Breitkopfischen Buchdruckerei, 1777). Reference: Hill, *Cartographical Curiosities*, 66.

Breitkopf was the first to apply his printing method to maps; at least three test maps are known, of which this "Kingdom of Love" is one example. Note that everything in this map, including the river lines, was printed with type. The method proved cumbersome and time-consuming, and was discontinued. But that did not deter Breitkopf from having fun with his subject.

On the left side of the map lies the country of those who believe in the power of love, bordered by the hopeless mountains; on the right is the country of bachelors, which is home to villages of stupidity and scandal. In the map's center sits a region of fixed ideas, where, among others, the restless live. At the bottom is the land of youth, where beautiful, carefree residents joke, kiss, and make wishes. Calm, reasonable sleepyheads (grandpas) live next door (bottom right). The largest territory (rosy-colored!), bordering the land of lusts, is for happy lovers, who feel secure, listen to each other, and evince a cheerful prospect—a place beneficial for children. Divorced, unwelcoming brawlers inhabit the drab region at the top center.

The map appeared in the midst of the Sturm und Drang ("turbulence and urgency") period (1760s–1780s) of German literature and music, which emphasized self-expression and extremes of emotion.

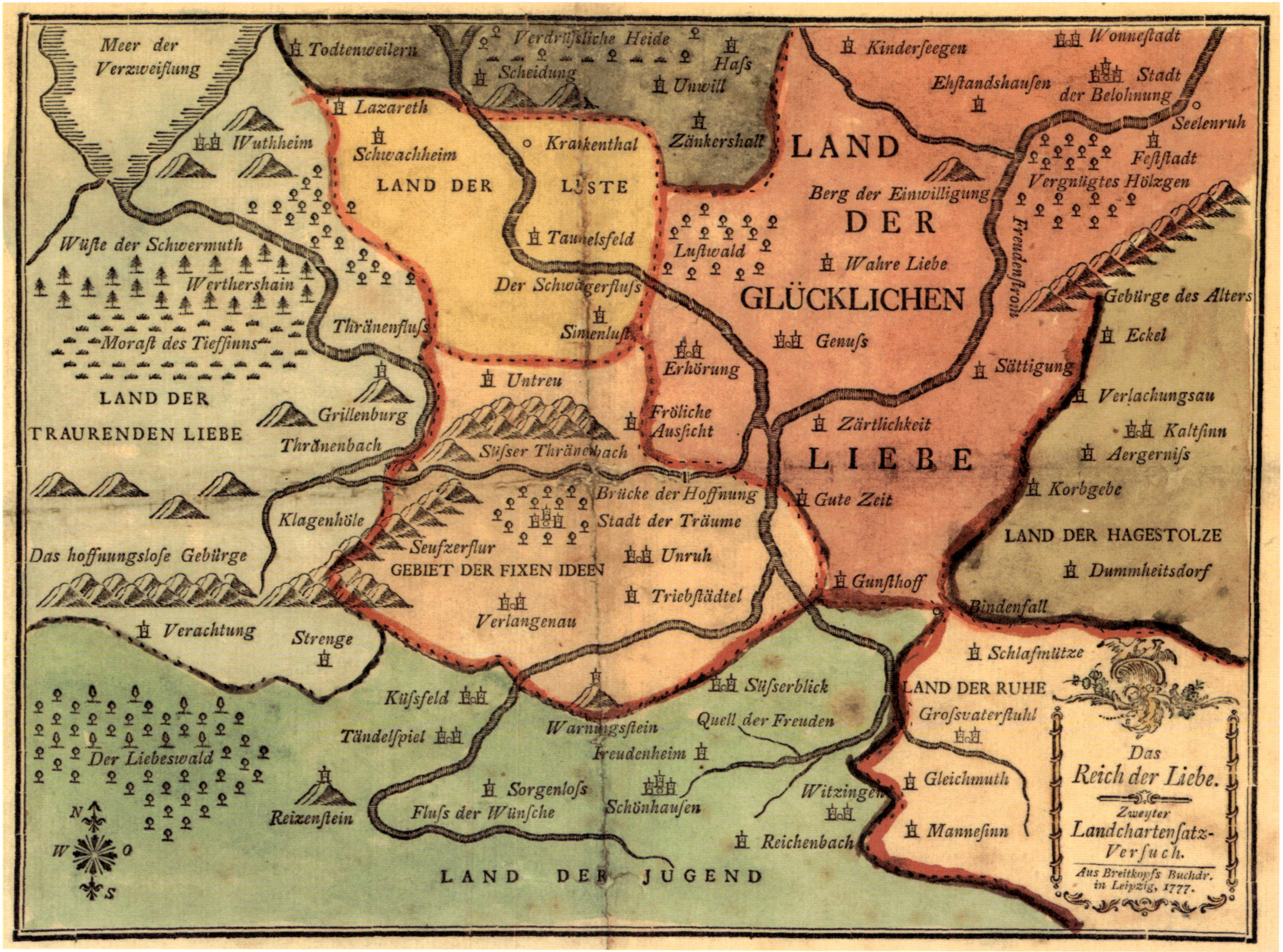

Das
Reich der Liebe.
Zweyter
Landchartensatz-
Versuch.
Aus Breitkopfs Buchdr.
in Leipzig, 1777.
Meer der
Verzweiflung
Todtenweilern
Verdrüssliche Heide
Scheidung
Hass
Unwill
Zänkershall
Lazareth
Schwachheim
Krankenthal
LAND DER
LÜSTE
Taumelsfeld
Der Schwägerfluss
Simenlust
Wuthheim
Wüste der Schwermuth
Werthershain
Morast des Tiefsinns
Thränenfluss
LAND DER
TRAURENDEN LIEBE
Grillenburg
Thränenbach
Klagenhöle
Das hoffnungslose Gebürge
Verachtung
Strenge
Der Liebeswald
Reizenstein
N
W
O
S
Kinderseegen
Ehstandshausen
Wonnestadt
Stadt
der Belohnung
Seelenruh
Feststadt
Vergnügtes Hölzgen
LAND
Berg der Einwilligung
DER
Lustwald
Wahre Liebe
GLÜCKLICHEN
Freudenstrom
Gebürge des Alters
Genuss
Erhörung
Sättigung
Eckel
Verlachungsau
Kaltsinn
Aergerniss
Zärtlichkeit
Fröliche
Aussicht
LIEBE
Gute Zeit
Korbgebe
LAND DER HAGESTOLZE
Dummheitsdorf
Untreu
Süsser Thränenbach
Brücke der Hoffnung
Stadt der Träume
Seufzerflur
Unruh
GEBIET DER FIXEN IDEEN
Triebstädtel
Verlangenau
Gunsthoff
Bindenfall
Schlafmütze
LAND DER RUHE
Grossvaterstuhl
Gleichmuth
Mannesinn
Küssfeld
Tändelspiel
Süsserblick
Quell der Freuden
Warnungsstein
Freudenheim
Sorgenloss
Schönhausen
Fluss der Wünsche
Witzingen
Reichenbach
LAND DER JUGEND

12 VTOPIAE INSVLAE TABVLA.

Amaurotū vrbs.

Fons Anydri. *Ostium anydri*

hythlodaeus.

UTOPIA

RECOGNIZED as a saint by the Catholic Church, English humanist Sir Thomas More is revered for resolutely refusing to accept King Henry VIII (1491–1547) as the supreme head of the Church of England, authority the king needed to annul his marriage to Catherine of Aragon so he could wed Anne Boleyn and, he hoped, produce an heir. More was imprisoned in the Tower of London for treason, found guilty of perjury, and subsequently beheaded—this, after years of loyalty and service to the king as an adviser and as Lord Chancellor.

✲ [*Opposite*] "Utopiæ insulæ tabula." Woodcut map, 17.9 × 11.9 cm. From More's *De optimo reip. statv, deqve noua insula Vtopia, libellus uere aureus, nec minus salutaris quàm festiuus* ... (Basel: Apvd Io. Frobenivm mense decembri an M.D.XVIII [December 1518]) [Rare Books Division]. Reference: Hill, *Cartographic Curiosities*, 22.

Map of Utopia from the work that originated the word. First published in 1516, the fictional work was further revised by More and issued in this Basel edition with a more elaborate map engraved by Ambrosius Holbein (ca. 1494–ca. 1519), brother of the well-known portraitist Hans Holbein, the Younger. As conceived, the island has the basic shape of a crescent moon. According to More, it is about two hundred miles broad at the widest point, with its ends or horns forming a strait that is eleven miles across. As a result, the interior forms a large harbor, affording residents easy commerce with one another. (However, that aspect is difficult to picture in this version of the map.) There are fifty-four city-states on the island, perhaps mirroring the number of shires in England and Wales (plus London) in More's time, and all are identical in languages, customs, and laws and similar in size, layout, and appearance.

More positioned his country somewhere in the New World (or, at least beyond the limits of the currently known world), for he states that his narrator, Raphael Hythlodaeus, participated in the last three of Amerigo Vespucci's four voyages. On the final voyage, Hythlo-

✲ Portrait of Sir Thomas More, 1478–1535. From his *A Dialogve of Cumfort against Tribulation* ... (Antwerp: apud Iohannem Foulerum, Anglum, 1573) [Rare Books Division].

daeus did not come home with Vespucci; rather, he continued his explorations and ultimately discovered Utopia, where he lived for five years before, miraculously, returning to Europe on a Portuguese vessel. Hythlodaeus's descriptions of his residence in Utopia provide the heart of the piece.

In More's Utopia, there is no private ownership. All the inhabitants must live in the countryside, working in agriculture, for two years at a time; they must also learn a necessary trade but only have to work at it for six hours a day. Necessities can be obtained freely from a storage warehouse; internal travel requires a passport; every household has two slaves (criminals or foreigners), who can be released for good behavior; and education and health care are free and universal. In the lower left of the map, Hythlodaeus and More are shown in conversation about the island, whose features certainly seem Old World in appearance: castles, spires, Christian crosses.

A recent article by M. Bishop (2005) interprets the map as a memento mori, also punning on More's name, in the form of a skull. To easily visualize this, begin at the toothy-looking side of the ship.

JOHANN BAPTIST HOMANN started his map publishing firm in Nuremberg in 1702. By 1715, the quality of his publications earned him the great honor of Imperial Cartographer of the Holy Roman Empire; the privilege also carried an early form of copyright protection for his works. His major opus, *Grosser atlas über die ganze Welt* (great atlas of whole world), contained maps that were scientifically-grounded, finely engraved, and sumptuously enhanced. It represented the high-water mark of German cartographic achievement. After his death, Homann's son Johann Christoph Homann (1703-1730) took over the firm, but he died suddenly a few years later. The business continued until 1848 under the name of Homann Heirs, often shown on maps as "Homannschen Erben," "Heritiers de Homann," or "Homannianis Heredibus."

✳ [*Overleaf*] "Accurata Utopiæ tabula: Das ist der neu entdeckten Schalck Welt, oder des so offtbenannten, und doch nie erkanten Schlarraffenlandes, neu erfundene lacherliche Land tabell, worinnen alle und jede laster in besondere Konigreich, Provintzen und Herrschafften ab getheilet, beyneben auch die negst angrentzende Länder der Frommen des zeitlichen Auff und Untergangs auch ewigen verderbens Regionen, samt einer Erklerung anmuthig und nutzlich vorgestellt werden" ([Nuremberg: Officina Homanniana, ca. 1720]) [Accurate map of Utopia: This is the newly invented, humorous chart of the World of Fools, frequently called the Land of Cockaigne which has never been found, showing and explaining in a beautiful and useful manner any and all vices by kingdom, province, and domain, also the border countries of the faithful as well as the regions of the beginning and end of time and eternal doom]. Copperplate map, with added color, 46 × 54 cm [Historic Maps Collection].

First state of the first of the "Schlarraffenland" (or the English equivalent "Cockaigne") maps, which parody

✳ Portrait of Johann Baptist Homann, 1663–1724. From his *Grosser atlas über die ganze Welt* ... (Nuremberg: Verlegung der Homannschen Erben, 1737). The atlas was first published in 1716.

paradise, depicted as a "land of milk and honey" where chickens fly around already cooked and each home is surrounded by a hedge of sausage. Schlarraffenland maps were popularized by German cartographers Homann and Seutter; this one is attributed to Homann. (See Seutter's map of love in this Theme Maps section.) Depicted here is paradise's opposite: the lands of vice. Each has its own kingdom, such as Pigritaria (Land of Indolence), Lurconia (Land of Gluttony), Bibonia (Land of Drink), Schmarotz Insula (Island of Spongers). Terra Sancta (in the north) is, of course, Incognita, whereas hell, at the bottom, is more accessible. The map's outlines roughly assume the shape of a fool's cap, with two peaks flopping down on the sides, dangling islands as their bells. In that interpretation, Iuronia

Regnum (Land of Oath-Swearing) locates the fool's throat appropriately below an open mouth (Venerea Meer).

The map has all the "normal" characteristics of a real map depicting a real country: latitude/longitude lines, a scale, topography (forests, rivers, lakes, mountains), place names, demarcated regions. But, of course, the devil is in the details. The longitude of this Schlarraffenland (from 360° to 550°) literally places it off the chart—its latitude situates it on the equator, where sin is not partial to day or night. The scale suggests that one of the country's big mouths ("Schlarrafische grosse Mäuler") equals two small venereal or arrogant mouths ("Kleine venerische oder Hoffärtige Mäuler"). There is much fun in decoding the map's cartographic humor, but, of course, there is always some sobering truth in something "funny"—in recognizing their own faults, viewers get the message: reform your sinful ways.

✱ Title cartouche of vice and folly from Johann Baptist Homann's Schlarraffenland map (see overleaf).

DAS TRAURIGEMEER
Cap Bonæ Spei
Cap Patientiæ
Fretum Poenitentiæ
POENITENTIA REGNUM
TERRA SA
UNBEKANTE LA
AMARA REG
IRRLANDIA
TERRA LABRADOR
CHYMICA
Sinus Melancholicus
Melancholia
der Melancholische Wald
KUMMERLAND
Tropicus Cancri
PRODIGALIA REGN
CREDIT GEBIET
SUPERBIA
DIE BIER INSUL
SCHLARAFFEN
SUMAGONIA
BENGELA
MARCOLPHIREN
BAUREN PARADEIS
DAS TOBACK LUDER MEER
ZULLERLAND
TOBACO
Luderstatt
SCHNUPFERLAND
DAS LURCONICUM
LAMPANIA
MULTALAUSIA
BULGARIA
SPURIA
INSULÆ
Tropicus Capricorni
NEGRO MANTICÆ Insulæ
RESPUBLICA
CHOREA
SPILMANNIA
LUDER MARE
DAS LUDER MEER MARE
LITTIGONIA
LUSORIA REG
BALGER REGNUM
Balgen
FECHT I.
IURONIA REG
TARTARIA
DAS HOLLISCHE
Teufels Küch
INFERUM
Schlarraffische große Mäuler
Kleine Venerische oder Hoffärtige Mäuler
Teutsche Geometrische Meilen
350
360
370
380
390
400
410
420
Zeitlicher Untergang der Weltleben

Accurata UTOPIÆ TABULA

Das ist
Der Neu entdeckten
SCHALCK WELT,
oder des so offt benanten, und doch nie erkanten
SCHLARRAFFENLANDES
Neu erfundene lächerliche Land tabell
Worinnen all und jede laster in besondere Königreich,
Provintzen und Norschafften abgetheilet
Beynebst auch die negst angrentzende Länder
Der FROMMEN des Zeitlichen AUFF und UNTERGANGS
auch ewigen VERDERBENS Regionen
samt einer erklerung
anmuthig und nutzlich vorgestellt werden
durch
Authorem anonymum

```
         ┌─────────────┐
         │  GEOGRAPHY  │
         └──────┬──────┘
      ┌────────┼────────┐
┌─────┴────┐ ┌─┴────┐ ┌─┴─────────┐
│ Physical │ │Social│ │Conceptual │
└──────────┘ └──────┘ └───────────┘
```

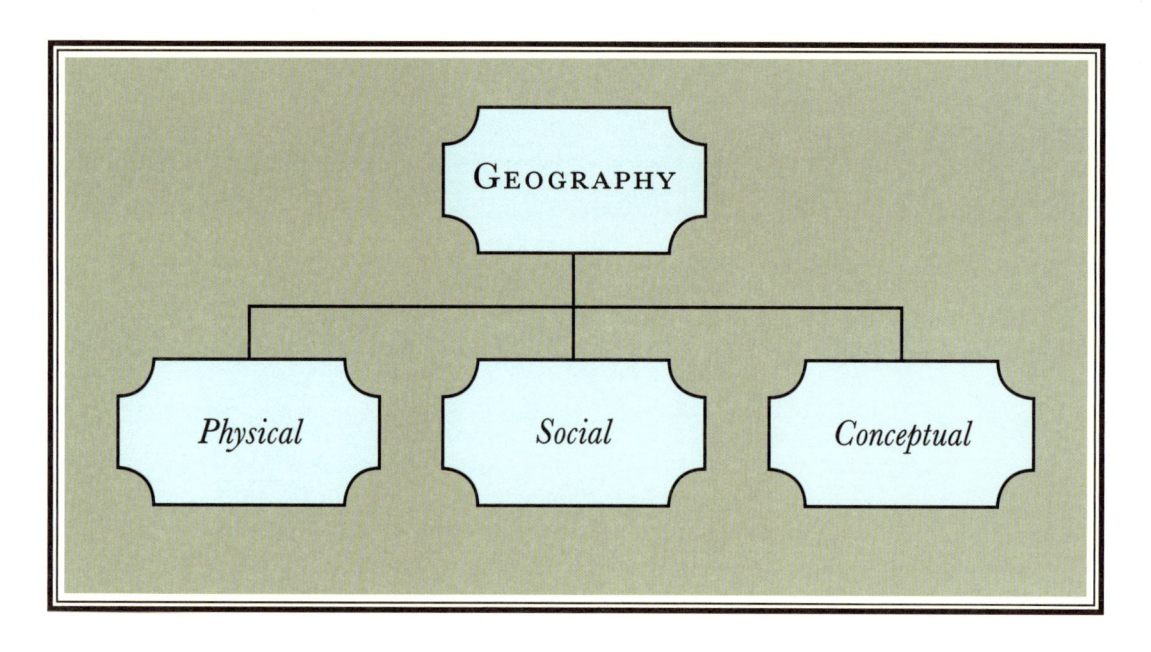

✽ To a thematic map, the chart of geography looks rather simple.

CONCLUSION

MAPS HAVE WALKED hand-in-hand with geography throughout the ages. As geographical knowledge has expanded, the handshake has tightened. They are now inseparable. Looking back over four hundred years, one appreciates the journey they have taken together.

✳ [*Overleaf*] Christophe de Savigny, ca. 1530–1608. "Geographie." Woodcut engraving, 40.2 × 31 cm. From his *Tableaux: Accomplis de tous les arts liberaux: Contenans brieuement et clerement par singuliere methode de doctrine, vne generale et sommaire partition des dicts arts, amassez et reducits en ordre pour le soulagement et profit de la ieunesse* (Paris: Par Iean & François de Gourmont freres, demeurants ruë Sainct Iean de Latran, 1587) [Rare Books Division]. Reference: Shirley, *Mapping of the World*, 159.

Geographically, the world in this sixteenth-century map is still very much a work in progress. What looks like Australia in the Pacific Ocean is really the mythical Southern Continent that would become a major goal of European explorers through the voyages of Captain James Cook in the 1770s. French humanist Savigny may have been encouraged to include the landmass by the discovery of the Solomon Islands in that general area by the Spanish explorer Alvaro de Mendaña de Neira (1542–1595?) in 1568.

The chart, or logic tree, presents the subject of geography in all of its basic hierarchical branches, dividing them by "superfice" (in English, "superficies" or surface) categories and qualities. For example, land is either a continent or an island; water is either flowing or standing. "Nouveau" land is labeled the "Northern," "West Indies," and "Southern or Magellanique" (after Ferdinand Magellan). Latitude is determined by the meridian of the sun, longitude by the motion of the stars; the only named astronomical instrument is the astrolabe, which dates from classical antiquity. Around the border are boxes of text, alternating with related scenes, that explain the gradual division of the realms of the earth into smaller and smaller units of measurement (provinces into regions, lands into acres, etc.), ending with "Les Espans en Doigts" (hands into fingers).

✳ [*Overleaf*] Richard Blome, d. 1705. "Geography: To the Rt. Honble. George Berkeley, Ld. Berkeley ... anno Dom. 1678." Copperplate engraving, with added color, sheet 38 × 24 cm. Plate 104 from his *The Gentlemans Recreation* ... (London: Printed by S. Roycroft, for Richard Blome..., 1686) [Historic Maps Collection]. Reference: Shirley, *Mapping of the World*, 479.

One hundred years later, in this seventeenth-century map, the west coast of Australia has been added to the world, following the explorations of Dutchman Abel Janszoon Tasman (1603?–1659). A finer, more accurate chiseling of the shape of the continents has occurred, though California is now an island. But the tree of geography remains virtually unchanged, except that the last divisions of measurement are "Feet into Inches" and "Inches into Barly-corns." (A barleycorn was an old unit of length equal to one-third of an inch.)

Still, as we know now, scientific inquiry had begun in earnest—Francis Bacon and like-minded others had sparked a new investigative approach—and, as a consequence, the first thematic maps had started to appear

{223}

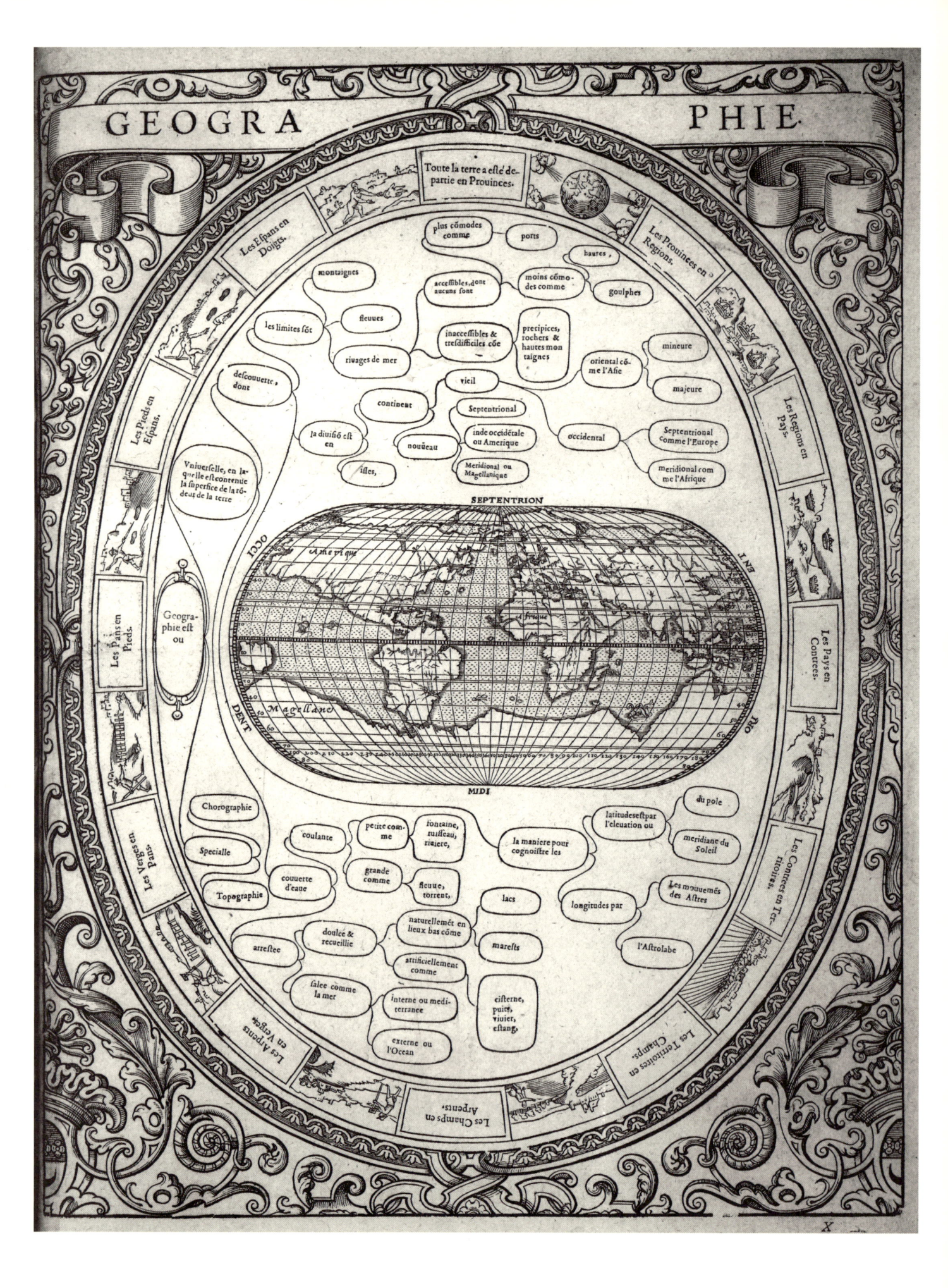

GEOGRAPHIE

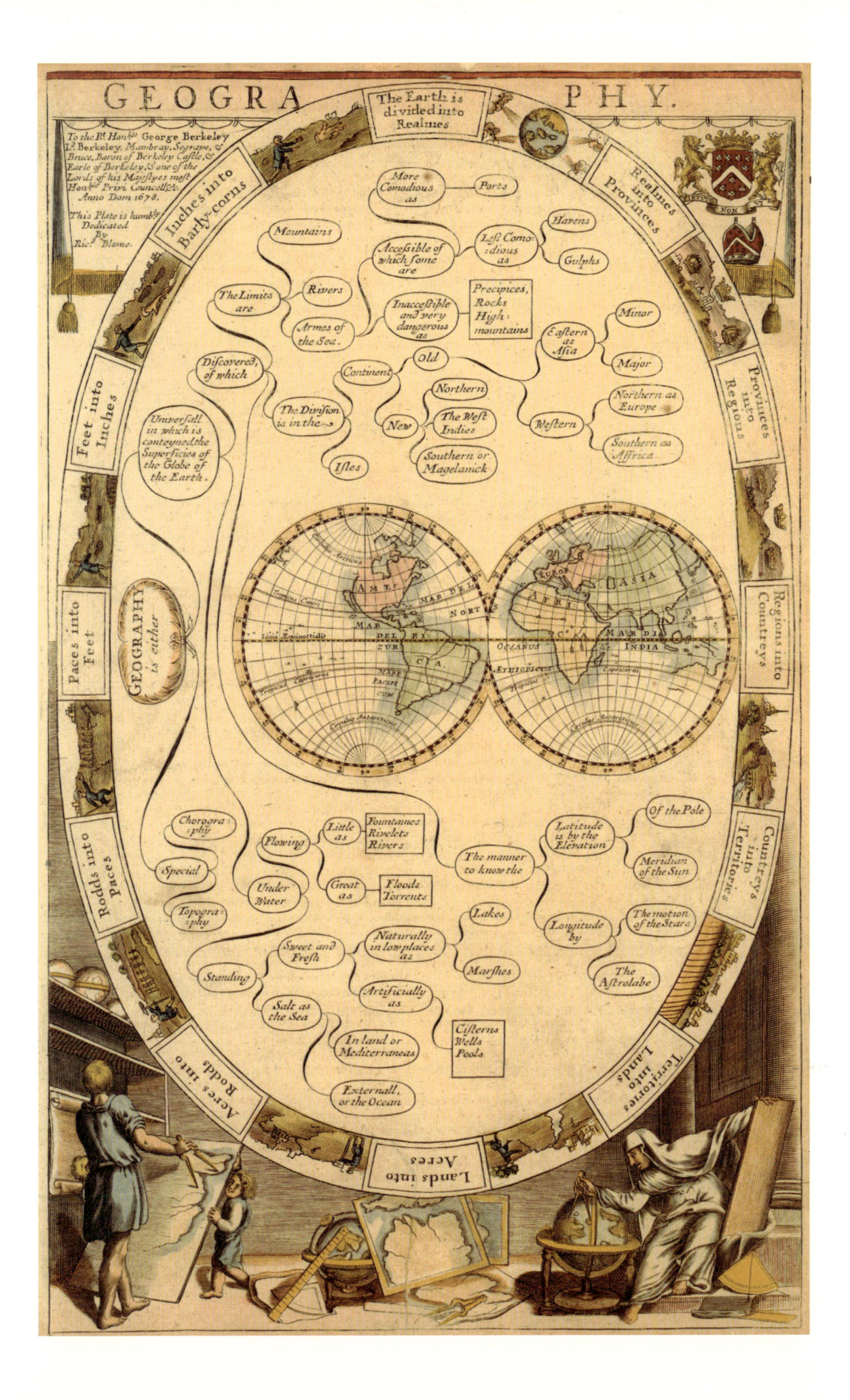

GEOGRAPHY.

To the Rt. Honble George Berkeley, Ld. Berkeley, Mawbray, Segrave, & Bruce, Baron of Berkeley Castle, & Earle of Berkeley, & one of the Lords of his Majestyes most Honble Privy Councell &c. Anno Dom 1678. This Plate is humbly Dedicated By Richd Blome.

The Earth is divided into Realmes
Realmes into Provinces
Provinces into Regions
Regions into Countreys
Countreys into Territories
Territories into Lands
Lands into Acres
Acres into Rodds
Rodds into Paces
Paces into Feet
Feet into Inches
Inches into Barly-corns

GEOGRAPHY is either

- **Universall** in which is conteyned the Superficies of the Globe of the Earth.
  - **The Limits are**
    - Mountains
    - Rivers
    - Armes of the Sea
  - **Discovered, of which**
    - **The Division is in the**
      - Continent — Old / New
        - Northern
        - The West Indies
        - Southern or Magelanick
      - Isles
  - **Accessible of which some are**
    - More Comodious as — Ports
    - Less Comodious as — Havens / Gulphs
  - **Inaccessible and very dangerous as** — Precipices, Rocks, High mountains
  - **Eastern as Asia** — Minor / Major
  - **Western** — Northern as Europe / Southern as Affrica

- **Chorography / Special**
- **Topography**

Standing
- Sweet and Fresh
  - Naturally in low places as — Lakes / Marshes
  - Artificially as — Cisterns, Wells, Pools
- Salt as the Sea
  - In land or Mediterraneas
  - Externall, or the Ocean

Flowing
- Little as — Fountaines, Rivelets, Rivers
- Great as — Floods, Torrents
Under Water

The manner to know the
- Latitude is by the Elevation — Of the Pole / Meridian of the Sun
- Longitude by — The motion of the Stars / The Astrolabe

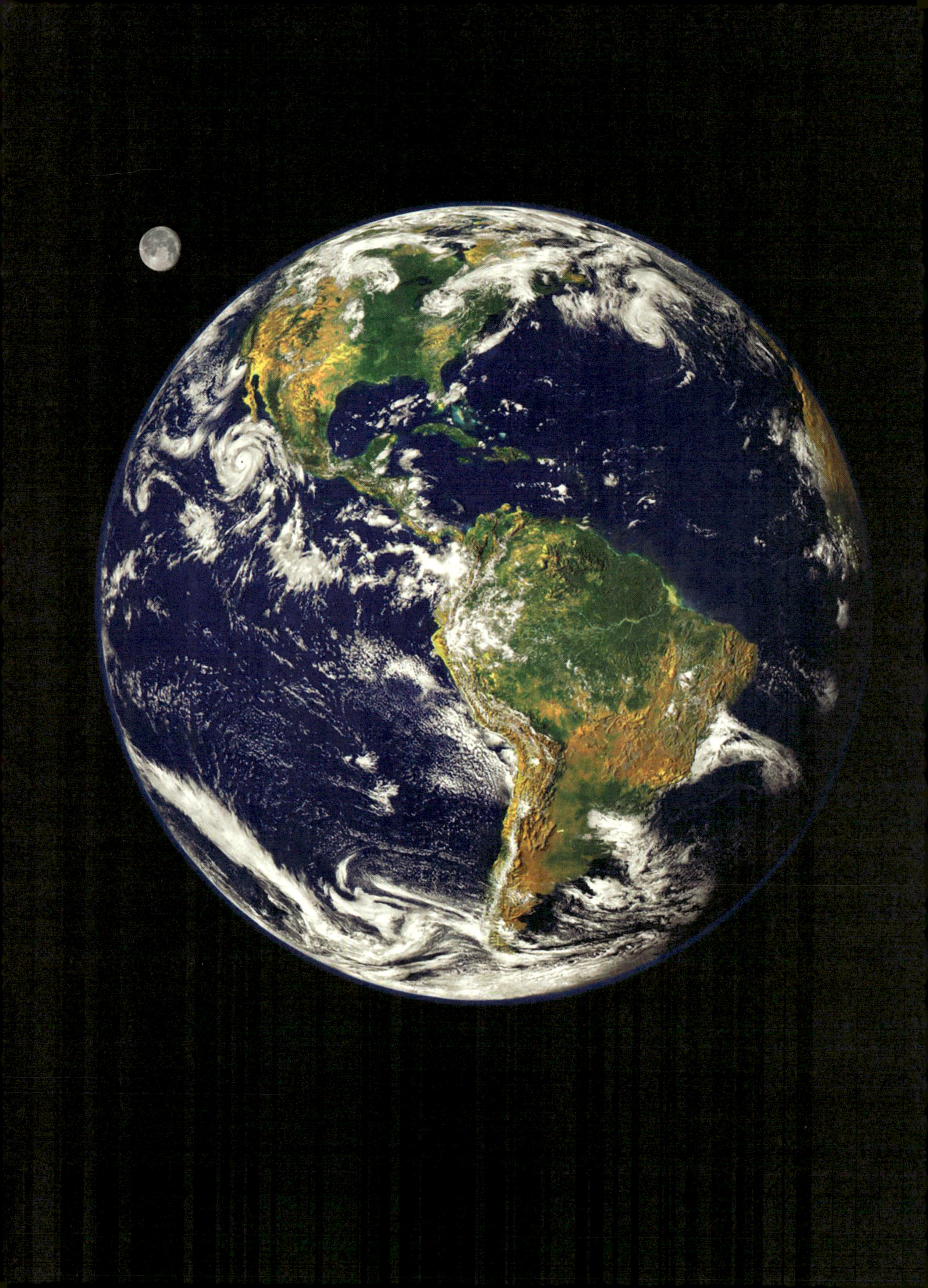

Conclusion 227

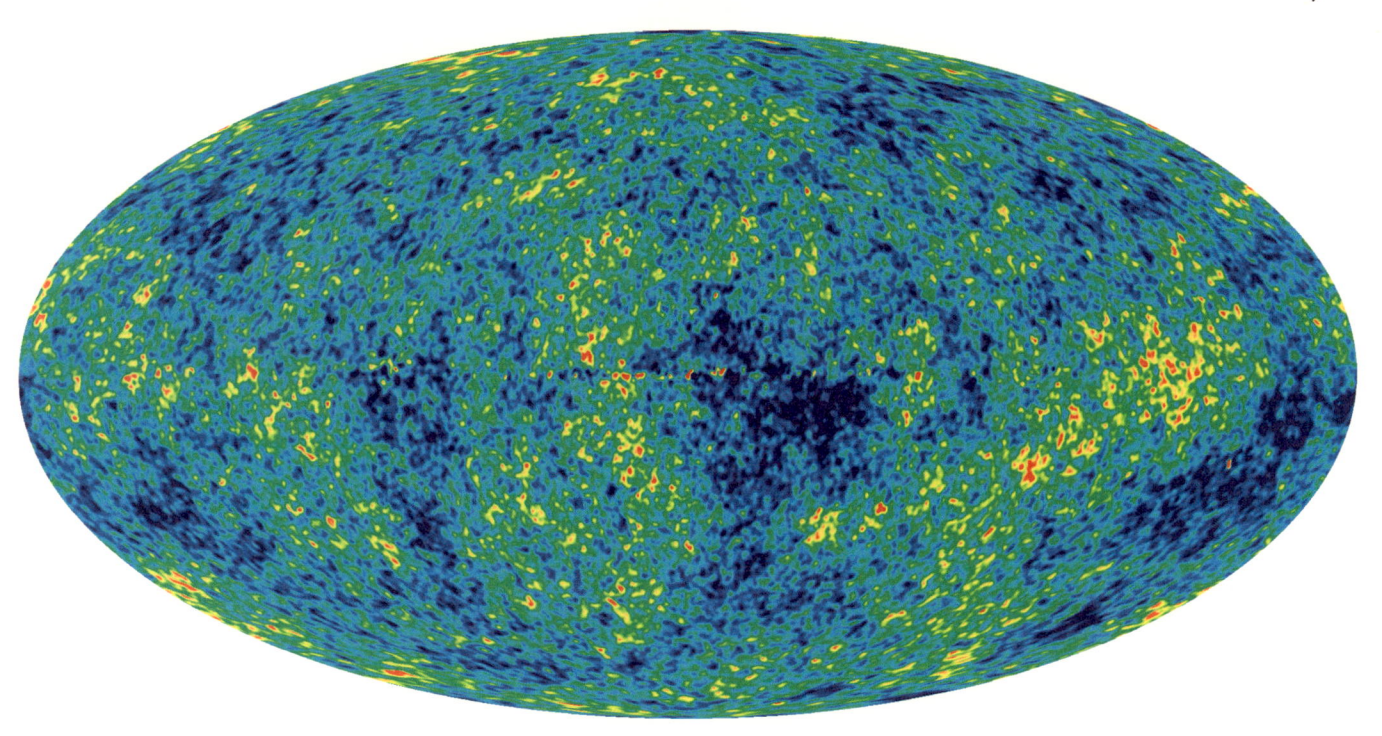

during the later part of this century. We have seen what would follow in the eighteenth and nineteenth centuries, preparing for their dominant cartographic role in the twentieth.

✳ ✳ ✳

Here at the beginning of the twenty-first century we confront this 3-D concept of the world. We have found and fitted in the geographical puzzle pieces of the planet and have begun turning our attention beyond Earth's horizon to the uncharted universe. Cartographically, in many respects, we must start at the beginning with basic reference maps that name "places" (stars, planets, etc.), locate them on a grid, and exhibit some of their topographic features. Thematic maps, of course, will play their essential part.

✳ [*Opposite*] Earth seen from space, with the moon in the background. From NASA.

✳ [*Above*] A thematic map of the infant universe created from five years of WMAP (Wilkinson Microwave Anisotropy Probe) data. The image reveals 13.7-billion-year-old temperature fluctuations (shown as color differences) that correspond to the seeds that grew to become the galaxies. This image shows a temperature range of ± 200 microKelvin. From NASA/WMAP Science Team.

✳ ✳ ✳

Yes, thematic maps are ubiquitous now. Think Google Maps. A weather map helps us plan for tomorrow, a geological map suggests where to explore for oil, a census map aids representative reapportionment. Obviously, it was not always so. The purpose of maps has followed a natural evolution—from where to what to why—from telling us where places are geographically located, to uncovering subject content of physical and social space, to forecasting and/or post-dating events to illustrate cause and effect. As tools, thematic maps help men and women make decisions for today and plan for tomorrow, *wherever* that may be.

Think of a topic and a place. By now you know, "There's a m/app for that."

—John Delaney, Curator
Historic Maps Collection
Princeton University Library

Standing

Acres into Rodds

SOURCES CONSULTED

BISHOP, M. "Ambrosius Holbein's *Memento Mori* Map for Sir Thomas More's *Utopia*: The Meanings of a Masterpiece of Early Sixteenth Century Graphic Art." *British Dental Journal* 199 (2005): 107–112.

BOTTING, Douglas. *Humboldt and the Cosmos*. New York: Harper & Row, 1973.

BULMER, Michael. *Francis Galton: Pioneer of Heredity and Biometry*. Baltimore: Johns Hopkins University Press, 2003.

Charles Dupin (1784–1873): Ingénieur, savant, économiste, pédagogue et parlementaire du Premier au Second Empire. Edited by Carole Christen and François Vatin. Rennes: Presses Universitaires de Rennes, 2009.

COOK, Alan. *Edmond Halley: Charting the Heavens and the Seas*. Oxford: Clarendon, 1998.

DENT, Borden D. *Principles of Thematic Map Design*. Reading, Mass.: Addison-Wesley, 1985.

DE VORSEY, Louis. "Pioneer Charting of the Gulf Stream: The Contributions of Benjamin Franklin and William Gerard De Brahm." *Imago Mundi* 28 (1976): 105–120.

EKNOYAN, Garabed. "Adolphe Quetelet (1796–1874)— the Average Man and Indices of Obesity." *Nephrology Dialysis Transplantation* 23, no. 1 (January 2008): 47–51.

EYLES, Joan M. "William Smith (1769–1839): A Bibliography of His Published Writings, Maps and Geological Sections, Printed and Lithographed." *Journal of the Society for the Bibliography of Natural History* 5, pt. 2 (April 1969): 87–109.

FEUERSTEIN-HERZ, Petra. *Der Elefant der neuen Welt— Eberhardt August Wilhelm von Zimmermann (1743–1815) und die Anfänge der Tiergeographie*. Stuttgart: Deutscher Apotheker Verlag, 2006.

FRIENDLY, Michael. "The Golden Age of Statistical Graphics." *Statistical Science* 23, no. 4 (2008): 502–535.

FRIENDLY, M., and D. J. DENIS. "Milestones in the History of Thematic Cartography, Statistical Graphics, and Data Visualization." 2001. Accessed December 15, 2011. http://datavis.ca/milestones/.

GEIKIE, Sir Archibald. *The Founders of Geology*. 2nd ed. London: Macmillan, 1905.

GILBERT, E. W. "Pioneer Maps of Health and Disease in England." *Geographical Journal* 124, pt. 2 (June 1958): 172–183.

GODWIN, Joscelyn. *Athanasius Kircher's Theatre of the World: The Life and Work of the Last Man to Search for Universal Knowledge*. Rochester, Vt.: Inner Traditions, 2009.

GOFFART, Walter. *Historical Atlases: The First Three Hundred Years, 1570–1870*. Chicago: University of Chicago Press, 2003.

GUERRY, A.-M. (André-Michel). *A Translation of André-Michel Guerry's Essay on the Moral Statistics of France (1833): A Sociological Report to the French Academy of Science*. Edited and translated by Hugh P. Whitt and Victor W. Reinking. Lewiston, N.Y.; Lampeter, Wales: Edwin Mellen Press, 2002.

HANKINS, Frank Hamilton. *Adolphe Quetelet as Statistician*. [New York: Columbia University, Longmans, Green & Co., agents; etc., etc.], 1908.

HILL, Gillian. *Cartographical Curiosities*. London: British Library, 1978.

HUMBOLDT, Alexander von. *Personal Narrative of Travels to the Equinoctial Regions of the New Continent, during the Years 1799–1804, by Alexander de Humboldt, and Aimé Bonpland*. Written in French by Alexander de Humboldt, and translated into English by Helen Maria Williams. 7 vols. London: Longman, Hurst, Rees, Orme, and Brown...; J. Murray...; and H. Colburn, 1814–1829.

JARCHO, Saul. "Yellow Fever, Cholera, and the Beginnings of Medical Cartography." *Journal of the History of Medicine and Allied Sciences* 25, no. 2 (April 1970): 131–142.

JONKERS, A. R. T. *Earth's Magnetism in the Age of Sail*. Baltimore: Johns Hopkins University Press, 2003.

KISH, George. "Early Thematic Mapping: The Work of Philippe Buache." *Imago Mundi* 28 (1976): 129–136.

KOCH, Tom. *Cartographies of Disease: Maps, Mapping, and Medicine.* Redlands, Calif.: ESRI Press, 2005.

KONVITZ, Josef W. *Cartography in France, 1660–1848: Science, Engineering, and Statecraft.* With a foreword by Emmanuel Le Roy Ladurie. Chicago: University of Chicago Press, 1987.

KOZÁK, Jan, and Jiří VANĚK. "Berghaus' Physikalischer Atlas: Surprising Content and Superior Artistic Images." *Studia Geophysica & Geodaetica* 46, no. 3 (2002): 599–610.

KUTZBACH, Gisela. *The Thermal Theory of Cyclones: A History of Meteorological Thought in the Nineteenth Century.* Boston: American Meteorological Society, 1979.

MACEACHREN, Alan M. "The Evolution of Thematic Cartography: A Research Methodology and Historical Review." *Canadian Cartographer* 16, no. 1 (June 1979): 17–33.

MORTON, Samuel George. *A Memoir of William Maclure, Esq. Late President of the Academy of Natural Sciences of Philadelphia. Read July 1, 1841, and Published by Direction of the Academy.* Philadelphia: Merrihew and Thompson, 1841.

MUNRO, James S. *Mademoiselle de Scudéry and the Carte de tendre.* [Durham, England]: University of Durham, 1986.

MUNROE, James Phinney. *A Life of Francis Amasa Walker.* New York: Henry Holt, 1923.

NEWTON, H. A. *Elias Loomis, LL.D., 1811–1889.* New Haven, Conn.: Tuttle, Morehouse & Taylor, printers, 1890.

One Hundred Years of Map Making: The Story of W. & A. K. Johnston. Edinburgh: Edina Works, [1925].

PALSKY, Gilles. "Origines et evolution de la cartographie thématique (XVIIe–XIXe siècles)." *Revista da Falculdade de Letras*—Geografia I série, 14 (1998): 39–60.

PORTER, Thomas M. *The Rise of Statistical Thinking, 1820–1900.* Princeton, N.J.: Princeton University Press, 1986.

REITINGER, Franz. "Mapping Relationships: Allegory, Gender and the Cartographical Image in Eighteenth-Century France and England." *Imago Mundi* 51 (1999): 106–130.

ROBINSON, Arthur Howard. *Early Thematic Mapping in the History of Cartography.* Chicago: University of Chicago Press, 1982.

ROBINSON, Arthur Howard. "The Thematic Maps of Charles Joseph Minard." *Imago Mundi* 21 (1967): 95–108.

SHIRLEY, Rodney W. *The Mapping of the World: Early Printed World Maps 1472–1700.* London: Holland Press, 1983.

SMITS, Jan. *Petermann's Maps: Carto-Bibliography of the Maps in Petermanns geographische Mitteilungen 1855–1945.* 't Goy-Houten: Hes and De Graaf, 2004.

Thematic Mapping.org. Website (and blog) devoted to issues of the thematic map issues and its techniques. http://thematicmapping.org/.

TUFTE, Edward. *The Visual Display of Quantitative Information.* Cheshire, Conn.: Graphics Press, 1983.

WAINER, Howard. *Graphic Discovery: A Trout in the Milk and Other Visual Adventures.* Princeton, N.J.: Princeton University Press, 2005.

WENZLIK, Roy. *William Playfair and His Charts.* [St. Louis?, 1950].

WINCHESTER, Simon. *The Map That Changed the World: The Tale of William Smith and the Birth of a Science.* London: Viking, 2001.

PRINTED IN
AN EDITION OF 1,000 COPIES BY
CAPITAL OFFSET COMPANY
CONCORD, NEW HAMPSHIRE

∞ THE PAPER OF THIS PUBLICATION MEETS
THE REQUIREMENTS OF ANSI/NISO Z39.48–1992
(PERMANENCE OF PAPER)

BOUND BY
ACME BOOKBINDING
CHARLESTOWN, MASSACHUSETTS

DESIGNED BY
MARK ARGETSINGER
ROCHESTER
NEW YORK